I0901816

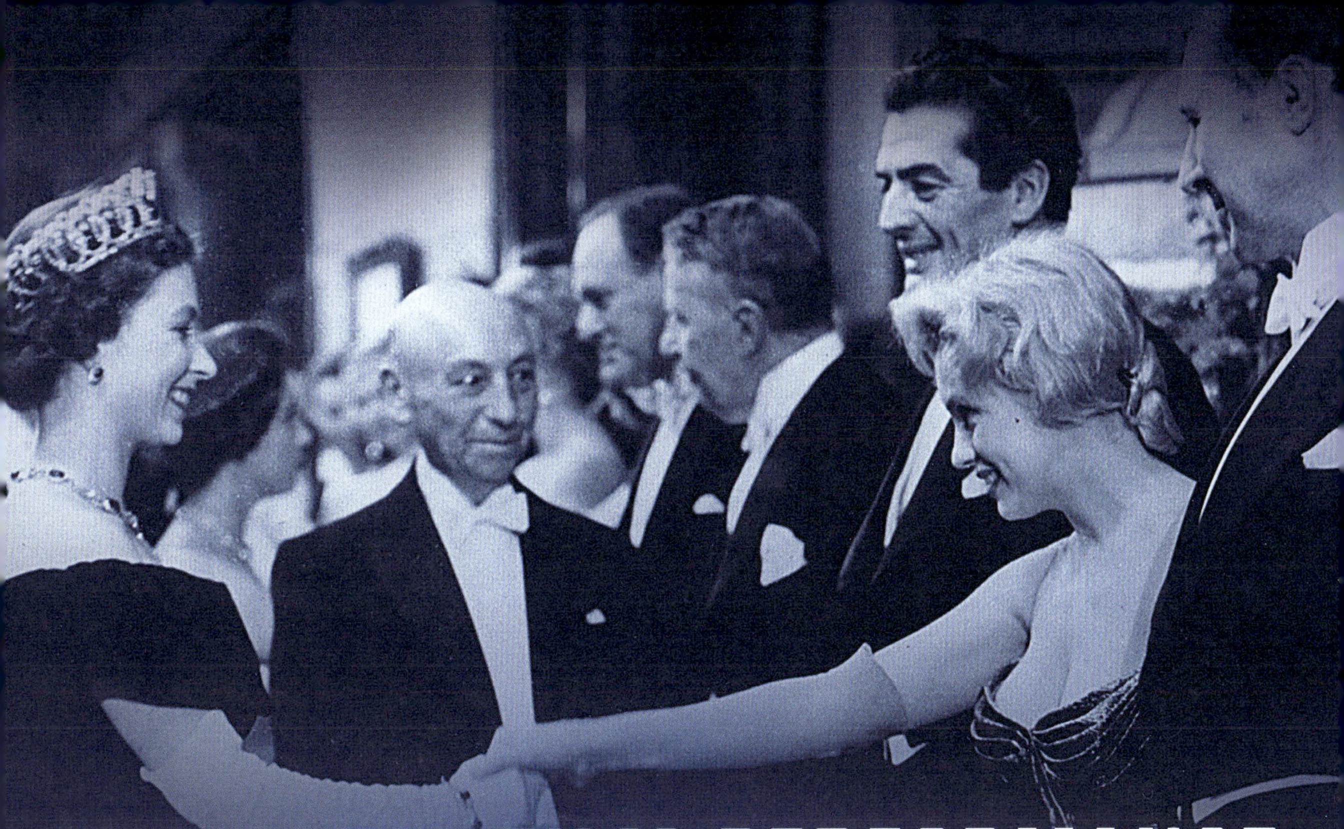

THE ROYAL FILM PERFORMANCE

A CELEBRATION

ROBERT SELLERS AND GARETH OWEN

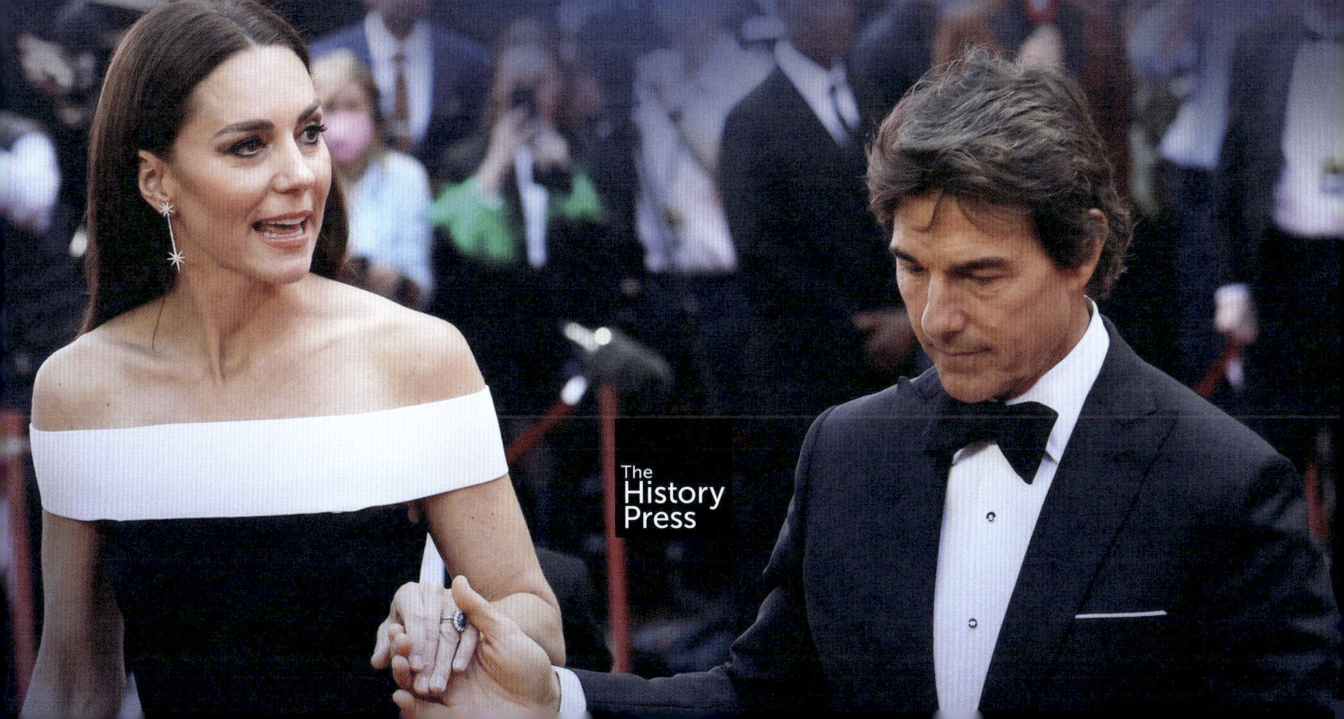

The History Press

Please note that quotations and press excerpts duplicated in the following pages are from sources dating back to the late nineteenth century onwards, and consequently the language and attitudes of the day do not necessarily reflect those of the charity or the authors today.

First published 2025

The History Press
97 St George's Place, Cheltenham,
Gloucestershire, GL50 3QB
www.thehistorypress.co.uk

British Library Cataloguing in Publication Data.
A catalogue record for this book is available from the British Library.

ISBN 978 1 80399 824 4

Typesetting and origination by The History Press
Printed and bound in Turkey by Imak

FSC www.fsc.org MIX Paper from responsible sources FSC® C111584

The History Press proudly supports
Trees for Life
www.treesforlife.org.uk

EU Authorised Representative: Easy Access System Europe
Mustamäe tee 50, 10621 Tallinn, Estonia
gpst.request@easproject.com

Contents

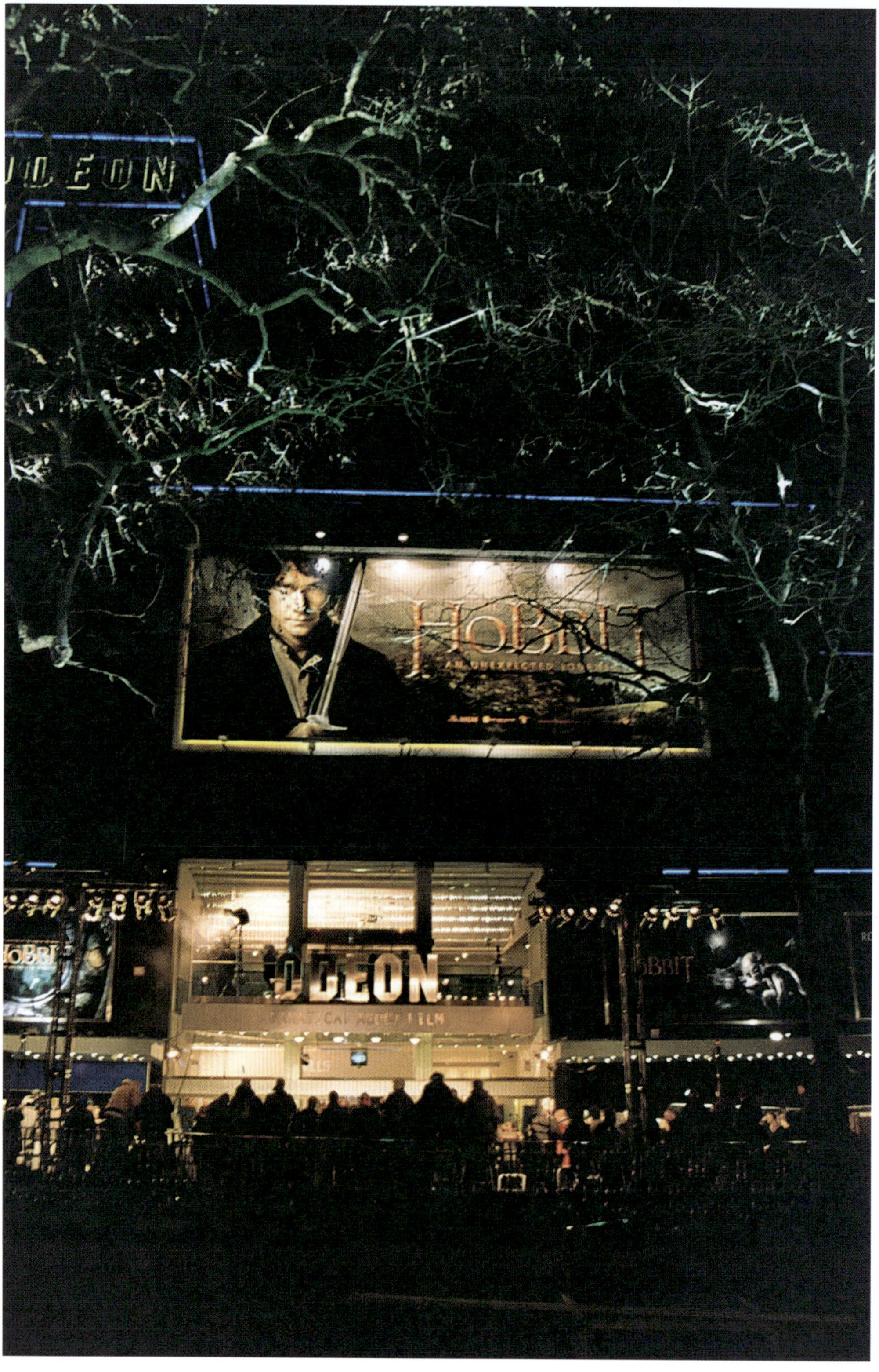
HOBBIT
ODEON

Foreword

THE ROYAL FILM PERFORMANCE has always been a special occasion – I can't remember a star, a director, a producer or a writer who wouldn't bust a gut to be present, and very few studio executives who weren't prepared to cross the Atlantic to be there. It's as if an extra layer of tinsel is added to Tinseltown!

The silent beneficiaries of the evening are not those who actually meet a member of the royal family, or whose names or logos are on the movie, but the hundreds, indeed thousands, of their fellow workers who have fallen on tougher times. Royal Film Performances have been held in support of a Film and TV Charity ever since the very first such occasion in 1946. Then called a Royal Command Performance, that first event was a screening of Powell and Pressburger's *A Matter of Life and Death*, attended by His Majesty King George VI, as well as Queen Elizabeth and the young princesses Elizabeth and Margaret.

Since then, there have been a further seventy such events over the years, ranging from classics like *To Catch a Thief* and *West Side Story* to more recent hits like *Titanic* and *Spectre*, and, most recently, the world premiere of Sir Ridley Scott's *Gladiator II*.

I've been fortunate to have enjoyed being part of half a dozen royal premieres, every one of them as special as a festival screening at Cannes, but only once have I had the privilege of producing a film selected for the Royal Film Performance: an experience which honestly outdoes all the rest of them.

It was 1981, and the film was *Chariots of Fire*, with the late Queen Mother in attendance. I have a clear memory of sitting next to her in the balcony of the Odeon Leicester Square and being aware of a slightly theatrical 'shudder' when David Yelland, playing the then Prince of Wales, made his first appearance on the screen – obviously old memories die hard!

It was in every way a totally amazing evening, topped off by a dinner at the Savoy with a performance by the Cambridge Footlights, starring, believe it or not, a young Emma Thompson, Stephen Fry, Hugh Laurie and Tony Slattery.

That was in every sense a Royal Film Performance to remember, but each year offers a new film and another special evening at which the industry gathers with members of the royal family to celebrate and support the wonderful world of cinema.

David Puttnam CBE, HonFRSA,
HonFRPS, MRIA,
2025

Introduction

FOR EIGHT DECADES, members of the British royal family have graced the red carpet to see the most eagerly anticipated films of the year. Since 1946, the Royal Film Performance™ has been an annual highlight of the entertainment social calendar with cinema's most famous icons coming face to face with royalty, and it is all organised by the Film and Television Charity, formerly known as the Cinematograph Trade Benevolent Fund and later the Cinema & Television Benevolent Fund (CTBF). Proceeds from Royal Film Performances as well as income from other fundraising events over the decades, such as cinema garden parties, Filmharmonic movie music concerts, London (fancy dress) parties, BAFTA comedy lunches, the *Daily Express* Balls, Christmas raffles and much more, have all helped those working behind the scenes in film, television and cinema with a range of practical, financial and mental health support.

Some of the previous Royal Film Performances have included memorable titles such as *Scott of the Antarctic* (1948), *To Catch a Thief* (1955), *West Side Story* (1962), *Born Free* (1966), *Love Story* (1971), *Kramer vs. Kramer* (1979), *Chariots of Fire* (1981), *A Passage To India* (1985), *Titanic* (1997), *Casino Royale* (2006), *The Hobbit* (2012) and *Top Gun: Maverick* (2022).

It was the centenary of the Film & Television Charity in 2024 and this book, which has the full backing of the charity along with exclusive access to their archives, is a celebration and testament to the great British institution and sets out the story in words and pictures of each Royal Film Performance, while offering a glimpse into the work of the charity and its many significant achievements along the way.

PART I: THE ROYAL FILM PERFORMANCE: A HISTORY

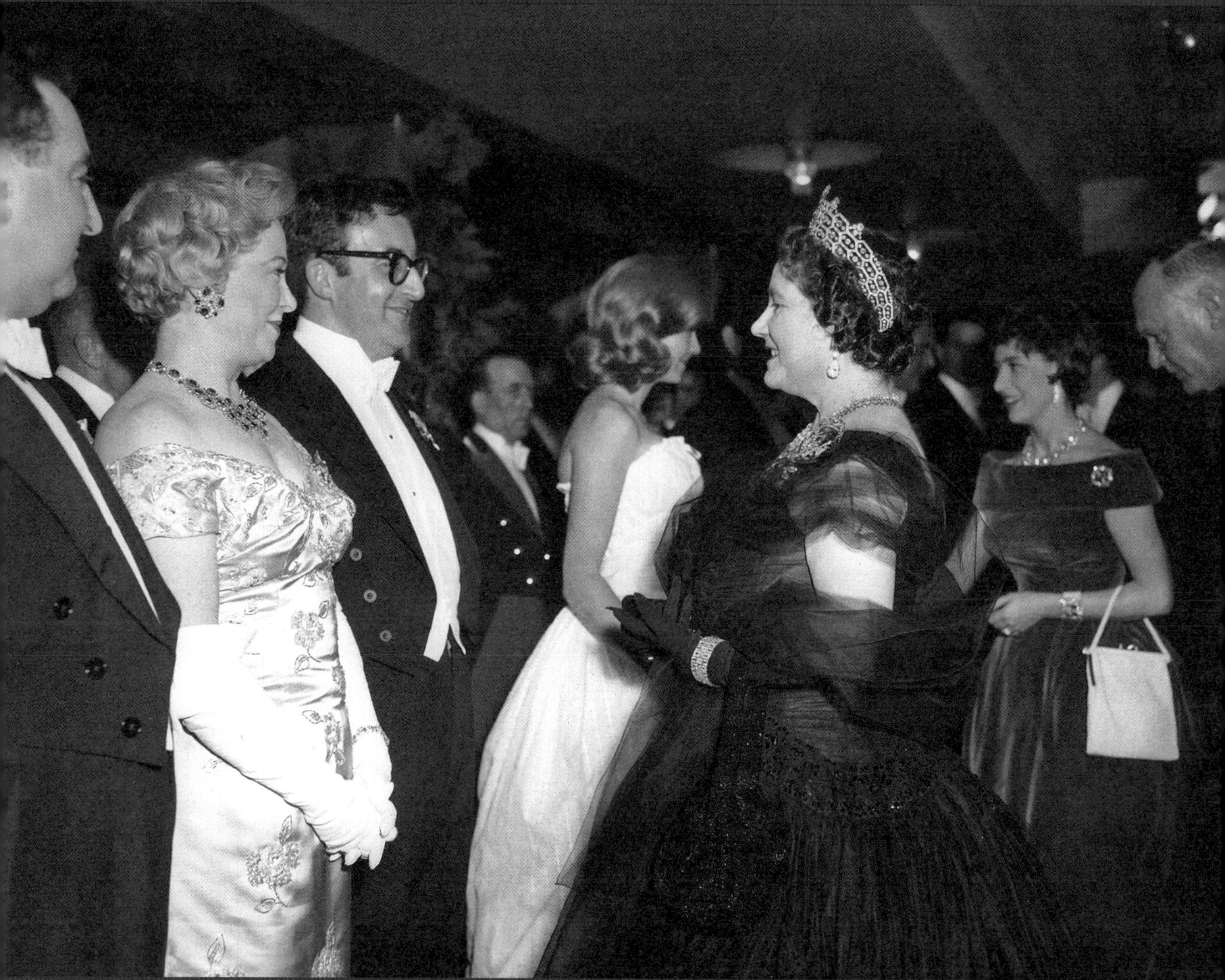

The Facts of Life (1961): The Queen Mother meets Peter Sellers, Brenda de Banzie and, far left, stage-show producer Vivian Cox.

1

The Royal Film

THE ROYAL FILM Command Performance was introduced as an annual event in 1946, and aside from a few exceptional years, it has remained such. Over seventy Royal Film Performances (as the event is now known) have taken place since, raising millions of pounds for the charity:

1946 *A Matter of Life and Death*
1947 *The Bishop's Wife*
1948 *Scott of the Antarctic*
1949 *The Forsyte Saga*
1950 *The Mudlark*
1951 *Where No Vultures Fly*
1952 *Because You're Mine*
1953 *Rob Roy: The Highland Rogue*
1954 *Beau Brummell*
1955 *To Catch a Thief*
1956 *The Battle of the River Plate*
1957 *Les Girls*
1959 *The Horse's Mouth*
1960 *The Last Angry Man*
1961 *The Facts of Life*
1962 *West Side Story*
1963 *Sammy Going South*
1964 *Move Over, Darling*
1965 *Lord Jim*
1966 *Born Free*
1967 *The Taming of the Shrew*
1968 *Romeo and Juliet*
1969 *The Prime of Miss Jean Brodie*
1970 *Anne of the Thousand Days*
1971 *Love Story*
1972 *Mary, Queen of Scots*
1973 *Lost Horizon*
1974 *The Three Musketeers*
1975 *Funny Lady*
1976 *The Slipper and the Rose*
1977 *Silver Streak*
1978 *Close Encounters of the Third Kind*
1979 *California Suite*
1980 *Kramer vs. Kramer*
1981 *Chariots of Fire*
1982 *Evil Under the Sun*
1983 *Table for Five*
1984 *The Dresser*
1985 *A Passage to India*
1986 *White Nights*
1987 *84 Charing Cross Road*
1988 *Empire of the Sun*
1989 *Madame Sousatzka*
1990 *Always*
1991 *Hot Shots!*
1992 *Chaplin*
1993 *The Man Without a Face*
1994 *Miracle on 34th Street*
1995 *French Kiss*
1996 *True Blue*
1997 *Titanic*
1998 *The Parent Trap*
1999 *Star Wars: Episode I – The Phantom Menace*
2000 *How the Grinch Stole Christmas*
2001 *Ali*
2002 *Die Another Day*

2003 *Master and Commander: The Far Side of the World*
2004 *Ladies in Lavender*
2005 *The Chronicles of Narnia: The Lion, the Witch and the Wardrobe*
2006 *Casino Royale*
2008 *The Other Boleyn Girl*
2008 *A Bunch of Amateurs*
2009 *The Lovely Bones*
2010 *The Chronicles of Narnia: The Voyage of the Dawn Treader*
2011 *Hugo*
2012 *The Hobbit: An Unexpected Journey*
2013 *Mandela: Long Walk to Freedom*
2015 *The Second Best Exotic Marigold Hotel*
2015 *Spectre*
2019 *1917*
2022 *Top Gun: Maverick*
2024 *Gladiator II*

Though the origins of the Royal Film Performance can be traced half a century earlier to 21 July 1896, when – during the infancy of the moving picture and long before the introduction of sound – forty royal guests gathered for the impending marriage of Princess Maud, the youngest daughter of King Edward VII and Queen Alexandra, to Prince Charles of Denmark. On the eve of her wedding, they assembled at Marlborough House in London's Pall Mall for a film show presented by Mr Birt Acres.

Six months earlier Acres, an American photographer and pioneering cinematographer who later developed the first 35mm film camera, gave a display of moving pictures to the Lyonsdown Photographic Society at the Lytton Road Assembly Rooms in his adopted London suburbs home of New Barnet. It was the first public film show to an audience in the United Kingdom. He went on to make several silent film shorts, including one about the Oxford and Cambridge Boat Race of 1895, but most significantly, in June 1896, he filmed Princess Maud's parents (then Prince and Princess of Wales) attending the huge Cardiff Industrial & Maritime Exhibition. The prince commanded Acres to bring the film to his home so that it could be screened for the extended family in a specially erected garden marquee. That, and twenty other shorts (many running just a few seconds), including *Tom Merry – Lightning Cartoonist*, *The Arrest of a Pickpocket* and *The Boxing Kangaroo*, proved so popular with the eager audience that they were run twice. This screening was termed 'The Royal Film' by the press of the day.

A year later, on 23 November 1897, the manager of the Empire Variety Theatre, H.J. Hitchens, presented a selection of Diamond Jubilee procession films, taken for the Lumière Cinématographe, to Her Majesty, Queen Victoria at Windsor Castle, accompanied by a full orchestra conducted by Leopold Wenzel. The programme comprised fifteen short films, including *The Czar of Russia in Paris*, *Spanish Dancers in Castille*, *Carnival at Nice* and *A Scene Taken from a Moving Train Near Clapham Junction*. Queen Victoria thus became the first sovereign to 'command' a film performance.

The Diamond Jubilee footage was distributed throughout Britain and the distant territories of the Empire and quickly demonstrated just how powerfully film could show the monarchy in a new, exciting – and immediate – medium. Queen Victoria's successors, Edward VII and George V, both came to the throne having grasped the potential of film. In fact, on 13 September 1902, the recently crowned King Edward VII and his wife, Queen Alexandra, welcomed their family to Balmoral Castle to enjoy an evening of Cinematograph Entertainment short films as part of their post-coronation summer holiday.

However, it was on 4 August 1916 that the first full-length feature film was presented by Royal Command. Cecil Hepworth's *Comin' Through the Rye* was shown before Queen Alexandra in the State Dining Room of Marlborough House, featuring stars Alma Taylor and Ralph Forbes in a story based on the 1875 novel of the same name by Helen Mathers, the title of which alluded to the 1782 Robert Burns poem 'Comin' Through the Rye'. Coincidentally, Cecil Hepworth had been present at the very first 'Royal Film' twenty years earlier, when he was assistant to Birt Acres. Eagle-eyed film fans might notice that a clip of *Comin' Through the Rye* can be seen in the Peter Sellers comedy movie *The Smallest Show on Earth* (1957), in which the elderly staff of the old 'kinema' tearfully watch silent films on their evenings off.

The first full-length feature film to be presented by command of the sovereign took place six months later, on 24 February 1917, when Lew Waren presented *Tom Brown's Schooldays* for King George V and Queen Mary at Buckingham Palace. Appropriately, the film had been made at Windsor Studios in south-east London.

It wasn't until three decades later that the Royal Film Command Performance was officially established. The charitable event was staged in aid of the Cinematograph Trade Benevolent Fund (CTBF, the forerunner of the Film & TV Charity). Although it had been first suggested in 1939, growing hostilities in Europe prevented it taking place and it wasn't until after the war, in 1946, that the idea was resurrected with Michael Powell and Emeric Pressburger's patriotic *A Matter of Life and Death* being chosen. The event was declared a huge success, and it was agreed it should become an annual addition to the royal calendar.

Of course, there have been many film premieres attended by members of the monarch's family over the years, but they are not to be confused with the Royal Film Performance, as there is – and can only ever be – one Royal Film of the year.

2

Foundations (1895–1939)

THE BIRTH OF CINEMA can be traced to the Lumière brothers' Cinématographe in 1895. French-born Auguste Marie Louis Nicolas Lumière and Louis Jean Lumière were manufacturers of photography equipment who had patented several processes, most notably 'film perforations as a means of advancing film through a camera'. They then devised and built a camera that could record, develop and project film, though at the time they regarded their new creation as little more than a curious novelty!

After they screened a forty-six-second film, *Workers Leaving the Lumière Factory*, on 22 March 1895 to a private audience of 200 members of the Society for the Development of the National Industry in Paris, they next organised a paid public screening on 28 December consisting of ten of their short films, each running for approximately fifty seconds, and cinema as we know it was born.

The first public performances of films to a paying audience in Great Britain were at the Polytechnic in Upper Regent Street, central London, on 21 February 1896. Consisting of short films by the Lumière brothers, the programme was so successful that it transferred to the Empire Music Hall in Leicester Square as one of the top items on the bill. A British inventor, R.W. Paul, showed films at Olympia the following month via his rival system, which was booked into the Alhambra Music Hall in Leicester Square and elsewhere. The third major variety theatre in London, the Palace, adopted the American Biograph system in March 1897.

The new marvel of 'animated pictures' spread rapidly through travelling fairs, showmen hiring local halls for special shows and music halls everywhere. Once film had demonstrated its lasting appeal, businessmen began taking over shops, halls and railway arches, painting over the windows and otherwise rather crudely converting them into full-time cinemas. A slightly more elaborate variation involved an auditorium resembling a railway carriage, presenting moving views ('Tours of the World') that had been photographed along railway lines.

The new medium's popularity exploded exponentially across the world, and in Britain, commercial-traveller-turned-film-pioneer Will Barker purchased two houses on Ealing Green in 1902 and created Ealing Studios. This first purpose-built – and now the oldest – British film production facility featured original stages constructed from very tall glass walls and roofs to make the most of the available light while keeping out the inclement British weather. Within ten years, it became the largest film studio in Britain – possibly Europe – and scores of films were released by Barker's Bulldog Films, leading the charge in quality British movies. Barker paid stage legends a small fortune to appear in his films, hired a composer to write music especially for them and was heralded as a 'big ideas man'.

Meanwhile, to accommodate the picture-going public's demand for his and other films, makeshift cinemas popped up everywhere from church halls and theatres to some more-unsuitable structures such as shops and even fairgrounds, which led to the government introducing the Cinematograph Act of 1909 requiring premises to be licensed by local authorities, particularly after nitrate film fire incidents increased – nitrate film when projected was highly flammable, and the Act required the construction of fire-resistant projection booths (occasionally positioned behind the screen, thus providing rear projection). This legislation saw purpose-built picture houses appearing in almost every town and village, many with flamboyant exteriors to catch the eye of passers-by and with box offices open to the street to take full advantage of impulse buying. The use of the word 'electric' in some of their names, such as the Electric Cinema in Notting Hill and the Electric Birmingham, was also a reminder that electricity was something of a novelty too – making a visit doubly appealing.

Performances were usually made up of short films, including travelogues and news items, and ran for anywhere between an hour to ninety minutes (feature films didn't arrive until 1914). Seating in these picture houses rarely accommodated more than a few hundred patrons and offered a range of prices, commonly starting at 3*d* and rising to 1*s*, with reduced prices for children. The best view in the house, with padded 'tip-up' seats, cost four times as much as the cheapest, basic wooden benches. However, common to all were unpleasant odours, dense cigarette smoke and a lack of fresh air. These issues were usually alleviated by opening windows and sometimes a ceiling dome or sliding roof during intervals.

A cinema-operator licence was not just based on issues of health and safety; it also allowed councils to grant or refuse cinemas according to the content of the films they presented, thereby indirectly – and, arguably accidentally – introducing censorship. In 1912, the British Board of Film Censors (BBFC) was set up by members of the film industry who had become frustrated by local government censorship, which had come to a head with the release of *From the Manger to the Cross* (1912), following a public and press outcry about how the life of Jesus should be treated as sacred and not used for commercial gain and entertainment – despite many of the complainants not actually having seen the film. In fact, when members of the clergy were invited to a private screening, they said there was nothing offensive or morally questionable in it. It was therefore agreed that a professional industry censorship body was urgently needed. Within a year of the BBFC's formation there were 3,000 cinemas in operation in Britain and new film studios were poised to open in Twickenham, Walthamstow, Isleworth,

Catford and Borehamwood to cater for the public's growing appetite for moving pictures.

Aside from the BBFC, the fast-growing film industry was largely unregulated and quite fragmented, leading in 1915 to the Cinematograph Exhibitors Association (CEA) being formed, which was swiftly followed by the Kinematograph Renters Society (KRS) coming into being, along with the Incorporated Association of Kinematograph Manufacturers (KMA) – all to help co-ordinate and supervise specific areas of the film and distribution industry. It soon became apparent to the organisations' executives that thousands of people working in the film industry, many of whom were described as 'gifted amateurs', were on low pay and often lived in poor conditions.

It was certainly not the wealthy or glamorous business it is today and there were no trade unions either – not until 1933 – and mindful of this, three senior members of the CEA, KRS and KMA decided to formulate a plan to establish a charitable organisation, similar to that of the Variety Artistes' Benevolent Fund (later, the Entertainment Artistes' Benevolent Fund), which had been founded in 1908 to 'provide care for entertainers who had fallen on hard times or were suffering ill health'. Those three executives – E.W. Pashley Peall, Reginald Charles Bromhead and J. Brooke-Wilkinson – drew up rules for a National Benevolent Fund and Provident Institution which was constituted in February 1924, and just over a year later, on Tuesday, 7 April 1925 at 3 p.m., the first General Meeting of the Cinematograph Trade Benevolent Fund took place at No. 33 Soho Square, London.

Twenty-five leading members of the film industry, along with trade press representative *Kine Weekly*, were present at the meeting, where Reginald C. Bromhead was appointed chairman. Bromhead reported:

> Subscribers to the Benevolent Fund, convened for the purpose of formally adopting the rules which have been prepared by Mr Brooke-Wilkinson and myself and approved by the Hon. Legal Advisers and of electing the Council and Trustees of the Fund. The Cinematograph Trades Council has been formed primarily with the object of fostering a Trade Provident Institution to which employers would subscribe and to supplementing the benefits to be given thereunder [...] we are very much indebted to Sir William Jury as a result of whose donation of £1000 we were able to hold a Garden Party last July, which proved very successful.

The first garden party, the CTBF's inaugural event, was held in the Royal Botanical Gardens on 19 July 1924 and proved a great success.

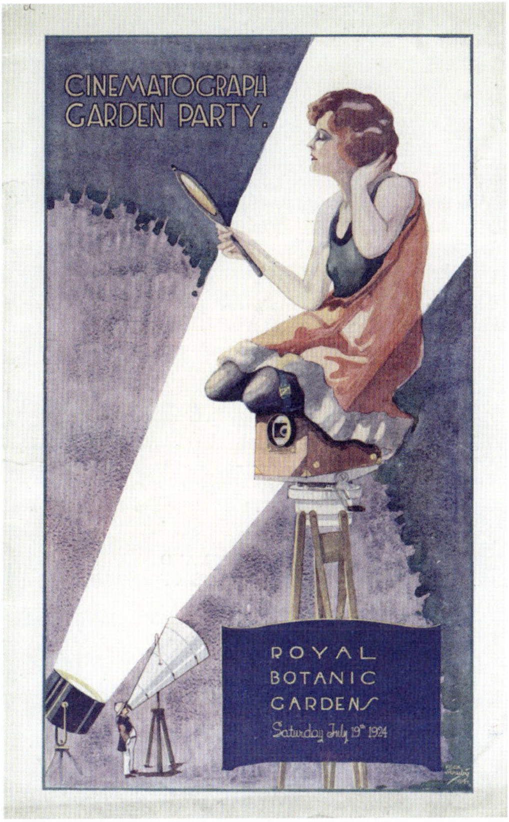

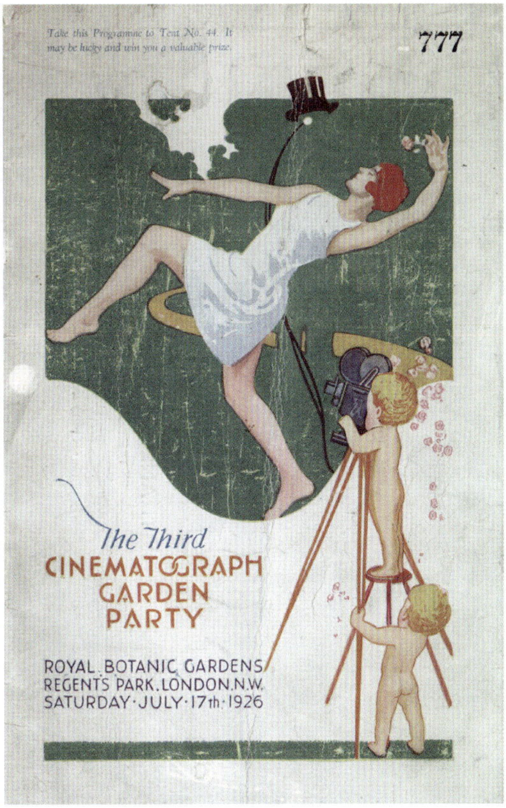

At the fund's first meeting, nine vice presidents, six life members and eleven annual subscribers were secured, with subscriptions varying from 1 guinea to £250. Each of the three trade organisations became vice presidents, along with a 'considerable number' of local branches of the CEA, with whom the management and control of the fund was to be entrusted. It was agreed that vice presidents would remain in office until the next Annual General Meeting, where management would be more formally established, and furthermore it was agreed that 'the Fund should offer financial relief without loss of self-respect and make a sincere effort to help those willing to help themselves'. A bank balance of £3,676 13*s* 2*d* was reported, with a further £2,551 13*s* 10*d* (the proceeds from the first Cinematograph Garden Party) being presented at the meeting, which itself included a £1,000 donation from Sir William Jury, head of Jury Imperial Pictures, a production company and leading renter (distributor) of British and American films throughout the colonies.

At the second Annual General Meeting in May 1926, the management of the CTBF was regularised and the first trustees were formally elected:

Sir William Jury, President and Trustee
Reginald Charles Bromhead, Chairman and Trustee
Alfred Claude Bromhead, Trustee
Headley M. Smith, Trustee
J. Brooke-Wilkinson, Hon. Treasurer
Reginald C.O. Vivash, Secretary

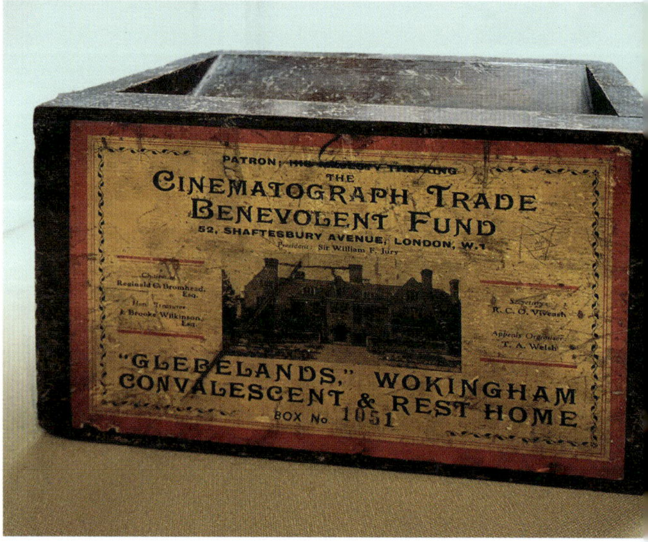

A couple of months later, the fund's second garden party was publicised in cinema newsreels with the tagline, 'Come to the Cinema Garden Party the jolliest Fete of the Year. You may be the lucky one to win this Clyno Motor Car for 2'6.' The car was raffled by Rootes Ltd of No. 141 New Bond Street, London, world exporters and distributors of the popular Clyno.

Post-event, the British Pathé silent newsreel reported, 'Theatrical stars give an excellent entertainment', in a short film featuring an audience sitting in the garden as the camera panned across them, to ladies dancing on the stage, then around a maypole with ribbons. It next focused on an actress reciting some prose on stage, before declaring one of the highlights to be a 'film face competition', the winner of which was a Miss Henchie, who was described as having 'big dark eyes and short dark hair under a cloche hat'. Though it's not clear if she was ever offered a film contract!

The officers of the CTBF were all wealthy, philanthropic film and distribution executives who drew no salaries or expenses from the charity. The Bromhead brothers established the British subsidiary of the French film company Gaumont and founded early newsreel Gaumont Graphic in 1910. Two years later, they opened a large factory in Shepherd's Bush, which supplied most positive prints of American and foreign films for the British market, and within a decade, the brothers had bought out the French interests, thus becoming an entirely British firm, with film studios at Lime Grove in Shepherd's Bush. By 1929, their company had become a conglomerate, controlling distribution and exhibition at 300 of their own cinemas. Incidentally, in 1956, a cinema was named after Reginald Bromhead inside the grounds of the Military College at Watchfield (Shrivenham) in recognition of his service to the Army Kinema Corporation as chairman.

Reginald C.O. Vivash, meanwhile, had joined the industry in 1910, first as an exhibitor and then in 1913 as a distributor with Gaumont-British. J. Brooke-Wilkinson was one of the founders of the Incorporated Association of Kinematograph Manufacturers, who was later appointed the first secretary of the British Board of Film Censors. Sadly, not much is known about Headley Smith apart from him being a member of the Cinema Exhibitors Association. In 1930, John Maxwell, founder of Associated British Pictures at Borehamwood, also joined as a trustee.

Meanwhile, in the first year of the CTBF's operation, seventy-nine people were awarded grants. The largest group of recipients were widows whose husbands had served in relatively lowly positions such as projectionists, door attendants and even a 'title writer'. They received cash gifts ranging from a few shillings to £5.

The third and last garden party took place in 1926 – the following year, it wasn't considered viable due to the underlying economic conditions in the UK. Instead, in 1927, the fund launched a raffle to win 'hundreds of prizes' with the top reward being a Morris car. Newsreel segments in cinemas suggested audiences could buy a ticket from the theatre manager or alternatively could send a postal order for 1*s* to the CTBF's address in Shaftesbury Avenue, London, W1.

In that same year, the Film Quota Act was introduced as a ten-year plan to reduce American dominance of UK cinemas by requiring 20 per cent of the films screened to be British-produced. The Act certainly came along with the best of intentions, but it was not a success and was in fact largely criticised within the industry for the emergence of opportunistic 'quota quickies' – mostly low-cost, low-quality and quickly produced films, commissioned by American distributors active in the UK or by British cinema owners purely to satisfy the quota requirements. It was often joked that only the cleaners and cinema ushers watched them!

Within two years of the Act, the whole business saw a massive change with the advent of 'talkies' introduced to the UK industry with Alfred Hitchcock's *Blackmail* (1929). Cinemas opened apace and donations to the CTBF consistently increased, particularly from the thirty individual CEA regional branches and KRS members with renters (distributors) making handsome and regular donations of anywhere between £50 and £500.

Yet, as income increased, so did the number of beneficiaries, and fundraising became uppermost in trustees' minds. To this end, on 10 March 1929, a Sunday benefit concert was held at the London Palladium and raised approximately £700; a Trade Carnival was held at the Astoria Dance Salon on 10 October, raising some £202 5*s* 7*d*, while a second Palladium Sunday concert took place on 19 January 1930, generating a further £324 15*s* 7*d*.

On 5 November 1930, the film division of the Federation of British Industries invited the CTBF to be co-beneficiary with the Royal National Lifeboat Institution of a gala performance of British films showcased for prime ministers at the annual British Empire and Dominions conference, which raised a further £817 2*s* 10*d*.

A Sunday evening entertainment programme was suggested as a next project to the fund by the manager of the London Hippodrome, but the Lord Chamberlain – mindful of the restrictive Sunday opening regulations of the time – refused permission, albeit 'with regret'.

In the 1931 annual report, salaries of £506 appeared for the first time in the accounts. This was no doubt due to the need for more staff to help administer the growing numbers of beneficiaries – again, the vast majority were widows, receiving single 'one-off' grants.

In 1932, the Federation of British Industries and the Trades Union Congress both expressed concern about 'the menace of Americanisation by means of film', suggesting that Hollywood imports acted as a threat to both Britain's financial interests and to 'English speech, customs, and cultural standards' – the very things the Quota Act of 1927 was supposed to prevent.

In fact, it had already been suggested that the government should increase the minimum quota of British films to at least 50 per cent of all cinema presentations to prevent the majority of box-office takings going to 'American Syndicates' – particularly as the development of sound had already caused unemployment of artistes, orchestra members and theatre stage staff with the rapid decline of variety theatre. However, with 5,300 cinema screens to fill, it was wisely suggested that excluding more American products would leave a massive shortfall in available films – plus cinemagoers actually enjoyed seeing lavish American movies.

In February 1935, 'The Power of Cinema as a Cultural and Propagandist Force', a talk chaired by the trade union leader (and future Foreign Secretary) Ernest Bevin, suggested that 'cinema is one of the most potent instruments for good or evil that man has invented, so powerful as to release a cultural force of unrivalled possibilities.'

In the meantime, other small fundraising events took place, and then, on 15 March 1934, the biggest event to benefit the fund was held. 'Midnight with the Stars' was a stage show featuring film personalities of the day with a live orchestra at the Empire Theatre, Leicester Square. In a filmed promotion that was run in cinemas ahead of the event, actor Sir Cedric Hardwicke said it would feature 'the greatest assembly of stage and screen stars ever gathered together', and for those unable to attend, he added, 'we have prepared a special gramophone record made by 24 stars, English and American ... the price is one shilling and sixpence of which one shilling goes to the Cinematograph Benevolent Fund. These records are on sale now at this theatre.'

The event and records raised approximately £14,000 and it was hoped it might become a regular extravaganza thereafter. Indeed, a second 'Midnight with the Stars' event was staged on Wednesday, 8 May 1935 at the Dominion Theatre in London's Tottenham Court Road and raised £7,111 14*s* 1*d*, including proceeds from gramophone record No. 2, 'featuring 27 front rank stars in excerpts from some of this season's outstanding successes.' Income prospects certainly seem bright for that year with £2,500 arriving in donations too.

By 1935, twenty-nine long-term beneficiaries appeared in the CTBF's annual accounts. These were people in sufficient need to receive regular, long-term payments.

King George V had been royal patron of the Variety Artistes' Benevolent Fund since 1921 and had stated, 'The Monarch or a senior member of the Royal Family, would attend an annual Performance, in aid of Brinsworth House and the Royal Variety Charity, once a year thereafter, to demonstrate the Royal family's love and support for the entertainment industry and its associated charity.'

It seemed a natural progression, as the CTBF and its work grew in stature and awareness, that the fund should seek a similar royal patronage. In 1935, Edward, Prince of Wales (later King Edward VIII) agreed to become patron. However, by the end of the following year he abdicated, leading to King George VI ascending the throne, and he immediately offered his patronage to the fund.

This exciting news coincided with more money-raising ideas coming from the trustees including releasing a series of 78rpm gramophone records called 'Voice of the Stars', between 1935 and 1937, containing vocal contributions of leading film actors of the time. Shirley Temple, Will Hay, Jean Harlow, Max Miller, Jessie Matthews along with Gary Cooper, Spencer Tracy, Clark Gable, Bette Davis, Errol Flynn and Bing Crosby appeared, among many others.

As mentioned, the Variety Artistes' Benevolent Fund had been established in the decade before the CTBF, and at its heart was a beautiful care home named Brinsworth House in Twickenham, described as being 'a place of safety, peace, happiness and tranquillity set within over three acres of land'. During the summer of 1935, Sir William Jury suggested to Reginald Bromhead that there was a need for such a convalescence and residential home for people in the film and cinema business who were either recovering from serious illness or might otherwise be made homeless, particularly by the death of a spouse. The two men visited Wokingham in September to view a large house that was for sale. Impressed by Glebelands and its 15 acres of grounds, and seeing its potential for perfectly fitting his brief, the generous Sir William Jury immediately made an offer to purchase the property and then gifted it to the fund in perpetuity.

Alterations and improvements were made, such as central heating being installed, all supervised by Frank Verity and Sam Beverley, renowned cinema and theatre architects, who were behind designs for the Plaza in Lower Regent Street and the Carlton in Haymarket, along with the Theatre Royal Windsor and many Paramount cinemas around the UK. They carried out work without any cost or charge to the fund.

Keen that the running costs of Glebelands should not be a drain on the CTBF itself, the trustees launched a campaign to raise a separate income purely for the upkeep and maintenance of the house and estate. Many existing donors contributed a few shillings to a few pounds, but there were some more sizeable individual gifts: £3,500 from the Gaumont-British Picture Corporation Ltd, plus Mr and Mrs A.C. Bromhead donated £1,000 personally. The CEA offered £1,170 towards running costs and distributors Columbia Pictures, Fox, MGM, Paramount, Radio Pictures, United Artists, Universal Pictures and Warner Brothers all donated £1,000 each. Another £1,500 was donated by Associated British Cinemas and the charity's own fund-raising subcommittees. All in all, £27,992 was raised to comfortably cover the £5,834 annual operating cost.

Nine months after its purchase, in June 1936 residents were accepted, and a few weeks later, the Lord Mayor of London Sir Percy Vincent officially cut the ribbon at Glebelands. He announced there were already fourteen occupants (with a capacity for seventy) and added, 'The very name of the home so generously provided by Sir William Jury, suggests peace and rest and shelter amongst natural beauty so fitting for the aged.'

In the *Cine-Technician* newspaper, Frank Canham, one of those first residents, wrote a letter asking to be remembered by all his old colleagues, and added how much he would appreciate visits from any who happened to be that way (Wokingham).

In further fundraising, the Broadway Melody Film Ball was held at the Wallington Public Hall by the South London Branch of the CEA in April 1936, featuring David Hayes and his ten Varsity Boys, while 2,500 collection boxes were distributed to cinemas the following year, with the tins being passed from row to row, raising £1,037 during the first year and up to £11,000 in loose change a decade later.

A further 'Midnight with the Stars' gala was staged on 6 May 1937 at the Empire Theatre, Leicester Square, as well as a regional performance organised by the Manchester branch of the CEA at the Paramount Theatre, Manchester, on 2 June the same year.

In 1938, a film-star jigsaw puzzle was advertised in cinemas to benefit the CTBF and paved the way for plans to be announced for an autumn 1939 Royal Cine-Variety Performance at the 4,000-seater Gaumont State Empire Theatre in Kilburn in the presence of the King and Queen. It is not recorded who came up with the idea of a 'Royal Film Performance', although given the King and other members of the royal family attended the annual Royal Variety Performance, it again seemed a natural and very appropriate progression for the CTBF to hold a gala film event.

However, just as plans were coming together, everything changed. Britain entered the dark days of the Second World War, and the proposed Royal Film event had to be postponed indefinitely. The expenses and preparations had unfortunately cost the fund £481 15*s* 2*d*, but it was a cost they had to bear – besides, greater worries lay ahead.

3

War and Peace (1939–45)

ALL CINEMAS AND PLACES of entertainment were immediately ordered to be closed at the outbreak of war in September 1939, with the government fearing aerial bombing of tightly packed spaces could wipe out hundreds, if not thousands, of people in a single incident. Some film studios faced the same fate, and for a brief time it looked as though the whole British film industry was about to come to a juddering halt – and with it, of course, income to the CTBF.

Within two days of cinema closures, George Bernard Shaw wrote a letter to *The Times* newspaper protesting the government order. He stated that denying entertainment to both soldiers and civilians was 'a masterstroke of unimaginative stupidity'.

A few weeks later, cinemas were allowed to reopen as the feared bombers did not come, though when the Blitz did begin in 1940 the devastation seemed so widespread and random that cinemas were not regarded as particularly dangerous places. In fact, during 1940, cinema admissions rose to just over 1 billion, across 5,000 screens, and continued rising steeply for the next few years, reaching over 1.5 billion in 1943, 1944 and 1945. People did not 'cower in darkness and terror', as Shaw put it – unless they were seeing a horror film – they laughed, cried, snickered and sighed at all manner of stories, and cinema-going became the country's primary leisure activity, proving also to be an indispensable means of instructing and educating the nation, while also building morale.

In 1940, the CTBF's annual accounts reported capital of £87,851, an income of £10,882 and an expenditure totalling £8,752 in salaries, assistance and grants. Far from income drying up, the fund's assets had actually grown exponentially.

On 2 October 1940, fund trustee John Maxwell died suddenly. At ABPC, Maxwell had built a vertically integrated company incorporating film production, film distribution and a large network of ABC Cinemas as well as becoming the biggest producer of British film by 1938. He owned 502 cinemas to support those productions and indeed was a staunch supporter of the CTBF. His presence was greatly missed, and his widow donated £2,000 in his memory.

The death of founder, president and fund benefactor Sir William Frederick Jury was felt even harder on 2 August 1944. His guiding hand, wisdom and generosity had made the formation of the charity possible, as well as Glebelands becoming a reality. Stepping into his large shoes, long-time trustee and chairman Reginald C. Bromhead assumed the presidency of the fund, while J. Arthur Rank, founder and chairman of the Rank Organisation, became a trustee.

In happier news during 1944, a fundraising campaign suggested cinema staff might contribute a penny a week from their salaries and the initiative raised £3,500.

The war years had certainly seen the British film industry bloom. Morale-boosting and flag-waving stories dominated the thousands of cinema buildings across the country as leading producers Michael Balcon (at Ealing Studios) and Alexander Korda (at Denham Studios) heightened spirits with the likes of *Went the Day Well* (1942) and *In Which We Serve* (1942).

Rising mogul and new fund trustee J. Arthur Rank purchased Gaumont-British Picture Corporation, making him the dominant force in the world of UK cinema, and with it, he created a stable of some of the top directors, writers and producers of the day under the umbrella of 'Independent Producers'. This talented and autonomous group of filmmakers included David Lean, Frank Launder and Leslie Gilliat, and The Archers (Michael Powell and Emeric Pressburger's company). Rank financed their productions and received great acclaim in return for the likes of *The Life and Death of Colonel Blimp* (1944), *This Happy Breed* (1944), *A Canterbury Tale* (1944), *Brief Encounter* (1945) and – in the immediate post-war period – the Archers' *A Matter of Life and Death* (1946) moved into production, inspired by a government request to improve Anglo-American relations. The latter became a truly significant film for the CTBF.

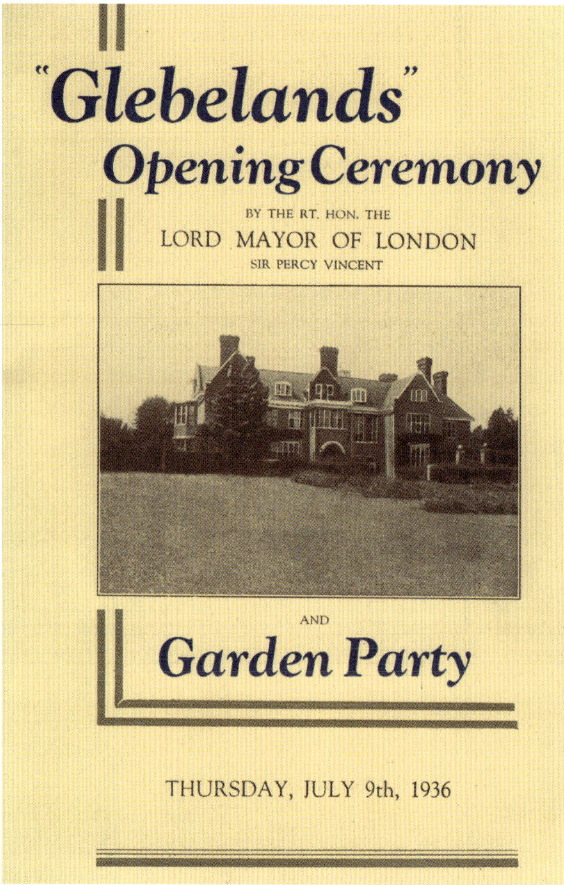

4

The First Royal Command Film Performances (1946–49)

BEING MINDFUL THAT THE CTBF was a national charity – not least as a significant amount of income came from regional CEA branches – in 1946, the trustees turned their attention to establishing a northern convalescence home, so that trade employees suffering illness or financial problems did not necessarily need to uproot and relocate to the south of the country to Glebelands. In November, the fund purchased a hotel on the promenade at Morecambe called 'The Craggs'. The purchase price and subsequent updating cost £26,000, and as with Glebelands, it was agreed that running costs should come from separate and independent fundraising, with the CEA Northern and Scottish branches being key contributors.

With the war ended, the trustees felt it was time to resurrect the idea of a Royal Film Performance. MGM agreed to loan their Empire Theatre in Leicester Square and Buckingham Palace confirmed that King George and Queen Elizabeth would attend, along with Princesses Elizabeth and Margaret. The date was set as 1 November 1946.

Taking inspiration from the popular 'Midnight with the Stars' galas, it was agreed the event should involve a stage show, devised and produced by Val Guest, who was assisted by a young actor named Peter Butterworth, who himself had just come to prominence after appearing in pantomime around the UK. Butterworth's first film appearance was in the Val Guest production *William Comes to Town* (1948) and the duo worked on a further seven films together during their careers.

'Cavalcade of the Movies', as the stage presentation was titled, was a glitzy and glamorously colourful event in what was a grey, rationed and bomb-damaged London of the time. Marius Goring kicked off the evening with some highlights from the 'Keystone Era' (Keystone Cops) before Will Hay introduced 'Chaplin Era' highlights. American actor William Eythe celebrated the 'Sound Era' with a couple of songs, before a series of other stars took to the stage with monologues and little sketches. Everyone, ranging from Diana Wynyard to Pat O'Brien, Bud Flanagan, Mai Zetterling and Ray Milland, offered their time. Recent Oscar winner Milland presented a scene from his triumphant movie *The Lost Weekend* and British director/writer Anthony Kimmins introduced a whole line-up of British film stars: Stewart Granger, Laurence Olivier, Margaret Lockwood, Valerie Hobson, Patricia Roc, Jean Kent, John Mills, Anna Neagle, Ralph Richardson and Deborah Kerr, among others, who all led the National Anthem ahead of the start of the film itself. It was certainly quite a prelude to the main event!

Later stage shows were also produced by Hollywood actor and former studio executive Ben Lyon, who became a familiar voice on BBC Radio, TV and stage, with the hugely popular *Hi, Gang!* and *Life with the Lyons*.

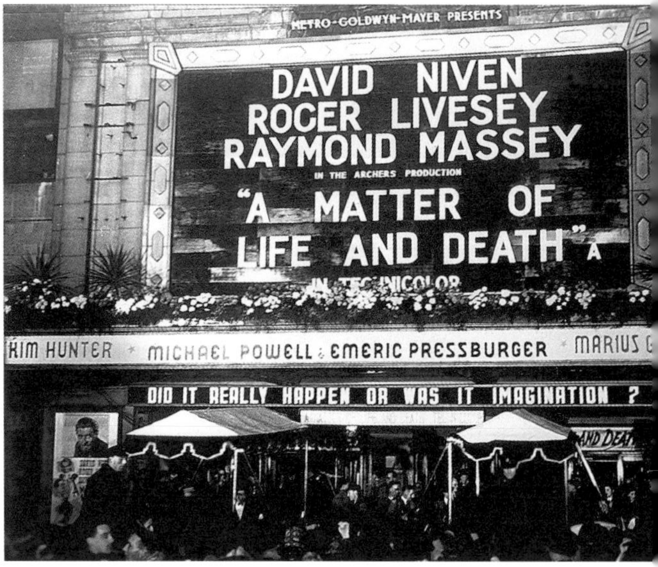

Incidentally, the choice of the Royal Command film was made by a 'viewing committee' consisting of exhibitors, producers and cinema companies and by whom the prospective candidates had already been narrowed down to three. Ahead of the evening, *The Picturegoer* magazine of 28 September 1946 reported:

> This will be an historic event. For many years, the stage and music hall have been honoured by Royal Command performances.
>
> Now the cinema receives equal recognition.
>
> As can be understood, it was no easy task to choose a film for this occasion.
>
> A special committee representing all sides of the industry saw all the films submitted by British and American producers. They were considered not only for their intrinsic merits but also in view of their suitability for this occasion. Finally, the entrants were narrowed down to three.
>
> These were Metro's *The Green Years*, which had very strong claims because of the nature of the story and its many British associations. *The Magic Bow*, a story of Paganini with Stewart Granger and Phyllis Calvert in the leading parts, and Yehudi Menuhin responsible for the violin playing. And *A Matter of Life and Death*, the Michael Powell – Emeric Pressburger picture starring David Niven, Raymond Massey, Roger Livesey, and Kim Hunter.
>
> After much careful consideration, the committee had decided on *A Matter of Life and Death*.
>
> This is an honour to British films of which we can be justly proud. We don't mean to suggest that we can beat the Big Drum and crow about scoring over Hollywood. Far from it. We can be modestly happy that we are producing pictures which are worthy of a Royal Command performance.

The scenery for the stage show was paid for by J. Arthur Rank and designed by 36-year-old George Ramon, an architect turned interior designer and acclaimed West End theatre set designer. The event was advertised in cinema newsreels in a special appeal fronted by Laurence Olivier, and throughout the film trade in newspapers and by word of mouth.

The performance generated a profit of £25,896 – the largest amount ever from an event organised by the CTBF – and it was immediately agreed that a follow-up Command Performance should be held the next year and indeed become an annual event thereafter. 'Command' was dropped ahead of 1949's premiere at the request of Buckingham Palace, to become 'The Royal Film Performance' as it was felt 'command' suggested the King had chosen the film.

James Chapman, writing in a 2016 issue of *Screen International* marking the seventieth anniversary of the Royal Film Performance, stated the event 'was one element in a bid to assert the cultural legitimacy of cinema in Britain in the late 40s. The other key event in this process was the establishment, in 1947, of the British Film Academy (later to become BAFTA).'

In the period immediately after the ending of the Second World War, the British economy, and particularly the balance of payments, was in such an acute state that by the summer of 1947 the Labour Government considered it necessary to restrict imports to reduce the outflow of funds. Of total spending on imports from the United States, films made up a relatively small 4 per cent, but on 6 August 1947 the Treasury imposed a 75 per cent customs tax on all film imports, which became known as Dalton Duty (after the Chancellor of the Exchequer, Hugh Dalton). The overwhelming majority of film imports came, of course, from the United States. US film company revenues from the UK had been more than $60 million a year ($68 million in 1946).

The following day, the Motion Picture Export Association of America (MPEA) announced that no further films would be supplied to British cinemas until further notice. The very legislation intended to stem the post-war dollar drain caused Hollywood to withhold new product, leaving Britain's biggest film conglomerate, the Rank Organisation, to feed over 600 cinemas. Rank hastily expanded production, only for the UK Government to reverse its policy five months later, exposing the modest British films that had just been completed to a huge backlog of competing Hollywood blockbusters, which, in turn, brought the Rank Organisation to its knees.

The next fundraiser for the CTBF was the *Daily Express* Film Ball at the Royal Albert Hall on 29 September 1947. Although it was unclear if any American stars or studio executives attended, home-grown talents such as Googie Withers, Michael Wilding and Anne Grey did.

Early in January 1948, President of the Board of Trade Harold Wilson led talks about an Anglo-American Film Agreement, which was announced two months later. In return for abolition of the duty, the American studios could again export films to Britain. Although there was to be no limit on the number of

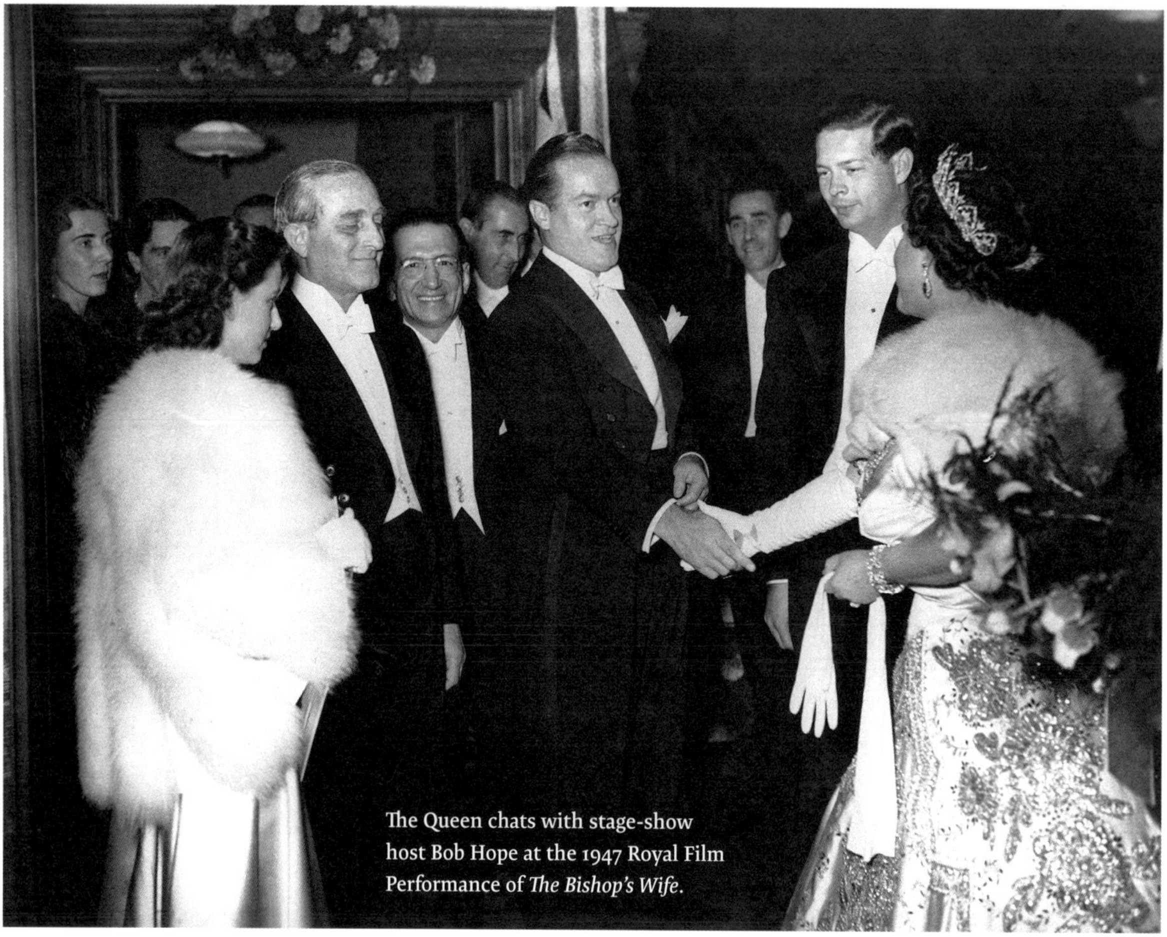

The Queen chats with stage-show host Bob Hope at the 1947 Royal Film Performance of *The Bishop's Wife*.

films that could be brought into the country, only $17 million of American films' earnings could be repatriated to the USA. Any surplus to that amount was to be blocked and would have to remain in Britain, but it could be used for investment in film production, rights acquisition, prints, advertising and even the purchase of studios and other properties (excluding cinemas). Furthermore, it was agreed that the amount that could be remitted to the USA could be increased by an amount equivalent to the earnings of British films from distribution in the USA. It was estimated that the saving to the British economy would be about $33 million.

On 21 November 1949, the Ritz Theatre in Birkenhead hosted a replica Royal Film Performance of *The Forsyte Saga* for local dignitaries after an impressive firework display. Celebrities such as Bebe Daniels, Ben Lyon, Gregory Peck, Margaret Lockwood, Valerie Hobson and Richard Todd made it the largest charity gala ever held in the north, which featured not only the regional premiere but also Nat Allen and his orchestra, jugglers and even the sand-dance trio of Wilson, Keppel & Betty in front of a capacity 2,500 crowd.

In 1950, another replica Royal Film Performance was organised, this time by the South Wales & Monmouthshire Branch of

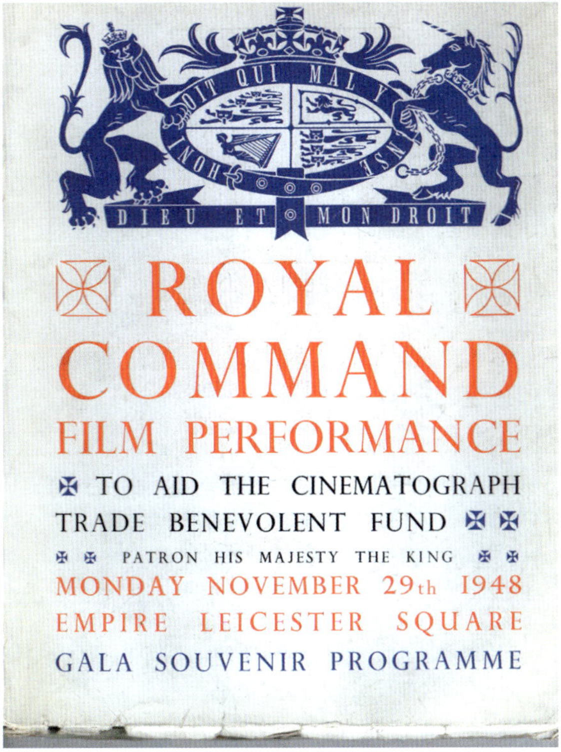

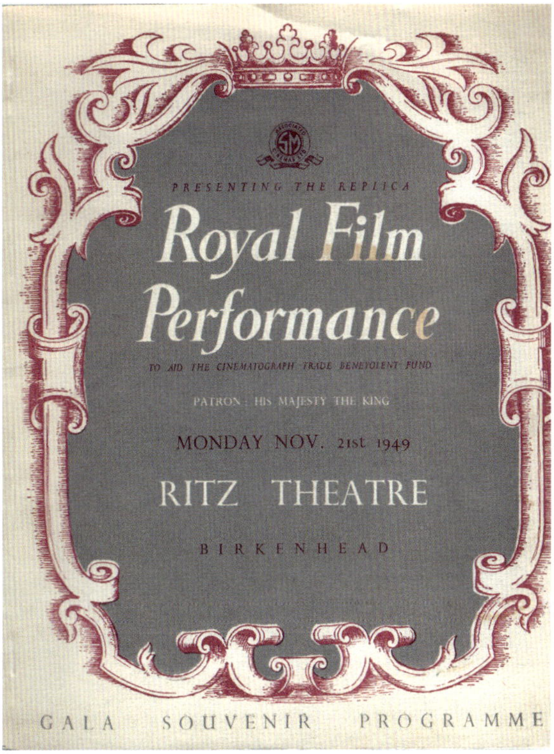

the Cinematograph Exhibition Association, who felt they'd like to share some of the London glamour associated with the Royal Film Performance of *The Mudlark*. Billed as the 'biggest event in the entertainment history of Wales' by local press, a rerun of the Royal Film Performance took place at the Empire Theatre, with tickets for the event costing £5 5*s*, £1 1*s*, and 7*s* 7*d* (for the cheap seats).

It was reported that a crowd of over 2,000 waited inside, while another 4,000 gathered outside on Queen Street in the drizzle, hoping to catch a glimpse of celebrities. Montgomery Clift was one of the first to emerge to the noise of girls screaming. Petula Clark, Jack Warner, Terry-Thomas, Googie Withers and Valerie Hobson followed, with Gloria Swanson the last to arrive. This was the year of *Sunset Boulevard* (her big hit movie), and the crowd surged forward, breaking through the police cordon in excitement and leaving twelve people injured. Following the film, the stars decamped to the nearby Park Hotel for a celebratory dinner dance.

All of the razzmatazz of Hollywood couldn't hide the fact that it had been a tough couple of years for the CTBF, having lost valued colleague J. Brooke-Wilkinson, who had been secretary and founding member of the fund as well as on the Board of Film Censors. He died in 1948, aged 77, and was said to have been found slumped over his desk.

But in 1952 greater sadness was to come with the news that King George VI had passed away. The trustees, like the rest of the nation, felt totally shattered. However, the charity was quickly reassured by the late King's eldest daughter, Elizabeth, who had immediately ascended to the throne. She wrote within a matter of weeks to confirm her wish to continue the royal patronage of the fund.

5

Premieres and Television (1950s)

THE DECADE OF THE 1950s brought an almost total change to the CTBF's long-term board of governance. Vivash retired in 1954, after thirty years of service, and Drummond-Scott took over the post of secretary – a position he held for seven years until his own death. Two years later, President Reginald C. Bromhead passed away and J. Arthur Rank (who was about to be ennobled as Lord Rank) immediately took over and served for five years until 1960. Bromhead's son Ralph Sidney was appointed chairman and held the position until it was abolished in 1971. The patronage of the new sovereign, meanwhile, ensured a familiar and steadying constant in the decades ahead.

Charles Moss Woolf formed the distribution company General Film Distributors in 1935. He later partnered with J. Arthur Rank and the logo for the company was the 'man with a gong' – which later graced all of Rank's films. Woolf had two sons, John and James. John became the sales manager of General Film Distributors until it was taken over by the Rank Organisation in 1942 upon their father's death. James worked for Columbia Pictures in Hollywood. Together, the brothers jointly formed Romulus Films in 1948, with early productions including *Pandora and the Flying Dutchman* (1951), *Moulin Rouge* (1952) and *Beat the Devil* (1953).

In the early 1950s, the Woolf family generously funded a group of cottages to be built on the grounds of Glebelands for those people in the business who were able to live independently but had fallen on hard times. The cottages were named the C.M. Woolf Memorial Cottages and the approach to Glebelands was renamed Woolf Drive.

Romulus Films won thirteen Academy Awards and featured some of the greatest talent of the era and were great supporters of the CTBF. Sadly, James suffered a fatal heart attack in 1966, aged just 46. John went on to be knighted in 1975 for his contribution to British film, and later became a trustee from 1982 to 1987, before being named life vice president in 1998.

Meanwhile, the Royal Film Performances continued annually throughout the 1950s, with the King (and subsequently Queen Elizabeth II) attending, joined occasionally by other members of the royal family. In 1952, regular photographer Harry Myers almost had an embarrassing moment with the Queen's sister at the premiere of *Because You're Mine*:

> In my rush to get one more photograph of the new Queen as she left the cinema, I ducked under a crash barrier and just as I came up Princess Margaret brushed by, and I was mortified I very nearly went up her skirt. She turned around and laughed heartily!

Taking a leaf from the CEA in south Wales, two years earlier, *Because You're Mine* was also screened regionally in Liverpool and Leeds with guest celebrities Jack Hawkins, Petula

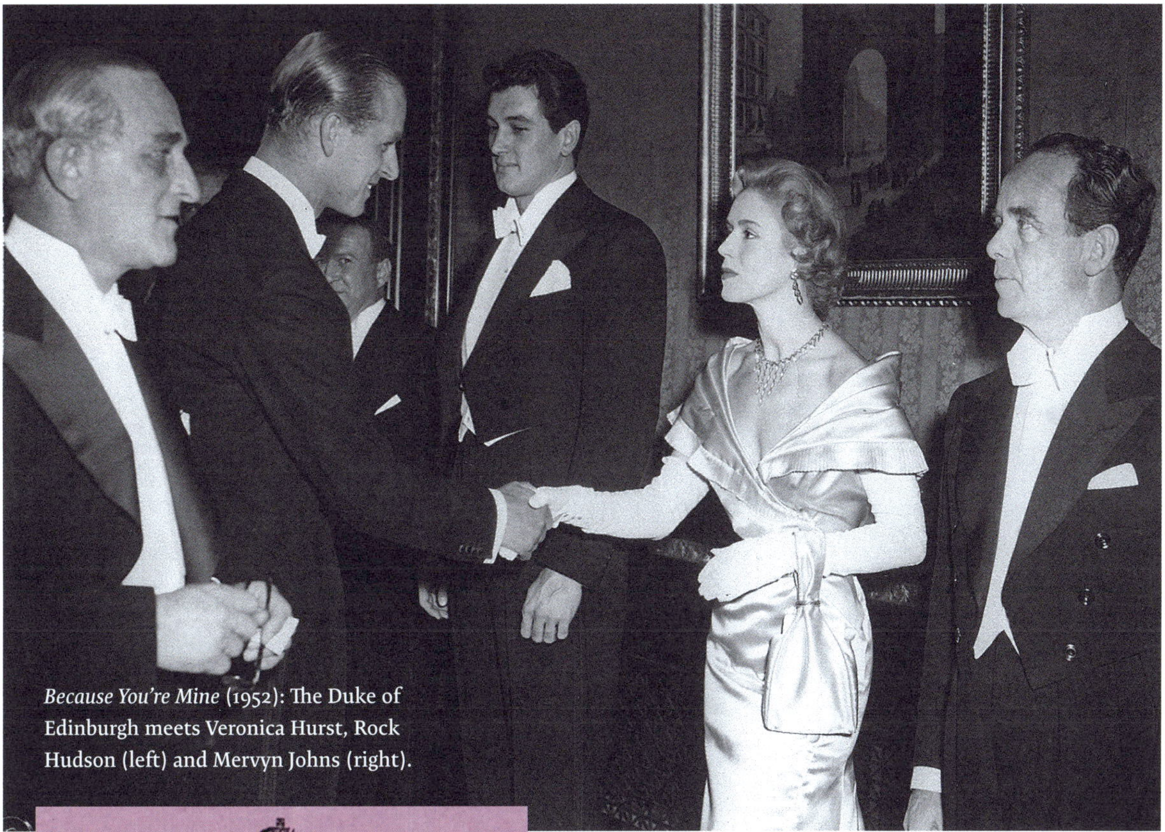

Because You're Mine (1952): The Duke of Edinburgh meets Veronica Hurst, Rock Hudson (left) and Mervyn Johns (right).

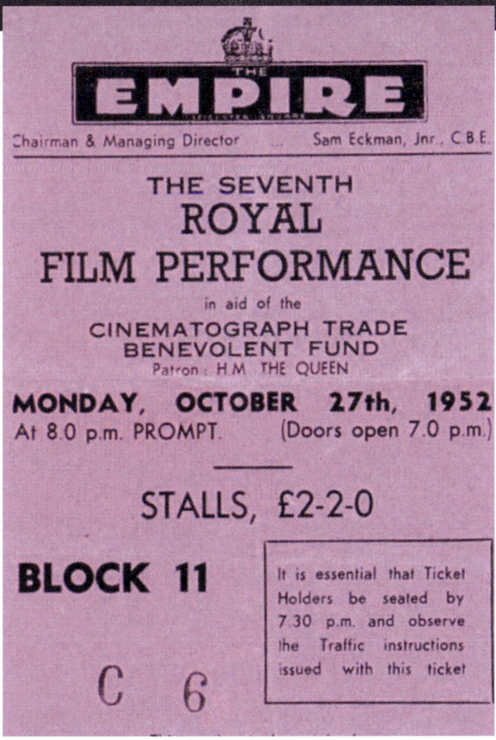

THE EMPIRE

Chairman & Managing Director ... Sam Eckman, Jnr., C.B.E.

THE SEVENTH
ROYAL
FILM PERFORMANCE
in aid of the
CINEMATOGRAPH TRADE
BENEVOLENT FUND
Patron : H.M. THE QUEEN

MONDAY, OCTOBER 27th, 1952
At 8.0 p.m. PROMPT. (Doors open 7.0 p.m.)

STALLS, £2-2-0

BLOCK 11

C 6

It is essential that Ticket Holders be seated by 7.30 p.m. and observe the Traffic instructions issued with this ticket

Clark, Peter Sellers, James Hayter and Lisa Daniely, among others, meeting local dignitaries and trustees of the fund.

The London events were usually held on Monday evenings in the early years so the stars could rehearse their parts for the stage show that preceded the film on Sundays (when theatre spaces were closed). That year, John Mills, Tyrone Power and Montgomery Clift performed Noël Coward's *Three Juvenile Delinquents*, which was hailed a great success, although the shows weren't always received so well. In fact, some proved embarrassingly bad, and unlike with the Royal Variety Performance, many film actor participants were not natural ad-libbers or comedians.

As the stage shows often ran longer than the films, resulting in the evening ending

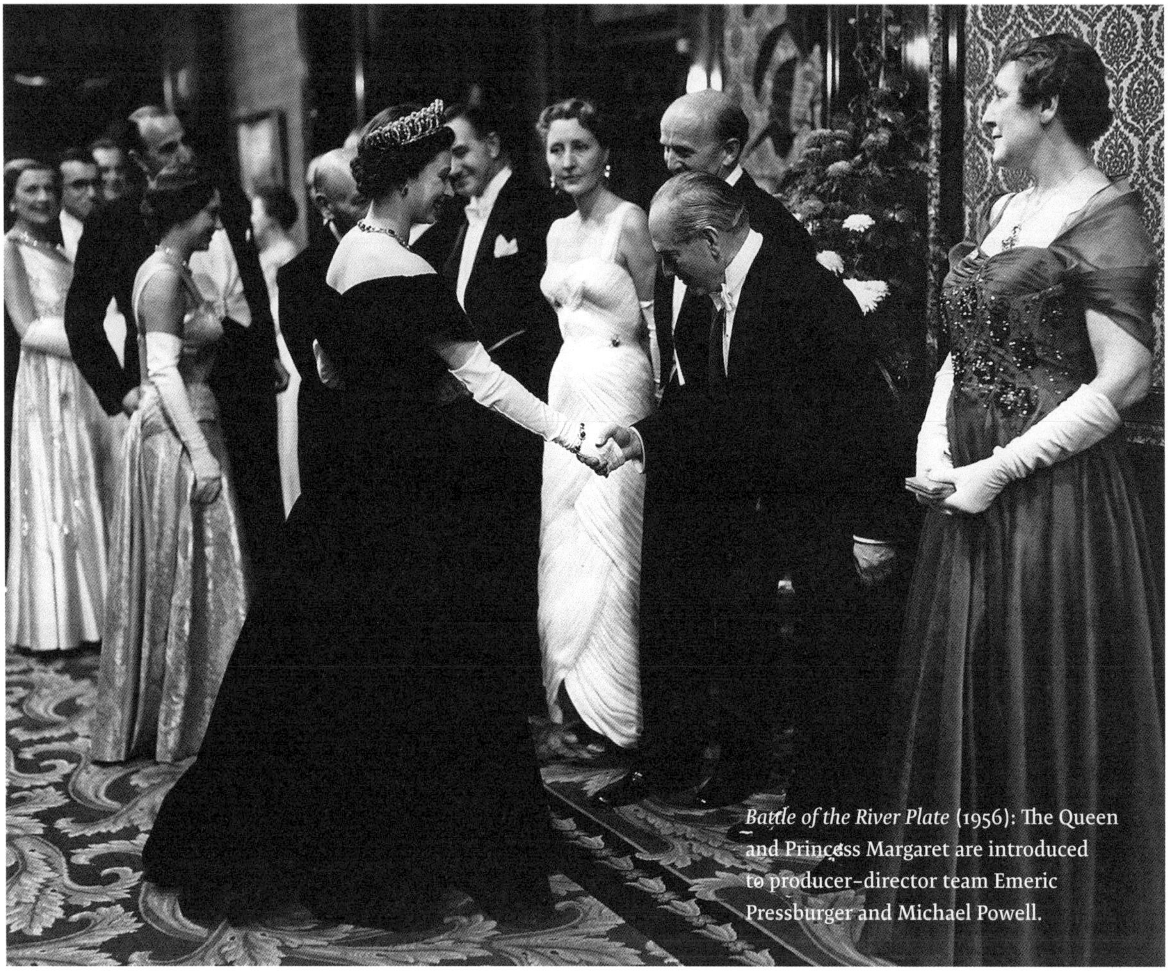

Battle of the River Plate (1956): The Queen and Princess Margaret are introduced to producer-director team Emeric Pressburger and Michael Powell.

around midnight, the Palace asked for this part of the Royal Film Performances to be dropped. However, to a much lesser degree (and shorter running time), the pre-show entertainment was revived in the 1960s under the supervision of producer Vivian Cox. He managed to recruit scores of top names to participate, including James Garner, Honor Blackman, Cliff Richard, George Peppard, Margaret Rutherford, Peter Finch, Peter O'Toole, Sean Connery, Deborah Kerr, Raquel Welch, Woody Allen, Rex Harrison, Roger Moore, Rachel Roberts, Peter Sellers, Maggie Smith, Peter Ustinov, Zero Mostel, Elizabeth Taylor, Mia Farrow, Tony Hancock, Yul Brynner, Sylvia Syms, Norman Wisdom, Jessie Matthews and Brenda de Banzie, to name but a few.

Of course, the red-carpet event was always a media highlight with both royal and film star attendees. Regular photographer Harry Myers – who covered the very first performance and every one up until his retirement fifty years later – commented that whenever Princess Margaret attended, she always asked to be supplied with a set of 8in × 6in photographs from the evening.

The chosen films tended to alternate between British and Hollywood productions

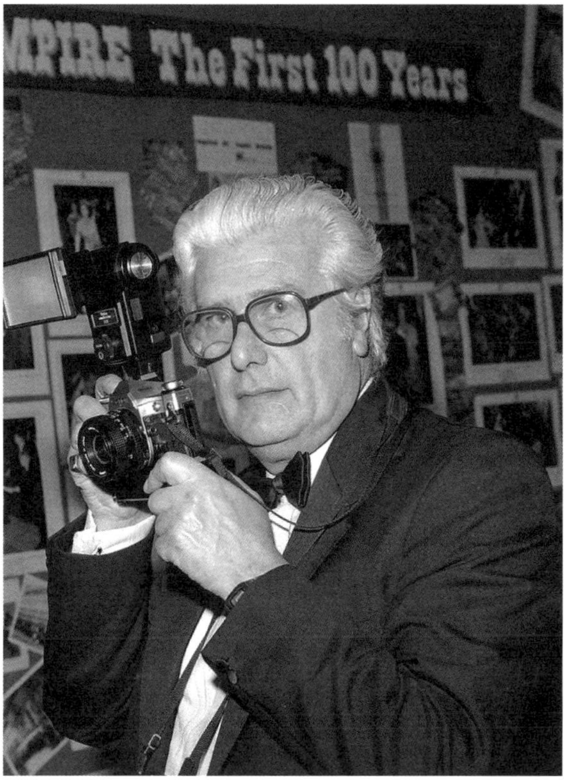

Photographer Harry Myers attended Royal Film Performances from the very first in 1946.

and in the coronation year of 1953, it was Disney's *Rob Roy* which took the honour. It was the shortest of any Royal Film Performance, running at just eighty-one minutes.

However, the next year led to some controversy when *Beau Brummell* premiered after the front-runner, *Seven Brides for Seven Brothers*, was ruled out for being a second American production in a row. The chosen film dealt with the story of the Queen's 'mad' ancestor, King George III, and in the line-up prior to the performance commencing, the Duke of Edinburgh asked star Stewart Granger if he thought the film was 'alright for Her Majesty?'

An embarrassed Granger replied, 'If you could manage to distract her attention when Robert Morley appears, it might be better, sir.'

When Cabinet papers were released thirty years later, they showed that the Queen had summoned Prime Minister Sir Winston Churchill to complain.

This was also the year closed-circuit TV was introduced (in 1957, sound was added) to allow the audience, who had to be seated ahead of the royal party arriving, to see what was happening outside the auditorium. It was also filmed for television, and TV lighting often caused problems for photographer Harry Myers in casting shadows, particularly as Harry worked without flash in the available light. A compromise in the number of lights used was usually found though.

With significant headline coverage, 1956's Royal Film Performance saw Marilyn Monroe – in town to film *The Prince and The Showgirl* (1957) – join the line-up. In 1957, the somewhat risqué *Les Girls* was chosen, though much to the delight of Leslie Phillips, who said in his 2009 autobiography *Hello*, 'My first Hollywood film was shown to the Queen and Prince Philip, and it turned out I was the only member of the cast able to make it, so I had Her Majesty all to myself.'

Visiting guest Jayne Mansfield did catch the eye of Her Majesty, however. 'You are so beautiful,' the star beamed upon being introduced.

It was decided to move the Royal Film Performance to a late autumn slot, as opposed to March, because of the prominence placed on the BAFTA and Oscar award-worthy promotion campaigns in the latter part of the year, with more quality films on offer, whereas the

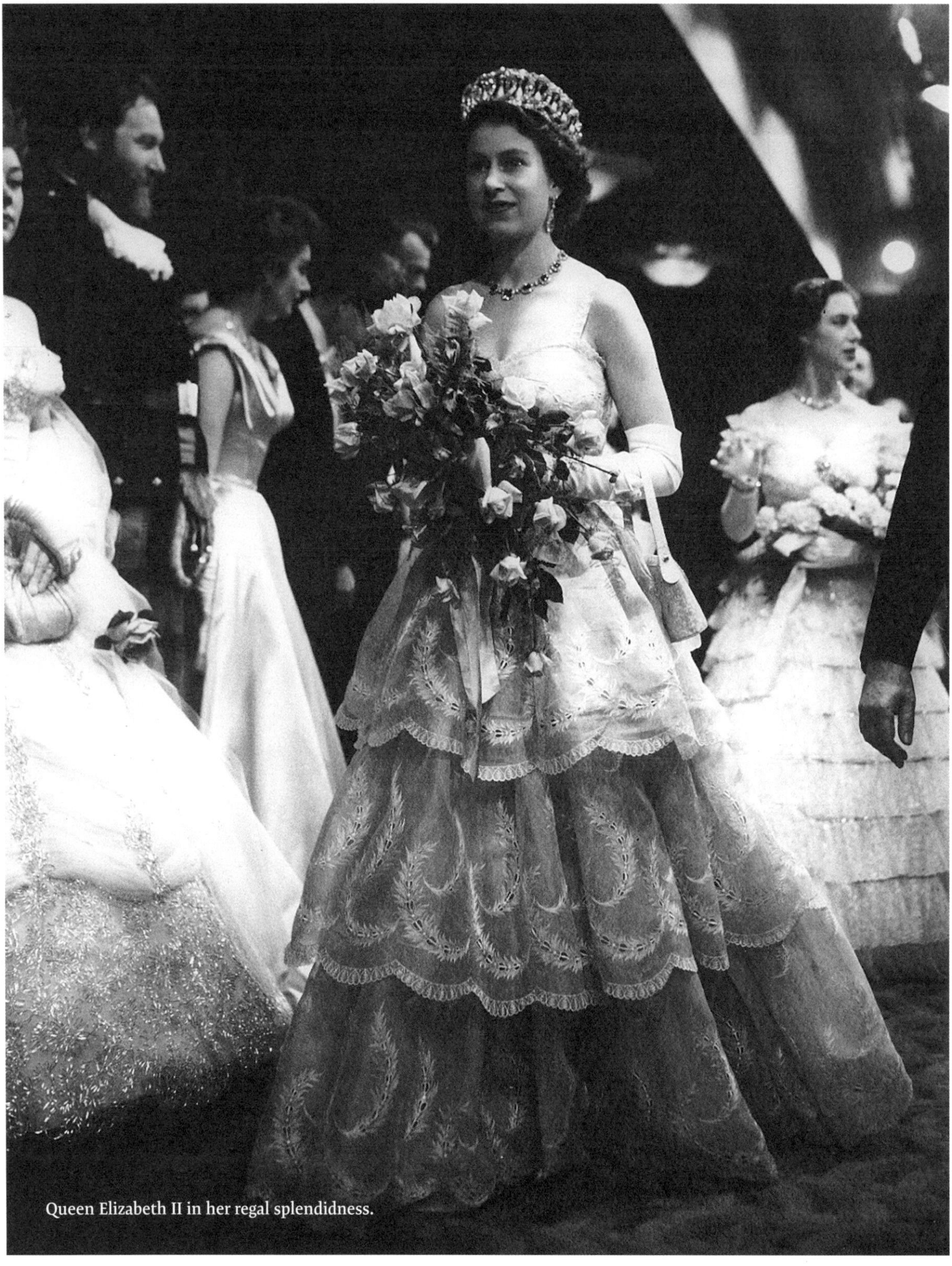

Queen Elizabeth II in her regal splendidness.

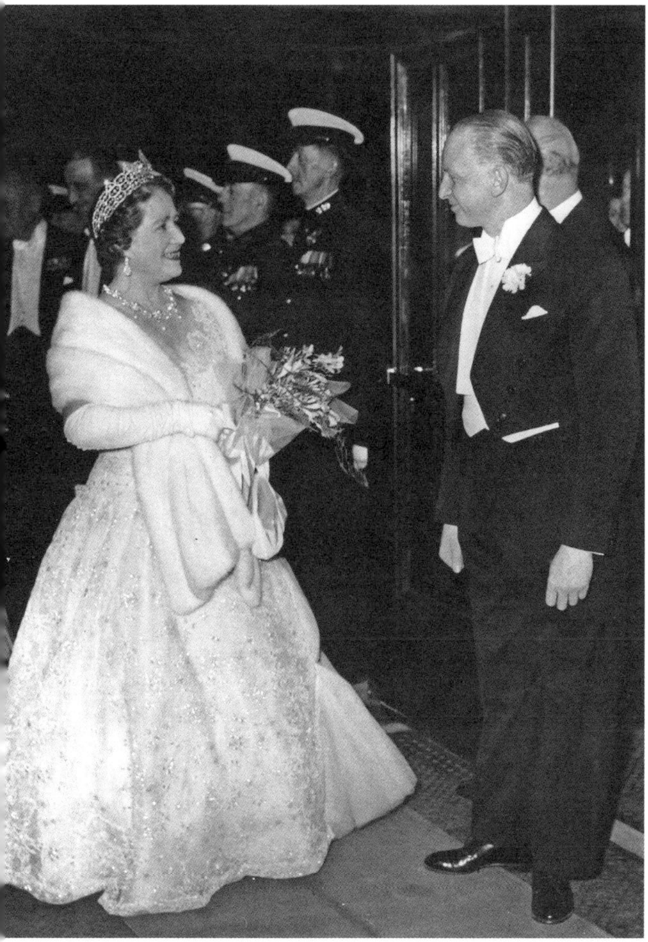

The Horses Mouth (1959): The Queen Mother is greeted by Empire Theatre's general manager, Mr A. Sidi.

early spring tended to see a glut of releases of not-so-notable titles. A November date seemed more commercial, and the Palace indicated Her Majesty had no objection to the re-siting of the event. However, a consequence of the move meant there was no Royal Film Performance in 1958, as reported in *The Daily Cinema* on 23 April 1958:

> The information received by Lord Rank, President of the Fund, indicates that Her Majesty has given careful consideration to her future program, and that, while maintaining her close interest in the work of the Fund and the well-being of the film industry generally, it is necessary for her to vary her engagements in such a manner as to cover the widest possible scope … Her Majesty and His Royal Highness wish the Royal Film Performance future success and look forward to attending it often in the future.

This suggested the Queen would not be available for every single Royal Film Performance going forward. In fact, she wanted to spread her patronage more widely with her attendance being shared by the Duke of Edinburgh, the Queen Mother, Princess Margaret and the Duchess of Kent.

The Queen didn't attend a Royal Film Performance again until 1961, which was also the year the CTBF's long-time secretary, C. Drummond-Scott died suddenly, just before Christmas. His passing led to John Davis, then managing director of the Rank Organisation, being appointed a trustee. The following March, Anthony Kilmister was promoted to the position of secretary, having joined the fund just months before, after responding to an advertisement in the *Daily Telegraph* for the post of deputy general secretary. He certainly didn't expect to take over from his boss so quickly, particularly when one of the secretary's main tasks was organising Royal Film Performances. Kilmister was certainly dropped in at the deep end but rose to the challenge brilliantly.

6

Evolving Times (1960s and 1970s)

THE LATE 1950S and early 1960s saw cinema admissions fall steadily across the UK following the growing popularity and affordability of television in homes. Picture-going was threatened to the point of many cinemas being shuttered or changed into bingo halls.

Research discovered that geographical areas of particular decline in cinema admissions were directly related to good TV reception. Rank's managing director, John Davis, warned of the growing threat of television at a CEA conference, saying he believed there would be a massive depreciation of the Rank Organisation's films if TV started broadcasting them. As such, none of Rank's contract artistes were allowed to work in television, though ironically, Lord Rank himself invested considerably in Southern Television, one of the first independent companies on the ITV network.

Trustees of the CTBF were mindful that television production could soon overtake film output in the UK and a growing number of new technicians and floor staff were not only being recruited by TV, but film veterans were transferring over to the medium from movie studios too. As such, in 1964, the trustees took the decision to change, update and modernise the name of the fund to embrace television – which they predicted could inject a new income into the fund too. The BBC aside (which had its own support arrangements for staff and former staff), it was felt that help, support and benefits should be extended to staff in independent television, where executives such as brothers Lew and Leslie Grade and Bernard Delfont had become the new giants on the scene.

The initials of the Cinematograph Trade Benevolent Fund (CTBF) were retained, but two key words were changed – 'Cinematograph' became 'Cinema' and 'Trade' became 'Television', thus the Cinema & Television Benevolent Fund was born, with all major independent television companies invited to become supporters. The National Association of Bingo Clubs was also invited to become a benefactor so that their employees (many of whom had transferred from cinemas) could benefit from the fund too.

Further embracing the fund's new inclusivity of television, Bernard Delfont, the agent and theatre impresario, who was then producing *Sunday Night at the London Palladium* for ATV, was invited to become a trustee in 1966 and swiftly helped ensure the charity was on a good financial footing by recruiting Granada TV's Cecil G. Bernstein as a trustee (and later president of the fund). Cecil was a very interesting man, and while he hadn't the huge personality or grandeur of his brother Sidney, he had great integrity and a marvellous nose for popular entertainment, including long-running soap *Coronation Street*, which became his baby.

Just prior to these appointments, the Screenwriters' Guild's own charity, the Screenwriters'

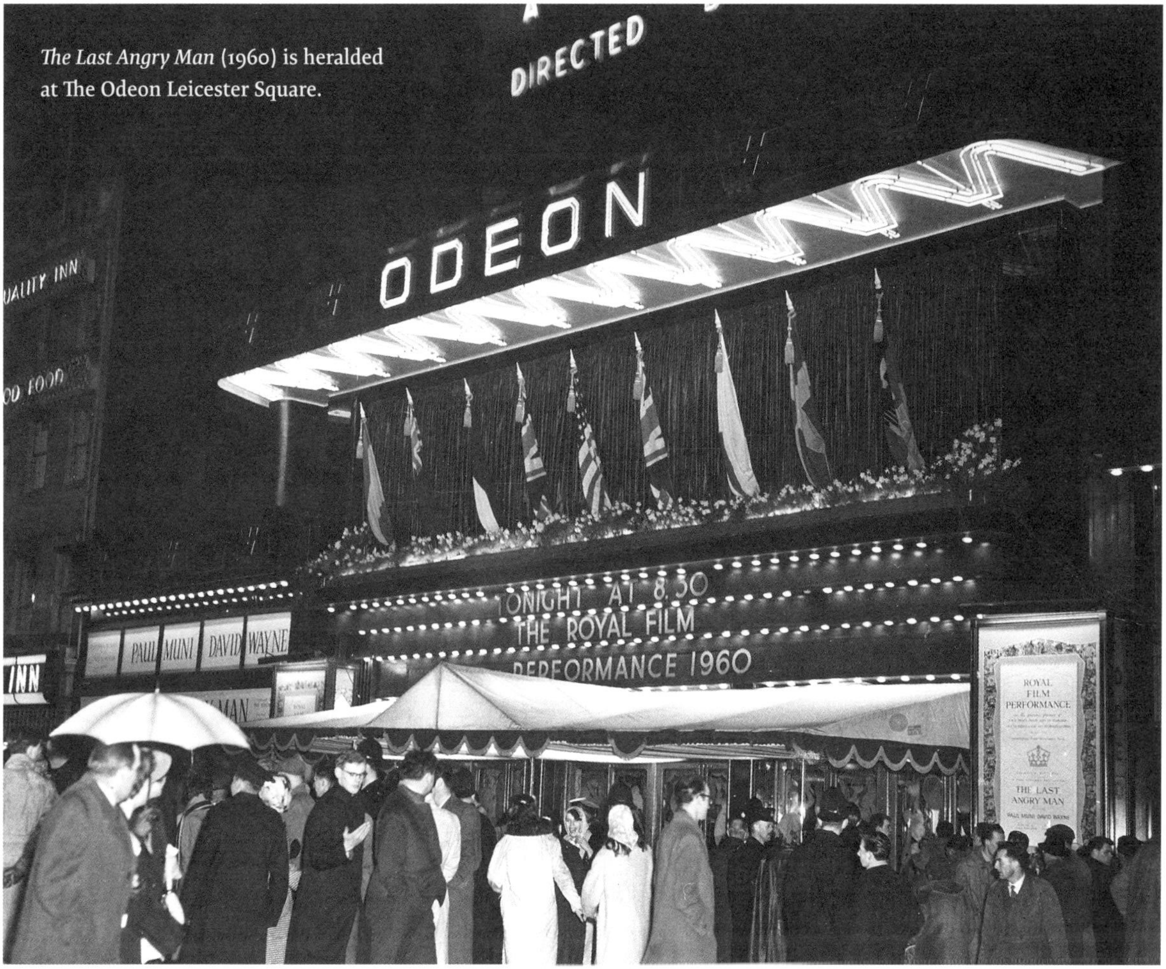

The Last Angry Man (1960) is heralded at The Odeon Leicester Square.

Benevolent Fund, merged with the (much larger) CTBF. A few years later, in 1970, Sydney Samuelson, a longtime supporter of the fund and its future president, came up with the idea of holding a concert of film music on a big scale at the Royal Albert Hall, helping to swell CTBF's income. Samuelson explained:

> I had been interested in music written for films for many, many years and when discussing fundraising options, I had the idea of putting on a concert of film music, with the ticket price earning us money for the Fund. Even though I had never produced a concert of music in my life, I did know about film music and said I could organise it. The team agreed to back me as far as the expenses were concerned and I set about putting on a concert at the Royal Albert Hall, no less, with of course the minimum amount of expense.
>
> In those days, you were able to rent the venue for a charity event (a Saturday night cost only £400 at that time), however the musicians didn't give an inch. Their payment was arranged by their union on the basis of a three-hour session, and I think there was an obligatory

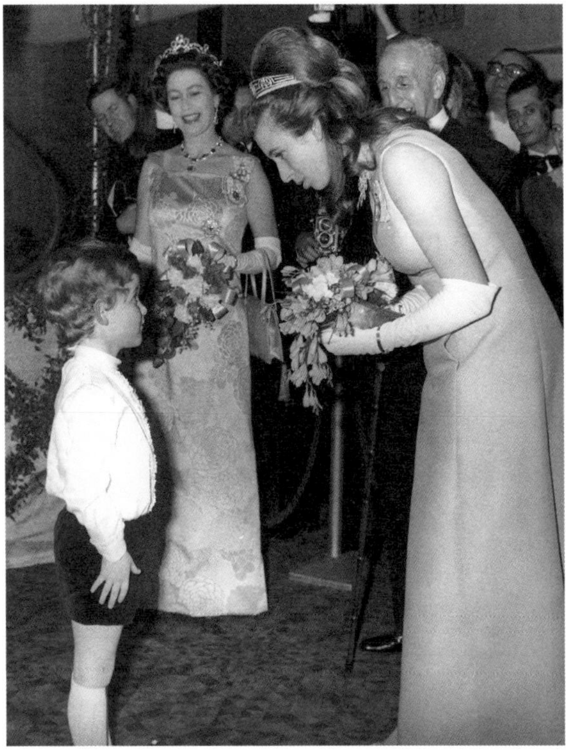

The Queen looks on as Princess Anne is given a bouquet at the 1970 Royal Film Performance of *Anne of a Thousand Days*.

twenty-minute break halfway through for them to go and have a cup of tea or a cigarette. You had to pay the same full rate for the rehearsal sessions, so it was expensive.

My plan was to invite composers of film music to conduct a symphony orchestra. Not me, but somebody else came up with the idea that we should call it 'Filmharmonic', one word.

I wanted the poster to advertise this 'concert of film music' and also say 'played by 100 musicians of the Royal Philharmonic Orchestra'. I also set about finding a star conductor to start off with, a composer of music who I felt would drag in the audience. I wanted someone everybody would know. I wanted Henry Mancini – the number one celebrity composer at that time. Mancini had already won two Oscars (for 'Moon River' from *Breakfast at Tiffany's* and 'Days of Wine and Roses' from the film of the same name). Mancini had many other works that he had composed for other films, and I managed to get in touch with him on one of my trips to Los Angeles and I put it to him.

And magic of magic, Henry Mancini said yes. I then revealed that I didn't have any money to pay him, but said we would provide him with return airfares. He interrupted me by saying 'first class – and for my wife as well'. I was always able to do a price deal with the hotels because I would say there will of course be publicity, and I would like to provide you with tickets for the concert. And so that was the way that it was done.

I formed the Film Concert Committee, which was full of friends of mine including the head of publicity for Paramount. One of the committee members came up with FILMHARMONIC – not Philharmonic – and that was brilliant. Everybody immediately agreed that it would be a marvellous name. Then somebody said that we should register the name, in case we wanted to do it again, which we did.

Filmharmonic 70 was the first concert, and I took the decision to have

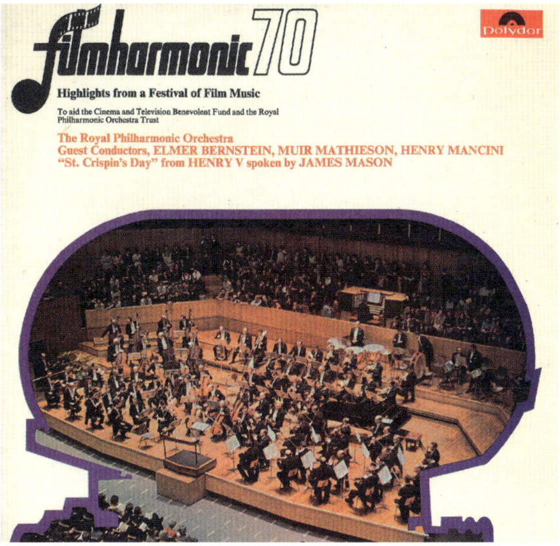

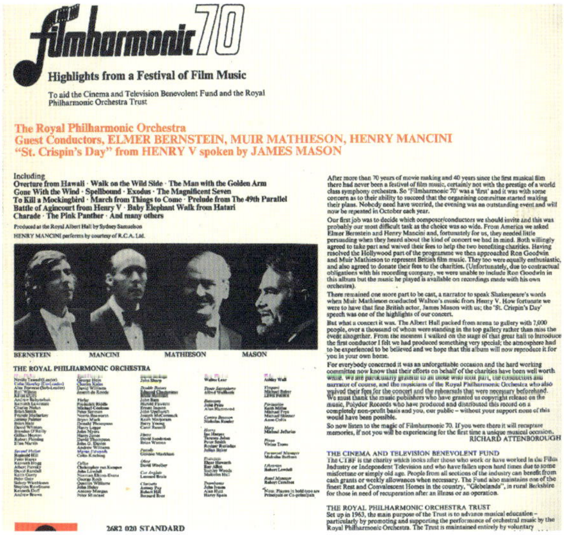

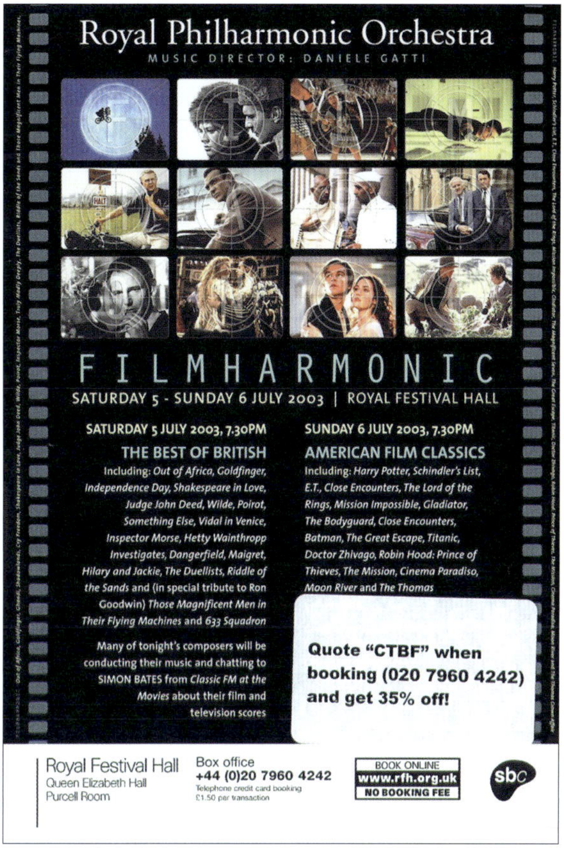

different composers/conductors in the same concert, and I gave the opening to Ron Goodwin.

I also had another American composer on the bill, quite a famous one, called Elmer Bernstein. I remember saying to him 'I will want you to open the second half' because that sounded less demeaning and better than saying 'I want you to go on third'. I had two sections for the first half and two for the second, but, obviously, the great Henry Mancini, the star composer/conductor, had to come on last.

The early sales did not go so well – and it didn't help that the Albert Hall with standing in the top balcony had 5,500 tickets to sell. Luckily, one of the chiefs of an independent television broadcaster was on the committee and suggested doing some commercials for Filmharmonic on ITV, around three weeks before the date of the concert. The commercials were only 30 seconds long but told the story of what it was all about: it sold out.

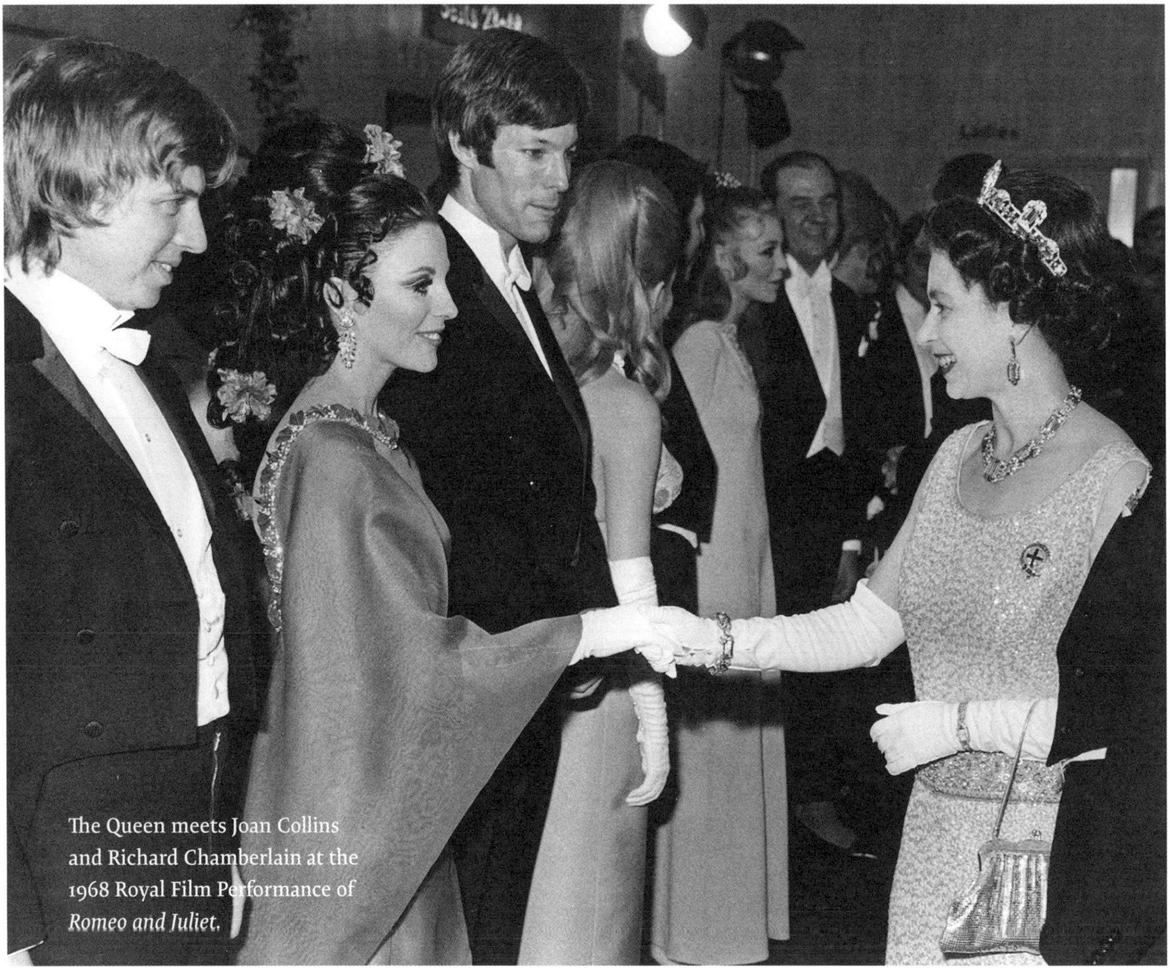

The Queen meets Joan Collins and Richard Chamberlain at the 1968 Royal Film Performance of *Romeo and Juliet.*

> Filmharmonic was a huge success, and I quickly started thinking about the following year.
>
> I think there were twelve of them all together. And do you know we never had an unsold seat.*

Over the years, Samuelson invited all the great film music composers: John Williams came twice, as did Henry Mancini. British film composers such as John Barry, Muir Mathieson and Ron Goodwin guested, and all without fees. 'I think on the last five occasions it was televised,' added Samuelson. He later ran the London Marathon at the age of 56 in aid of the CTBF, raising £22,000.

A further period of change came as the fund grew and expanded its day-to-day operation, because it had become too big for the part-time (and honorary) role of chairman. As such, in 1972 the position was discontinued and, in its place, the salaried role of executive director was introduced to take over the daily running and management of the charity while reporting directly to the president and trustees.

* This and all quotes from Sydney Samuelson are from an interview with the British Entertainment History Project, May 2002. Unless otherwise stated, all quotes are from charity press releases or interviews with the authors.

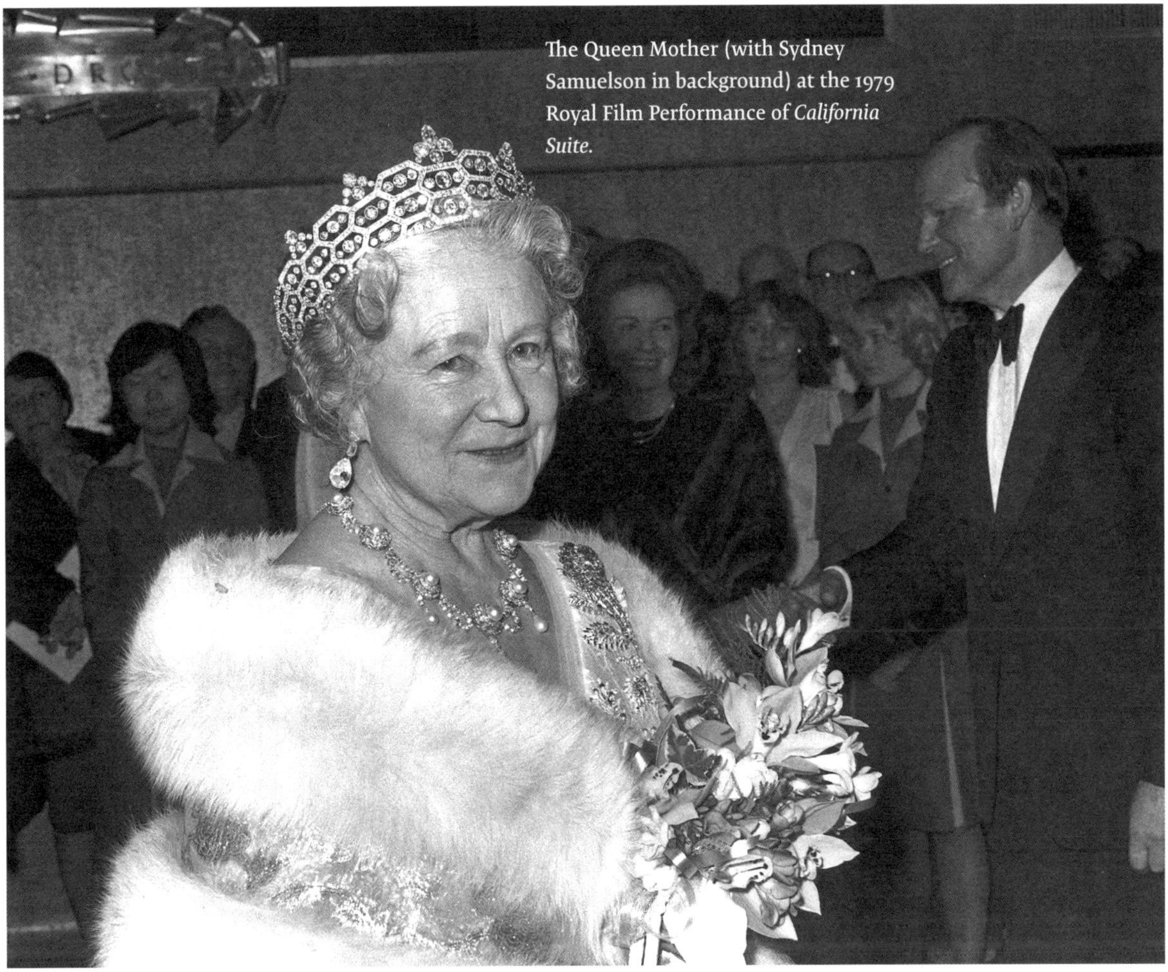

The Queen Mother (with Sydney Samuelson in background) at the 1979 Royal Film Performance of *California Suite*.

The first appointment in the role was Major General Casimir Michael Grigg CBE, a retired British Army officer who had won the Military Cross in Sicily in 1943. His appointment coincided with Anthony Kilmister retiring as secretary and the new position of secretary of finance and administration was created.

Grigg examined all areas of the charity and reported to the trustees that the northern convalescent home, The Craggs, only had twelve residents and the running costs were considerable with very little income; it surely made sense to close that home and transfer everyone to Glebelands. The Craggs seafront site was subsequently redeveloped as flats.

Positive changes were sadly overshadowed by the death of former fund president Lord Rank in March 1972, and although the mogul had stepped back from the day-to-day running of his organisation in favour of his feared managing director John Davis, he remained a larger-than-life figure within the industry and indeed within the charity.

Sydney Samuelson recalls another sad death within the CTBF, which led to John Davis succeeding Lord Rank in the CTBF as well as in his business empire:

> When serving President Cecil Bernstein died in 1977, he just dropped down dead I think on the pavement, John Davis was asked if he would take over the Presidency [of the Fund].
>
> I'm absolutely sure that those who'd been there a very long time witnessed a degree of fear in his appointment in so much as 'Well I suppose we better ask John Davis to do it'. And so the next thing I found was that John Davis was the President.
>
> 'Well, that's ok, we can carry on,' I thought, but the first thing that happened under his tenure was that a submission was put in to close down Glebelands!

There were reportedly only sixteen long-time residents of the home, with new applications dwindling. With the fund's northern convalescent home having closed, the news of Glebelands rarely being full resulted in John Davis suggesting that the fund should instead concentrate on providing help for people in their own homes, where they'd lived all their lives and where their roots were. His proposal met with strong opposition, not least from the technicians who had given up their own homes – in some cases years before – and moved into Glebelands.

John Davis summoned a gathering at the Rank Organisation's HQ, as explained by Sydney Samuelson, who was firmly against Glebelands' closure:

> The meeting was called at South Street of all those concerned, I had two people with me – in other words, on my side – and we prepared to speak up against John Davis; the Chief Executive, or General Secretary I should say of NATKE and Alan Sapper of trade union ACTT.
>
> The answer to Glebelands' so-called problem of not enough residents was surely to make it better known what we had on offer. Because there were bound to be lots of people who would be so much better off if they had someone to look after them. But then it was said that nursing care is only available up to a certain point. And then if people got really sick, they were shunted off to a fully equipped nursing home.
>
> I said, 'What we need is to put in the extra care that is needed, not throw them out'. And I'm sure that a lot of people at that time didn't come to Glebelands because they realised that when they became really unwell, they would have to be sent somewhere else. My main point, that we should keep it open, make it better known, and keep all the residents, assure them that they are never going to be moved on and to fund the building of an extra care wing.

Davis realised he had lost the argument:

> He then said, 'I want silence in respect of the death of Cecil Bernstein', and of course everybody was silent for two minutes or whatever it was. And then he added, 'I've been asked if I will take over. I will only take over until the end of the term of three years that Cecil had to run'. Which I think was about a year and a half. 'And meanwhile we must appoint my successor and I'm going to ask Sydney Samuelson if he will consider succeeding me as President of the Fund'.
>
> I was absolutely dumbfounded because we'd had so many run-ins, especially because of Glebelands. But that's how I became the President of the CTBF.

Although Samuelson didn't particularly enjoy a close friendship with John Davis – no one did – he and his wife were often invited to dine at Davis's home and to his plush office in South Street:

> On several occasions I had lunch with him. And we used to sit at this ginormous Rank Organisation board room table, just the two of us, and that of course was all butler service and so on. But you never arrived late. I remember before he became President, he was in charge of the Finance Committee, and there was a meeting where he was Chair – handling all the investments for the CTBF – amounting to millions. I got held up and arrived late, the meeting had just started but I would say I was a good ten minutes delayed. Davis said, 'Late, interfering with someone else, were you?' All because he felt I'd interfered with the proposed Glebelands closure.

Far from closing Glebelands, once Sydney Samuelson took over as president in 1978, he oversaw the extra-care wing being built. 'I remember Countess Mountbatten came and opened it,' Samuelson recalled, 'and nobody disappeared from Glebelands, elsewhere, ever again'.

He also made minor but important improvements, such as new decoration and removing the brass plaques above beds – 'this bed was endowed by …' – stating, 'They'd been sponsored years before and none of the people involved were still around plus I felt it was demeaning. A touch of the workhouse, isn't it?'

By the end of the 1970s, CTBF assets stood at an impressive £2,857,175, but more fundamental changes were about to come.

7

Flying the Flag (1980s)

IN 1981, THE ROYAL FILM Performance was *Chariots of Fire* from which producer David Puttnam generously donated a percentage of the box-office receipts to the CTBF. Its theme of hope, honour and belief seemed very fitting for Britain in the early premiership of Margaret Thatcher.

Soon afterwards, and for the first time since the charity's founding in 1924, the AGM of 1982 saw a vote for fixed terms for key roles: the position of president was to be fixed for three years, while trustees would only serve for a maximum of four years and the honorary treasurer term would be fixed for five years. The number of trustees was also increased to six and, as with other roles, was subject to a vote of approval by members at each AGM. This was to ensure the CTBF was governed independently and with members having the power of appointments, rather than a select group of existing executives, many of whom had already served thirty-plus years in office.

With the new extra-care wing at Glebelands open, the home was full and had a waiting list of new potential residents. Further improvements such as rewiring, upgrading the central heating system, new furniture and telephones in all residents' rooms had made Glebelands a desirable and modern place.

Meanwhile, there were now 452 long-term beneficiaries of the fund, making Royal Film Performance income very important, although the British film industry had fallen into a slump with fewer movies made in 1980 and 1981 than in any year since 1914. In the 1970s, there were over 1,500 cinemas in operation, but by the 1980s there were just 650. Many had closed in favour of bingo halls, while others had just been shuttered due to dwindling attendance.

A new hope came on 2 November 1982, when Channel 4 Television launched and committed to a film strand. Its first production, Stephen Frears' *Walter*, starring Sir Ian McKellen, was commissioned to broadcast on the channel's opening night. Film on 4 (now Film4) helped relaunch and support British films to an international audience after the bleakness of the late 1970s, often tackling gritty domestic subjects at the same time. Early successes included *My Beautiful Laundrette*, *The Company of Wolves*, *Mona Lisa*, *Letter to Brezhnev* and Derek Jarman's *Jubilee* and *Sebastiane*.

However, the Film Act of 1985 saw the Conservative Government of the time remove support for the industry: tax rules were tightened and the Eady Levy, which reinvested a percentage of box-office sales back into production via the National Film Finance Corporation (NFFC), was abolished, as was the NFFC itself.

Somewhat ironically, 1985 was declared 'British Film Year' and a special ident with accompanying music composed by Vangelis ran in cinemas with the aim of promoting

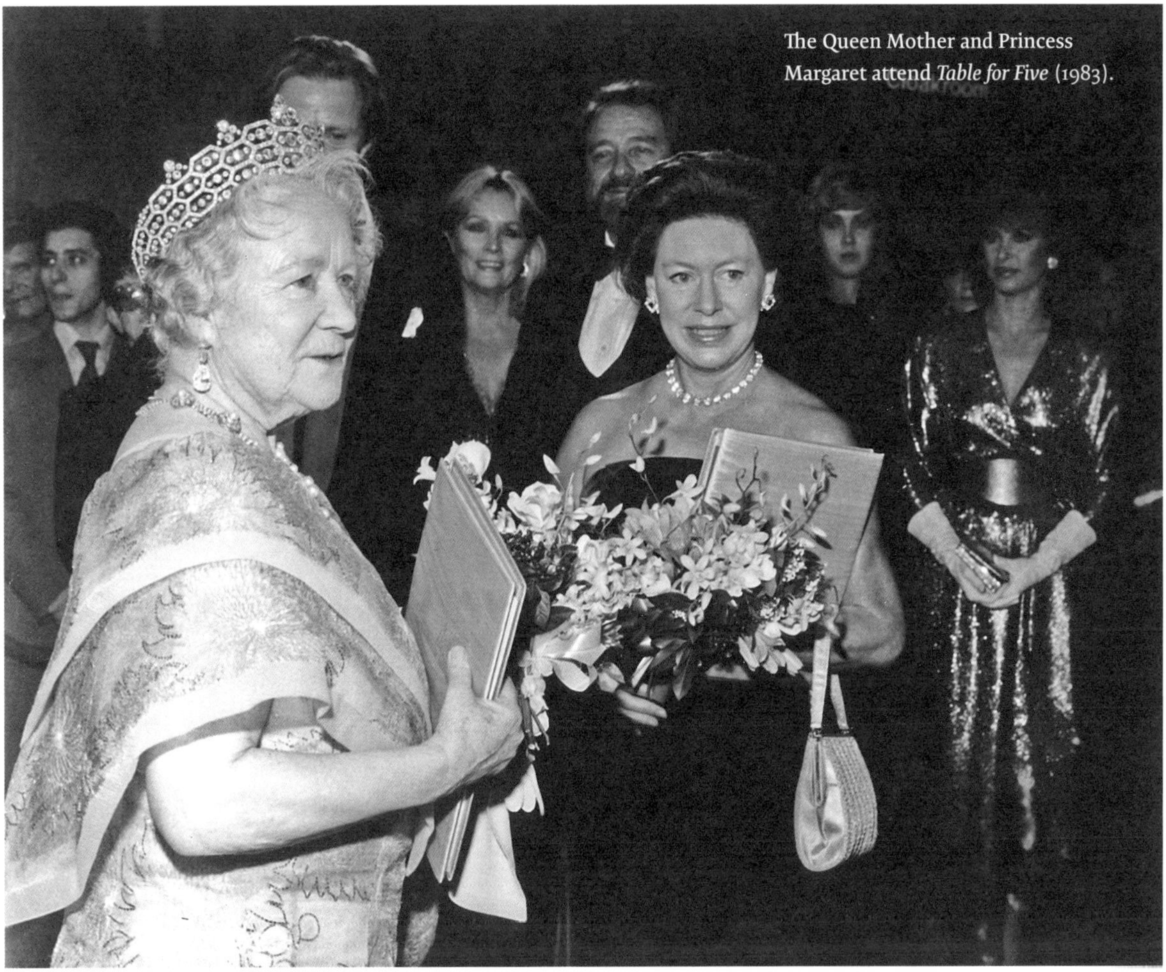

The Queen Mother and Princess Margaret attend *Table for Five* (1983).

both film production and cinema attendance – at a time when it was estimated that people in the UK went to the pictures on average just once a year, with a total annual attendance estimated at 50 million. Of course, all this came at a time of increasing popularity of home video rentals too.

The Film Year initiative had hopes of boosting attendance by 4–5 per cent at a time when cinemas were closing or changing use at a higher percentage. Roadshows were planned, with a gala launch event at Leicester Square in London supported by a roster of film-world dignitaries and British stars, including John Hurt, Tom Conti, Terry Jones and Fiona Fullerton. Film Minister Norman Lamont launched the initiative with a flurry of red, white and blue balloons and named twenty-five cities as destinations. Special screenings, exhibitions and lectures were planned in each.

Bucking the trend of cinema closures was the first cinema multiplex opening in Milton Keynes. The Point offered ten different screens and paved the way for less-expensive edge-of-town cinema complexes. The front part of the Point building had a distinctive mirrored, crystal ziggurat shape framed by external steel beams at each corner and joined at the apex.

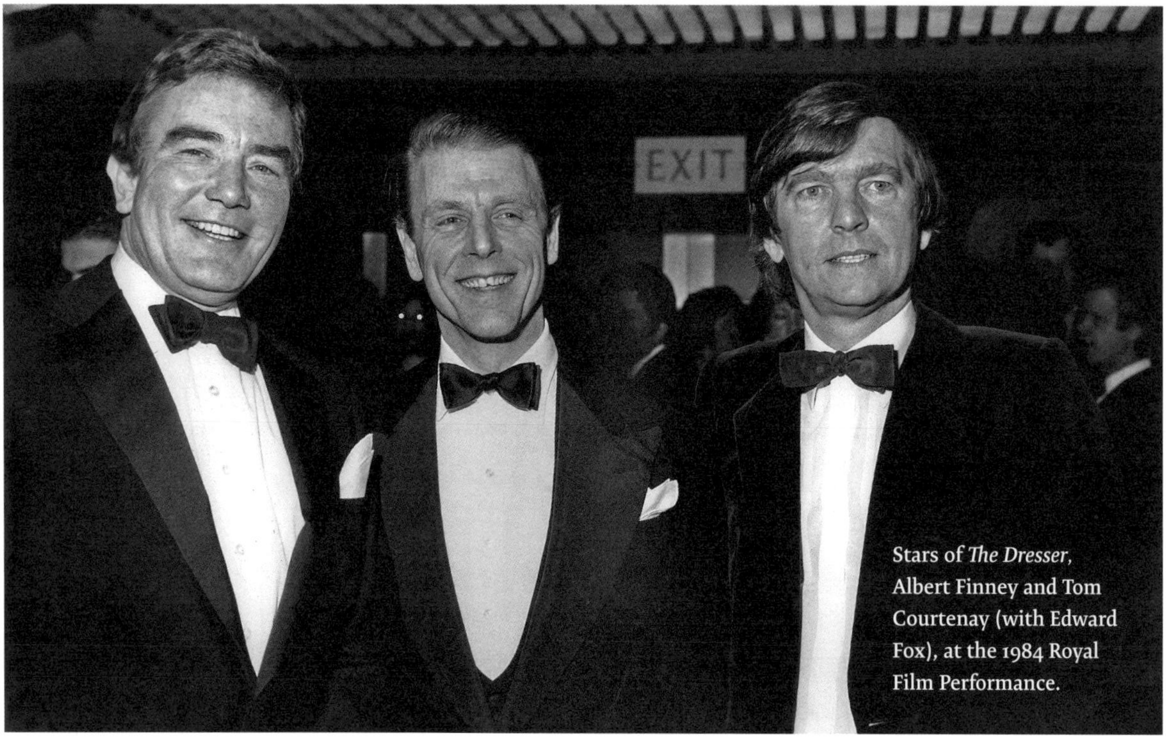

Stars of *The Dresser*, Albert Finney and Tom Courtenay (with Edward Fox), at the 1984 Royal Film Performance.

Originally, it had red neon lights connecting the apexes at each side, so that it looked like a pyramid at night.

Rather appropriately for British Film Year, John Brabourne, the film-producer husband of Lord Mountbatten's daughter Patricia, became a trustee of the fund and brought with him his latest epic, *A Passage to India*, for the Royal Film Performance in March. The premiere was particularly notable for the significant royal presence of the Queen Mother and Princess Anne, along with the Prince and Princess of Wales – marking Princess Diana's debut at the event. She dazzled the crowds in an off-the-shoulder emerald-green gown.

Newspapers were also quick to centre on popular TV stars of the day Michael Brandon and Glynis Barber (aka *Dempsey and Makepeace*) pretending to have an argument on the red carpet to throw off rumours of a romance. In fact, they married four years later.

The return of 'Filmharmonic' was also heralded in 1985 after a short break (due to lack of sponsorship and a TV broadcast deal of the 1981 concert). The revived musical celebration of cinema primarily featured music from films made at Thorn EMI (formerly ABPC) Studios in Elstree. Sir Richard Attenborough introduced the conductors, John Gregory, John Scott, Stanley Black and John Williams, who, in turn, led the London Symphony Orchestra. Forty attending residents from Glebelands received a particularly special welcome from Sir Richard.

In 1987, plans were confirmed for the CTBF to sell 10 acres of the gardens surrounding Glebelands for a private housing development, generating £6 million, thus allowing the fund to move from rented offices at Royalty House in London's Dean Street to a new freehold office building at No. 22 Golden Square. However, fund staff had very little time to enjoy their new offices when a further slump in UK production forced studios to contract – Pinewood Studios went four-walled (dry hire) from previously being a fully staffed facility, while Elstree Film Studios was sold off by Thorn-EMI to Brent Walker. Both moves saw mass redundancies and coupled with a jobs shortage, the CTBF swung into action with a range of measures from offering grants and loans to providing invaluable expert advice and moral support. Thankfully, the earlier land sale helped boost fund assets from £2.8 million in 1980 to £16.3 million in 1990, placing it in a strong position at a time of ongoing crisis in the film industry.

The television business seemed buoyant, however, with advertising revenue steady and a good balance of indigenous productions versus imported programmes. In fact, the CTBF benefited directly from a TV drama when producer Sarah Lawson wrote at the end of 1989 asking the trustees if they'd grant permission for the LWT drama *Life After Life* to use Glebelands house and grounds for filming. The story revolved around a 70-year-old man (George Cole) moving into a retirement home. Helen Burns, Renée Asherson and Leslie Phillips co-starred and 'after various negotiations' (according to the fund's annual report), the production moved in between 19–29 September, offering to send the younger residents of Glebelands to a hotel in Hastings for a holiday for the duration!

Also that year, a special luncheon was hosted at BAFTA for 133 beneficiaries of the charity and was followed by a screening of *Goodbye Mr Chips* in the presence of cinematographer Freddie Young. In 1991, George Cole returned to Glebelands to draw the annual Christmas raffle, which raised over £35,000.

8

Changing Times (1990–2010)

WHILE THE UK FILM INDUSTRY limped along with a couple of dozen films in production during 1990, it sadly went without the anticipated third James Bond film to star Timothy Dalton, due to legal wranglings between the parent studio MGM and producer Cubby Broccoli. The planned *Batman* sequel for which Pinewood kept the huge Gotham City set from 1989 standing on the backlot was lost when Tim Burton decided to relocate to America, somewhat influenced by Jack Nicholson, who played the Joker in the first film, stating the UK's strict withholding tax laws made filming in the UK very unappealing to Hollywood stars.

A real-life protagonist shook the UK independent TV business meanwhile. The Broadcasting Act (1990) was introduced to liberalise and deregulate the British broadcasting industry – in particular ITV, which had been described by Prime Minister Margaret Thatcher as 'the last bastion of restrictive practices'. It led directly to the abolition of the Independent Broadcasting Authority, which was replaced with the Independent Television Commission and the Radio Authority (both themselves now replaced by Ofcom). More significantly, it reformed the system of awarding ITV franchises via a silent auction. Thames, TVS, TSW and TV-am lost out on 6 October 1991, not necessarily because they bid lower than other companies, but also based on the perceived quality of their programming plans. Admittedly, financial offerings were the key factor: Carlton bid £43.2 million for the London weekday franchise versus Thames bidding £32.7 million, while GMTV bid £34.6 million to TV-am's £14.1 million. Many staff transferred across to new franchise operators, redundancies were again made and the fund swung into action once more to support behind-the-scenes staff facing an uncertain future.

The all-important annual Royal Film Performance received global attention in 1991 when the Prince and Princess of Wales attended *Hot Shots!* after a four-year absence from the event and helped raise over £81,000. However, in a reflection of the troubling times facing both the film and television industry, it proved to be the lowest amount generated in a decade, which was particularly unfortunate as it was reported there were now 1,200 people being supported by the charity.

Happily, the following year, Richard Attenborough's biopic of Charlie Chaplin, simply titled *Chaplin*, was the Royal Film Performance and raised a higher sum of £106,000. Robert Downey Jr starred and earned an Academy Award nomination, although as he has since revealed it was a challenging time for him personally. Happily, he credits sobriety for the phenomenal career momentum he has enjoyed over the past few years, and Richard Attenborough's suggestion he might choose to model himself on Anthony Hopkins rather than Peter O'Toole!

In 1993, it was Hollywood's turn to supply a blockbuster for the Royal Film Performance and Mel Gibson's directorial debut *The Man Without A Face* was chosen. The Loyal Address was given by Stephen Fry, who said:

> It has fallen to me to welcome you to the 47th Royal Film Performance: I don't propose to keep you long, but I do want to say one or two words about this business we call show.
>
> Those of us who are lucky enough to appear in front of the cameras from time to time are, as the world knows, hugely overpraised, over-primped and overpaid. It's a world of glamour, money, lax moral standards, disgusting table-manners and a worrying disregard of core values.
>
> It is well known, however, that actors form only a tiny minority of the personnel that go to make films and television. The number of drop-dead handsome, petite, ivory-toothed, slim-thighed, firmly muscled, internationally acclaimed, doe-eyed beauties like myself is surprisingly small. We are but the tip of the iceberg. The majority of film and television personnel working behind the cameras in this country, the ones who have contributed so much to Britain's reputation in the techniques of film making are invisible. The film technician is truly 'The Man Without A Face'. That is usually how they like it: they are craftsmen and women of the highest order whose pleasure lies in their work.
>
> The Cinema and Television Benevolent Fund in whose aid this screening is being given, if I can slip on my serious trousers for a moment, exists to make sure that the once valued craftsman does not become The Man Without A Place, for it is alarmingly common for workers in this industry to fall upon hard times. I believe it is not only fitting that the enormous well of affection and respect that all of us in Cinema and Television feel for these men and women be reflected in a decent and well-run benevolent fund that can provide for a happy retirement.
>
> So that old cinematographers don't find their light fading therefore, so that retired script girls receive the continuity they have earned, so that old dolly operators don't lose their grip, so that old clapper boys aren't clapped out, so that old electricians don't lose their sparks, so that chippies don't chip and boom operators don't go bust. The CTBF has a beautiful retirement home near Wokingham and a professionally managed fund of money with which to help workers in an industry which is all about life and hope and

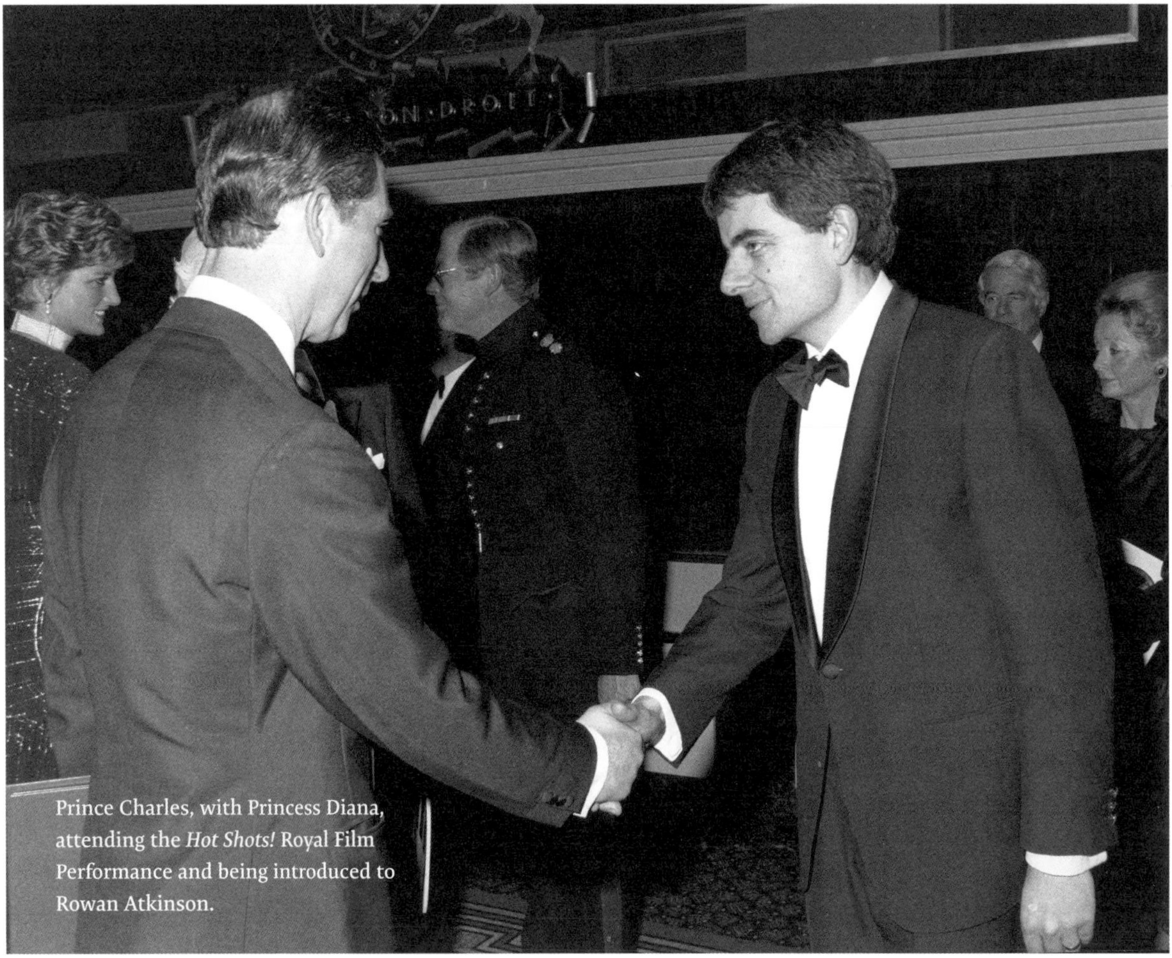

Prince Charles, with Princess Diana, attending the *Hot Shots!* Royal Film Performance and being introduced to Rowan Atkinson.

beauty and promise, to help them earn their just reward, living, if they wish, amongst their fellows and remembering old shoots, old locations and old triumphs in peace and comfort.

There is a phrase cameramen use for a certain time of day, the gloaming, the early twilight, when it is neither day nor night, that dusky time towards the evening which photographs so beautifully: they call it the Magic Hour. In order to make the twilight of those heroes of cinema and television a true Magic Hour the CTBF needs, like any film star, money, and a good profile. We are all immensely grateful to you, Your Royal Highness, to Mr Mel Gibson, the star and director of the film we're about to enjoy, to the management of this wonderful cinema and to all of you who have supported this beloved industry and its craftsmen by being here tonight. We hope you will never forget this evening and never forget the CTBF and the work it does every day of the year.

But, as the Archbishop of Canterbury likes to say, that's enough tedious offal, let's party. Your Royal Highness, my Lords, Ladies and Gentlemen, settle back in your comfy Odeon seats, pop some corn, lick some lollies, and enjoy tonight's Royal Film – *The Man Without A Face*. Thank you.

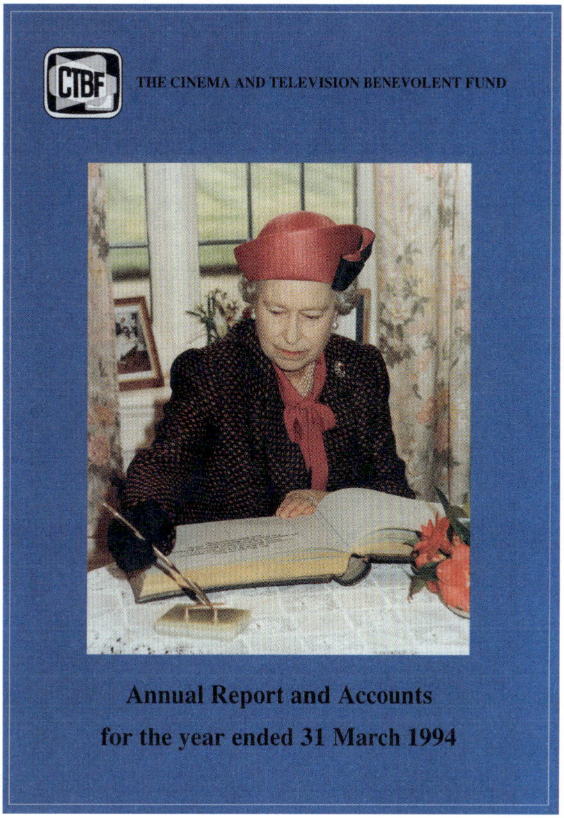
THE CINEMA AND TELEVISION BENEVOLENT FUND

Annual Report and Accounts

for the year ended 31 March 1994

On 12 April 1994, the Queen and the Duke of Edinburgh visited Glebelands to mark the seventieth anniversary of the fund and meet residents. They also officially inaugurated the Jeremy Woolf Memorial bungalows, the David Pratt Summerhouse and the Kate Philips Gate Wing.

Later that same year, the royal couple attended the Royal Film Performance, which again centred around Richard Attenborough – albeit this time starring in *Miracle On 34th Street*. The film's release coincided with the National Lottery launching in the UK, and thanks in no small part to the personal intervention of the recently ennobled Lord Attenborough, it was agreed by the government that a percentage of the good-causes money raised would be set aside for film production. Funds were initially administered by the Arts Council, then by the UK Film Council and now by the British Film Institute, and the Lottery has helped fund more than 600 films, winning 504 awards, including sixteen Oscars, 124 BAFTAs and thirty-three Cannes titles along the way.

This crucial financial support certainly helped bolster the film business at its introduction and a few years later in 1997, a new Labour Government additionally introduced Section 48 tax relief, which provided a write-down of UK production expenditure (netting approximately 20 per cent of a budget) which in turn prompted a tenfold increase on the average of twenty British films made annually in the decade prior. Things seemed to be on the up again!

Fun initiatives to help raise awareness of the CTBF (as well as funds) were launched in the new millennium. The London Party was a lively themed dinner, with entertainment and disco, and it soon became the fund's second-most important fundraising event after the Royal Film Performance.

Meanwhile, in 2004, the CTBF celebrated its eightieth anniversary, and to mark the occasion, a special fundraising lunch party was organised at the Corinthia Hotel in central

2006 Comedy Lunch guests Greg Davies and Lucy Porter.

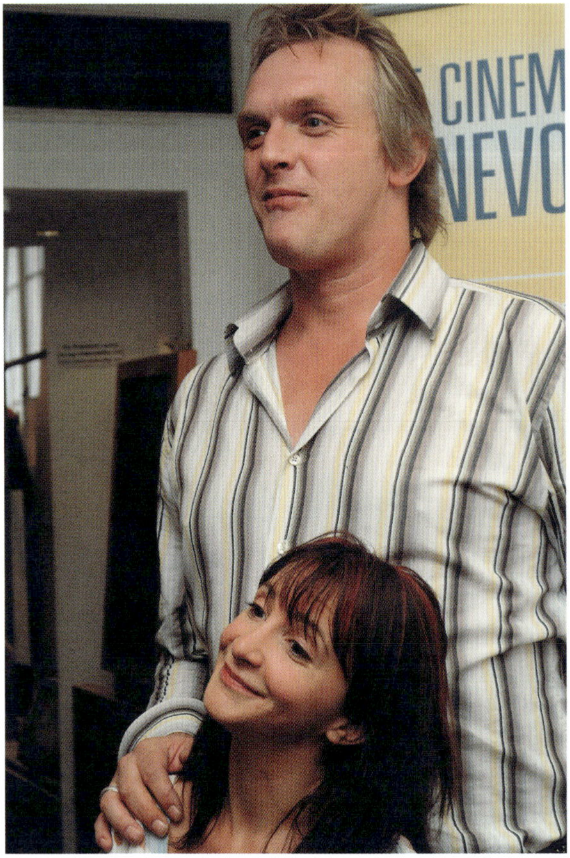

London. Each table was hosted by a film industry legend in their eighth decade, and included actors Sir Roger Moore KBE, Sir John Mills CBE, Sir Donald Sinden CBE, Lord Richard Attenborough and Richard Todd OBE; cinematographers Oswald (aka Ossie) Morris, Sir Sydney Samuelson CBE and Jack Cardiff OBE; producers Leslie Gilliat and Peter Morley OBE; production designers Peter Murton and Sir Ken Adam; director Roy Ward Baker; costume designer Julie Harris; and script supervisor Elaine Schreyeck.

Also in 2004, the charity was incorporated as a company, registered in England and Wales and limited by guarantee. It was a move to protect the people running the organisation from personal liability against any debts that might have been incurred and enable the charity to tap into potential funding streams that were only open to incorporated charities.

In 2005, a regular Best of British Comedy Lunch was born and hosted at BAFTA's Piccadilly headquarters in association with the Comedy Store. Funny people, old and new, gathered for an afternoon of hilarity, chat, stand-up and more. For over a decade, comedy glitterati such as Galton & Simpson, Victor Spinetti, Rufus Hound, Andrew Sachs, Paul Merton, Barry Cryer, Lucy Porter, Katherine Ryan, Stephen K. Amos, Ed Byrne, Sarah Millican, Sanjeev Bhaskar, Jason Manford and many more all guested.

After long-time fund supporter and producer Lord Brabourne passed away in 2005, his family approached the CTBF with the idea of introducing an initiative to provide financial support to individuals facing difficulties in progressing their careers. John Brabourne, whose credits included *Murder on the Orient Express* (1974) and *A Passage to India* (1984), had always tried to support upcoming talent. It was agreed that the John Brabourne Awards would run twice a year, providing up to £5,000 to cover expenses ranging from development and training to production and living costs, and would be aimed at helping upcoming talent overcome barriers, realise career-changing projects and take vital next steps in the industry.

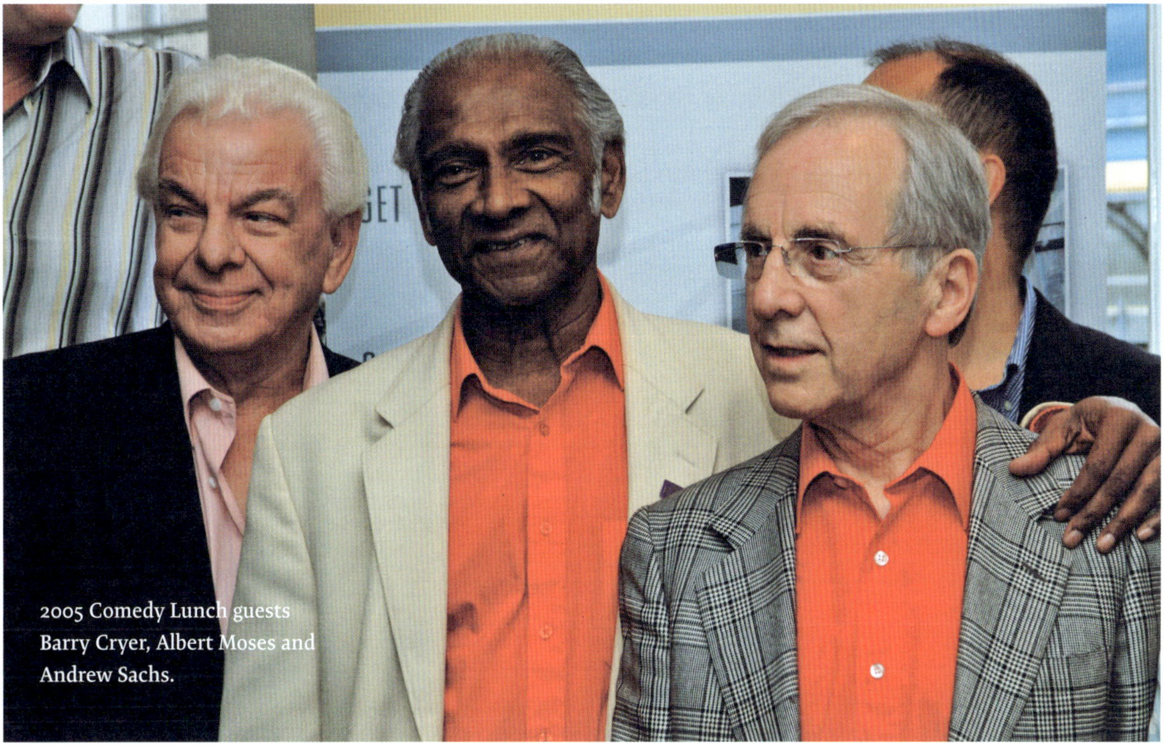

2005 Comedy Lunch guests Barry Cryer, Albert Moses and Andrew Sachs.

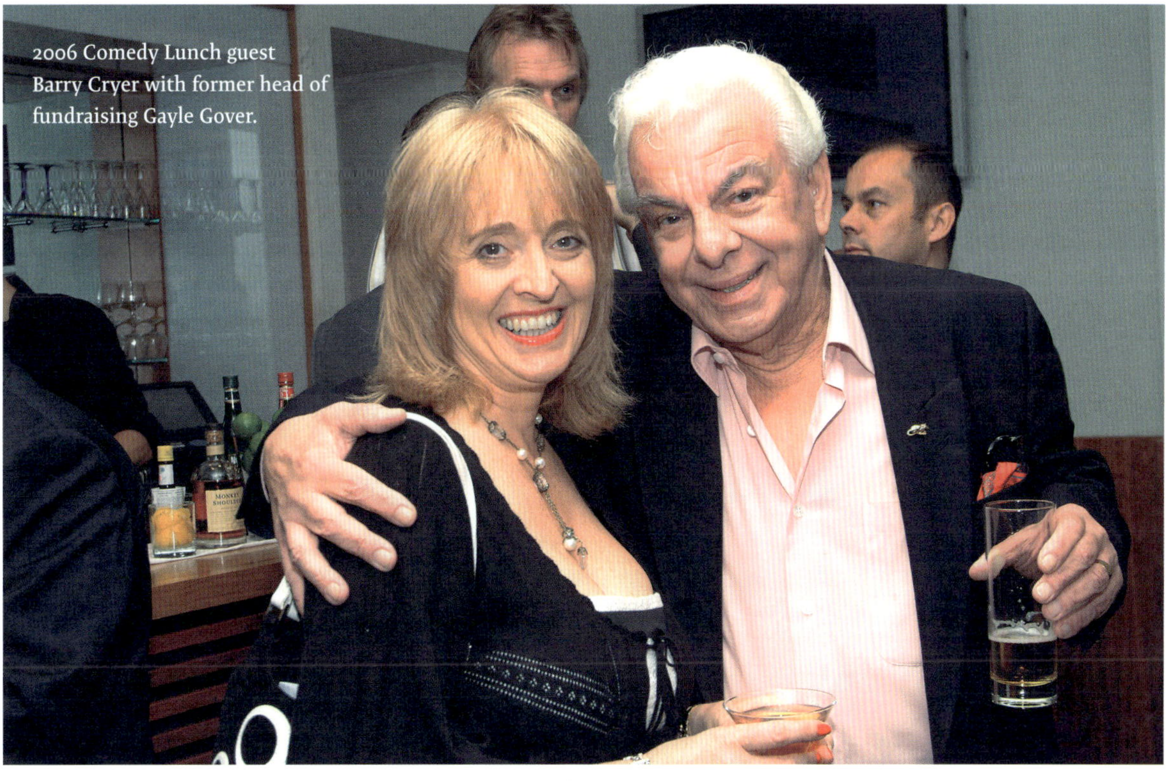

2006 Comedy Lunch guest Barry Cryer with former head of fundraising Gayle Gover.

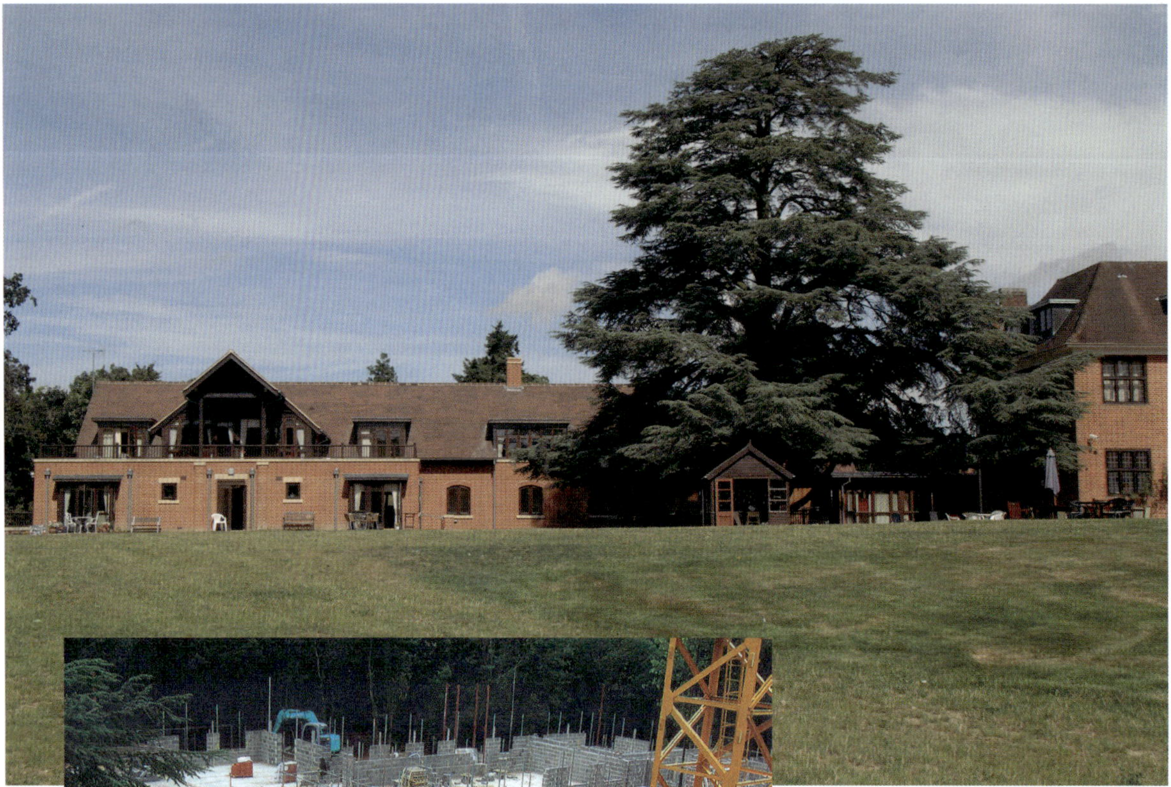

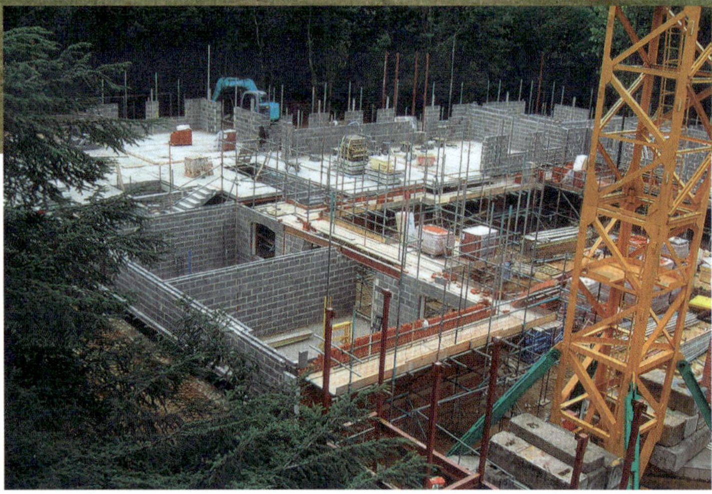

Glebelands new wing in 2006, which became the Broccoli Cloisters.

Along with direct support from the Brabourne (and Knatchbull) family, the awards pool received initial financial backing from companies such as ITV and Kodak, and in its inaugural year, it distributed £25,000–30,000 in assistance, with grants of up to £5,000 each supporting young filmmakers. Over its fifteen-year history it helped scores of young people achieve their big break in the industry.

In 2021 the charity announced:

In recent months the charity has been reviewing our discrete grants programme and have taken the decision that the alignment of the John Brabourne name with a single award will end. Instead, we will be offering high value grants to those in greatest need as part of our Always

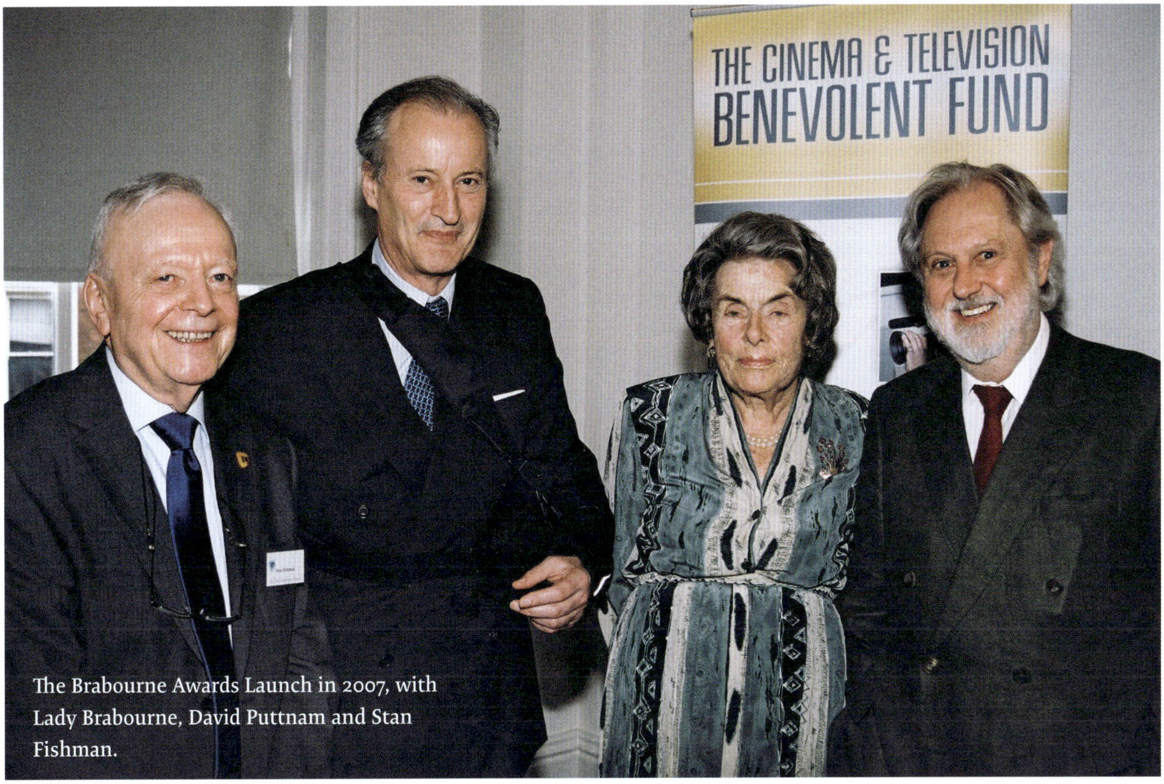

The Brabourne Awards Launch in 2007, with Lady Brabourne, David Puttnam and Stan Fishman.

On core service, with financial support enhanced by new wraparound wellbeing and practical support so that we are best placed to help individuals move forward in the industry. Our hope is that a shift to accessible support 365 days of the year means we will be able to help a much larger proportion of those experiencing challenges that may be preventing them from reaching their full potential. This aim is further enhanced by the fact that 30% of all our grants budgets are now ring-fenced for Black, Asian and Minority Ethnic applicants and 15% are ring-fenced for disabled applicants.

The Royal Film Performance of 2007 was set to be *Brick Lane*, an adaptation of Monica Ali's bestseller. However, as the autumn date approached, media reports suggested ongoing protests about the film might embarrass Prince Charles, who was scheduled to attend.

The charity announced the event was cancelled because of scheduling problems. '*Brick Lane* was chosen, but we have been informed that the date no longer works in the royal diary and for this reason there will be no Royal Film Performance this year,' CEO Peter Hore told the *Sunday Telegraph*. There had already been protests over the book by members of the Bangladeshi community, who claimed that it presented them as backward and uneducated and had mounted a successful campaign to force production company Ruby Films to find an alternative location.

Instead, two Royal Film Performances were scheduled for 2008 – *The Other Boleyn Girl* in February with Prince Charles and *A Bunch of Amateurs* in November in the presence of the Queen. It was suggested the Queen enjoyed the fun of the film so much that she requested a copy to be shown to her family at Sandringham over Christmas.

John Brabourne was not the only producer whose legacy helped the CTBF continue its work. In 2009 *Carry On*'s Peter Rogers passed away, a decade after his late wife Betty Box, and both left a considerable part of their estates, including the royalties from their films to the charity. Peter Hore, CTBF chief executive, said:

> Peter Rogers had always been a tremendous supporter of the fund and didn't hesitate to contribute towards our fundraising activities. The legacy which he has left to the CTBF is a tremendous gesture for which we are truly grateful. We intend to honour this legacy and mark the passing of a great British film producer.

Perhaps the most notable American producer to work within the UK was the James Bond franchise's Albert R. 'Cubby' Broccoli. At Glebelands in Wokingham on Monday, 7 April 2009, a special plaque was unveiled by his children, Barbara Broccoli and Michael G. Wilson following their donation of £1 million from the Dana and Albert R. Broccoli Foundation, and the plaque officially marked the renaming of the Cloisters building at

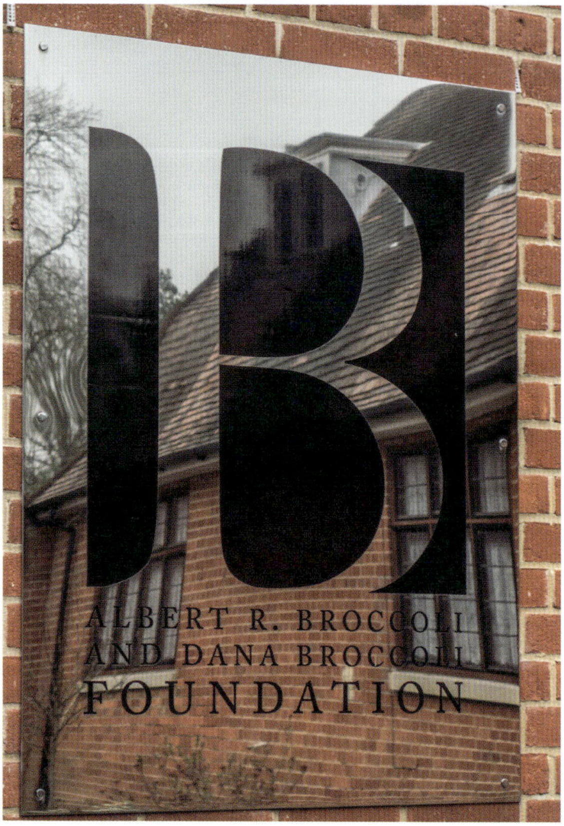

Glebelands as the Broccoli Cloisters. At the event, Barbara Broccoli said:

> The Bond films were made in Great Britain, they were started by my father Albert Broccoli, he moved to the United Kingdom in 1952 and felt England was home. He felt that he was very lucky and had a wonderful professional career here and always wanted to support the people in the industry that helped make him a successful producer.

Joining them on the day was Samantha Bond, who played Miss Moneypenny in the Pierce Brosnan Bond films, and Lewis Gilbert, who directed *You Only Live Twice*, *The Spy Who Loved Me* and *Moonraker*. Gilbert said:

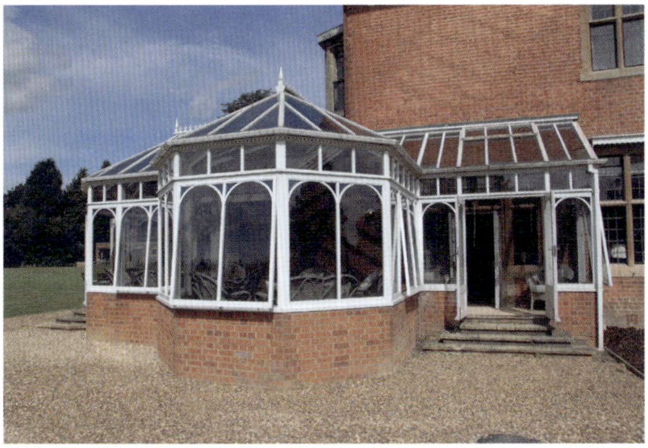

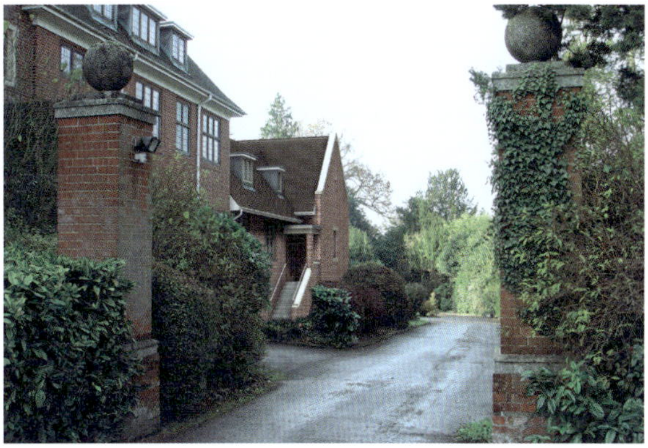

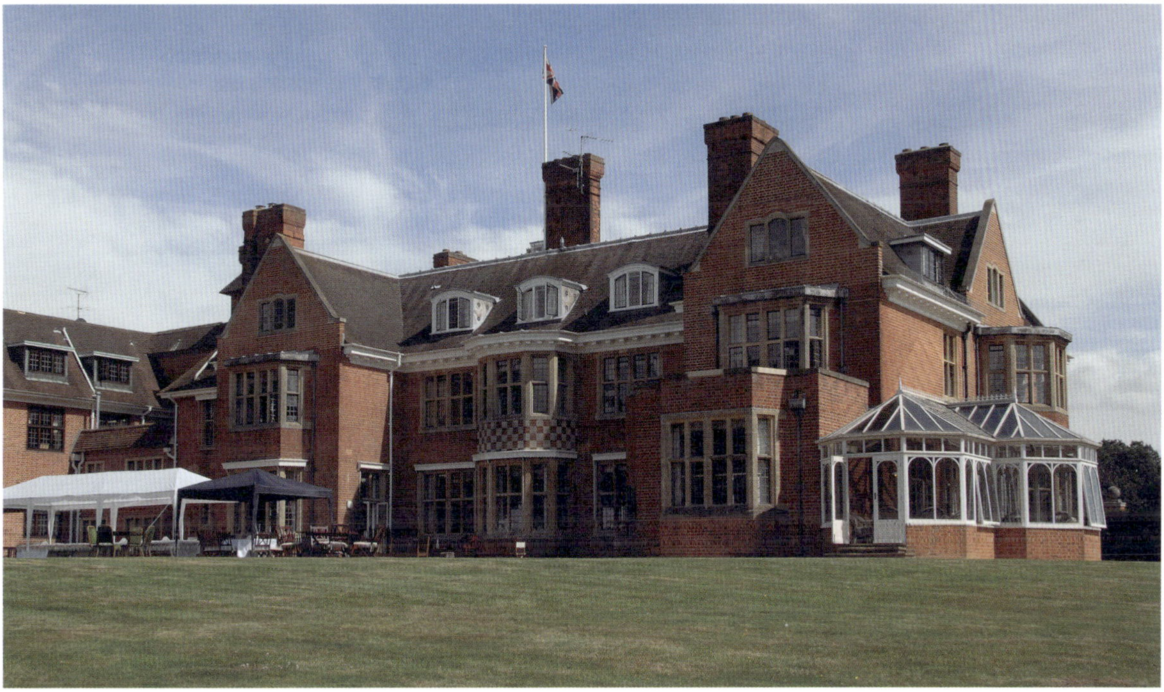

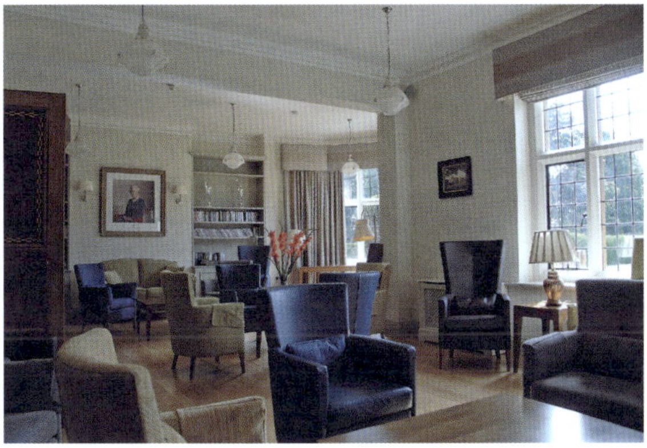

The Glebelands conservatory, main building, new wing and sitting room in 2008.

I directed 40 films, but why is it that the three Bond films that I worked on – they live in my memory so much. It's because of something very unique in the film industry and that was Broccoli himself – he cared, he cared for the unit, he was unique in the way he behaved with the unit and the way the unit loved him. Units don't love the producer, he's there to bully them and make them work harder, but Broccoli had this unique way of talking to people, you knew he cared whether you were happy or unhappy.

Michael G. Wilson added:

I think it's been fantastic to come out here and see this place, we met the residents, we looked in the rooms, this is something that Cubby and his wife Dana would've loved to have seen. They were always interested in the welfare of the people in the industry, they were always lending a helping hand. Cubby was a governor of the CTBF, and this is something that he would have been very proud of.

The James Bond Golf Society had also been long-time supporters of Glebelands and had raised funds to donate a minibus to the home for residents' outings – which included everything from trips to London, not least to attend Royal Film Performances, to outings at local shopping centres and Thames moorings for river trips.

In June 2009, a new chief executive joined the CTBF – the first non-military appointment in the role – when former chief financial officer of Sony UK Brian Robertson was appointed and brought a fresh perspective:

I felt the charity needed modernising to make it more relevant to the industries it supported. A lot of long-established organisations, which are cash rich, can fall into a 'this is how we do things' way of working and thinking. I questioned, purely from a business point of view, whether things could be done better and more effectively.

I wanted to forge more direct contact with the film and television businesses too so, for example, acquired tickets to popular TV shows and awards ceremonies and sold them on behalf of the charity – which increased awareness of who we were and what we did, as well as raised funds.

I went out to visit beneficiaries to see how we could help first hand, and I wanted to try and ensure the charity became self-financed through events and initiatives, rather than draw on reserves.

9

Changing and Evolving (2010–24)

PETER ROGERS' ESTATE included many letters and papers, as well as production and marketing materials, which Brian Robertson offered to the BFI. 'But they didn't want them,' he added, somewhat puzzled. Plans are now afoot, a decade or so later, for the archive to be put to use and while *Carry On* humour and stereotypes may be considered 'of their time', there is still a huge fondness for the films – as is demonstrated by the continuing residuals into the charity. 'Peter also owned film rights to several books which he bought years ago, which had never moved into production, and were more or less forgotten,' Brian Robertson explained. 'One of which saw an enquiry come in from Steven Spielberg's company about purchasing an option!'

The question of whether Glebelands was still relevant to the charity was regularly raised, and it was a matter close to Brian Robertson's heart. 'We never really had the expertise to run the home ourselves and I had many meetings about bringing in a care company to manage it on our behalf,' he added. However, at that point, the status quo was maintained.

The Royal Film Performance of 2010, *The Chronicles of Narnia: The Voyage of the Dawn Treader*, turned out to be the last attended by the Queen – not through design, but rather purely through her diary availability and an absence of some Royal Film Performances during the decade. Prince Charles and the Duchess of Cornwall, along with Prince William and Princess Catherine, took on duties for the six other premieres that decade.

'The Queen was always very good, whatever film we presented she would go along with it,' says former 20th Century Fox and Paramount executive Cameron Saunders:

> Usually, the chair of the charity would visit the Palace and discuss the Royal Film Performance with an equerry and generally speaking it would be a little mood dance around when a Royal party would be available, and what films were coming up. Generally the Queen was pretty relaxed and happy to see most films, whereas I think with Charles and Camilla they are much more active in their choice: they are more passionate about film and would be interested about who is in the movie and its storyline.

Indeed, this was the case in 2023 when Queen Camilla suggested a film that might have been chosen for the Royal Film Performance – but alas, the actors' strike meant the whole event had to be postponed.

Former CEO Brian Robertson said to the authors:

> The most important thing in planning was always to meet the Queen's equerry, Sir Christopher Geidt, six months

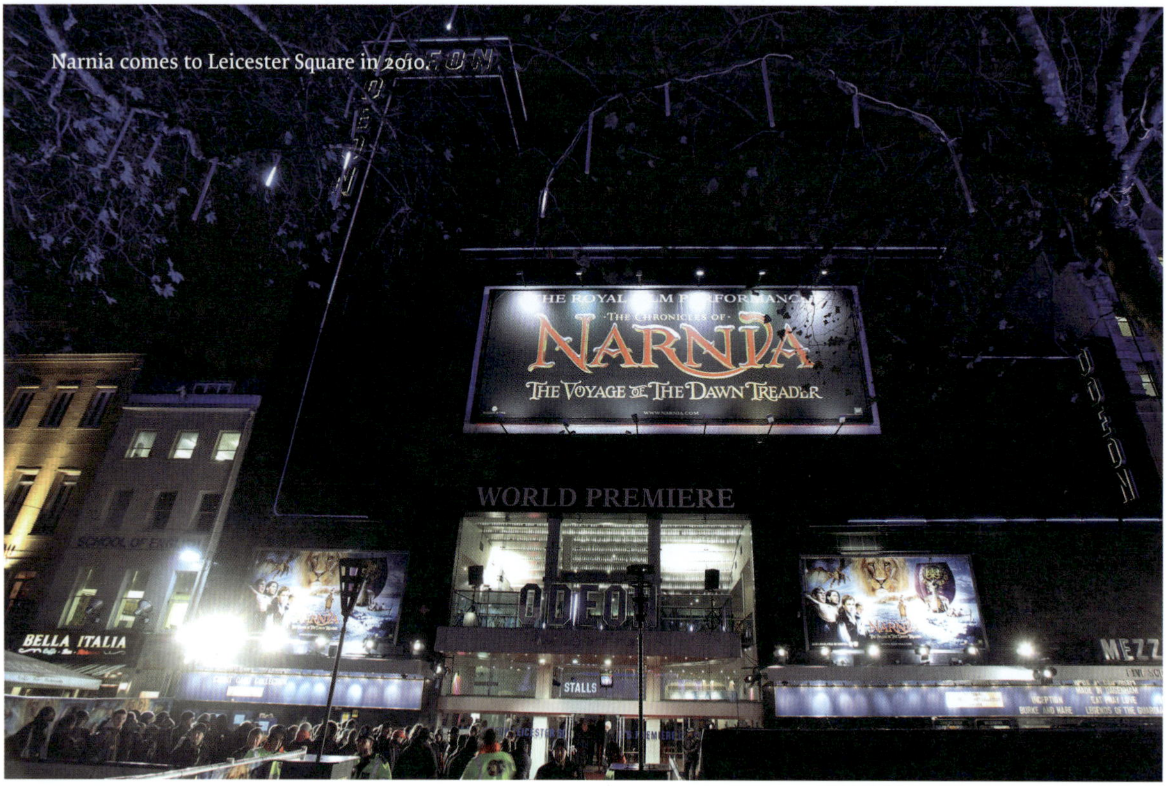

Narnia comes to Leicester Square in 2010.

before the premiere to fix a date in the Royal diary. I went to the Palace with a list of possible films to meet with Sir Christopher, and *Narnia* was mentioned as directed by Michael Apted.

'Ah yes her Majesty met Mr Apted in Washington and liked him immensely.' So that settled, we fixed a date.

Though we didn't know it was going to be a 3D film, which necessitated glasses initially so I immediately phoned Sir Christopher to ask if it would be an issue. 'No, no issue,' he reassured me.

The manufacturers of the glasses did later somewhat mischievously enquire if Her Majesty could be used in the promotion of their eyewear – a request Brian Robertson felt duty-bound to pass on, despite the expected answer. 'They said "no"!' Robertson added, with a wry smile.

Just before going into the auditorium at the premiere, Brian Robertson was standing with Her Majesty and the wife of the president of the US Studio (backing the movie) on the balcony. 'His wife was quite furious as he'd nipped in to the gents loo and not realising the Queen was completing her line-up meant HM was left, figuratively, tapping her watch much to the huge embarrassment of the executive when he finally emerged!' Incidentally, there was always an exclusive rest room set up for the royal party in the event they wanted to freshen up.

One amusing incident relating to security at the venue was also recalled to the authors by Brian Robertson:

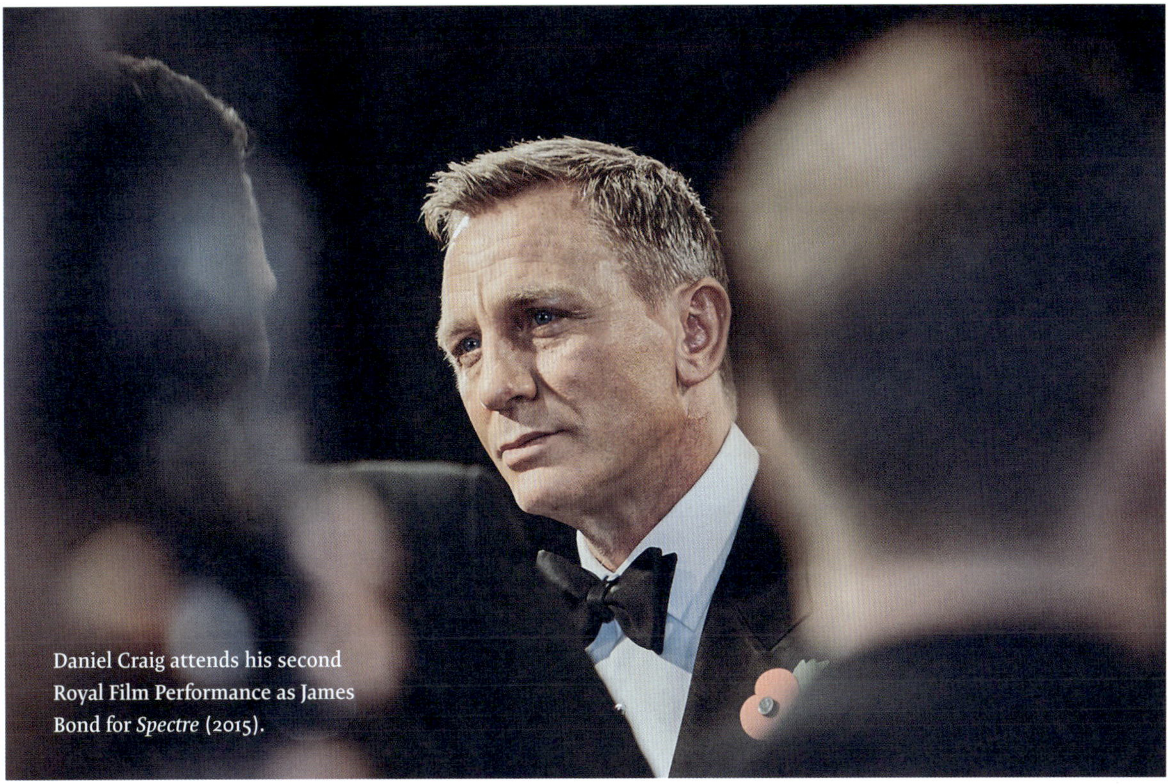

Daniel Craig attends his second Royal Film Performance as James Bond for *Spectre* (2015).

The biggest challenge we had with the security sniffer dogs – who were sent in ahead of the film to check for any bombs and firearms that might have been hidden – was when pick 'n' mix was left in goodies bags on seats one year, as a welcome gift to patrons; it drove the dogs absolutely wild! The instructions thereafter from the protection team was 'no pick 'n' mix please!'

In the changing and expanding world of television following the 2012 'switch off' of analogue TV broadcasting and the explosion in digital channels, the CTBF hosted a premiere screening of *Downton Abbey*, Series 5; the first time in its ninety-year history that the charity had staged such a grand-scale TV event. 'This is the perfect example of where we want to go as a charity,' newly installed CTBF chief executive Richard Wilson said. 'It's got a cross-platform feel to it and that's exactly what we are as a charity. We don't want to be thought of as *just* cinema or television … we're really focusing in strengthening our links with the rapidly changing television sector.'

On 25 February 2015, an Extraordinary General Meeting was called to vote on changes to the CTBF's Articles of Association, proposing to dissolve the membership element of the charity and instead allow trustees to make all the decisions going forward without the need to ask for members' approval. Some eyebrows were raised at the unquestioned autonomy the fund now had, but it was considered important in a fast-changing and evolving business that the charity could react quickly when needed and without the need to continually consult an ageing membership.

The charity launched the Betty Box and Peter Rogers Comedy Writing Programme initiative in 2016. The chosen emerging comedy writers were each to be offered £10,000 and take part in a personalised script-development programme in partnership with Big Talk Productions and LOCO (London Comedy Film Festival). The press release stated:

> Four writers will be funded and awarded a personalised 7-month programme of industry support to develop a comedy feature film screenplay or a pilot script for a narrative comedy television series.
>
> At the end of the development period, the feature screenplays and television pilots will be presented as a live, full cast table read to an industry audience at a special LOCO event in spring 2017.
>
> The programme honoured the legacy of Betty Box and Peter Rogers, the producers of the *Doctor* and *Carry On* series who, as previously mentioned, had left endowments in their wills to the CTBF.
>
> Barry Jenkins, President of the CTBF, commented: 'The Betty Box and Peter Rogers Comedy Writing Programme provides an exciting opportunity to discover those hidden gems of comedy writers who need support to realise their creative potential. Both Big Talk and LOCO are at the very forefront of the UK's thriving comedy landscape, ideally placed to support the next wave of talent in the genre. We're excited to see what this year's entrants will produce, and we're certain the programme will prove a fitting legacy for Peter and Betty – two titans of British comedy.'

Christine Robertson, Laura Kirwan-Ashman, Meryl O'Rourke and Sasha Collington were announced as the winners later in the same year, having been selected from over 600 applications. Kenton Allen, Big Talk Productions CEO, said:

> We are thrilled to be part of such a generous and unique programme for new comedy writers. Without writers, Big Talk would immediately cease to exist, so what the CTBF have made possible here, along with the LOCO Film Festival and ourselves, is a financially and professionally supported programme for talented individuals to focus on their craft over a concentrated period of time. It's impossible to put a price on what a difference this could make to these writers, some of whom are juggling two or three freelance jobs to pay their rent while trying to find the time to pursue the career they are clearly gifted enough to succeed at.

In early 2016, the CTBF took over the assets and support of the Scottish Cinematograph Benevolent Fund (a previously unrelated body) due to dwindling numbers of beneficiaries. Meanwhile, the CTBF ran a campaign to appeal for legacies, fronted by Stephen Fry and supported by Dame Helen Mirren and Lord Michael Grade, to help contribute towards CTBF grants that were now made to more than 1,000 individuals every year. The chief executive, Richard Wilson, a former TV executive who had stepped in as an interim in 2012 and later became a permanent staff addition, was forced to stand down due to ill health and sadly passed away in late 2015, aged just 58. D'Arcy Myers stepped into the position as interim CEO until a new full-time officer could be recruited – the year-long search meant a Royal Film Performance could not be organised in 2017.

It was a time of continuing change for the charity and in March 2017 the CTBF announced it had sold Glebelands care home to Greensleeves, a care home charity which looked after more than 750 residents at twenty homes across England. The sale was part of the CTBF's ongoing review of the support it provided to people working behind the scenes. The charity had launched its National Care Plan two years earlier in partnership with Anchor, which allowed beneficiaries and their parents to choose any Anchor care home in England at a preferential rate. Anchor operated more than 120 care homes and retirement housing at 700 sites across England. With fewer beneficiaries choosing Glebelands, the CTBF sought better ways of securing the home's future for current and future residents.

Former chief executive Brian Robertson had earlier explored the possibility of a care provider, such as BUPA, coming in to run Glebelands as previously mentioned, but a few years later, interim CEO D'Arcy Myers stated:

> The needs of our beneficiaries have changed, so this is an opportunity for us to focus our services to better meet those changing needs. It will also secure Glebelands' future as a care home which can continue to offer a high-quality care option for CTBF beneficiaries and their loved ones, and for people in the local community.
>
> This agreement with Greensleeves means we can focus on supporting our beneficiaries as best we can knowing that Glebelands is in safe hands.

Plans for a Royal Film Performance shifted to an autumn 2018 date, but with structural and staff changes at the charity, the date of the next Royal Film Performance had to be delayed. Meanwhile, in February 2017, Raising Films, the pioneering organisation for parents and carers in the UK film and television

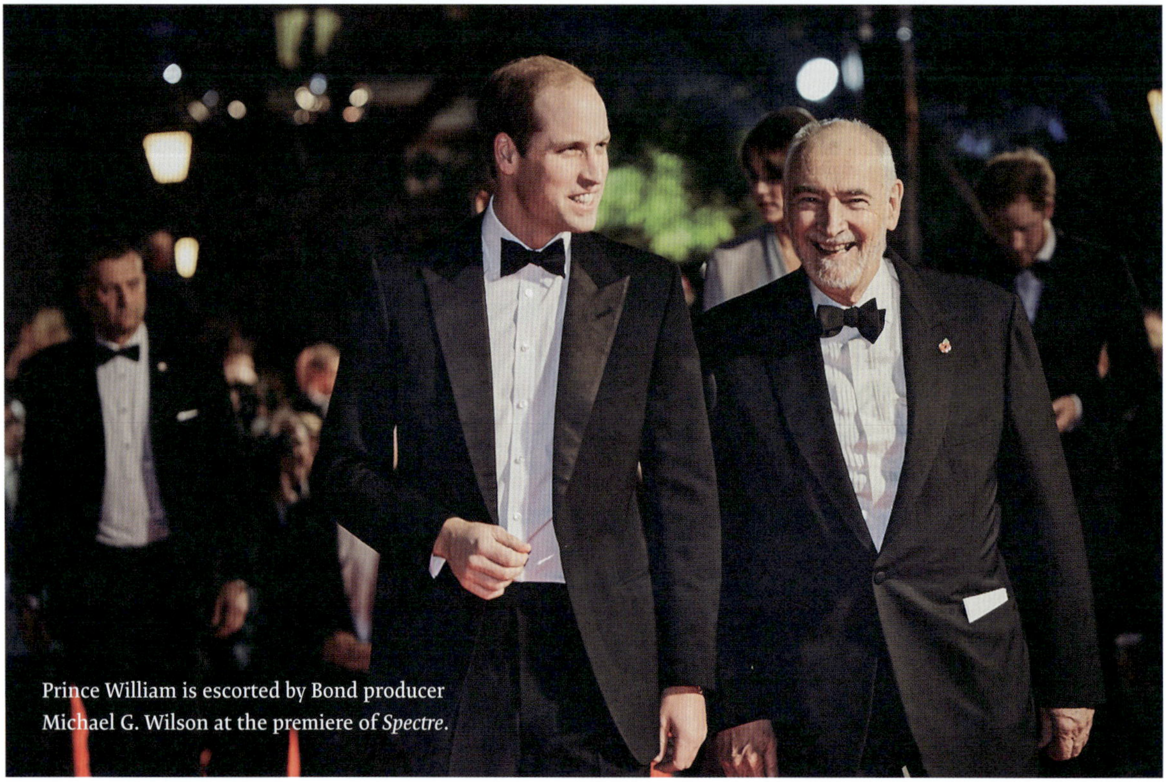

Prince William is escorted by Bond producer Michael G. Wilson at the premiere of *Spectre*.

industry, launched the Family Support Fund with the backing of the CTBF, with the aim of providing short-term financial support to registered members of Raising Films by contributing up to £75 a day to help cover the cost of childcare arrangements. Beneficiaries were able to claim a total of £1,500 a year and could make multiple applications. 'We are thrilled to be partnering with Raising Films to launch the Family Support Fund as we further our commitment to supporting more people from our industry who face barriers to work throughout their career journey,' said D'Arcy Myers.

The Family Support Fund ran as a twelve-month pilot scheme. It was the first time there had been a dedicated fund for caring costs aimed at UK screen professionals.

In March 2018, the charity relaunched with a new mission and a new name. Feeling the word 'benevolent' was old-fashioned and one which didn't amply represent the charity – which offered everything from the John Brabourne Awards nurturing young talent to bullying and mental health advice – any longer, it became the more succinctly titled Film & Television Charity (FTVC).

A new 24/7 helpline was introduced to offer confidential advice to workers dealing with problems ranging from bullying and harassment to mental health concerns, bereavement, addiction and substance abuse, while a new travel fund, Going Places, a UK-wide scheme offering to cover travel expenses for training, interviews and pitches, was also introduced to support the well-being of all those who work within the film, television and cinema sectors. The phone line took 2,000 calls in its first year.

'We're radically looking to increase our reach and our impact, the charity currently helps around 600 individuals a year,' said new CEO Alex Pumfrey, before adding:

> It has the potential to do much more as it reacts to challenges currently facing the sector, including the culture of sexual misconduct, as well as concerns around mental health. There's very little support there for anyone at the moment in what is a tough and lonely place, particularly for freelancers.

In the year following its launch, the helpline saw the number of people supported by the charity quadruple. The helpline was now viewed as the 'front door' to the charity.

Exciting plans were announced to refurbish No. 22 Golden Square, and the Royal Film Performance of 2019 saw the premiere of Sam Mendes' acclaimed First World War drama *1917* in December. The director said:

> I am delighted that the World Premiere will take place in my hometown, London, in aid of the Film and Television Charity. I couldn't have made the film without the skill and dedication of the many talented craftspeople working in the UK industry – the very people who the Film and Television Charity does so much to support on a daily basis. This film is a hugely personal project for me, and it's an honour to have it chosen as the 71st Royal Film Performance.

Around the same time, rumours of a pandemic were escalating. Nobody could have predicted what was to come and how it would bring the film and cinema industries to a halt. The charity swung into action, raising a staggering £6.3 million in donations in those first few months of the pandemic. By rapidly reorganising to focus on the Covid-19 response, they were able to help over 7,000 people (one in twenty-five people working in the industry), while the support line offered practical and emotional support and was called more than 6,000 times. Over 2,300 people were awarded grants through two Covid-19 funds with one in five of the recipients saying it prevented them losing their home. In total, the charity distributed support of £7.94 million in the 2020–2021 accounting year.

The BBC donated £700,000 to the charity in 2020 to 'assist those affected by the hiatus in film and television production caused by the coronavirus pandemic'. The corporation said £500,000 would go towards the new Film and TV Covid-19 Emergency Relief Fund in partnership with the British Film Institute (BFI), while the other £200,000 would go into the charity's two-year mental health action plan, known as the Whole Picture Programme, to address the mental health crisis found in the sector.

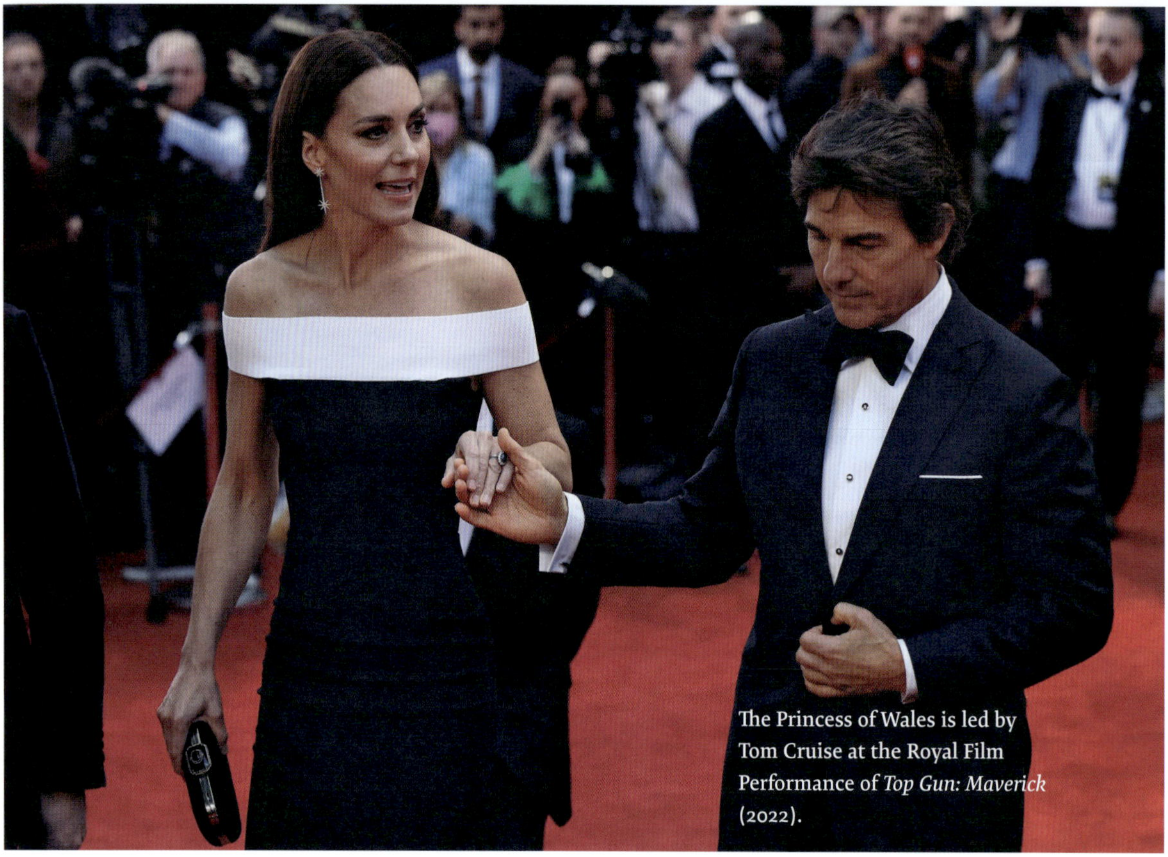
The Princess of Wales is led by Tom Cruise at the Royal Film Performance of *Top Gun: Maverick* (2022).

The funds came principally from the BBC's commercial production and distribution arm, BBC Studios, with contributions from public service commissioning teams, including BBC Content. BBC Content director Charlotte Moore said, 'Freelancers are the lifeblood of our industry, keeping our shows creatively brilliant for all audiences. At times like these it is critical we stand by them. We are proud to contribute to the Film and Television Charity, to support our industry's freelance community during these unprecedented times.'

BBC Studios CEO Tim Davie (later director general of the corporation) added, 'I hope that this will play a part to ease the difficulties some are facing and protect those who help to make the UK's creative sector the envy of the world.'

As the pandemic restrictions began to lift in 2021 and the industry slowly returned to full swing, £3.11 million was distributed in aid. This was a time when 200,000 people were calculated to be working in film, television and cinema, and this prompted the charity to unveil 'Strategy 2030' – a refreshed mission to build a community of support, while improving the quality of working life and to provide support to an anticipated 15,000 people a year in a variety of ways, not least the people facing a cost-of-living crisis in the wake of the Ukraine invasion, which pushed up wholesale prices across fuel, energy and food markets. The charity estimated that an additional 5,000 film and television workers were now at risk of in-work poverty.

In helping fund the important work of the FTVC, London Weekend Television (LWT) made a significant donation and transfer of assets totalling £116,000 from their charitable trust, which was winding up, having provided support to LWT employees for more than thirty years, believing the FTVC was better placed to carry on its work.

Also in 2021, the Bullying Advice Service was launched in support of anyone who had witnessed or experienced bullying or harassment. But it was the following year, 2022, that was perhaps most significant to the charity when it lost its patron, Queen Elizabeth II, who passed away on 8 September. The charity had benefited from Her Majesty's presence at many events from 1946, throughout her long reign up to her last Royal Film Performance, *The Chronicles of Narnia: The Voyage of the Dawn Treader* in 2010.

More than £1.7 million was raised in 2022 by the charity, thanks to corporate partners BBC Studios, Channel 4, ITV, Sky and the Walt Disney Company along with the 'Industry Friends' scheme that was launched to give smaller organisations the chance to show their support – Hat Trick, Gaumont and Headline Pictures were among the first to sign up.

The Sir Horace Ové Fund created a dedicated grant for Black and Global Majority people in the industry facing barriers. That income, coupled with legacies, royalties and a record-breaking Royal Film Performance with £185,000 generated by *Top Gun: Maverick*, meant the charity was well placed to tackle the unpredictable nature of the industries.

10

In Focus

IN JULY 2023, the charity welcomed its new chief executive, Marcus Ryder MBE, and its new chair of trustees, Claire Tavernier. Marcus had previously been Head of External Consultancies at the Sir Lenny Henry Centre for Media Diversity, which was set up to explore and increase diversity across the media industry. Claire was Fremantle's Global Head of Digital for over a decade, working with shows such as *American Idol*, *X Factor* and *Neighbours*, where she dedicated herself to building and expanding successful content and digital businesses. Marcus Ryder explained:

> I was very aware of the charity before I joined and I was also aware of the RFP. Although I had never joined up the two in my mind.
>
> I knew the charity as a force for good before Covid, though its importance really became clear to the entire industry during the pandemic and its research around mental health also was a major factor which personally changed its image to me, and I think the entire industry, from a 'nice' benevolent fund to one that shaped the conversation as to how we can create a better industry for everyone.

Claire Tavernier was equally aware of the charity before joining, having worked in the film and television industry for several decades, although, as she too explained, 'It was its work during the pandemic, and around mental health in the industry, that really caught my eye. The charity is unique and essential, and more importantly has evolved dynamically to meet the changing demands of our creative sector'.

The new chief executive highlighted his initial priorities as:

> Making certain that our mission is clear both internally and externally. I think we need to make sure everyone knows how we are helping to create a better industry for all. Our activities should be tied to addressing the physical, financial, and mental health of everyone working in the industry. Though I am constantly surprised how many people come to an event at 22 Golden Square [the charity HQ] and say they have not heard of us before. A large part of that is likely because despite being around for 100 years the workforce is quite young. But that awareness is changing, and I think the actors' strike in 2023 was a tipping point where thousands of people accessed our grants.

In fact, in August 2023, the charity rolled out an unprecedented extra £500,000 fund to help UK film, TV and cinema workers in urgent financial need as the industry faced severe economic conditions caused by US actors' and writers' strikes, coupled with the cost-of-living crisis and pressures on scripted and unscripted production budgets. It all resulted in an 800 per cent surge in grant applications to the charity. Worryingly, 46 per cent of workers surveyed were said to have less than £1,000 in savings to fall back on. The BBC, Channel 4, Paramount (Channel 5), Amazon Prime Video, Sky, Warner Bros Discovery and Banijay all agreed donations to the charity to launch this emergency assistance.

But what of the immediate years ahead? 'Right now, the most pressing needs are our counselling services and hardship grants,' said Marcus Ryder:

> But our services must meet need and, for example, in 2023 there was a rise in anti-Semitism and Islamophobia in wider society that was also reflected in our sector; we pivoted to directly address that problem. By the time this book is published I am sure there will be other factors impacting workers in the industry and our job is to keep on identifying those needs and then helping people affected.

'Our help is different from what it might have been several decades ago,' added Claire Tavernier:

> ... but it is no less essential. Faced with fast-changing business models and content consumption trends, challenging financial conditions and increased global competition, our industry is working hard to develop pathways and solutions and ensure that the UK remains the creative powerhouse it has always been.
>
> The next few years will be challenging: the overlap of a cost-of-living crisis with a downturn in UK film and television production has created a particularly harsh environment for those working behind the scenes in the industry, many of whom have had little or no work in recent times.

However, in positive news, the charity's recent research shows encouraging signs of better mental health support in the industry, something it is passionate about and will continue to champion and support, although of course, funding is needed for this and all their other work. Balancing the books is a challenge every charity faces, and thankfully, the Royal Film Performance is a significant contributor to the FTVC's income.

Before becoming CEO, Marcus Ryder confessed that he hadn't attended a Royal Film Performance but added enthusiastically, 'It is literally all my 7-year-old son talks about since I started at the charity!'

Although focusing very much on the future, the charity is also keen to celebrate and build upon its past, as Alan de Sousa Caires, who joined as director of finance and operations in 2019, explained:

> Part of my role is looking after our office building, including our off-site storage facility where all our archives are kept. When I first visited the unit and found many wonderful items, I knew that they had to have the dust blown off of them to be enjoyed. Admittedly the Covid-19 period put a temporary halt on things, but coming out of lockdown I realised that our centenary year was fast approaching and that we should be sharing these treasures as part of celebrating a charity with a long history.

But what treasures are there exactly? Alan continued:

> Out of the blue I received an email from a gentleman in Scotland saying that he'd found a ticket for the 1924 garden party [the first charity fundraiser] in a suitcase of items that he picked up at a car boot sale. I didn't hesitate to ask to take it on loan; it's a wonderful piece of history, and that made me wonder what else was out there. I then typed 'Cinematograph and Trade Benevolent Fund' into the eBay search bar and there was no turning back … a 1926 garden party brochure, along with a 1924 one, a 1938 cinema collection box, and, after searching for three years, I finally acquired the brochure for the first Royal Command Film Performance (we had the other seventy brochures already), and it came with a lovely story.

Memorabilia bequeathed to the charity include a pair of red shoes from the acclaimed Powell & Pressburger film *The Red Shoes* (1948) by its assistant editor Noreen Ackland – a long-time resident of Glebelands – and Herbert Wilcox's 1940s National Film Awards (the forerunner to BAFTAs), both 'definite highlights', according to Alan. However, the most amazing wow! moment for Alan has been speaking to Julian and Alistair Mead, the grandchildren of founder Reginald C. Bromhead, and then meeting them in person to read the memoirs that Bromhead's daughter wrote during the latter part of his life.

The FTVC remains committed to building on its long history of grant-giving as well as striving to improve well-being – mental, financial, social and physical. Its lean but effective staff count and the dedicated trustees who guide and focus the charity remain as committed as those who went before them for over a century. In the financial year ending March 2023, charitable activities amounted to £3.34 million, underlining just how relevant and needed it still is.

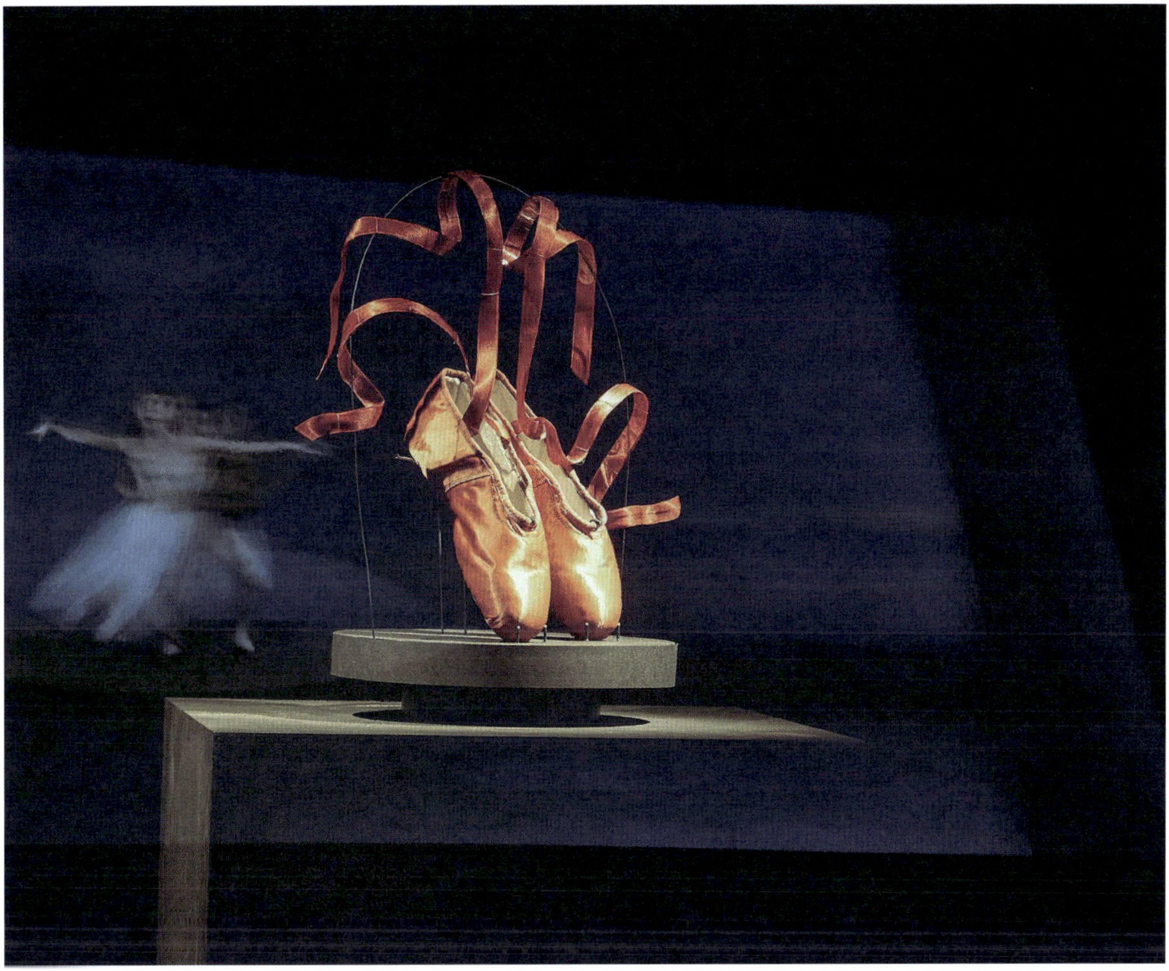

The bequeathed red shoes. (Courtesy of Sarah J. Duncan, BFI)

Chief executive Marcus Ryder offers the final thought:

> Our celebrations give us a brilliant opportunity to raise funds as we raise our profile, and we look forward to working with partners old and new to do just that. If anyone reading this does just one thing to help us celebrate our 100 plus years, please let it be the simple act of spreading the word so we can help everyone in film, television and cinema to thrive.

www.filmtvcharity.org.uk

PART II: ROYAL FILM PERFORMANCES

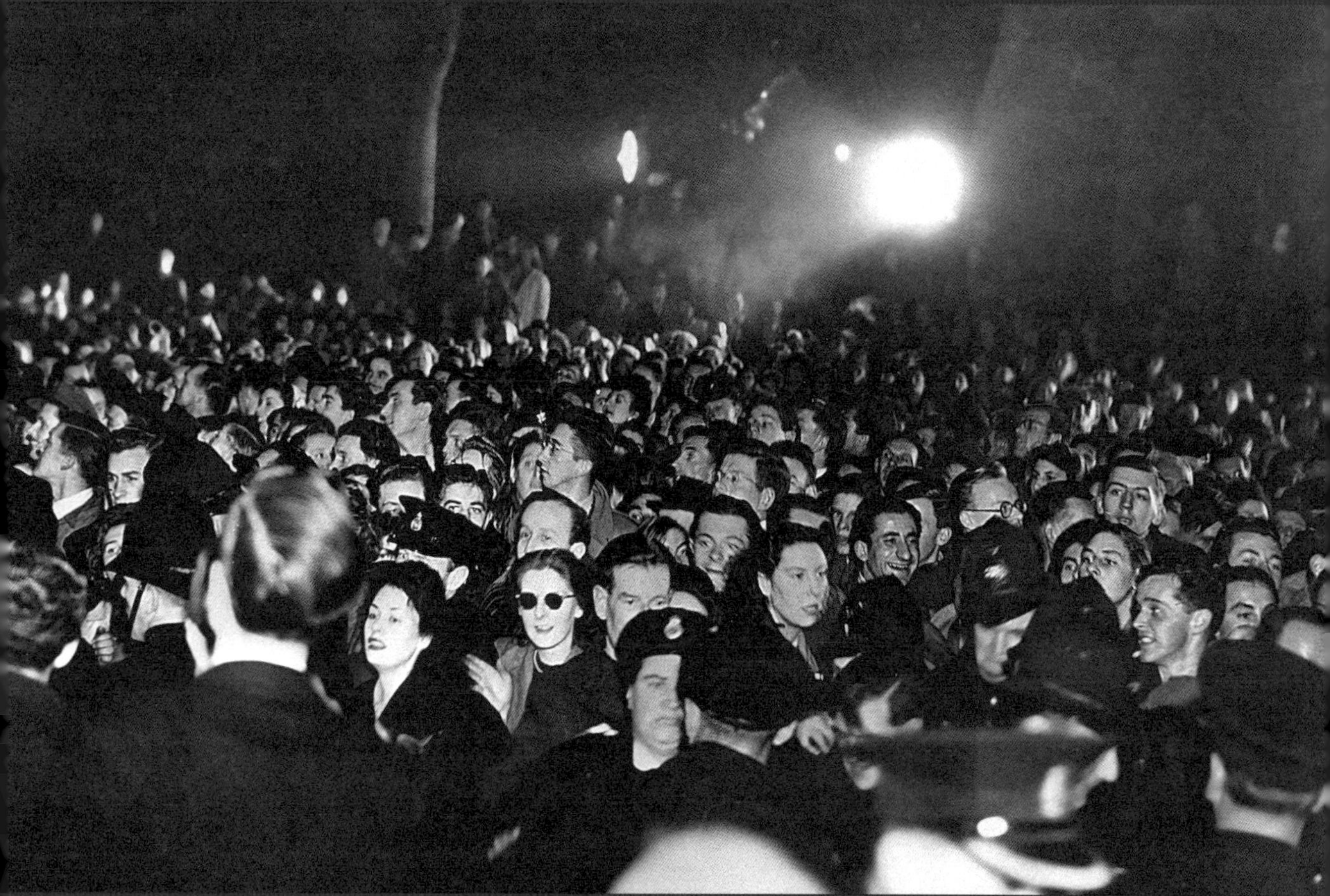

1946 *A Matter of Life and Death*

The first Royal Command Film Performance took the West End by storm. Everyone within the film industry was determined to make it a success. A special viewing committee was set up representing all sides of the industry, including Reginald Bromhead, president and chairman of the CTBF, and J. Arthur Rank. Numerous films had been submitted by hopeful producers and distributors and it was the committee's job to consider them, not only on artistic merit but also in view of their suitability to be seen by royalty. It is fitting that the picture chosen has since become a British classic – Powell and Pressburger's *A Matter of Life and Death*.

The event certainly drew the interest of the public. The West End had never seen anything quite like it before. Hours before the royal party was due to arrive, large crowds began to assemble. By 7.30 p.m., an estimated 50,000 people had packed into Leicester Square and its environs. The police struggled to keep the route open for the arrival of ticket holders, many of whom had to forcibly make their way through the crowds to get into the Empire Theatre.

An emergency dressing station was set up in the foyer attended by staff of the St John Ambulance to care for women who had fainted in the crush outside. Some eighty people were treated, with three taken to hospital with possible fractures. 'But for the courage and endurance of the police there would have been a major disaster,' Joe Grossman, district staff officer for St John Ambulance, told the press. Film star Dorothy Malone fought her way to a side door and got through the crowd by holding a camera and claiming to be a press photographer. The sitting prime minister

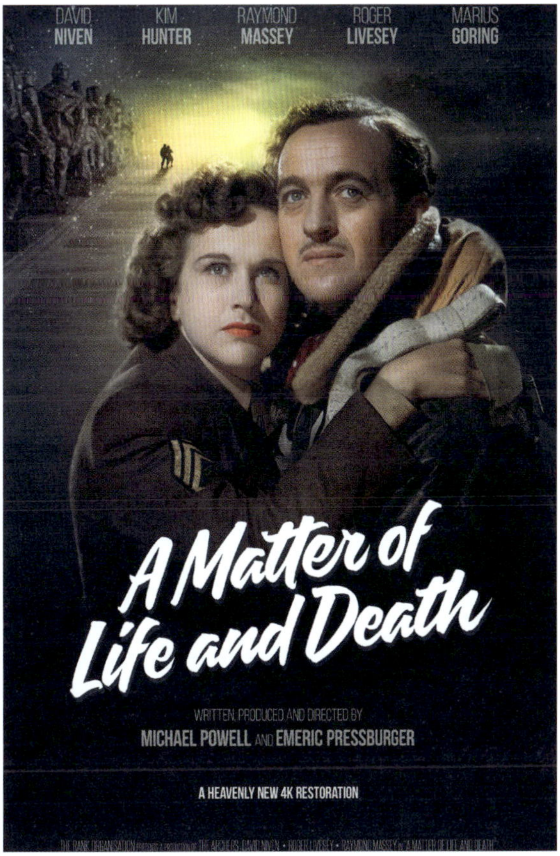

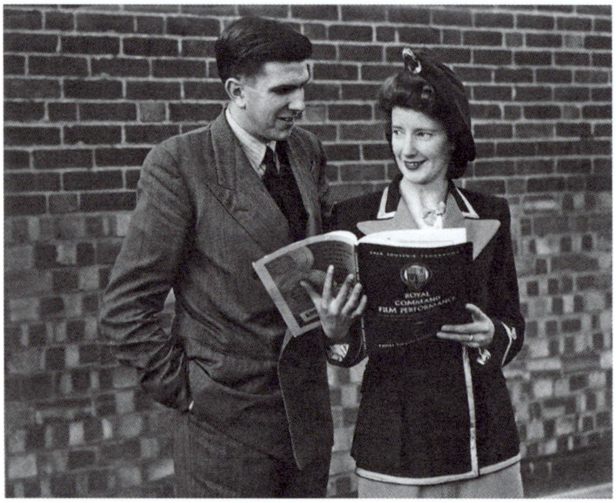

Violet Nelson (with her husband), who was selected to be an usherette for the very first Royal Film Performance in 1946.

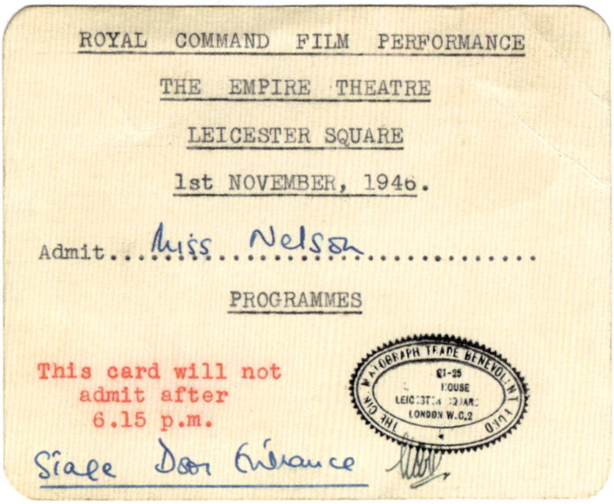

ROYAL COMMAND FILM PERFORMANCE

THE EMPIRE THEATRE

LEICESTER SQUARE

1st NOVEMBER, 1946.

Admit........Miss Nelson..............

PROGRAMMES

This card will not admit after 6.15 p.m.

Stage Door Entrance

Usherette Violet Nelson's ticket for *A Matter of Life and Death.*

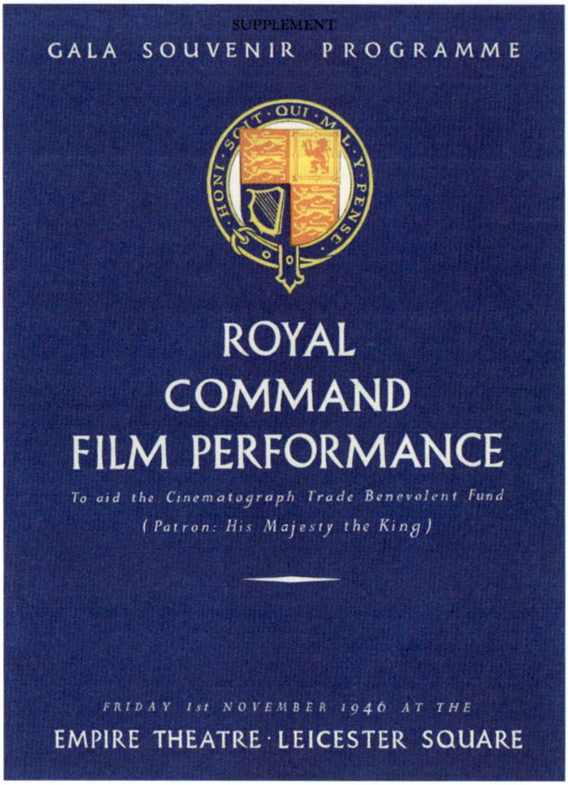

Mr Attlee slipped in unnoticed. Actor Pat O'Brien said, 'Hollywood has never seen anything like this. It's unbelievable.'

When the cars containing King George VI and Queen Elizabeth, along with their party, including Princess Elizabeth and Princess Margaret, neared the square, the crowd broke through the cordons and closed around them. Officers on horseback had to force a way through for the royal motorcade to proceed and then back their horses on to the steps of the cinema to keep the way clear for the manager to escort the royals into the foyer. The King later admitted, 'I thought we were nearly going to be casualties ourselves.' In the auditorium some 3,000 people stood in silence to receive the royal party and the National Anthem, after which the King and Queen and the princesses took their place on gold-painted armchairs in the flower-bedecked Royal Box that had been specially erected in the Royal Circle.

Following the screening of *A Matter of Life and Death*, there was a stage show devised and produced by Val Guest. British and American stars took part in a pageant celebrating the movies, from the *Keystone Cops* to the present day. Will Hay introduced a clip from a Chaplin short, there was a special appearance by Bessie Love, a great star of silent film, and

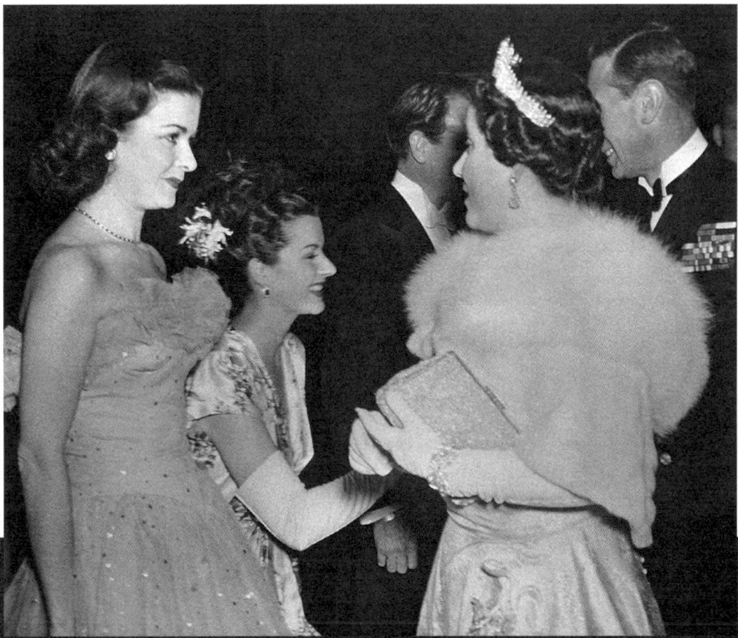

The Queen talks to American actress Joan Bennet while Margaret Lockwood curtseys to the King.

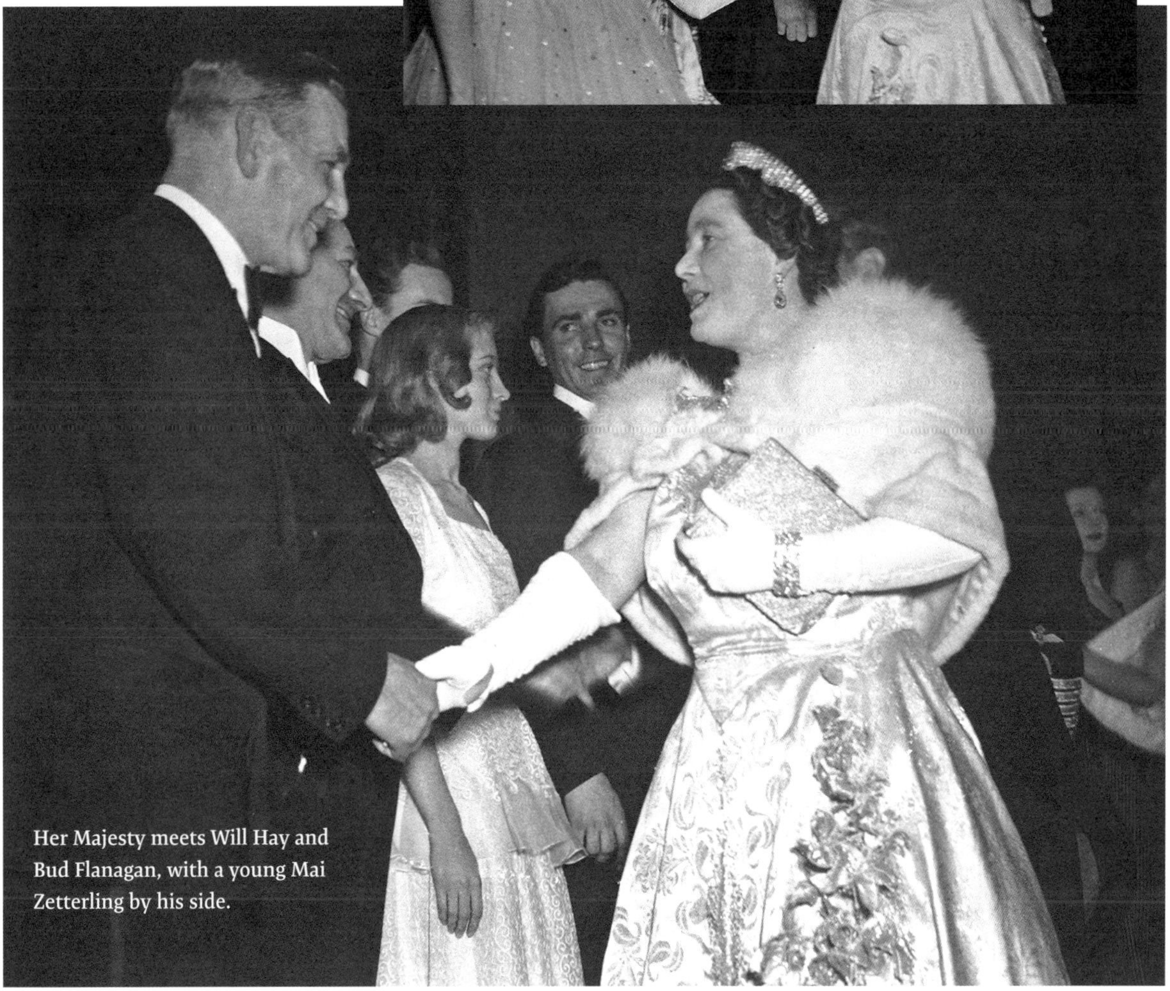

Her Majesty meets Will Hay and Bud Flanagan, with a young Mai Zetterling by his side.

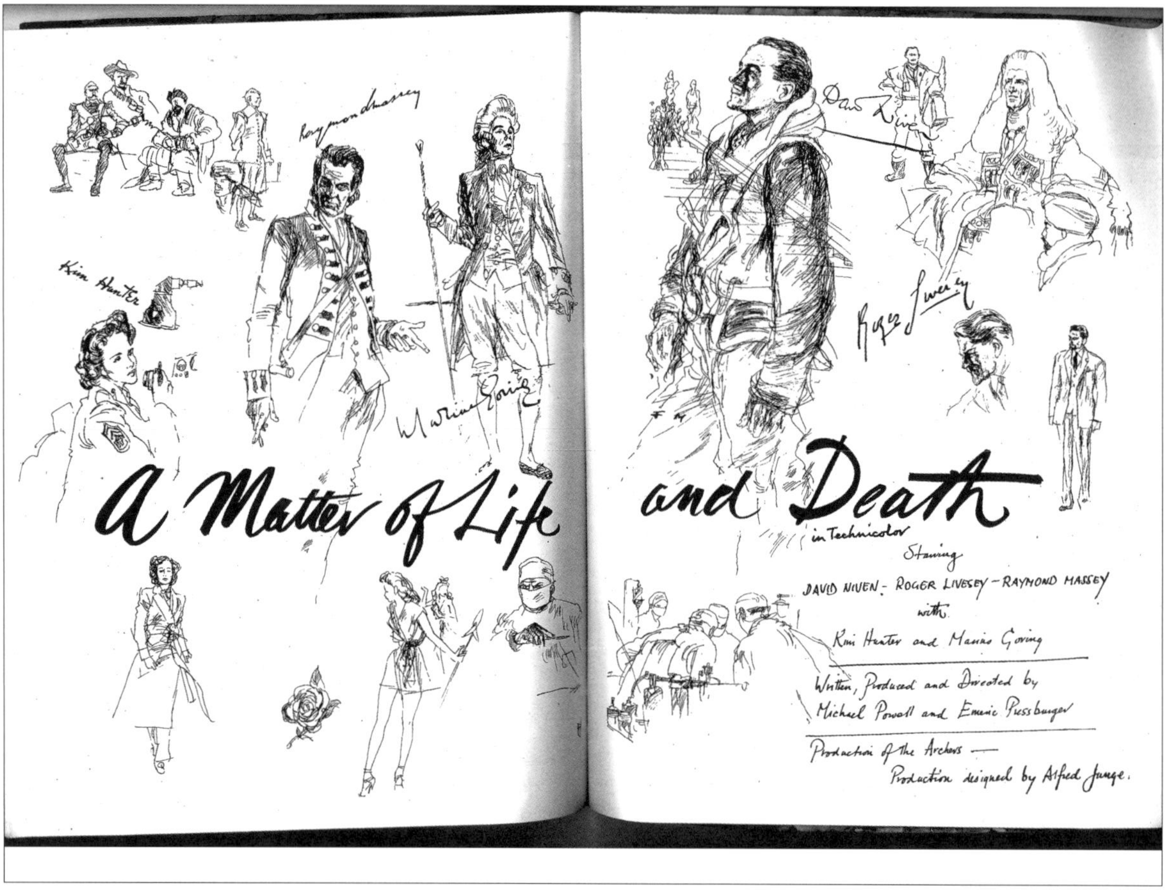

Ray Milland amused the audience by recalling the various battlefields he had visited during the war, adding, 'And tonight I was in Leicester Square'.

After the show, Their Majesties were presented to the likes of Robert Donat, Stewart Granger, Valerie Hobson, Deborah Kerr, Vivien Leigh, Margaret Lockwood, John Mills, Anna Neagle, Laurence Olivier, Michael Redgrave and Ralph Richardson. The star of the film, David Niven, did not attend. He stayed at home because his wife was due to give birth, which she did five days later.

The event raised a net profit of £25,895, easily the highest figure ever achieved at a single event organised by the CTBF. The general view was that this first Royal Film Command Performance was a success and showed off the film industry at its best.

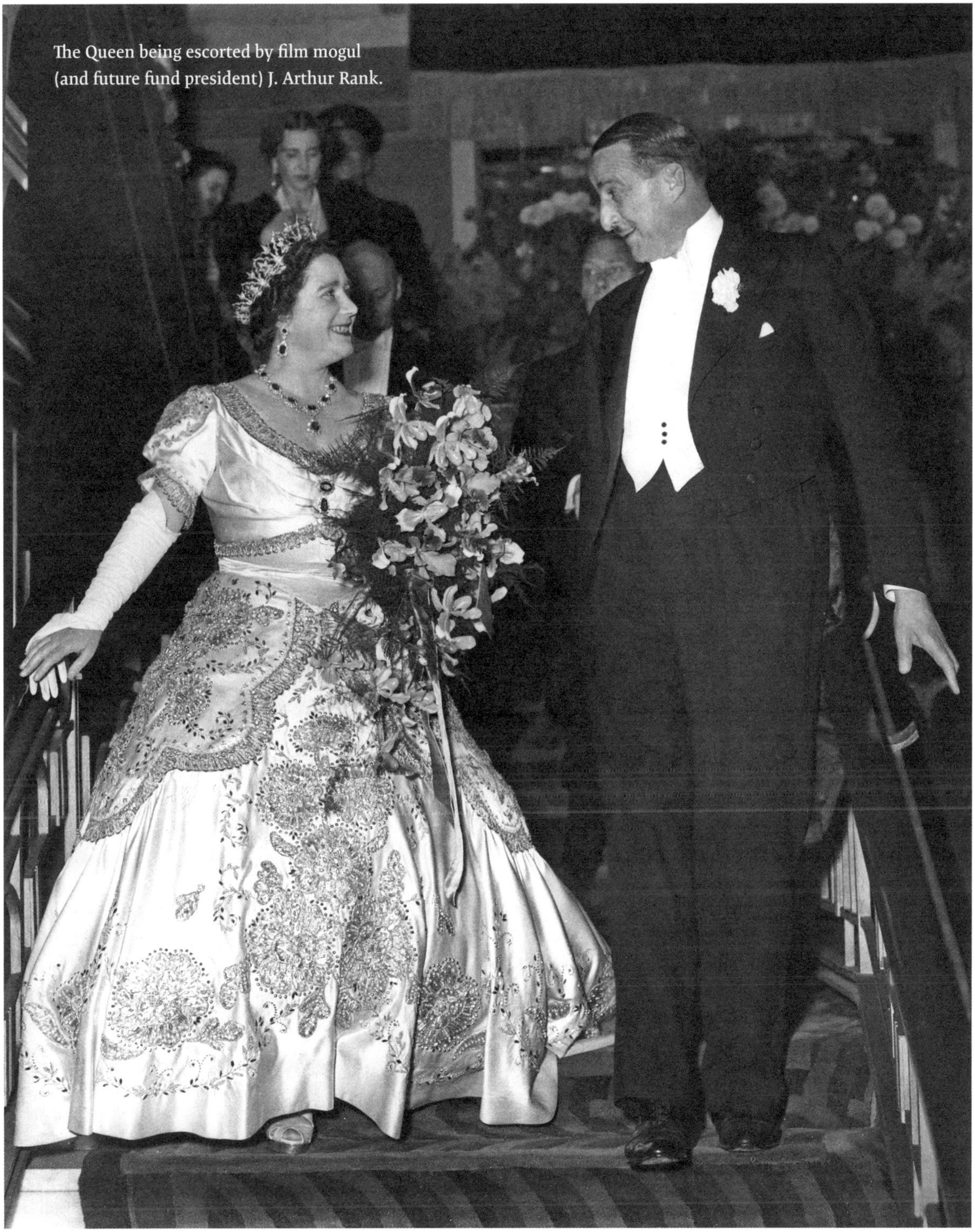

The Queen being escorted by film mogul (and future fund president) J. Arthur Rank.

1947 *The Bishop's Wife*

Lessons had certainly been learnt from the previous year's 'Battle of Leicester Square', as the press had called it. A much larger police force was on duty this time, crush barriers were erected and no car or taxi that didn't bear an official sticker stood any chance of getting near the Odeon Cinema. (Until the 1960s, the Royal Film would alternate between the Odeon and Empire theatres.)

Only in its second year, the Royal Command Film Performance had already acquired a prestige and importance in the entertainment and social calendar of the nation. The chosen film, *The Bishop's Wife*, was a lightweight but beguiling seasonal comedy starring Cary Grant, David Niven and Loretta Young. It was about an angel who assumes human form to help a bishop repair his marriage and build his dream cathedral. There were mild rumblings of discontent from sections of the British film industry that a Hollywood production had been selected, but the idea was to always alternate between British and American films.

The royal party received a tremendous ovation as they drove into Leicester Square. Attending was King George VI, Queen Elizabeth, wearing a crinoline gown of ivory satin, and Princess Margaret. It was the royal family's first public appearance since the wedding of Princess Elizabeth to the Duke of Edinburgh just a few days before. As the royal party were presented to leaders of the film industry, the band and trumpeters of the Royal Military School of Music played in the auditorium entertaining the audience. The royal party occupied an open box in the centre of the Royal Circle decorated with white and bronze chrysanthemums.

Following the presentation of the film there was another stage show, hosted by Bob Hope. The royal party were then presented to two stars of the film, Loretta Young and David Niven, along with those who had participated in the 'live' entertainment, including Phyllis Calvert, Rex Harrison, Vivien Leigh, Margaret Lockwood, Laurence Olivier, Ralph Richardson, Ann Todd and Michael Wilding. Bob Hope presented Princess Margaret with an album of signed photographs of Hollywood personalities. As Hope flicked through them, the King leaned over his daughter's shoulder, 'Look, he's hurrying to get to his own picture.'

'Why not?' cracked Hope. 'He's the prettiest.'

The evening was regarded as a total success. The highlight was the presentation of a three-reel colour film of the royal wedding of Princess Elizabeth and Philip Mountbatten, which stopped the show. It had been edited and processed overnight to be available in time. The large screen bristled with scenes of magnificent pageantry and the press reported that the audience reaction was one of almost constant applause.

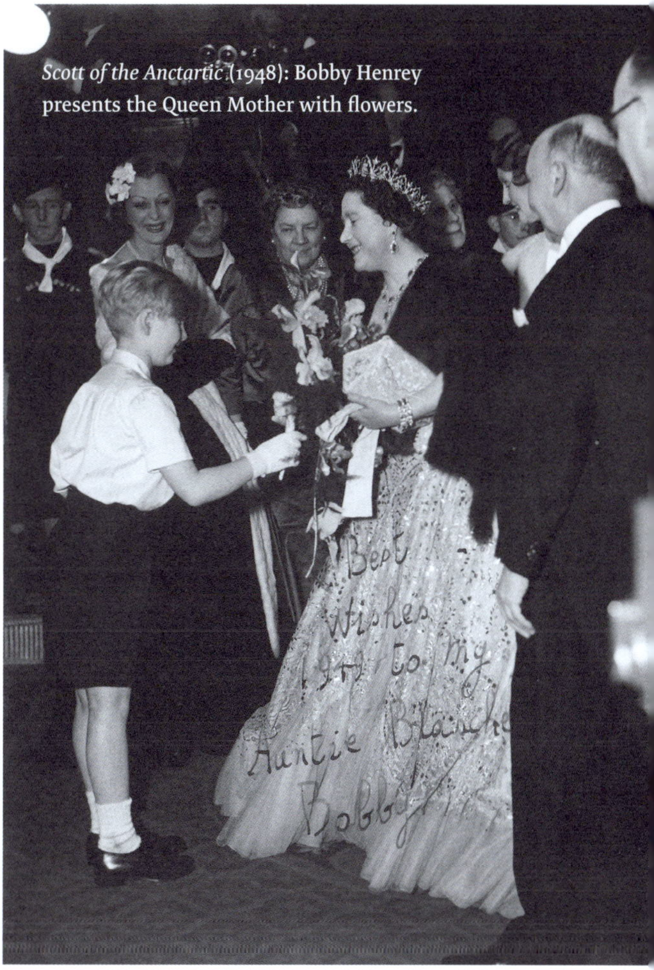

Scott of the Anctartic (1948): Bobby Henrey presents the Queen Mother with flowers.

1948 *Scott of the Antarctic*

Now in its third year, the Royal Command Film Performance had risen yet more in significance, as stated by *Kinematograph Weekly*, 'The occasion has become the most important trade social event of the year. Practically everybody who is anybody in trade circles makes a point of being present.'

Despite the gloomy weather and heavy fog, thousands lined the official route to the Empire, Leicester Square. Due to illness, the King did not attend, but the crowds were delighted to see the Queen, Princess Margaret and the Duke of Edinburgh and roared their approval. Princess Elizabeth was also absent, having recently given birth to a baby boy, christened Charles. During the evening the theatre audience were delighted to see a short colour film commemorating the birth.

In the foyer, the Queen was presented with a bouquet of orchids by Bobby Henrey, the 9-year-old star of the acclaimed recent film *The Fallen Idol*:

> It was a very special evening. When I presented my bouquet to the Queen, I was told what to do and I don't have any memories of being nervous about it. I was born in a village in France and my picture with the Queen was in the newspapers and immensely popular in the village. Some of the local merchants put it up in their shop and people said, 'Look, he shook hands with the Queen, this local kid'.

Scott of the Antarctic, on paper, was a fitting choice, representing as it did a true British hero and a film of supreme British craftsmanship from a studio that had begun to capture the hearts of the nation – Ealing. But the picture itself, detailing the doomed expedition, was too reverential of its subject and a touch plodding. However, reports say it was warmly received on the night. The film's star, John Mills, was introduced on stage by Laurence Olivier and greeted with a storm of applause.

The British entertainer Jack Hulbert produced the stage presentation. The set was an exact reproduction of the Empire foyer, and the likes of Cary Grant, Alan Ladd, Vivien Leigh, Myrna Loy, Ronald Reagan, Elizabeth Taylor and Robert Taylor were introduced to the audience by broadcaster Richard Dimbleby and the BBC radio sports commentator Raymond Glendenning.

Other stars did little skits. Sid Field performed his famous character 'Slasher Green', the Cockney 'wide boy', and Anna Neagle and Michael Wilding performed a dance routine. Laurence Olivier read out a telegram from the King wishing the evening goodwill. The climax of the show was a tableau in which all the stars gathered on stage and turned towards the Royal Box to pay homage.

A final treat was the novelty of seeing newsreel of the royal party arriving in the foyer captured by Pathé's cameras earlier in the evening. The film was rushed to a developing plant in Wardour Street and rushed back to the cinema just in time.

The Queen spent almost an hour chatting to the stars after the show. As the youngest of the American contingent, Virginia Mayo was chosen to convey to the Queen everyone's sympathy with the King and their hopes for his speedy recovery.

1949 *The Forsyte Saga*

The absence of the King had been keenly felt at the previous year's Royal Command Film Performance and so it was with a mixture of relief and excitement that he was making a welcome return. As he was still plagued by ill health, a new venue was chosen, the Odeon Marble Arch, because there was only one step from the foyer to the Royal Box. Joining the King and Queen were Princesses Elizabeth and Margaret.

Once again, thousands waited outside for the arrival of the stars and the royal party, held back by a strong police presence. The crowd was in good spirits, but even so, thirty-seven women were reported to have fainted. One wonders how many did so due to the appearance of matinee idol Errol Flynn, who was one of the stars of the chosen film, *The Forsyte Saga*, MGM's version of the famous novel by John Galsworthy. The title was changed in America to *That Forsyte Woman*, after a survey found that many Americans did not know the meaning of the word 'saga'.

Jack Hulbert returned to produce the stage show, this time with a modern take on 'Cinderella'. Jean Simmons appeared as Cinderella, who wishes to go to the Royal Film Performance; her fairy godmother, played by Moira Lister, grants the wish. Richard Attenborough was Buttons and Ralph Richardson played the 'demon king'.

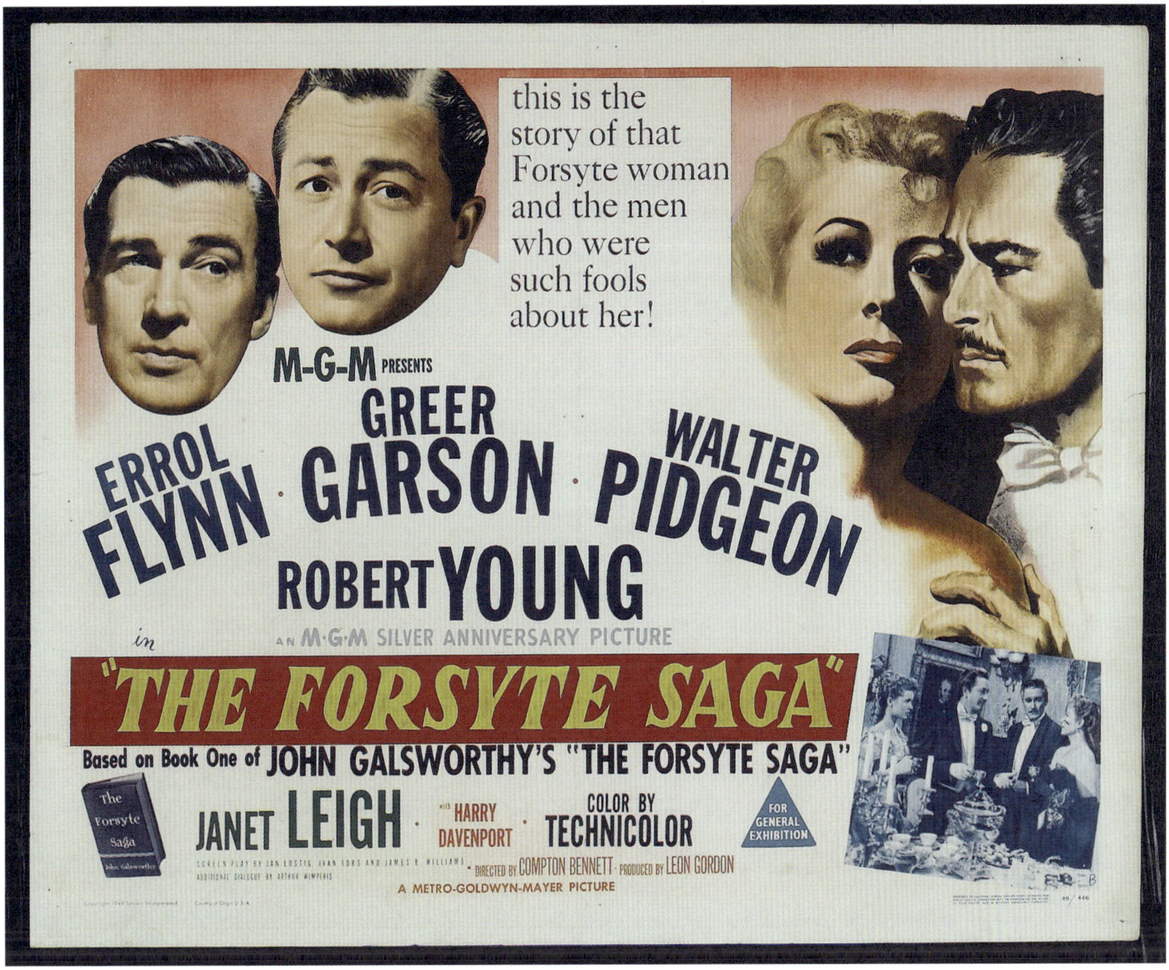

Other highlights of the stage presentation included Carol Reed introducing a performance by Anton Karas, the man who famously played the zither on the director's film *The Third Man*. Rosalind Russell, Douglas Fairbanks Jr and Gregory Peck (reported to be Princess Margaret's favourite film star) also featured. And there was much amusement, too, in the on-stage byplay between Errol Flynn and Stanley Holloway. Ben Lyon was the compère. Anna Neagle perhaps had the evening's most coveted job, to address the royal party and on behalf of all the artistes to congratulate the King on his recovery, a task she carried off with expected regal poise.

At the after-show line-up, the royal party chatted for some forty minutes to the likes of Alec Guinness, Valerie Hobson, Trevor Howard, John Mills, Richard Todd and Jack Warner. Many of the artists were delightfully surprised at how much the royals knew about their movies. The Queen was heard to compliment Rosalind Russell on her comedy singing on the stage and suggested she should do more of it in films.

The King was seen laughing and joking with Errol Flynn. Referring to the controversy that surrounded his 1945 war film *Objective, Burma* (which largely snubbed the British involvement in that campaign), the King asked, 'Are

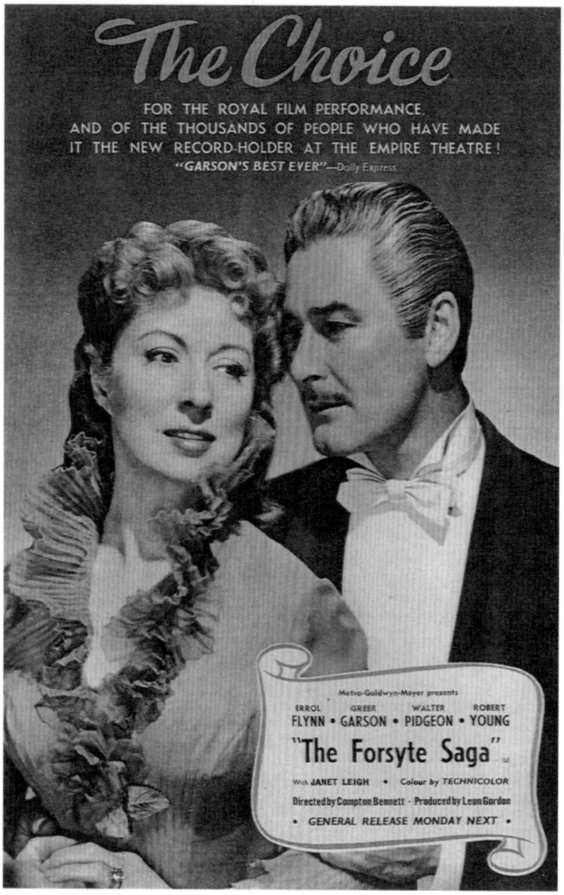

you still having problems with Burma?' Errol cracked, 'Yes indeed, sir. She's pregnant.' Before leaving, the Queen was presented with a specially bound copy of the Galsworthy book.

A few nights later, a replica Royal Film Performance took place at the Ritz Theatre in Birkenhead, Merseyside. The press called it the biggest-ever charity performance staged in the north. Thousands jammed all approaches to the cinema to catch a glimpse of the likes of Gregory Peck, Margaret Lockwood and Richard Todd. Wilson, Keppel & Betty entertained the audience as part of the stage show.

1950 *The Mudlark*

This year, eleven films were under consideration and the press reported that the selection committee spent all weekend 'literally locked in a private theatre' to watch the films and decide. In the end, *The Mudlark* was selected, a fictional account of how a young street urchin, played by Andrew Ray, finds a locket of Queen Victoria, then still in mourning for her beloved Prince Albert, and journeys to Windsor Castle to see her.

Leicester Square was packed with 10,000 people, in some places twenty deep, despite the freezing drizzle. The biggest cheer of the night was for the royal party. The King and Queen, and Princesses Elizabeth and Margaret were dressed in black for the court mourning ordered by the King following the death of King Gustav V of Sweden. The Queen was in a crinoline-skirted black velvet gown, with tiara, earrings and a necklace of diamonds.

Before entering the auditorium of the Empire, the Queen was presented with a bouquet by 11-year-old Andrew Ray, dressed in an Eton suit with shining white collar. 'You're the mudlark, aren't you?' asked the Queen. Andrew nodded.

There was speculation about how the royals might receive some of the dialogue in the film. But the King and Queen were seen to exchange amused glances as they heard Windsor Castle referred to as 'Those blasted old lodgings'. Some doubts had been

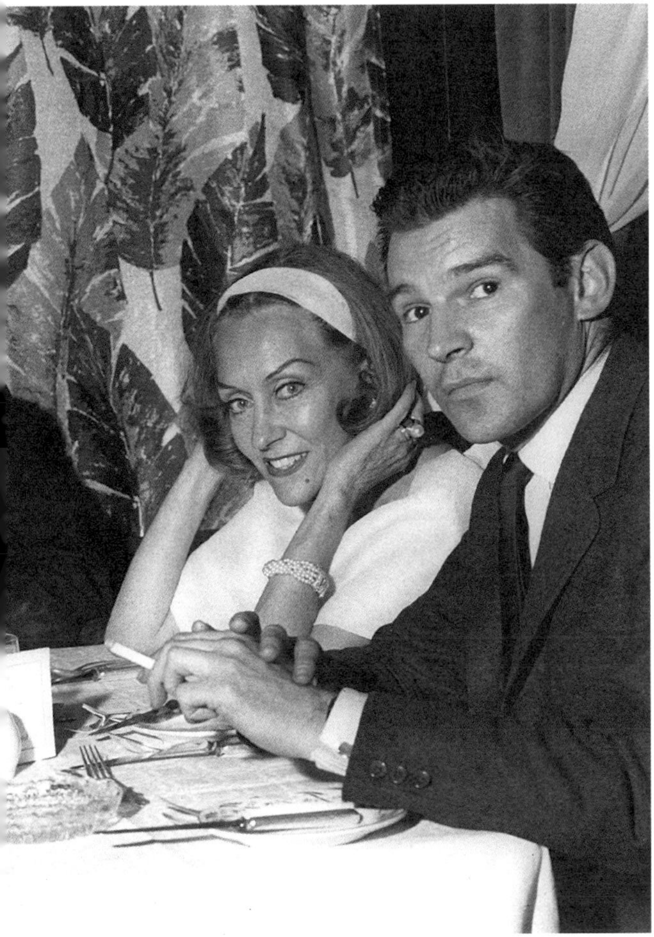

The Mudlark (1950): Gloria Swanson.

expressed about the propriety of showing a film depicting Queen Victoria so informally and that a Palace view was reportedly sought. The King said, in effect, that he would prefer to see the film as the public saw it, without cuts.

The stage show, produced by Nat Karson, included John Mills, Tyrone Power and Montgomery Clift singing Noël Coward's 'Three Juvenile Delinquents'; Terry-Thomas in a sketch spoofing the man who strikes the famous Rank gong, stripped to the waist and in leopard-skin shorts; twenty-four chorus girls dancing in gleaming sequin uniforms and white busbies and Marlene Dietrich performing 'Lili Marlene', which brought the house down. Also performing were Claudette Colbert, Gloria Swanson, James Stewart and Richard Todd.

Afterwards, the stars were presented to the royal party. Princess Elizabeth asked Andrew Ray if he enjoyed making the film.

'Oh yes, I did very much.'

At which his father, the comedian Ted Ray, nudged him and whispered, 'You should say, "Your Highness."'

The Princess waved the apology aside. 'It's very difficult to remember all these things, isn't it?' she said, putting the young lad at ease.

The King also congratulated actress Irene Dunne on looking so uncannily like his great-grandmother, Queen Victoria – the result of two hours in make-up every day.

There were 4,000 people still outside the cinema when the show ended. The star with the biggest cheer upon leaving was Gloria Swanson as everyone made their way to a party at the Savoy.

Once again there was a replica Royal Film Performance, this time in Cardiff and attended by Montgomery Clift, Gloria Swanson, Jack Warner and Terry-Thomas wearing one of his customary outlandish waistcoats.

1951 *Where No Vultures Fly*

In this year of the Festival of Britain, it was decided that the chosen picture had to be British made. In any case, this year saw the end of the original agreement to alternate between British and American productions. Now pictures from all countries were eligible. The winner turned out to be Ealing Studio's colourful adventure, *Where No Vultures Fly*, shot on location in Kenya and inspired by conservationist Mervyn Cowie, who pioneered wildlife protection.

With the King once again absent due to illness, the Queen was joined by Princess Margaret, the Duke and Duchess of Gloucester and the Duchess of Kent. They arrived to cheers from the crowds and were escorted into the brightly lit foyer of the Odeon, Leicester Square, that was banked high with great bouquets of gold, mauve and bronze chrysanthemums and white heather.

After meeting leading figures of the British film industry and trustees of the CTBF, the royal party proceeded upstairs to the circle lounge to be introduced to the stars of the film, Anthony Steel and Dinah Sheridan, along with the film's producer Sir Michael Balcon. Also in the line-up were the stars taking part in the stage show, including Petula Clark, Burt Lancaster, Peter Lawford, Herbert Lom, Fred MacMurray, Merle Oberon, Jane Russell, Margaret Rutherford and Lizabeth Scott. This was a change from tradition. In previous years, the royals met the artists at the close of the evening.

Before entering the auditorium, the Queen received a bouquet from William Simons, the 12-year-old boy star of the film, while Princess Margaret received a floral tribute from Jeremy Hanley, the 6-year-old son of Dinah Sheridan (and later chairman of the Conservative Party). Inside, the trumpeters of the Metropolitan Police Central Band blew a fanfare of welcome.

Following the film, there was the stage presentation produced by Ben Lyon. The opening had the American stars arriving by boat at Southampton, a clever way of introducing them to the audience. 'Naturally enough, Jane Russell seemed to get the lion's share of attention,' said the *Daily Film Renter*. Other highlights included a barn dance featuring a host of British stars, Fred MacMurray surprising many with his saxophone solo and Orson Welles performing a magician act. The finale, where all the female stars paraded across the stage in their sparkling gowns, went down especially well.

At the conclusion, Sir Ralph Richardson stepped forward and addressed the Queen personally, offering her and the King 'the leaves of our loyalty and the flowers of our affection'.

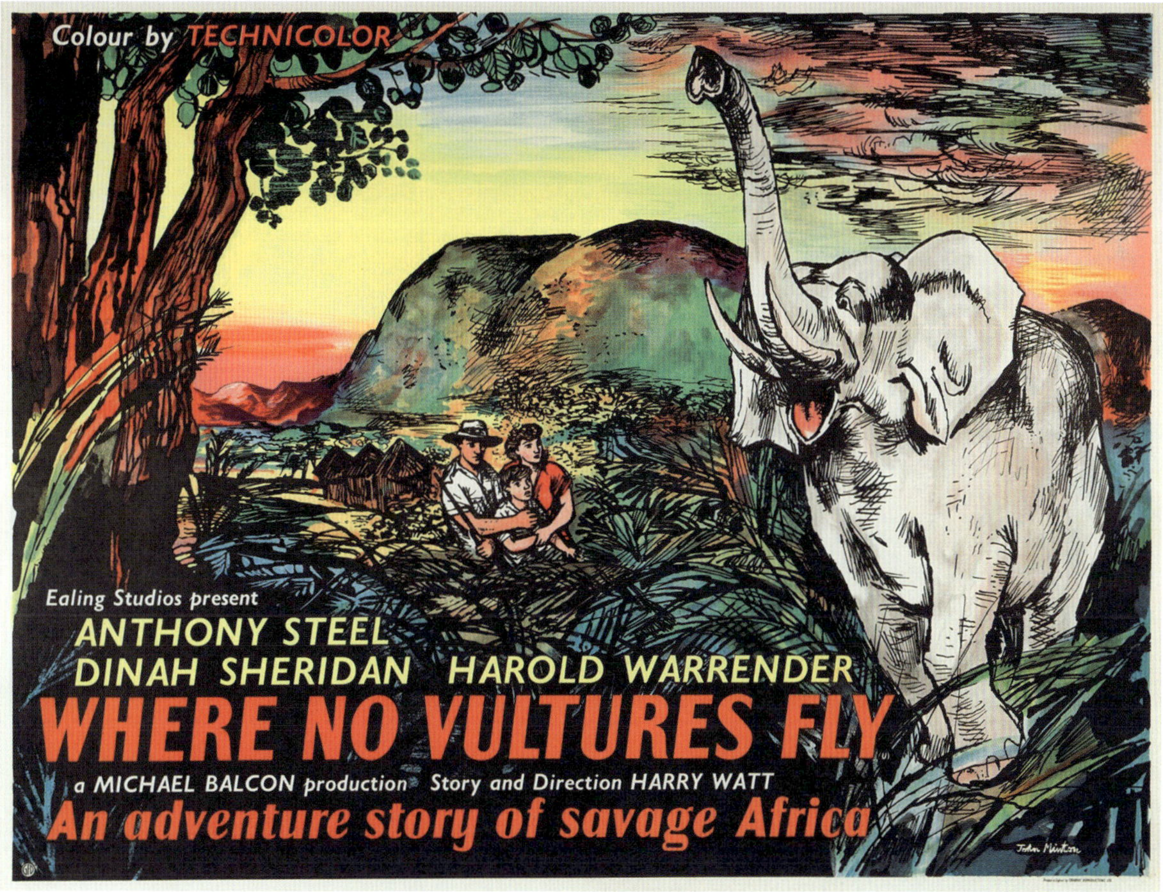

The packed audience then joined in the National Anthem, with markedly more fervour than usual, given the absence of the King and a desire for his quick recovery.

It was certainly a starry evening with many other popular artistes appearing such as Richard Attenborough, Hermione Baddeley, Peggy Cummins, Dulcie Gray, Joan Greenwood, Jack Hawkins, Valerie Hobson, Glynis Johns, Margaret Leighton, Peter Ustinov and Googie Withers.

This year also saw the last time the event went by the name of the Royal Command Film Performance. At the request of the Palace, the word 'command' was dropped as it suggested that the King chose the film.

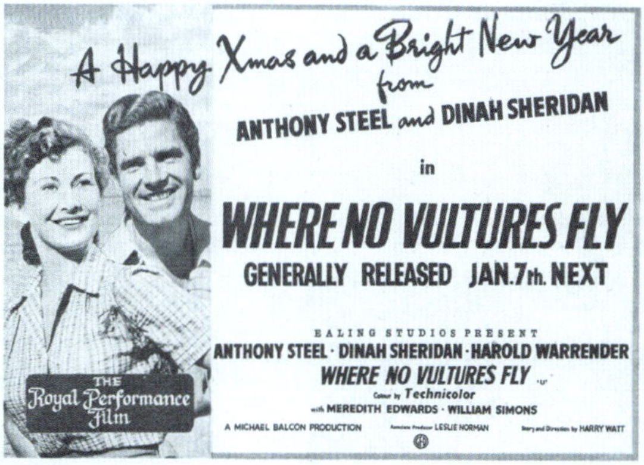

1952 *Because You're Mine*

With the sad passing of the King earlier in the year, this marked the first Royal Film Performance attended by the new Queen. As the royal car approached the Empire Cinema, Prince Philip was seen to lean over and speak to the driver. Suddenly, the lights went on in the car so the huge crowds could see the royal couple inside.

Elizabeth had often followed her mother to these film occasions, now, as Queen, she headed the royal party. Dazzling in black and white silk and wearing the famous 'Girls of Great Britain and Ireland' tiara, the Queen was presented to a line-up of stars including Kirk Douglas and Rock Hudson. There was Maurice Denham too, who, years before, had mended the lifts at the royal family's old home at No. 145 Piccadilly. And Gene Kelly. 'I saw *Singing in the Rain* six times,' Princess Margaret told him.

Undoubtedly the biggest film personality of the night was Charlie Chaplin, in London to publicise his new film *Limelight*. The Queen told him she had yet to see the picture. 'I hope, ma'am, that you will,' he said.

The cinema foyer was ablaze with a mass of flowers sent by air from twenty-two countries, rare orchids from Singapore, flame flowers from Brazil and carnations from Italy. After the show, at the Queen's special request, the flowers were sent to Charing Cross Hospital.

The film to be shown, however, was largely deemed to be not up to the magnitude of the occasion: 'not Royal quality', according to *Picturegoer* magazine. *Because You're Mine* starred the famous tenor Mario Lanza, playing an opera singer drafted into the army. Trading on the success of Lanza's previous box-office hit, *The Great Caruso*, this was a film that even the singer didn't want to make. Nor did Lanza show up for the Royal Film Performance, which the US press saw as a snub to Her Majesty. Many reasons exist why Lanza was a no-show: that he was at the time suspended by MGM, that he had a fear of flying and his schedule didn't allow him to make the boat trip over. Most likely, it was due to his wife being pregnant and not wanting to leave her side. Lanza sent his sincere apologies to the Palace.

The stage show, entitled 'Let's Go to the Pictures', began with clips from old silent movies. Celia Johnson and Trevor Howard acted out a scene from *Brief Encounter*, and Laurence Olivier and Vivien Leigh did likewise from *That Hamilton Woman*. Gene Kelly thrilled the audience with a dance routine and there was a skit about a couple of studio canteen workers played by Googie Withers and Peggy Cummins. When Douglas Fairbanks Jr introduced Chaplin there was a loud ovation. When the applause died down, there was a cry

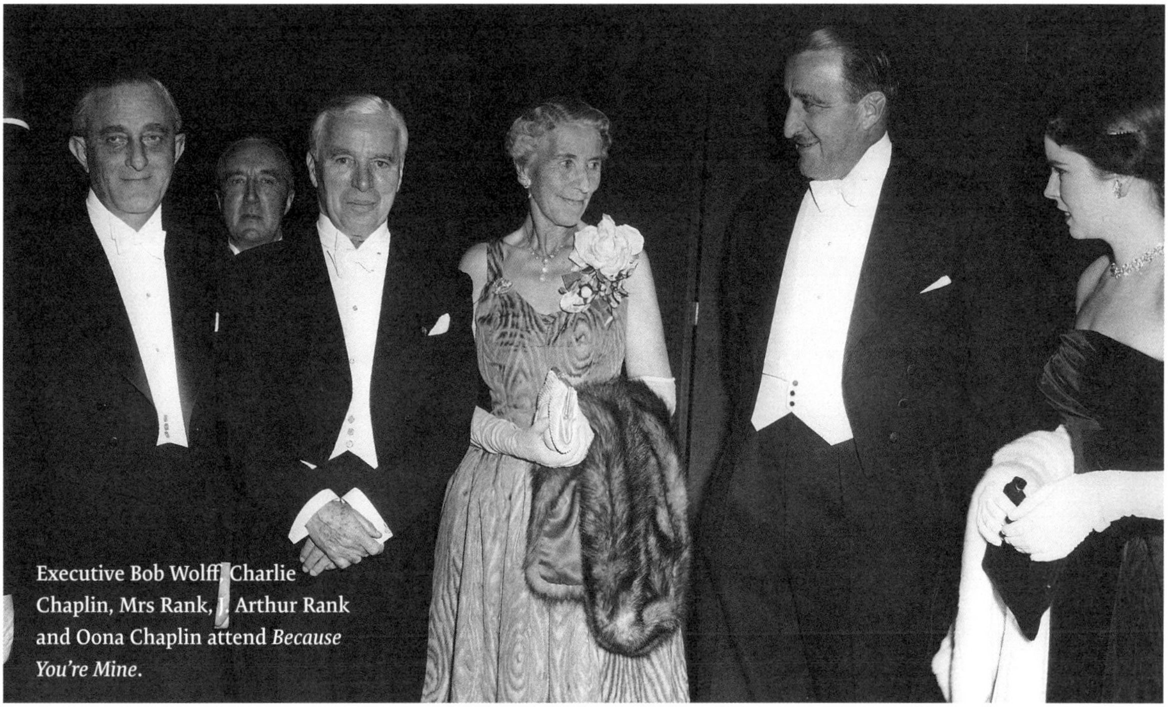

Executive Bob Wolff, Charlie Chaplin, Mrs Rank, J. Arthur Rank and Oona Chaplin attend *Because You're Mine*.

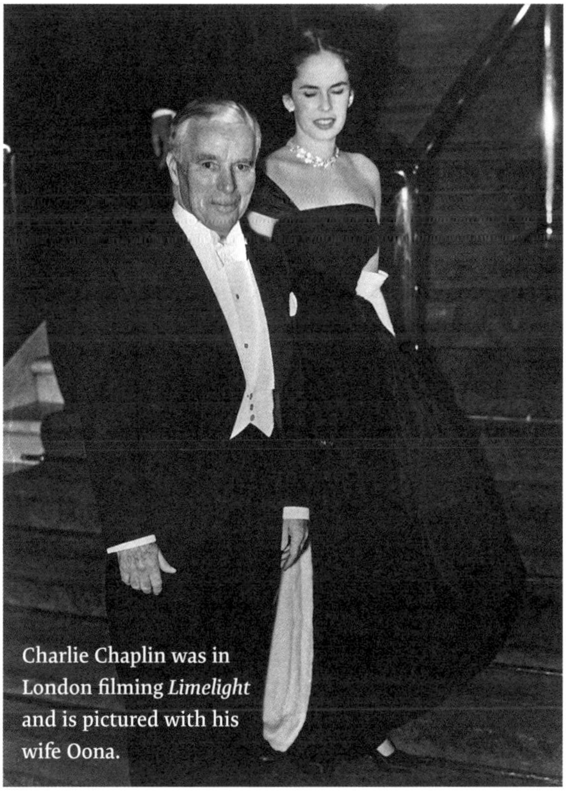

Charlie Chaplin was in London filming *Limelight* and is pictured with his wife Oona.

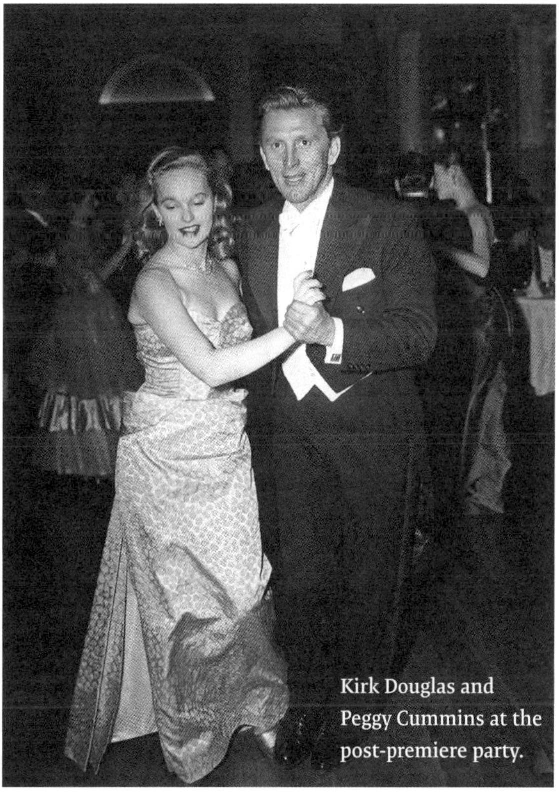

Kirk Douglas and Peggy Cummins at the post-premiere party.

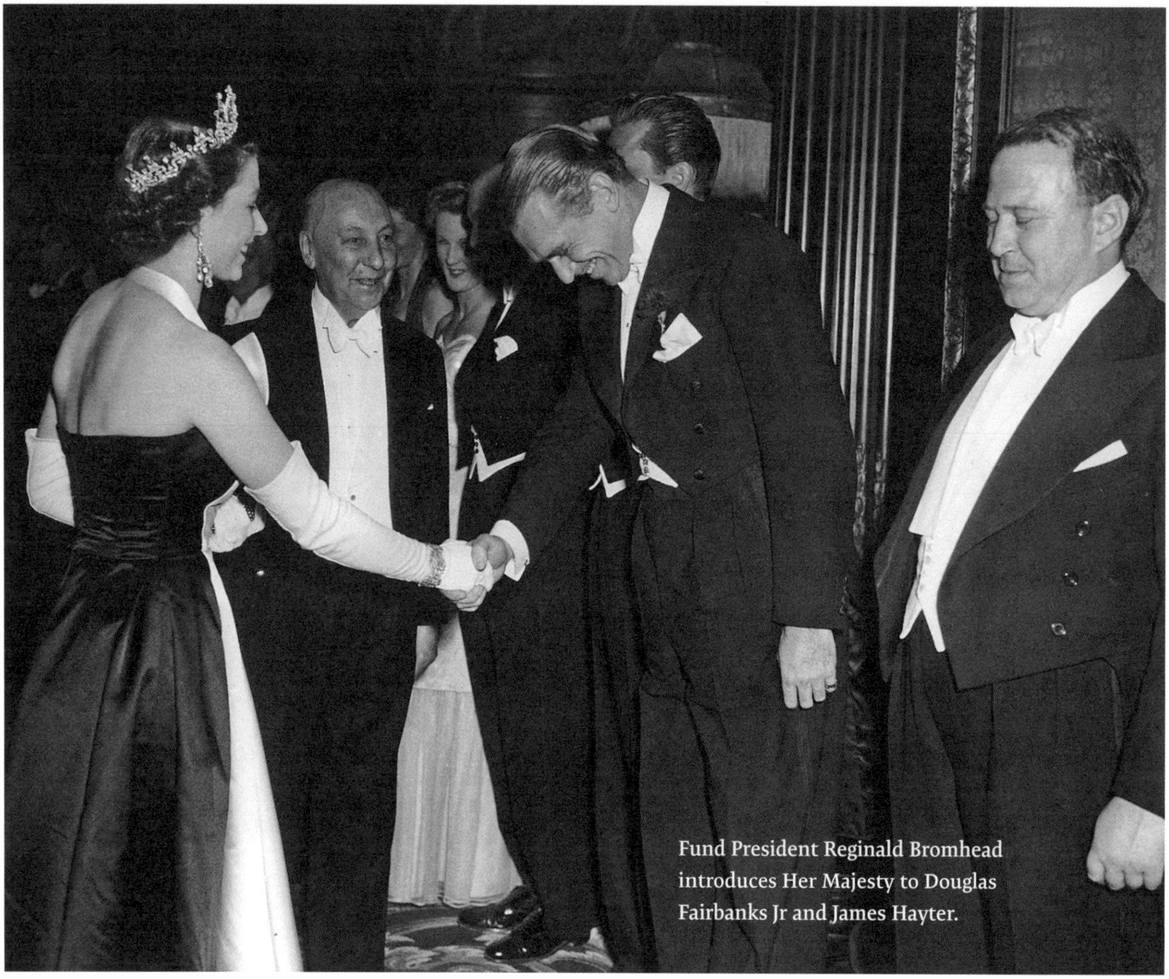

Fund President Reginald Bromhead introduces Her Majesty to Douglas Fairbanks Jr and James Hayter.

of 'Good old Charlie!' Shyly, the little tramp returned thanks.

The royal address was given by John Mills who spoke of an 'adventurous Elizabethan age'. Some commentators sensed a special atmosphere about this occasion, perhaps due to the youthfulness of the royal party. Mills finished with, 'We give you, ma'am, our allegiance and our love and say, with all our hearts, God save the Queen.' Trumpeters of the Household Cavalry in their heraldic tunics sounded a fanfare and the evening closed with the National Anthem and applause for the Queen.

This time, there was not one but two replica Royal Film Performances, in Liverpool and then in Leeds. The police had a job keeping order as stars such as Petula Clark, Peter Sellers and Jack Hawkins were introduced to the enthusiastic crowds outside each of the theatres.

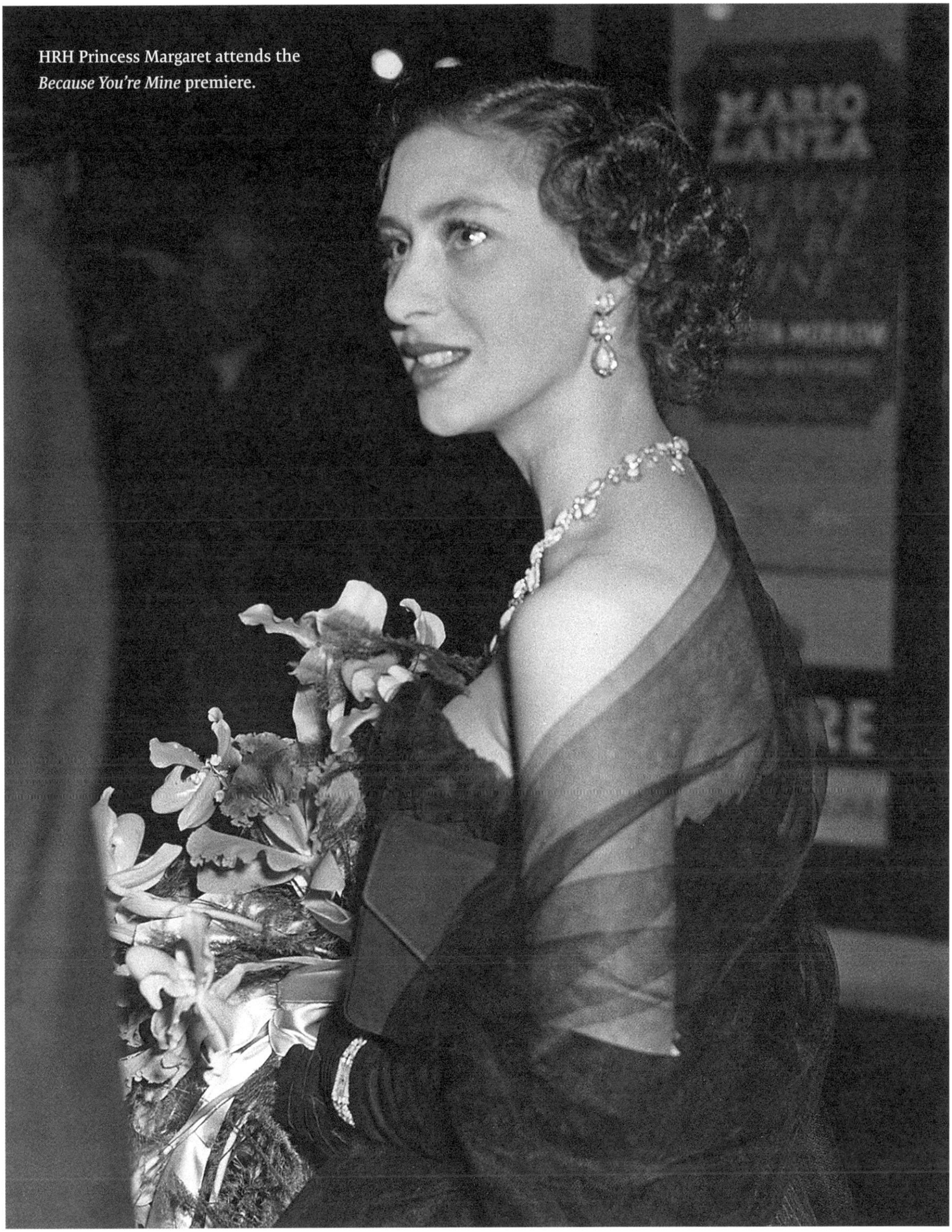

HRH Princess Margaret attends the *Because You're Mine* premiere.

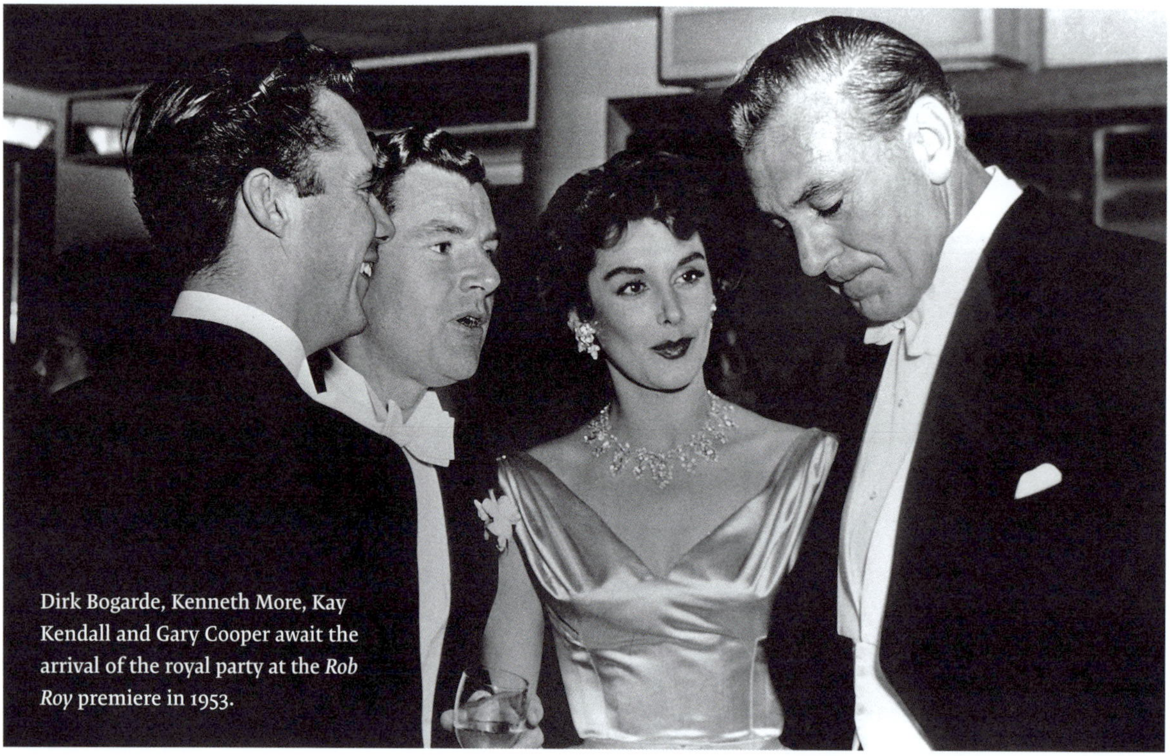

Dirk Bogarde, Kenneth More, Kay Kendall and Gary Cooper await the arrival of the royal party at the *Rob Roy* premiere in 1953.

1953 *Rob Roy: The Highland Rogue*

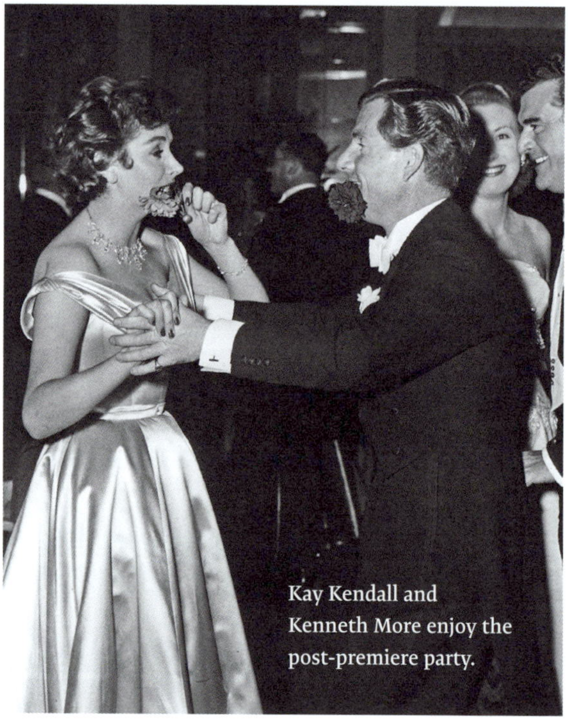

Kay Kendall and Kenneth More enjoy the post-premiere party.

Taking place as it did in coronation year, this Royal Film Performance took on added significance. Fittingly, large crowds gathered outside the Odeon, Leicester Square, to see the arrival of the Queen, dressed in a tiered gown of lilac organdie, a white ermine stole and a pearl and diamond tiara which once belonged to Queen Mary. She was accompanied by Prince Philip and Princess Margaret.

The film chosen was the colourful, rip-roaring adventure *Rob Roy*, made by the Disney studio. Based loosely on the Sir Walter Scott novel about the famous Scottish Highland leader, it was shot on location in Scotland where soldiers of the Argyll & Sutherland Highlanders, fresh from the conflict in Korea, were recruited for the battle scenes, doubling as red coats and Rob Roy's men. Director

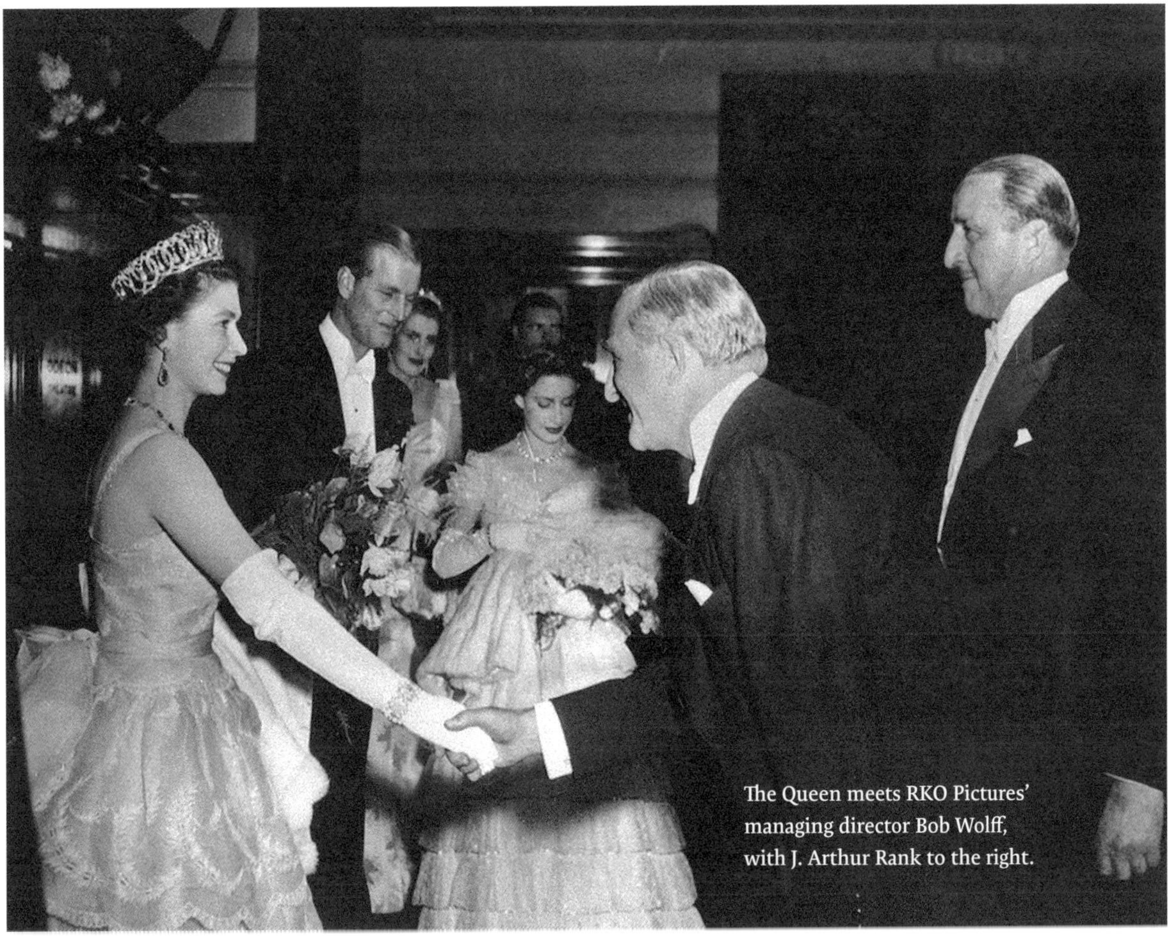

The Queen meets RKO Pictures' managing director Bob Wolff, with J. Arthur Rank to the right.

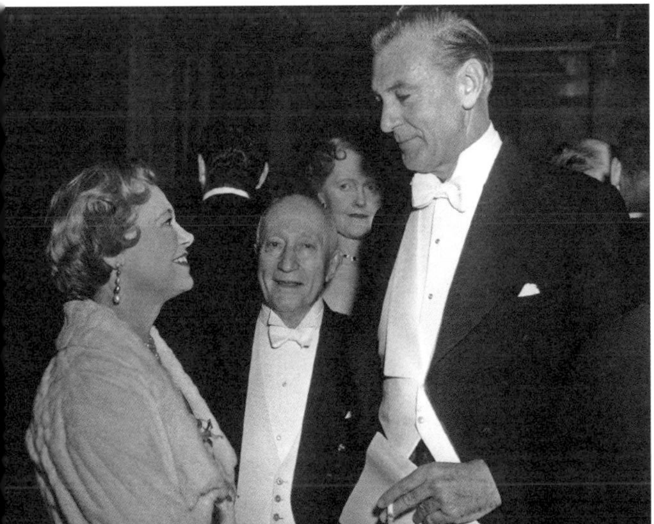

Harold French summed up the film to the Queen as 'A western in kilts, Your Majesty'.

The Queen was presented to a host of stars: Dirk Bogarde, George Cole, Gary Cooper, Gloria Grahame, Alec Guinness, John Ireland, Kay Kendall and Kenneth More, along with the stars of the film, Richard Todd, Glynis Johns and James Robertson Justice, resplendent in full Highland regalia. For those due to be presented to the Queen, their invitation specified, 'Full evening dress. No gloves for gentlemen. White gloves for ladies.'

Rob Roy premiere: Toots Bounds, Adolph Zukor (Chairman of Paramount Pictures) and Gary Cooper.

There was a change in the way the stage show was to be presented. The previous year the Queen was heard to say, 'What a lot of trouble they must have taken to put on a show like that just for one night'. It was the view of many that maybe the stage show was too long and that it might be markedly improved by being shorter and snappier. After all, this wasn't a variety show, the film itself should be the main attraction of the evening. With the stage presentation pruned of its length, a selection of short films could be included in the programme for the first time.

The sixteen-man pipe band of the Royal Canadian Air Force swung onto the stage playing the march 'Scotland the Brave', creating a suitable atmosphere for the showing of *Rob Roy*. They were led by Jack Hawkins.

Each performer was also presented with a medallion of the occasion by 9-year-old Mandy Miller, star of the recent Ealing drama *Mandy*. Earlier, Mandy had presented Princess Margaret with a bouquet of flowers. David Douglas-Mead, the grandson of Reginald Bromhead, did likewise with the Queen. Sadly for David, he wasn't allowed to stay and watch the film, but when he left, the crowds mistook him for a child actor and gave him a resounding cheer.

1954 *Beau Brummell*

This Hollywood dramatisation of the bon viveur Beau Brummell, who was friend to the Prince Regent, later George IV, was no doubt selected because of the belief that nothing interested royalty more than royalty. Starring Stewart Granger and Elizabeth Taylor, the choice was to backfire badly.

The Queen arrived at the Empire, Leicester Square, wearing a full-skirted, strapless gown of white tulle, with a diamond and emerald tiara. She was accompanied by Princess Margaret. For the first time, the waiting audience inside the auditorium was able to watch the arrival of the royal party and events inside the foyer via closed-circuit television beamed onto a screen.

In the line-up to meet the Queen were eighteen stars including Peter Finch, Stewart Granger, Anna Neagle, Michael Redgrave, Jane Russell, Jean Simmons, Donald Sinden and Shelley Winters. Italian actress Valentina Cortese was visibly shaking and when the Queen took her hand, she burst into tears. The Queen asked if she was alright. 'Yes,' Valentina replied, 'but I'm too emotional for this kind of thing.'

Jane Russell had originally planned to wear a red dress, but this was considered 'unsuitable' for the occasion. A theatrical costumier was hurriedly asked to copy the dress in velvet and gold, and it was delivered, unfinished, at Jane's hotel suite just minutes before she was due

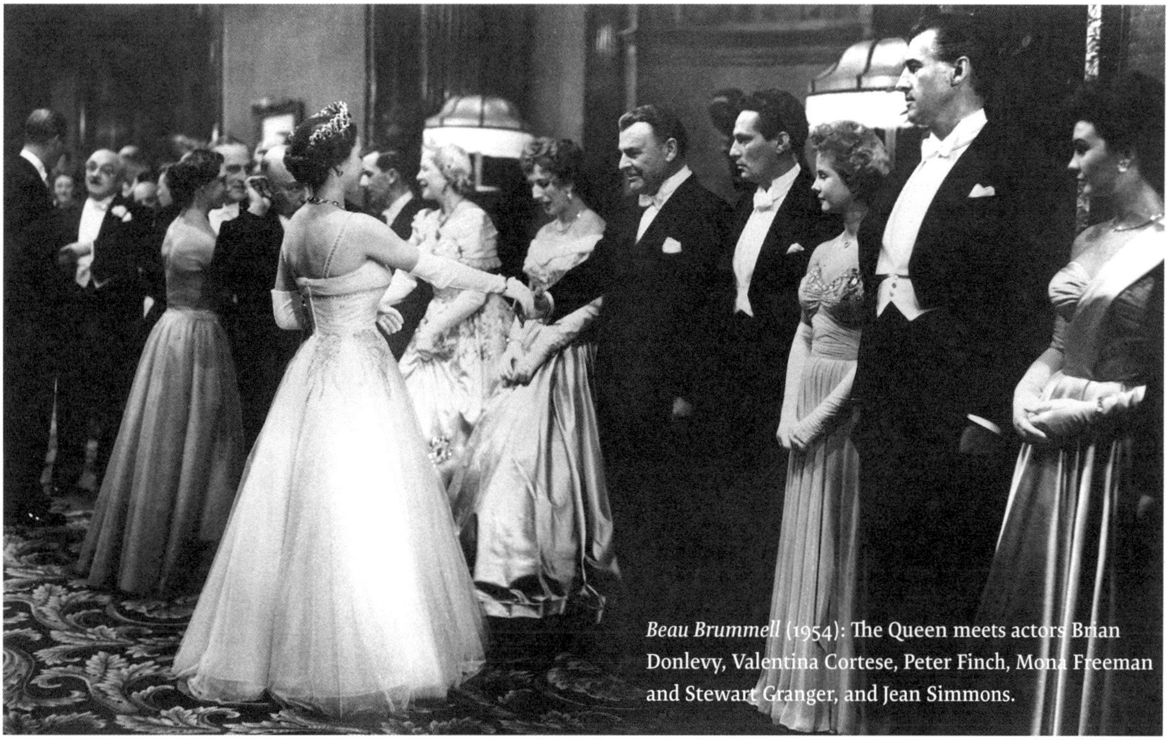

Beau Brummell (1954): The Queen meets actors Brian Donlevy, Valentina Cortese, Peter Finch, Mona Freeman and Stewart Granger, and Jean Simmons.

to leave. After meeting the Queen, the final stitches were added in the cinema's kitchen.

Further down the line-up, screen tough guy Brian Donlevy informed Prince Philip that he was filming at Bray Studios. 'Oh, I know the country round there pretty well,' said the duke. 'If you pop in at the Hind's Head there, give my regards to Mrs Williams, the landlady.'

Peter Ustinov was producer of the stage show, whose theme was 'All the World's a Cinema'. It took place in front of a backcloth tracing the course of the Queen's recent tour of the Commonwealth. Jane Russell sang 'Buttons and Bows' and Anna Neagle posed in a historical tableau. Ustinov himself was seen as the highlight, doing a funny commentary over a newsreel.

The following morning the papers were full of stories that the Queen was far from amused with the film, due to lurid scenes depicting a mentally ill George III. It was reported that Prince Philip said in private he was 'flabbergasted' by the 'poor choice'. This was the first occasion since the start of the Royal Film Performance that the royal family had been known to express a negative view at the choice of picture. Reginald Bromhead told the *Daily Express*, 'The Palace is impartial about the films which are selected for royal showing. It is accepted that the Palace will take what is provided.'

With the whole selection process being called into question by the press, an inquest within the charity was held days later. It was reported to have been 'very lively'. Even the government exerted pressure to get things sorted. The outcome was a new selection committee headed by an independent chairman, Lord Radcliffe.

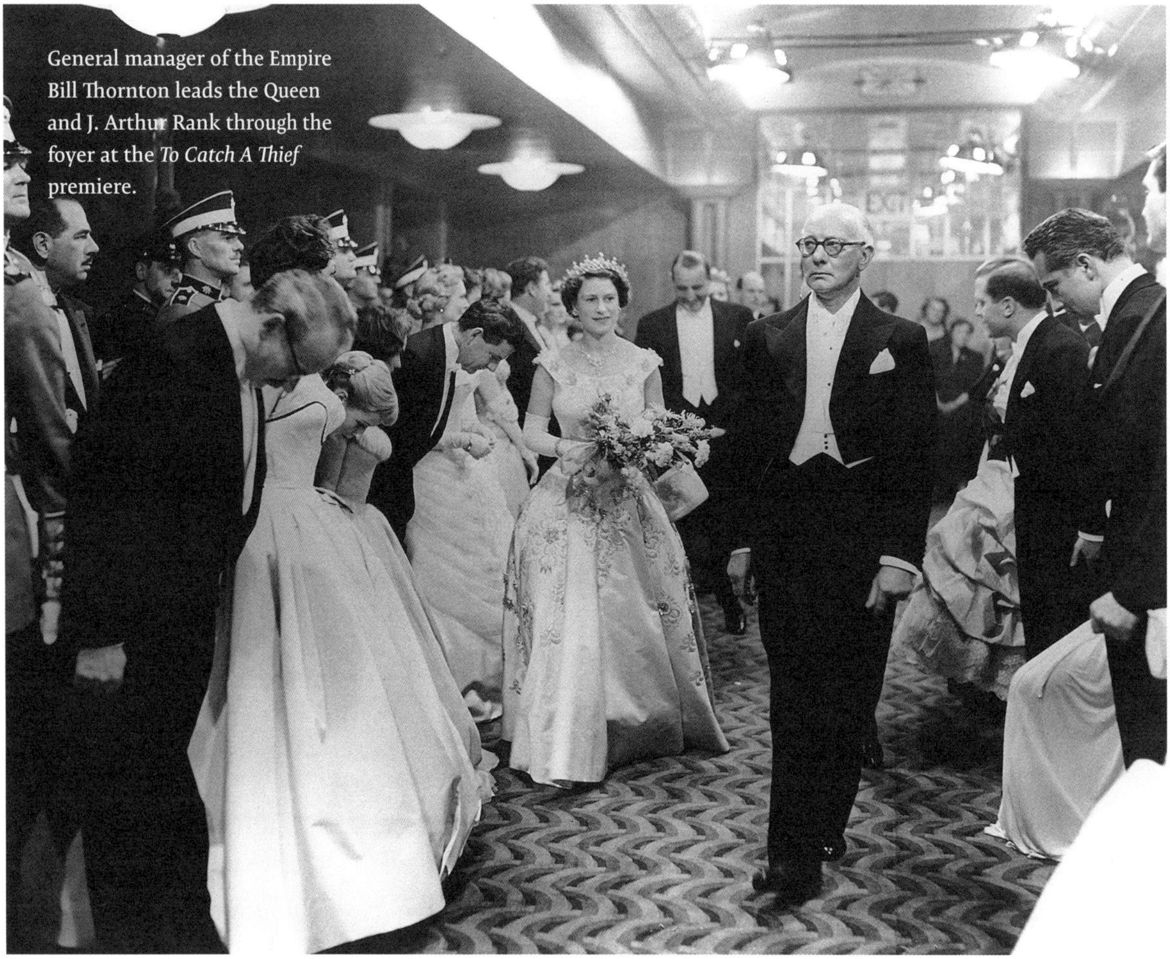

General manager of the Empire Bill Thornton leads the Queen and J. Arthur Rank through the foyer at the *To Catch A Thief* premiere.

1955 *To Catch a Thief*

The new selection committee, which for the first time included a couple of film critics, came up trumps this year with the classic Alfred Hitchcock romantic drama *To Catch a Thief*, starring two of Hollywood's most photogenic specimens in Cary Grant and Grace Kelly. Sadly, neither star was available to attend due to filming commitments, but the presence of Hitchcock himself more than made up for their absence.

The favourite in the press to land the coveted Royal Film that year, the publicity value of which was calculated to be worth £1 million, had been Laurence Olivier's *Richard III*. But after the previous year's debacle, it was decided to steer clear of a film that depicted a former King of England as one of history's darkest villains.

Thousands braved a chilly night and lined the route from the National Gallery to the Odeon, Leicester Square. The Queen, smiling, turned twice and waved to the crowds before entering the foyer. For the first time since 1946, Princess Margaret was missing due to a

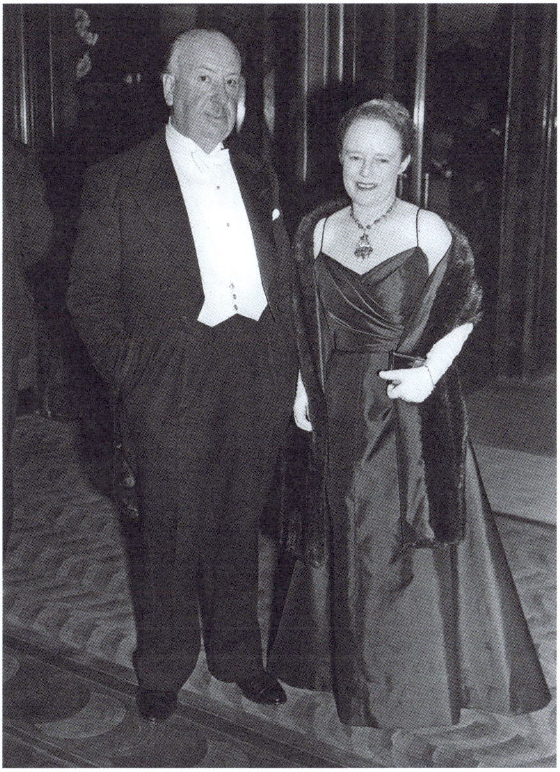

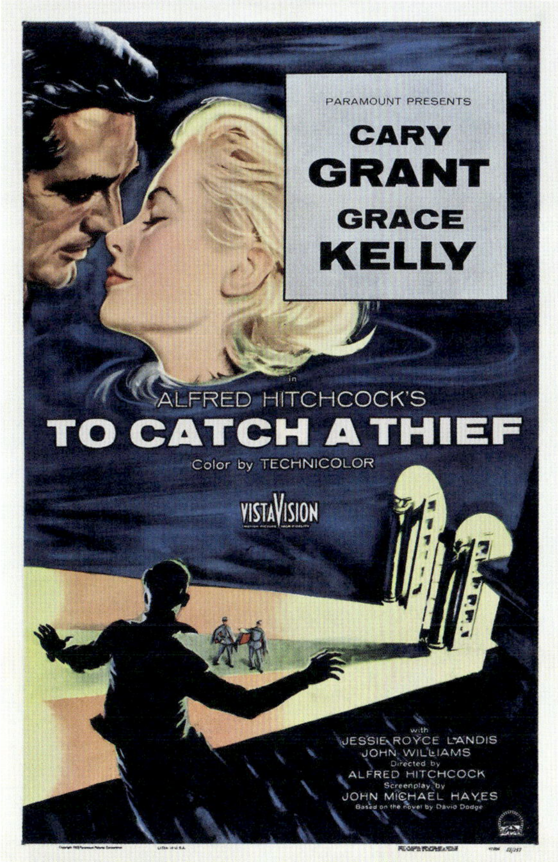

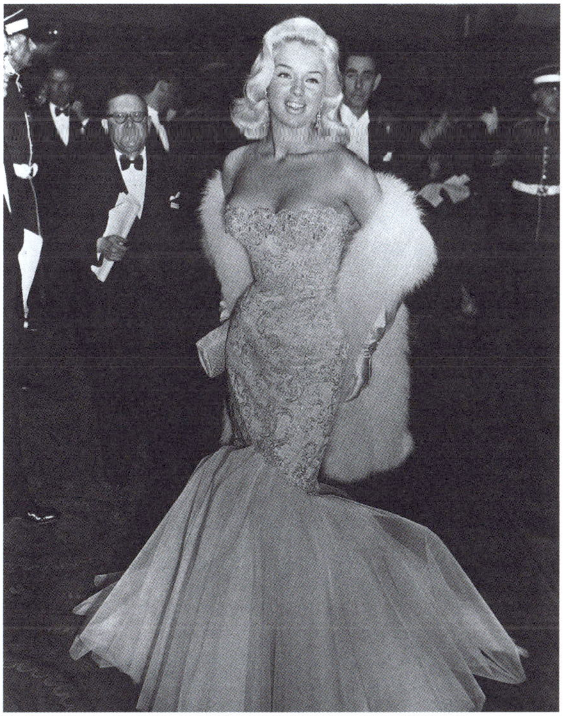

(Above left) Director Alfred Hitchcock, with his wife Alma, arrive at the cinema.

(Left) Diana Dors was known as the 'British Marilyn Monroe'.

trauma in her private life. That evening, she released a statement of her intention not to marry Group Captain Peter Townsend. No doubt concerned for her sister, the Queen put on a brave show.

One reporter counted forty people in three tight ranks waiting to be introduced, flanked by fourteen members of the Coldstream Guards in their flame-coloured tunics. Again, the stars were left impressed by the royals' film knowledge. The Queen knew the title of Diana Dors' forthcoming film and commiserated with Gina

Lollobrigida for her luggage being misplaced at Heathrow Airport. Italian star Rossano Brazzi had wanted to kiss the hand of the Queen, Continental style, and wrote to Buckingham Palace for advice. 'No, sir,' was his reply: this was not within the bounds of protocol.

When Prince Philip approached Kenneth More in the line-up, he talked about the film he was then making about Douglas Bader, *Reach for the Sky*, and if he did any of the flying. 'No, sir,' said More. 'Every time I get near an airplane the insurance people haul me out.'

Other stars in attendance were Belinda Lee, Virginia McKenna and Ava Gardner, whose dress was so tight she was forced to bow rather than curtsey, which raised a few eyebrows.

There was no stage show this year, which most commentators saw as a good thing, as it always seemed to drag out the evening to an often-execrable length. Instead, Jack Hawkins merely introduced the stars to the audience, one by one, on the stage. Diana Dors brushed past Hawkins wearing white fox furs, leaving a powdering of white fluff on his midnight-blue dinner jacket. 'Oh bother,' he was heard to mutter. 'Now I've got Diana Dors all over me.'

1956 *The Battle of the River Plate*

This year's Royal Film Performance made headlines around the world, thanks to the meeting of two great icons from two very different worlds, the Queen and Marilyn Monroe. Monroe, wearing a gown of gold, Grecian in style, that looked as if it had been sprayed on, drew huge cheers from the crowd and for two minutes stood and waved from outside the Empire Theatre. When asked by a reporter if she had attended anything quite like this before, the starlet answered, 'Well, we don't have the Queen of England back home.'

Monroe was noticeably nervous in the line-up. Her eyes never seemed to part from her husband, Arthur Miller, standing close by. Standing next to Monroe was Victor Mature, equally nervous and tense, wiping perspiration from his brow. On the other side of Monroe was Anthony Quayle, the embodiment of composure and calm. In the country filming *The Prince and the Showgirl* with Laurence Olivier, Monroe was renting a house in the village of Englefield Green, on the edge of Windsor Great Park. 'Then we are neighbours, how nice,' said the Queen. Asked how she liked living there, Monroe said, 'We love it', explaining how she and Miller went for bicycle rides in the park.

During Monroe's chat with Princess Margaret, Anthony Quayle butted in to ask whether she might come and see Arthur

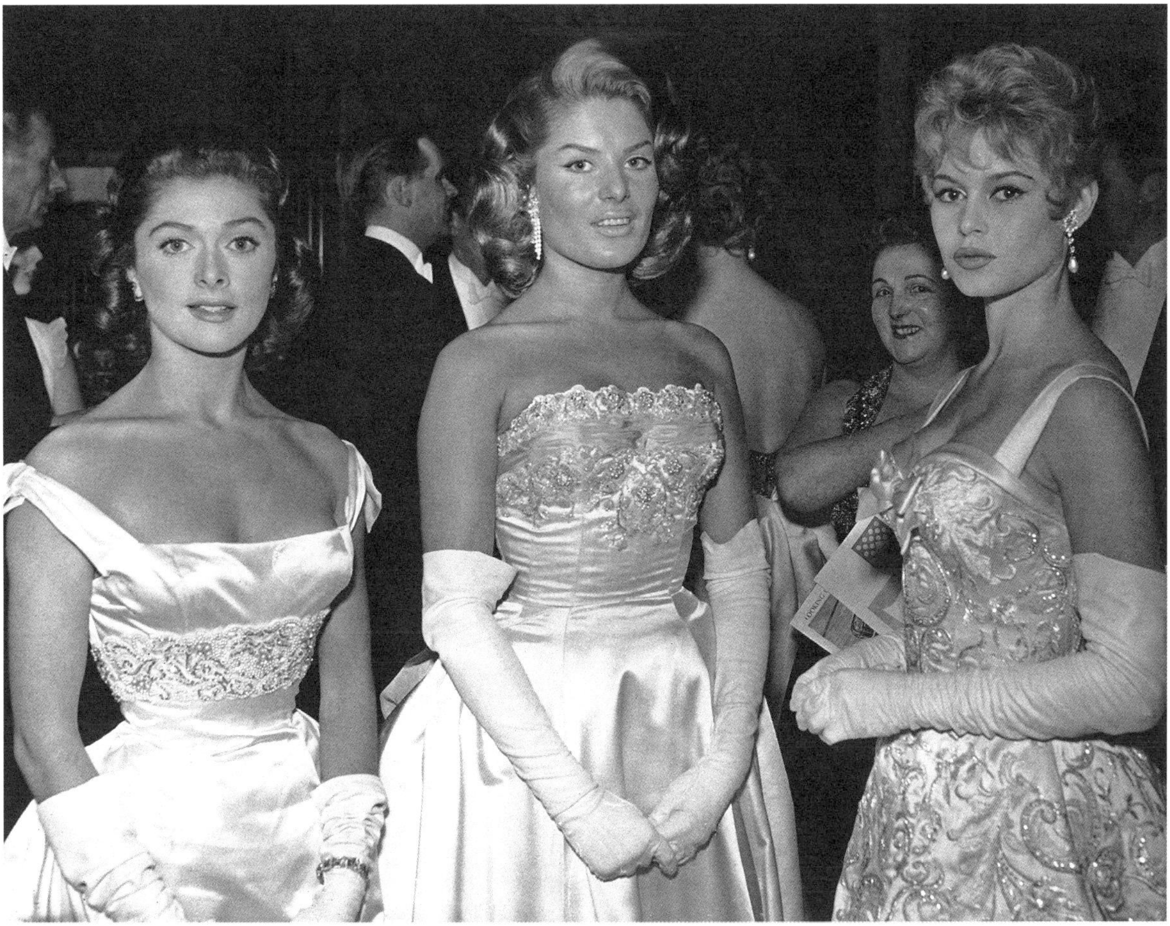

At the premiere of *Battle of the River Plate*, Brigitte Bardot is pictured with Rank starlets Maureen Swanson (Countess of Dudley) and Belinda Lee.

Miller's new play, *A View from the Bridge*, in which he appeared. 'Of course I mean, ma'am, that we would be delighted to see you if you were allowed to see a banned play.' The Lord Chamberlain, England's puritanical public censor, had banned *A View from the Bridge* and it was being performed in a theatre club.

'I hope you will come and see it,' said Marilyn.

'Well,' said Princess Margaret, 'perhaps I might be able to come … I shall have to see about it.' The princess did indeed attend a performance.

When the royal party moved into the auditorium the stars in the line-up could relax. Some headed for the bar. Joan Crawford collapsed in a chair, asking for iced water. She had been nervous all day. 'Never again, brother,' she said. 'I hope I'm asked, but I couldn't take it a second time.' So nervous had she been that waiting in line, she suddenly made a break for it and her husband, Alfred Steele, had to push her back in.

With Monroe all but stealing the show, the film itself was almost relegated to a supporting role. This year, the choice was a Powell and

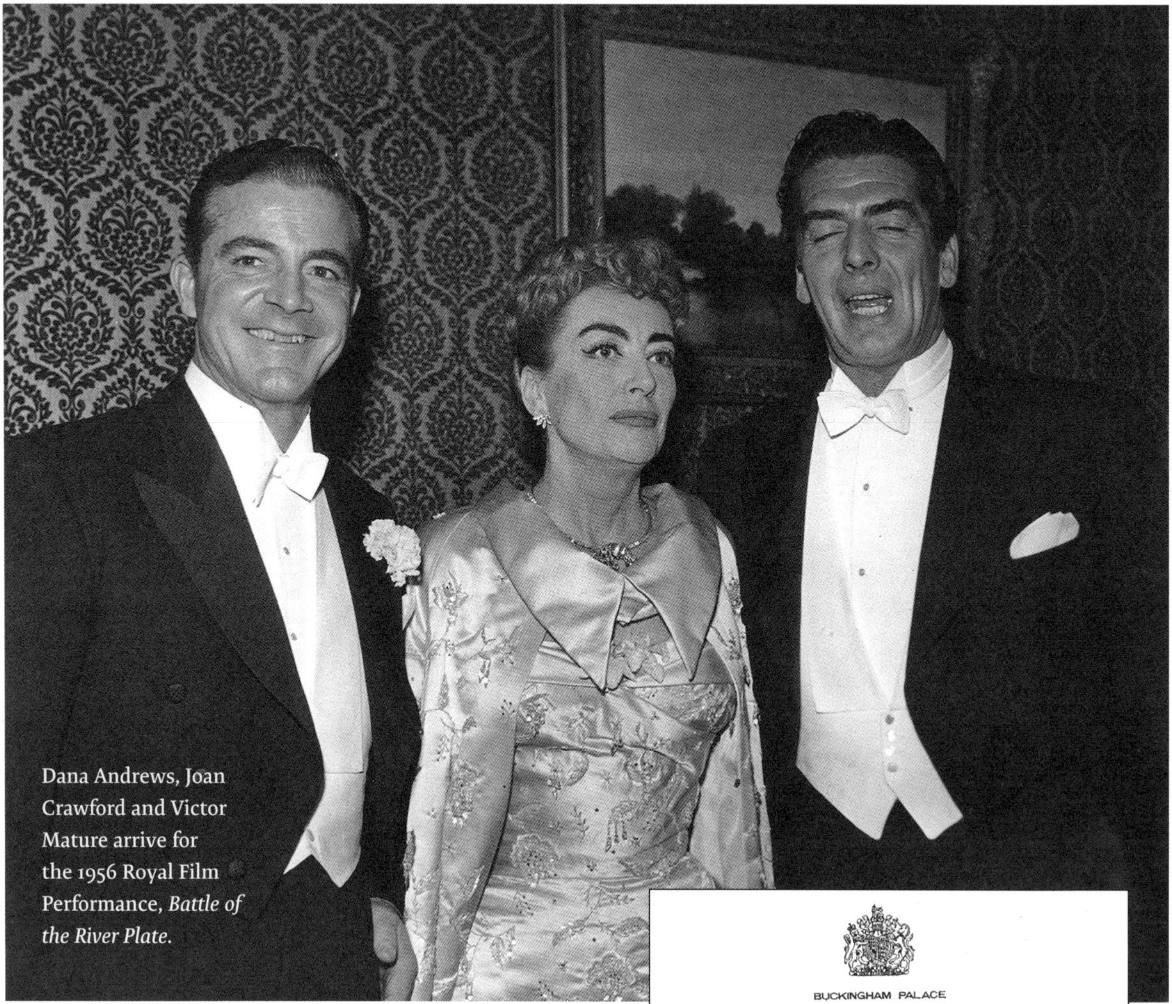

Dana Andrews, Joan Crawford and Victor Mature arrive for the 1956 Royal Film Performance, *Battle of the River Plate*.

Pressburger production, *The Battle of the River Plate*, which told the story of an early naval engagement in 1939 between a Royal Navy force of three cruisers and the German pocket battleship *Admiral Graf Spee*. It starred Peter Finch and Anthony Quayle

Again, instead of a stage show, the stars were merely presented to the audience, asked to walk on stage, one by one, turn left, then right, bow or curtsey, then make their

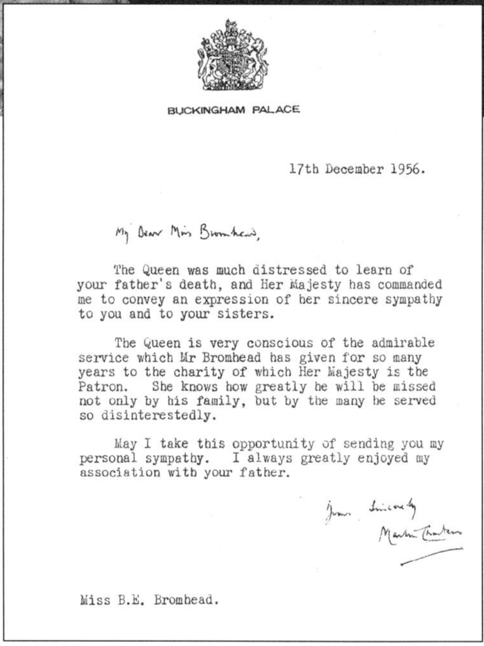

BUCKINGHAM PALACE

17th December 1956.

My dear Miss Bromhead,

The Queen was much distressed to learn of your father's death, and Her Majesty has commanded me to convey an expression of her sincere sympathy to you and to your sisters.

The Queen is very conscious of the admirable service which Mr Bromhead has given for so many years to the charity of which Her Majesty is the Patron. She knows how greatly he will be missed not only by his family, but by the many he served so disinterestedly.

May I take this opportunity of sending you my personal sympathy. I always greatly enjoyed my association with your father.

Yours sincerely

Martin Charteris

Miss B.E. Bromhead.

Letter from the Palace regarding Reginald Bromhead's passing

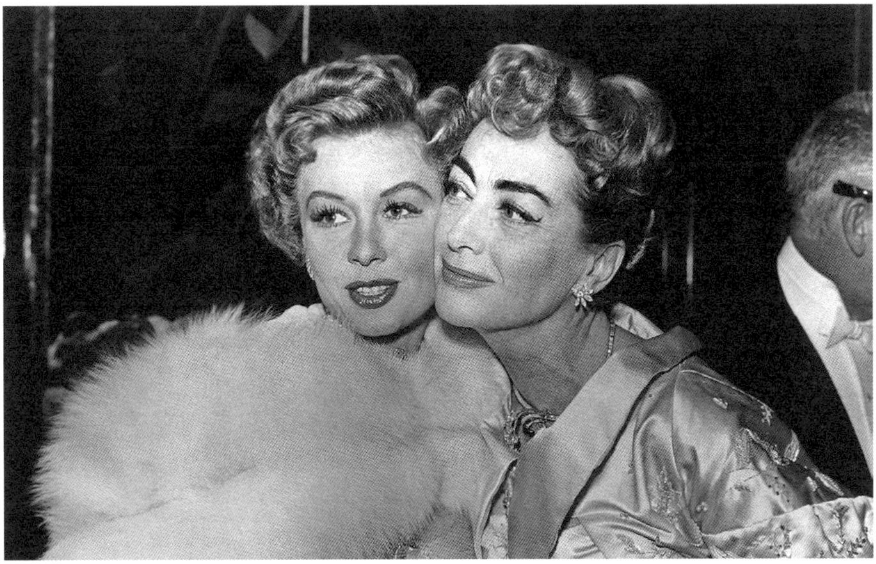

Vera Ellen and Joan Crawford cosy up 'cheek to cheek' for a photo at the 1956 Royal Film Performance.

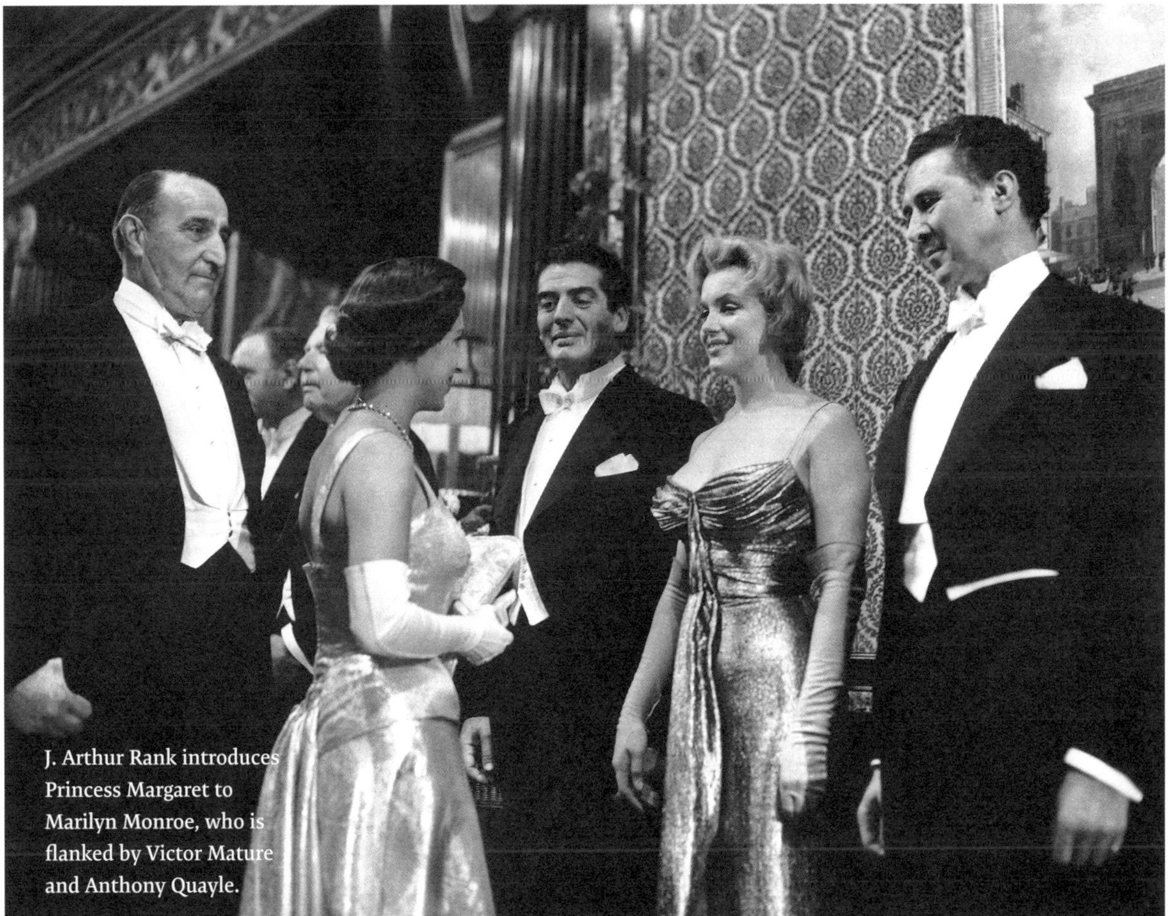

J. Arthur Rank introduces Princess Margaret to Marilyn Monroe, who is flanked by Victor Mature and Anthony Quayle.

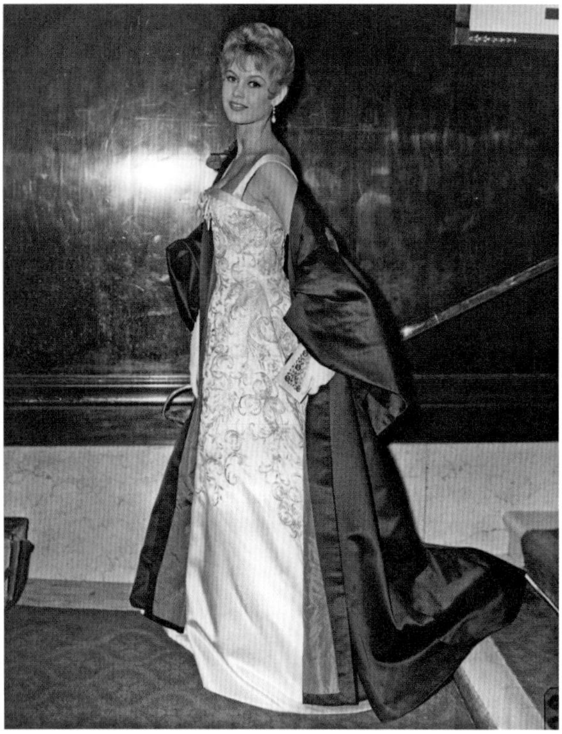

French star Brigitte Bardot fresh from her success in starring in *Doctor at Sea.*

way off. Because Marilyn had been unable to attend rehearsals, she had no idea what she was required to do and kept asking Quayle. Despite explaining several times, Monroe was so nervous she kept forgetting. About to go on, Monroe asked Victor Mature what she should do. 'Fall on your ass, baby,' he said, before making his own entrance. Seconds later, Marilyn was introduced and managed to get everything right.

Other stars in attendance that sparkling evening included Ian Carmichael, Anita Ekberg, Laurence Harvey, Anthony Steel, Mary Ure and Norman Wisdom. Also making headlines was 22-year-old rising French starlet Brigitte Bardot, who confessed to practising her curtsey before being presented to the Queen.

1957 *Les Girls*

Les Girls was generally seen to be a good choice – something lightweight and entertaining as only an old-fashioned MGM musical can be, with the bonus of music and lyrics by Cole Porter. Crowds began to gather outside the Odeon, Leicester Square, from midday, despite the inclement weather, and by the evening numbered in their thousands as the rain came teeming down. There were squeals of joy at the star arrivals, the biggest of which were for new music sensation Tommy Steele. The Queen, accompanied by Prince Philip and Princess Alexandra, dazzled in a white gown decorated with silver sequins and fur trim and a diamond tiara. As was the custom, pictures of the stars arriving in the cinema foyer were beamed live to the audience in the auditorium, for the first time with sound.

The stage show was back, and for once, the spotlight shone on the people on the other side of the camera. Entitled 'Meet the Movie Makers', it was produced by Vivian Cox and compèred by Kenneth More. Set on a busy soundstage, stars introduced those who worked behind the scenes, from the smallest studio worker to the director. Keeping with this theme, two veterans of the industry were presented to the Queen: Mr Joseph Rogers, 85, a former model-maker and stage carpenter and a permanent resident at Glebelands, and H. Langley Merritt, 81, a former projectionist and cinema manager. It was a nice touch.

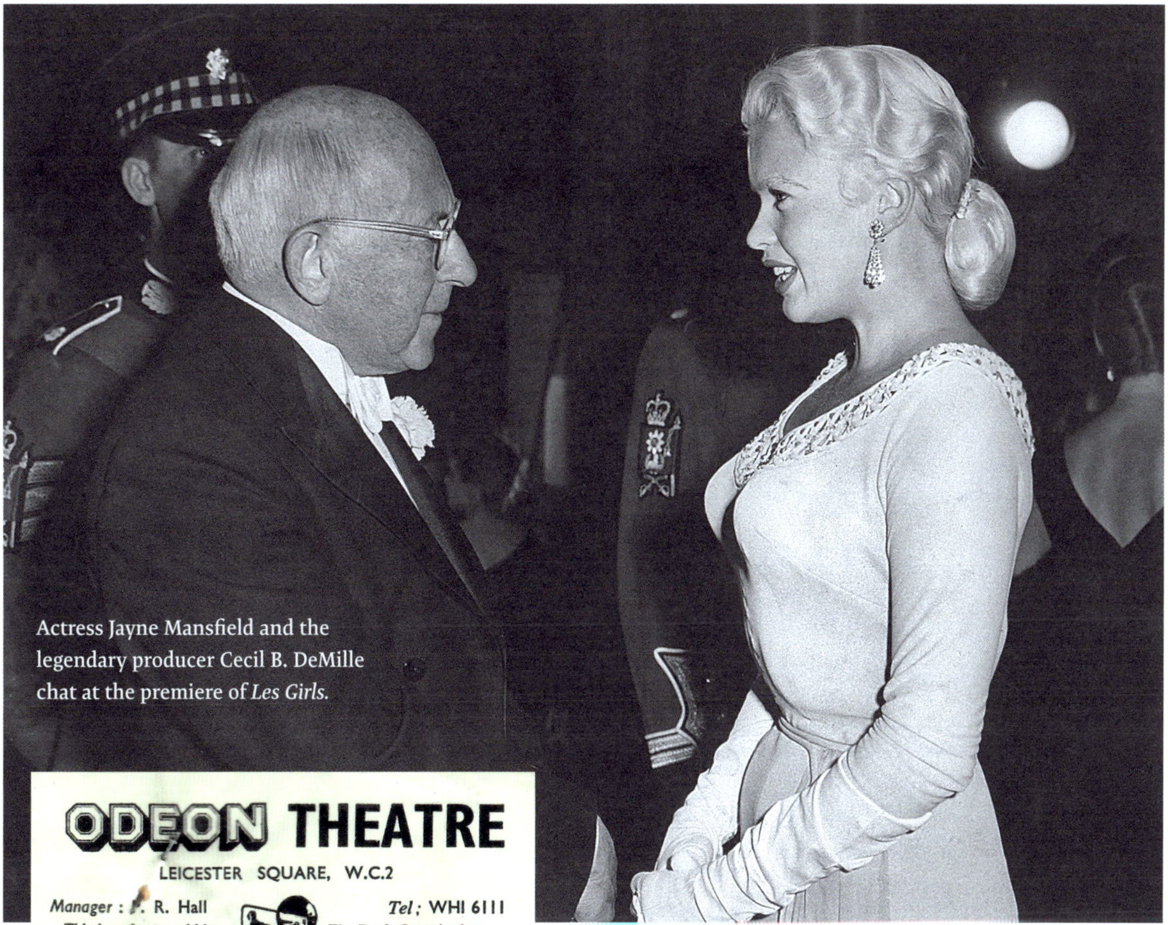

Actress Jayne Mansfield and the legendary producer Cecil B. DeMille chat at the premiere of *Les Girls*.

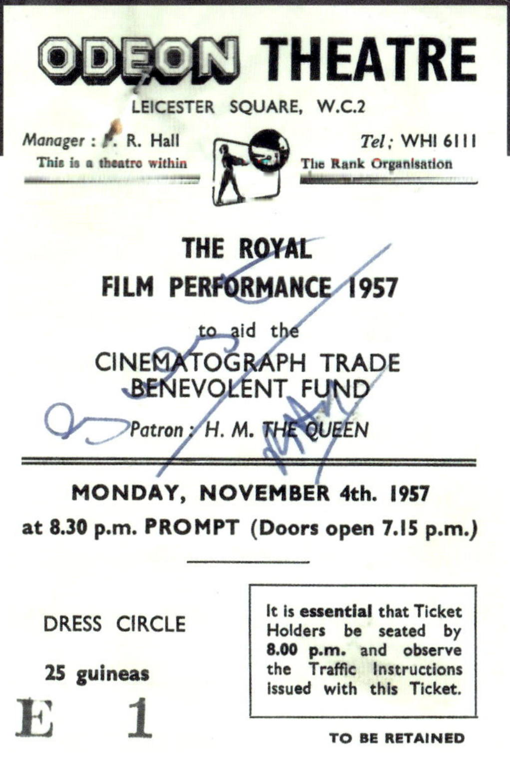

ODEON THEATRE
LEICESTER SQUARE, W.C.2
Manager : F. R. Hall Tel: WHI 6111
This is a theatre within The Rank Organisation

THE ROYAL
FILM PERFORMANCE 1957
to aid the
CINEMATOGRAPH TRADE
BENEVOLENT FUND
Patron : H. M. THE QUEEN

MONDAY, NOVEMBER 4th. 1957
at 8.30 p.m. PROMPT (Doors open 7.15 p.m.)

DRESS CIRCLE
25 guineas
E 1

It is essential that Ticket Holders be seated by 8.00 p.m. and observe the Traffic Instructions issued with this Ticket.

TO BE RETAINED

The royal party entered the Royal Box, which was emblazoned with the coat of arms, and the whole audience stood up as the state trumpeters of the Life Guards sounded a fanfare. As the show began there was a big laugh at a spoof newsreel, featuring a commentary by Terry-Thomas that included a few sly digs at the Duke of Edinburgh.

After the main film, some of the stars were presented to the Queen, including Stanley Baker, Michael Craig, Jack Hawkins, Anne Heywood, William Holden, Sophia Loren, Tommy Steele and Dorothy Tutin. The Queen was also presented to famed Hollywood director Cecil B. DeMille. Jayne Mansfield wore a champagne-coloured floor-length gown that

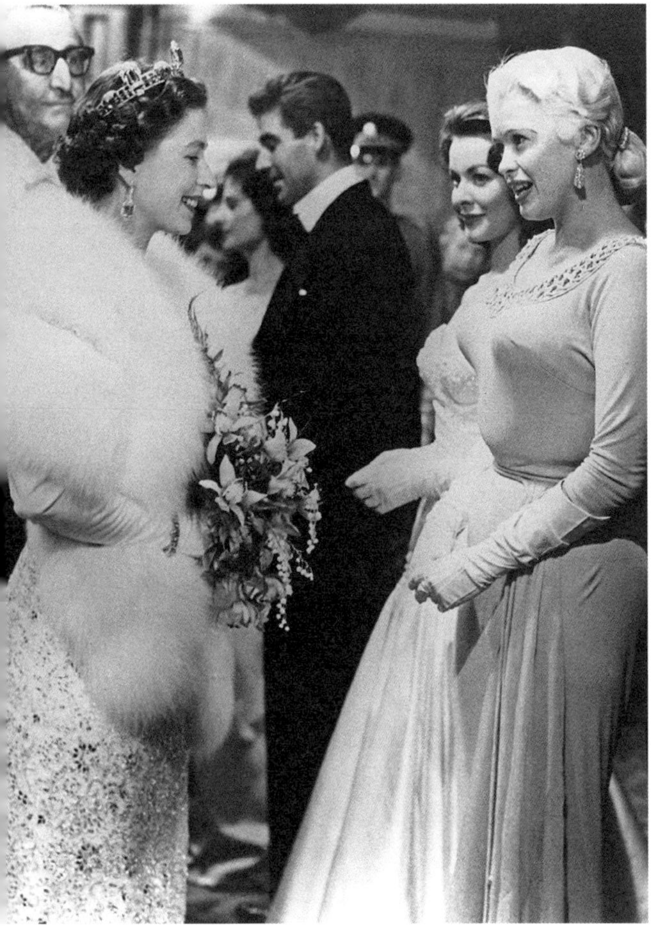

Jayne Mansfield meets the Queen.

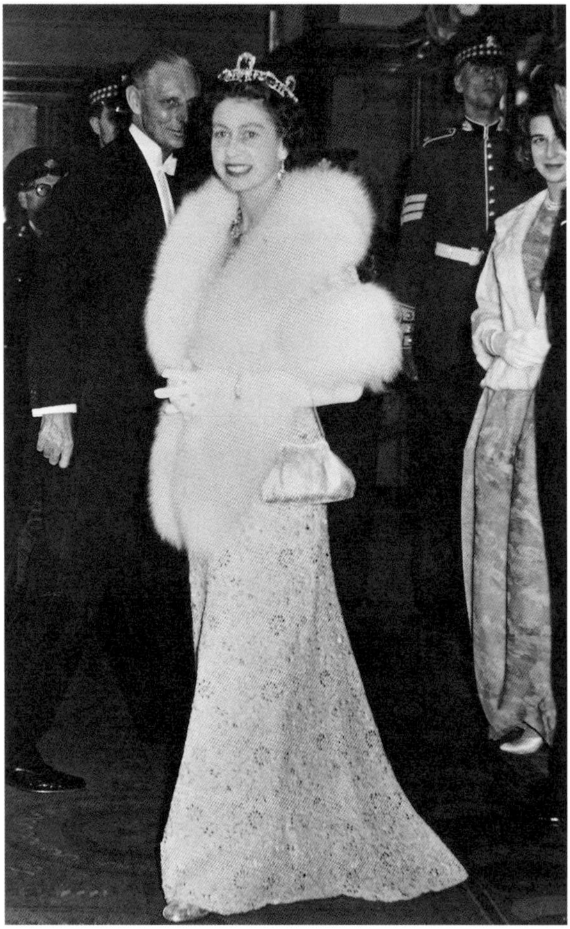

Her Majesty looks radiant.

was so tight it split down the back. Before meeting the Queen, it was hastily stitched up.

'Your Majesty, you're looking so beautiful,' gushed the star.

The Queen said, 'Thank you so much. You're so kind. I understand you have been travelling on the Continent. Did you come here to meet me especially?'

Mansfield replied, 'Yes, Madam, and I was never so excited in all my life.'

A bouquet was presented to the Queen by Sarah More, Kenneth More's 4-year-old daughter.

The evening was another unqualified success but soon news broke that there would be no Royal Film Performance in 1958. The Queen had made it known that she wished to vary her engagements to cover the widest possible field of charitable events and spread her patronage in future years to other members of the royal family. In this way, there would always be a Royal Film Performance, regardless of her availability. As it turned out, the Queen did not attend another one until 1961.

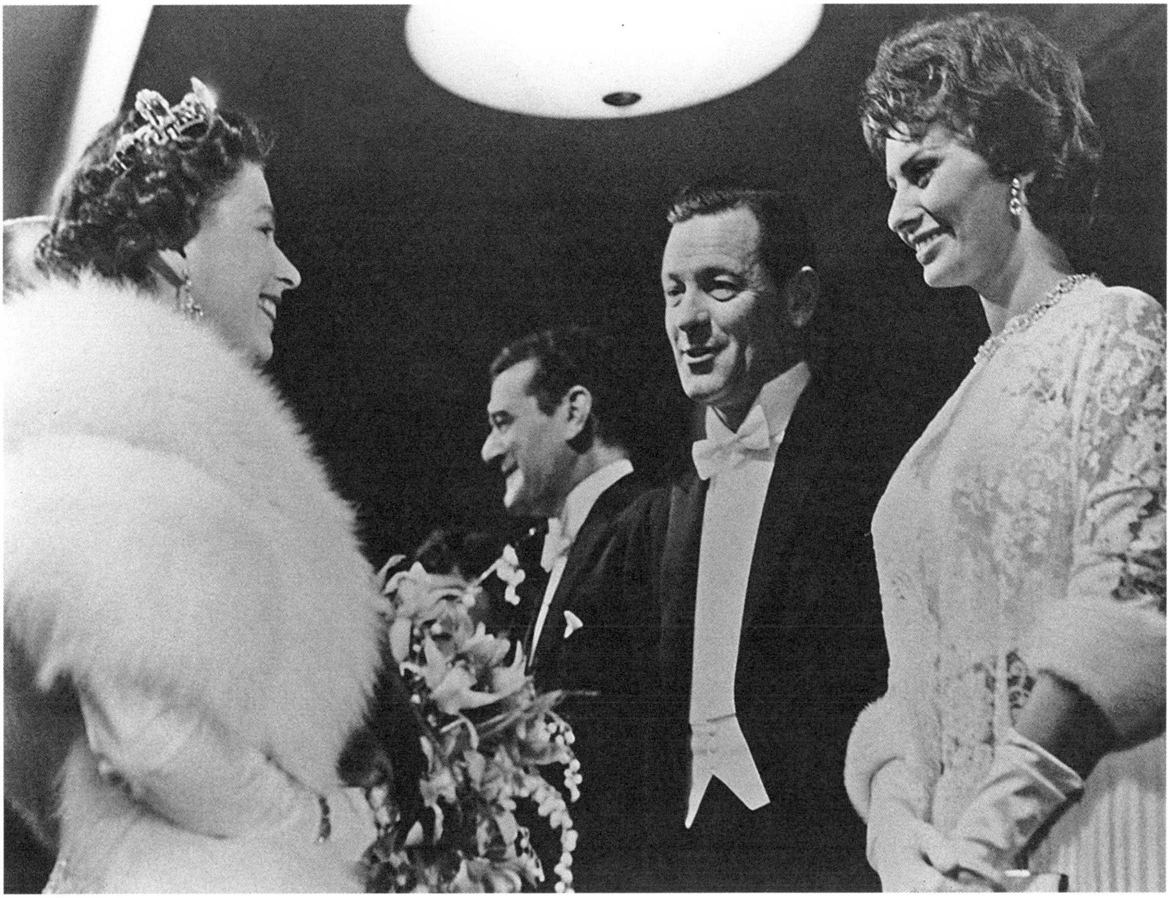

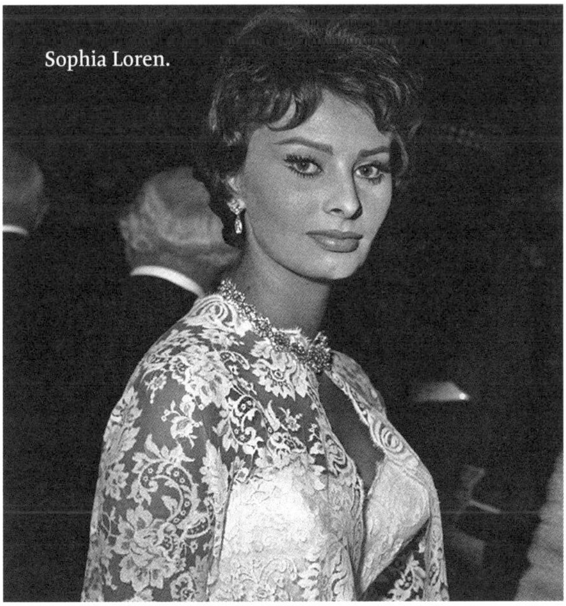

Sophia Loren.

Miss Loren and William Holden chat with the Queen. Jack Hawkins is in the background.

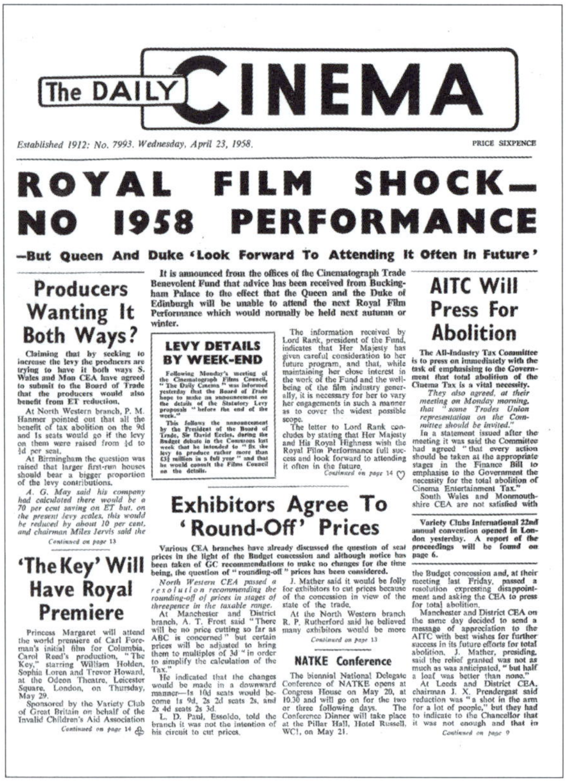

The DAILY CINEMA

Established 1912: No. 7993. Wednesday, April 23, 1958. PRICE SIXPENCE

ROYAL FILM SHOCK— NO 1958 PERFORMANCE

—But Queen And Duke 'Look Forward To Attending It Often In Future'

It is announced from the offices of the Cinematograph Trade Benevolent Fund that advice has been received from Buckingham Palace to the effect that the Queen and the Duke of Edinburgh will be unable to attend the next Royal Film Performance which would normally be held next autumn or winter.

The information received by Lord Rank, president of the Fund, indicates that Her Majesty has given careful consideration to her future program, and that, while maintaining her close interest in the work of the Fund and the well-being of the film industry generally, it is necessary for her to vary her engagements in such a manner as to cover the widest possible scope.

The letter to Lord Rank concludes by stating that Her Majesty and His Royal Highness wish the Royal Film Performance full success and look forward to attending it often in the future.

Continued on page 14

Producers Wanting It Both Ways?

Claiming that by seeking to increase the levy the producers are trying to have it both ways S. Wales and Mon CEA have agreed to submit to the Board of Trade that the producers would also benefit from ET reduction.

At North Western branch, P. M. Hanmer pointed out that all the benefit of tax abolition on the 9d and 1s seats would go if the levy on them were raised from ½d to ¾d per seat.

At Birmingham the question was raised that larger first-run houses should bear a bigger proportion of the levy contributions.

A. G. May said his company had calculated there would be a 70 per cent saving on ET but, on the present levy scales, this would be reduced by about 10 per cent, and chairman Miles Jervis said the

Continued on page 13

LEVY DETAILS BY WEEK-END

Following Monday's meeting of the Cinematograph Films Council, "The Daily Cinema" was informed yesterday that the Board of Trade hope to make an announcement on the details of the Statutory Levy proposals "before the end of the week."

This follows the announcement by the President of the Board of Trade, Sir David Eccles, during the Budget debate in the Commons last week that he intended to "fix the levy to produce rather more than £3¾ million in a full year" and that he would consult the Films Council on the details.

AITC Will Press For Abolition

The All-Industry Tax Committee is to press on immediately with the task of emphasising to the Government that total abolition of the Cinema Tax is a vital necessity.

They also agreed, at their meeting on Monday morning, that "some Trades Union representation on the Committee should be invited."

In a statement issued after the meeting it was said the Committee had agreed "that every action should be taken at the appropriate stages in the Finance Bill to emphasise to the Government the necessity for the total abolition of Cinema Entertainment Tax."

South Wales and Monmouthshire CEA are not satisfied with the Budget concession and, at their meeting last Friday, passed a resolution expressing disappointment and asking the CEA to press for total abolition.

Manchester and District CEA on the same day decided to send a message of appreciation to the AITC with best wishes for further success in its future efforts for total abolition. J. Mather, presiding, said the relief granted was not as much as was anticipated, "but half a loaf was better than none."

At Leeds and District CEA, chairman J. X. Prendergast said reduction was "a shot in the arm for a lot of people," but they had to indicate to the Chancellor that it was not enough and that in

Continued on page 9

Variety Clubs International 22nd annual convention opened in London yesterday. A report of the proceedings will be found on page 6.

Exhibitors Agree To 'Round-Off' Prices

Various CEA branches have already discussed the question of seat prices in the light of the Budget concession and although notice has been taken of GC recommendations to make no changes for the time being, the question of "rounding-off" prices has been considered.

North Western CEA passed a resolution recommending the rounding-off of prices in stages of threepence in the taxable range.

At Manchester and District branch, A. T. Frost said "There will be no price cutting so far as ABC is concerned" but certain prices will be adjusted to bring them to multiples of 3d "in order to simplify the calculation of the Tax."

He indicated that the changes would be made in a downward manner—1s 10d seats would become 1s 9d, 2s 2d seats 2s, and 2s 4d seats 2s 3d.

L. D. Paul, Essoldo, told the branch it was not the intention of his circuit to cut prices.

J. Mather said it would be folly for exhibitors to cut prices because of the concession in view of the state of the trade.

At the North Western branch R. P. Rutherford said he believed many exhibitors would be more

Continued on page 13

'The Key' Will Have Royal Premiere

Princess Margaret will attend the world premiere of Carl Foreman's initial film for Columbia, Carol Reed's production, "The Key," starring William Holden, Sophia Loren and Trevor Howard, at the Odeon Theatre, Leicester Square, London, on Thursday, May 29.

Sponsored by the Variety Club of Great Britain on behalf of the Invalid Children's Aid Association

Continued on page 14

NATKE Conference

The biennial National Delegate Conference of NATKE opens at Congress House on May 20, at 10.30 and will go on for the two or three following days. The Conference Dinner will take place at the Pillar Hall, Hotel Russell, WC1, on May 21.

There wasn't a Royal Film Performance in 1958, as headlined in the trade press.

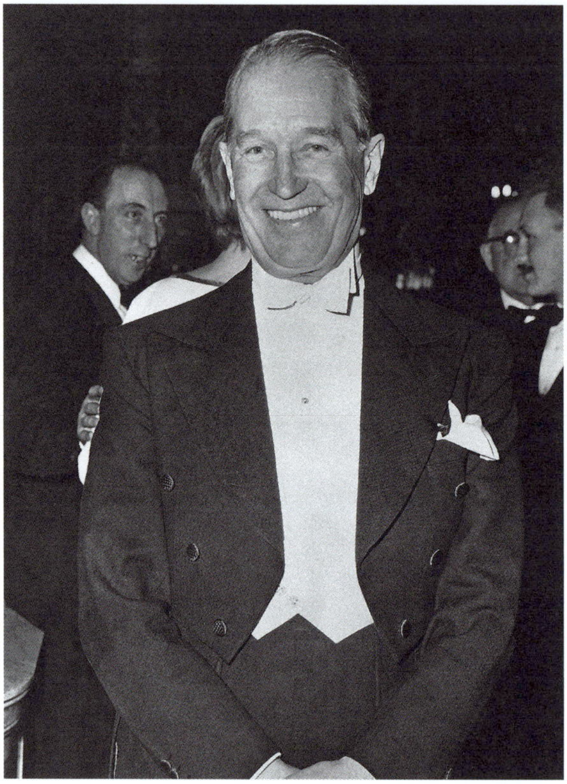

French star Maurice Chevalier arrives for *The Horse's Mouth*.

1959 *The Horse's Mouth*

Following a year's absence, the Royal Film Performance returned, and in the place of the Queen was the Queen Mother, accompanied by Princess Margaret in a satin dress of light delphinium blue. The chosen film was *The Horse's Mouth*, an Ealing-type comedy starring Alec Guinness as an anarchic and egotistical painter.

Guinness, who spent a long time chatting to the crowds outside the Empire Theatre, was among the many stars presented to the royal party. Others included Richard Attenborough; Lauren Bacall, who confessed that she was dying of fright while waiting in line; Max Bygraves; Diane Cilento; Peggy Cummins; Juliette Gréco; Peter Sellers; Simone Signoret; Richard Todd; and Frankie Vaughan.

Princess Margaret was heard to ask Sellers what he was up to these days. 'Still tiddly-winking,' he replied. The previous year, the Duke of Edinburgh had appointed the Goons as his royal champions for a tiddlywink match against students at Cambridge University. A bit puzzled, the princess asked what his plans were for the evening. 'That's all in preparation,' said Sellers, mysteriously. The princess moved on.

Maurice Chevalier happened to be in London for the opening of his film *Gigi* and was delighted when the Queen Mother spoke

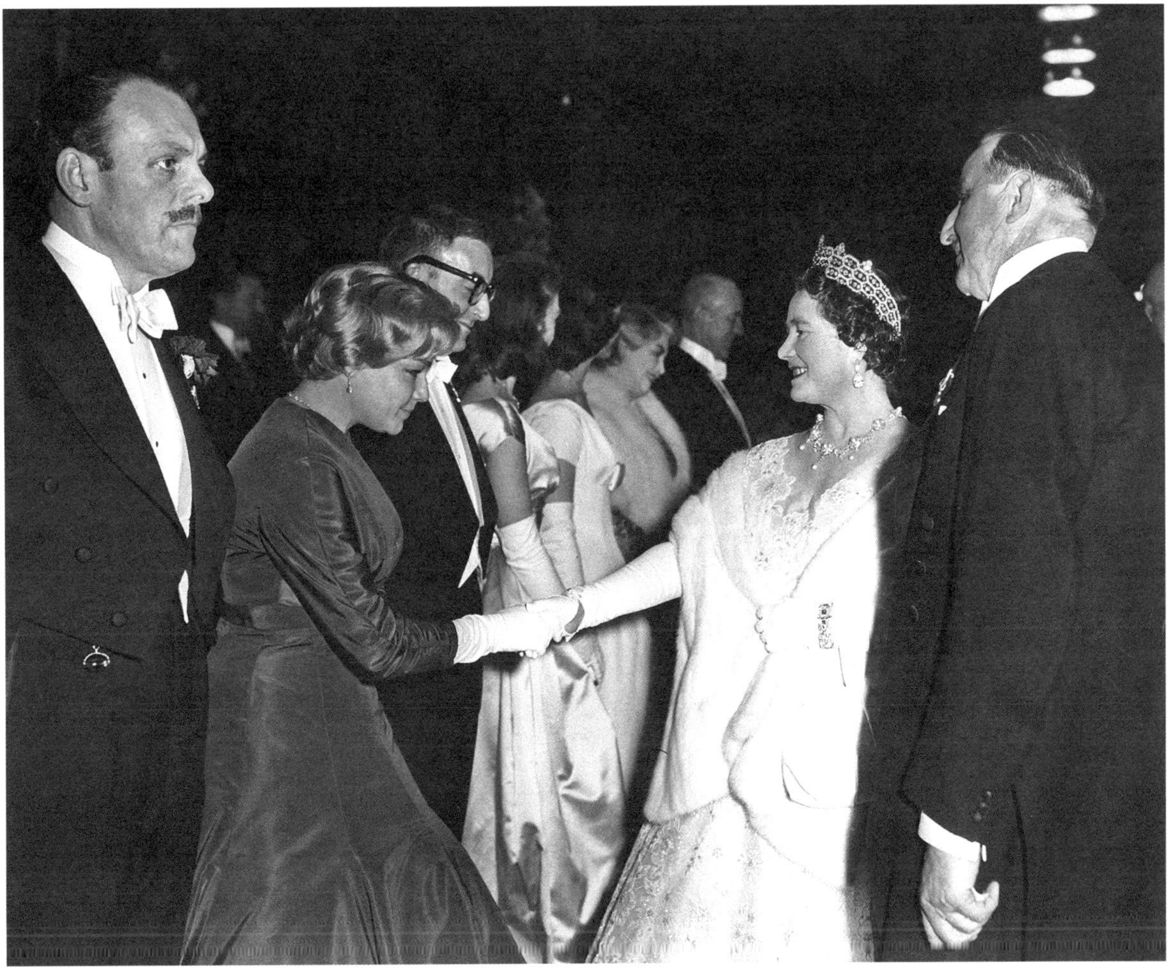

to him in perfect French. Princess Margaret told him she had already heard the record of *Gigi* several times and loved it.

Terry-Thomas arrived with a diamond-studded cigarette holder, which was insured for £2,000. His jacket sported a row of medals and a carnation. 'I have boobed dreadfully, old boy,' he told a friend. 'Apparently a carnation with gongs is a terrible clanger.'

Princess Margaret told the comedy star how much she enjoyed his performance in the recent film *Tom Thumb*. 'I made that in terrible agony,' he explained. 'I had lumbago at the time.' The Princess laughed and winced in sympathy.

The recently ennobled Lord Rank introduces the Queen Mother to Simone Signoret, Terry-Thomas and Peter Sellers at the premiere of *The Horse's Mouth*.

The highlight of the stage show was when Maurice Chevalier came on stage and spoke about his love for the British public that had lasted some fifty years. Then Max Bygraves rushed on with Chevalier's famous straw hat on a golden cushion, complete with gold tassels, and handed it to him. The veteran French entertainer led the stars in a chorus of his old song 'Louise' and the audience hummed along.

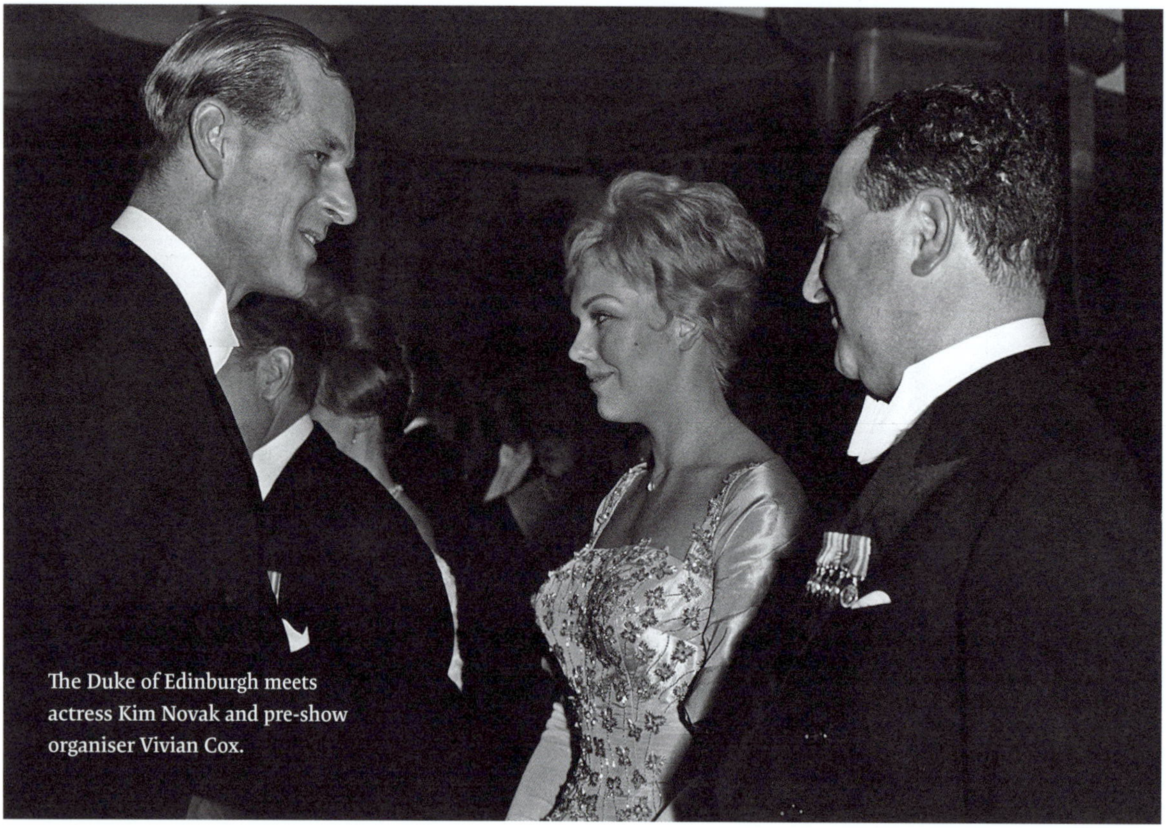

The Duke of Edinburgh meets actress Kim Novak and pre-show organiser Vivian Cox.

1960 *The Last Angry Man*

The story of 1960's Royal Film Performance was the late arrival of the royal party due to, of all things, a lift getting stuck at Buckingham Palace. After dining with the Queen and Prince Philip in their private apartments on the first floor of the palace, the Duchess of Kent and Princess Alexandra, escorted by Philip, took a lift down to a waiting car to take them to the Odeon, Leicester Square. The Queen was not attending, having recently given birth to Prince Andrew.

The lift was one of those old-fashioned cage-type affairs and it hesitantly began its descent, only to jerk to a halt between floors. Buttons were frenziedly pressed. It would not budge. Philip tried the emergency phone, that wasn't working either. There was no choice but to shout for help. Servants came running and a mechanic was called. 'Someone had to get a handle and wind us down,' Philip was to relate.

Meanwhile, guests and organisers were worriedly looking at their watches. At last, the royal car was sighted, twenty minutes late. Prince Philip apologised profusely and confessed his embarrassment. When he heard what happened, Noël Coward roared with laughter.

Despite his late arrival, Philip was in a genial and chatty mood, instantly putting people in the line-up at ease. A nervous Kim Novak, who had flown in specially from California, admitted to being dreadfully worried about her curtsey. She'd rehearsed it five times and was making a mess of it. When Philip reached her, he asked,

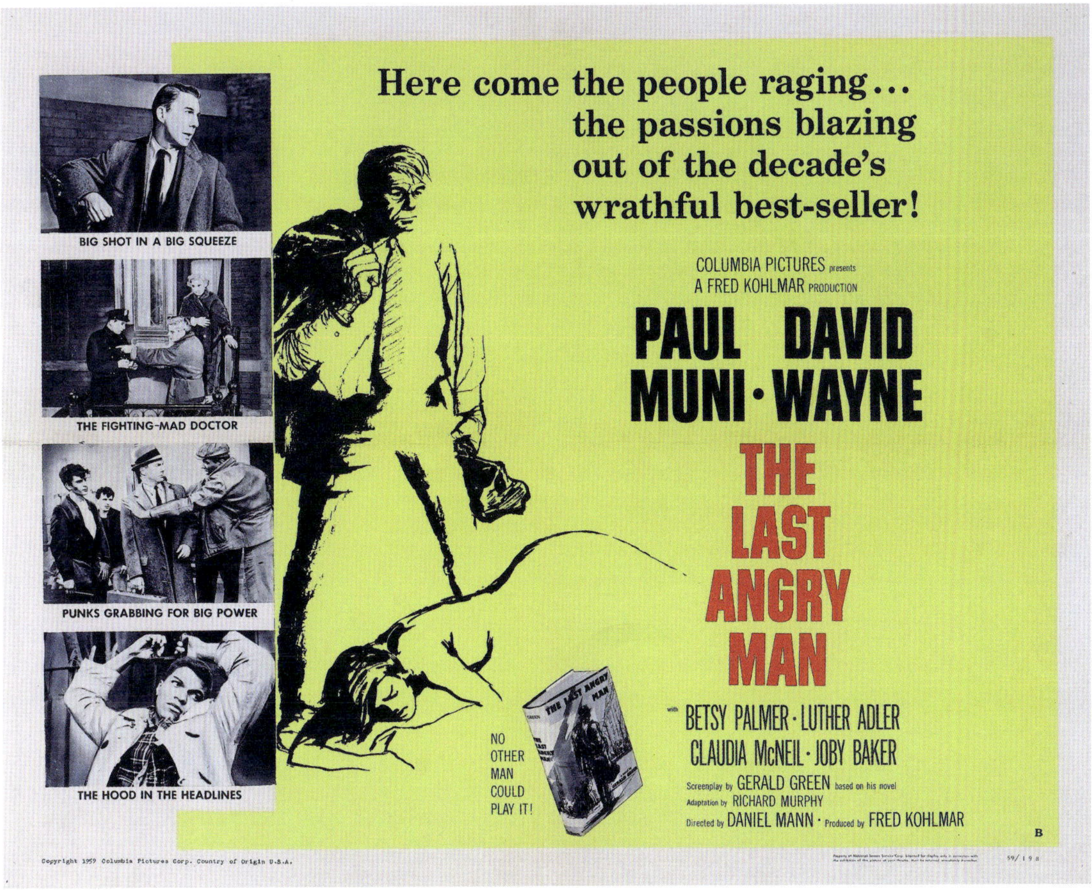

'Have you been dragged all the way here just for this?' What else could Kim say but 'Yes'?

Most of all, Prince Philip seemed to enjoy a chat with a 90-year-old resident of Glebelands, a Mr F. Pereira. It had become a tradition in the line-ups to present to the royal party one of the pensioners the charity helped support. He had been a cameraman in the early days of the industry and happily explained to the prince what it used to be like to crank the camera by hand.

The brief stage show, produced by Vivian Cox, involved British stars such as Charlie Drake, Kenneth More and Anthony Newley introducing artists from overseas, including Leslie Caron, Yoko Tani and Mai Zetterling, all of whom stood against a cycloramic background of scenes from their various countries.

The main film was, it must be said, a strange choice. *The Last Angry Man* was notable as the last film of Paul Muni, here playing a crusading doctor. Commentators thought the film was not distinguished enough and surely there had been better options. This led to one organiser of the event saying, 'It seems to be a tradition that whichever film they pick is deemed unsuitable by the press.'

Even so, it was another starry evening. Other guests included Nancy Kwan, Richard Todd and Terry-Thomas. Along with rising pop sensation Cliff Richard, Noël Coward got the biggest cheers of the night from the waiting crowds.

1961 *The Facts of Life*

As preparations began for this year's Royal Film Performance, the charity was rocked by the news that its president, Lord Rank, was regretfully resigning, due to too many other work and voluntary commitments. He had been a trustee for sixteen years and president for three. His replacement was Sir Philip Warter, chairman of the ABPC (Associated British Picture Corporation).

Warter's first task was to select a suitable film for the charity's biggest annual occasion. His choice of *The Facts of Life* courted some mild controversy with its theme of adultery and sex outside marriage, although it starred two of Hollywood's least-controversial stars in Bob Hope and Lucille Ball. This didn't stop the press from making such headlines as 'The sauciest film ever to be shown at a Royal Film Performance'. But speaking from Hollywood, Bob Hope reassured that there was nothing in the picture that would offend Her Majesty. Indeed, many saw the film as an improvement on the previous year's offering and tickets sold much faster.

The Facts of Life was an enjoyable enough comedy, very much a commercial product as opposed to a critic's one. As Lord Radcliffe explained, 'We tend to choose gay rather than grave films because they usually provide more entertainment.'

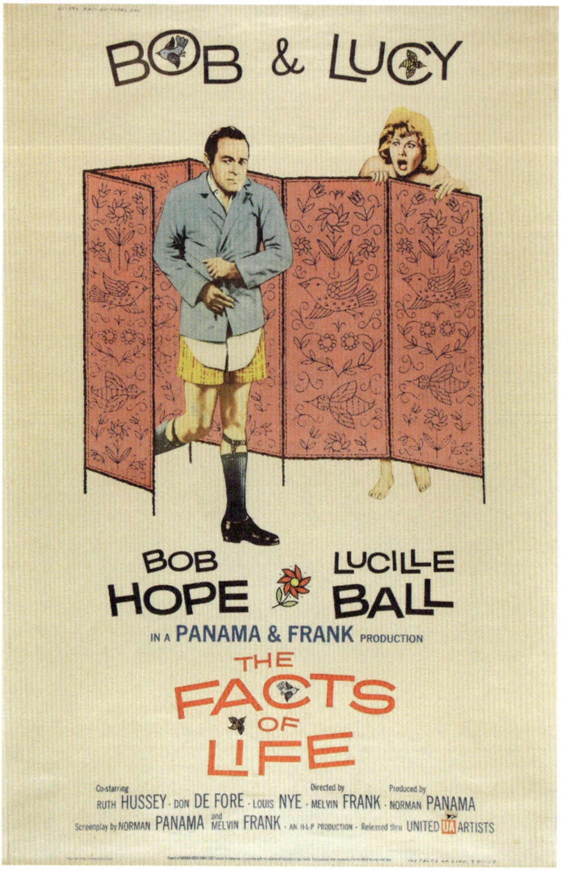

TV cameras covered the event at the Odeon, Leicester Square, with Nicholas Parsons interviewing the arriving celebrities. And then came the royal party, Queen Elizabeth the Queen Mother with Princess Margaret and her husband, the Earl of Snowdon.

Once again, taking charge of the stage show was Vivian Cox, who revealed that the most difficult aspect of the job was setting the mood for the entire evening. He also revealed that he only had six hours to meet and then rehearse the twenty or so performers for both the stage show and the presentations to the royal party – quite a task. Often, revealed Cox, there would be arguments about who would be

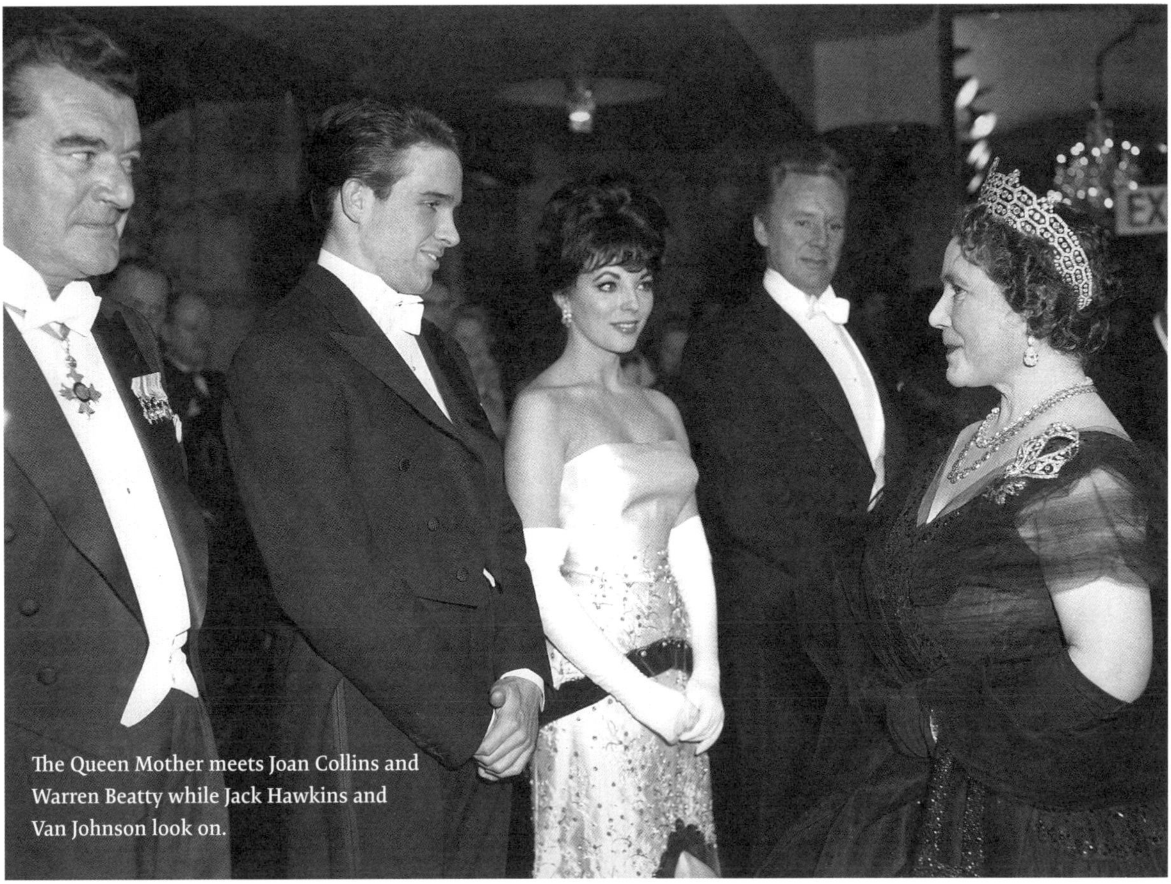

The Queen Mother meets Joan Collins and Warren Beatty while Jack Hawkins and Van Johnson look on.

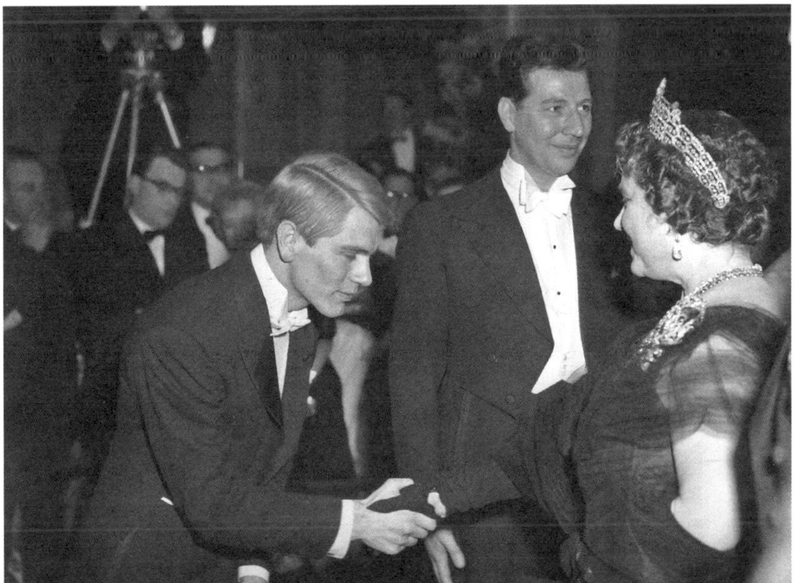

The Queen Mother greets singing stars Adam Faith and Max Bygraves at *The Facts of Life* premiere.

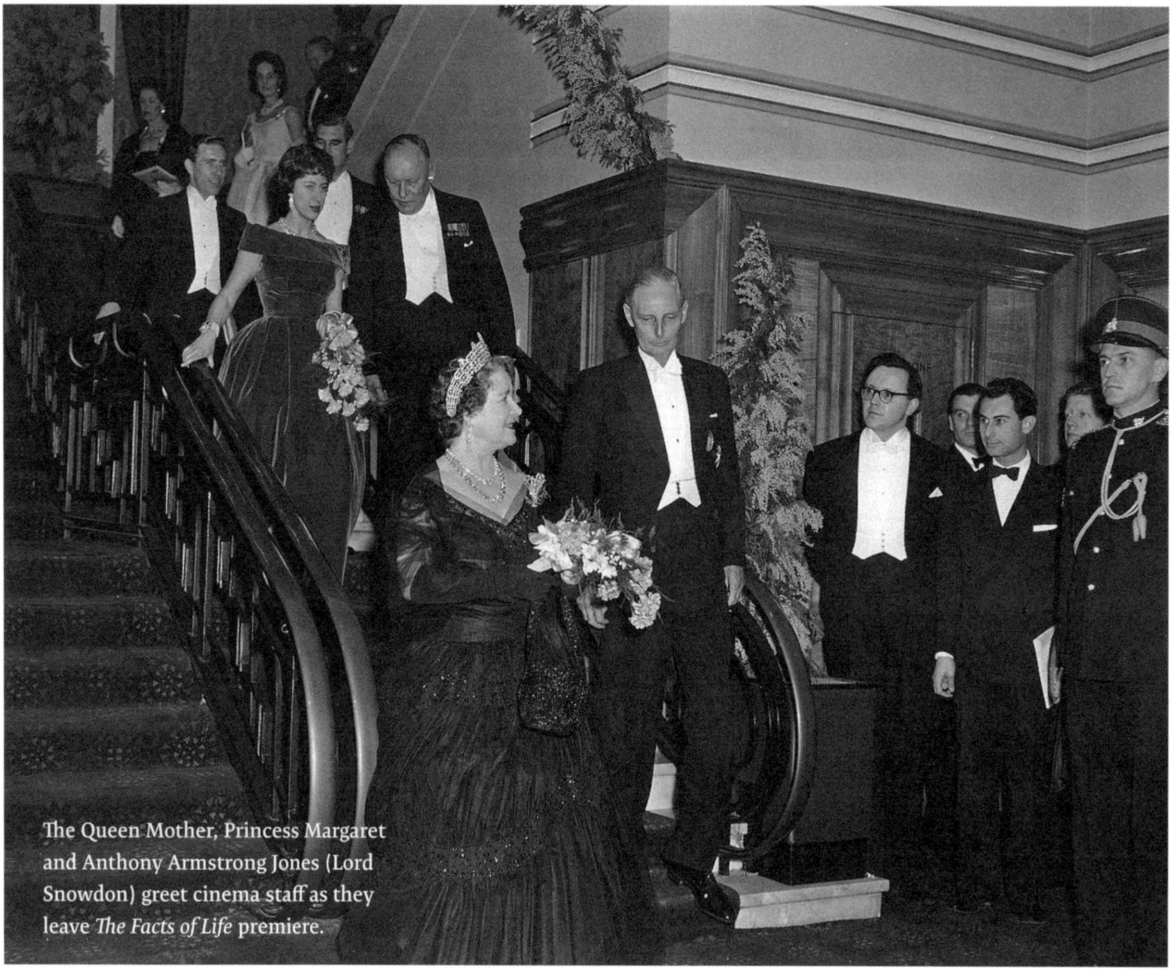

The Queen Mother, Princess Margaret and Anthony Armstrong Jones (Lord Snowdon) greet cinema staff as they leave *The Facts of Life* premiere.

first in the line-up and who would be last. On one occasion, Cox had all the stars lined up in alphabetical order. Unfortunately, that meant two well-known Hollywood actresses who were not on speaking terms being placed next to each other. Hurriedly, they swapped places with someone else.

Those presented to the royal party at the end of the evening included Max Bygraves, Joan Collins, Adam Faith, Shirley Anne Field, Tony Hancock, Jack Hawkins, Sidney James, Van Johnson, Warren Beatty and Peter Sellers.

1962 ***West Side Story***

For the first time since *Les Girls* in 1957, the Queen was to attend a Royal Film Performance. Nothing less than a spectacular film was required to mark the occasion and the smash-hit musical *West Side Story* more than fitted the bill. Lord Radcliffe confirmed that the selection committee reached its unanimous decision immediately after seeing the picture.

The Odeon really pulled out all the stops for the Queen's return with floral decorations ranging from orange groves to banks

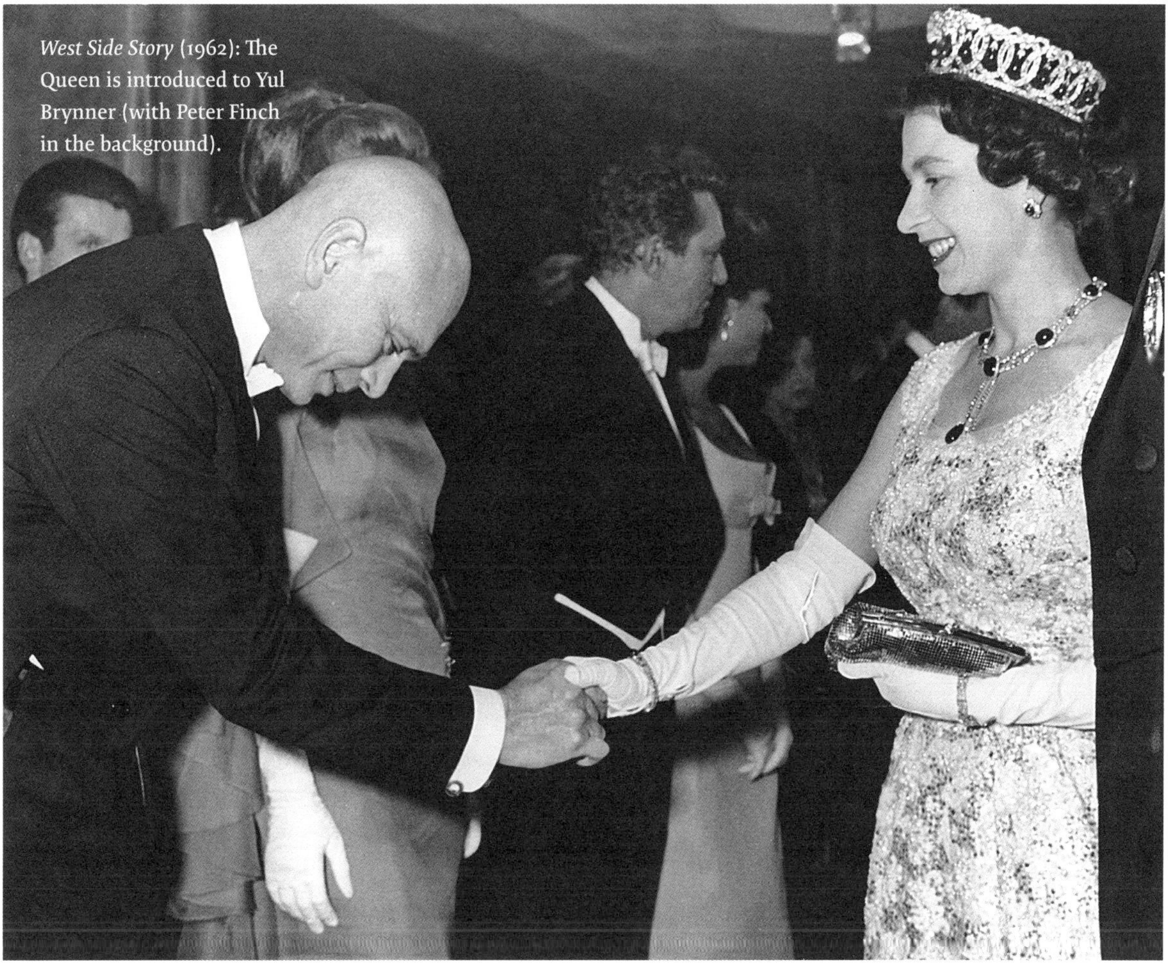

West Side Story (1962): The Queen is introduced to Yul Brynner (with Peter Finch in the background).

of carnations and hyacinths, and a luxurious new proscenium curtain of ice blue with gold tassels. When the drapes parted to reveal the giant curved screen, there was an audible gasp from the audience.

The Queen dazzled in a slender dress of silver lace, embroidered with pearls and gold and mounted on gold tissue, along with an emerald and diamond tiara. She was accompanied by Princess Margaret, the Earl of Snowdon and Lord Mountbatten.

Sixteen stars were presented to the Queen, including Yul Brynner, Horst Buchholz, Pat Boone, Claudia Cardinale, Leslie Caron, Peter Finch, Cliff Richard, who escorted his mother to the event, and Peter Sellers, who received the biggest cheer from the waiting crowds outside. Three of the stars of *West Side Story* flew in from the United States – George Chakiris, Richard Beymer and Russ Tamblyn – as did the director, Robert Wise.

The evening began with a surprise item, a twelve-minute newsreel of the Duke of Edinburgh's ongoing tour of South America, which had been flown in the day before. It proved a delight to the audience, and no doubt Her Majesty, to see what her husband had been getting up to.

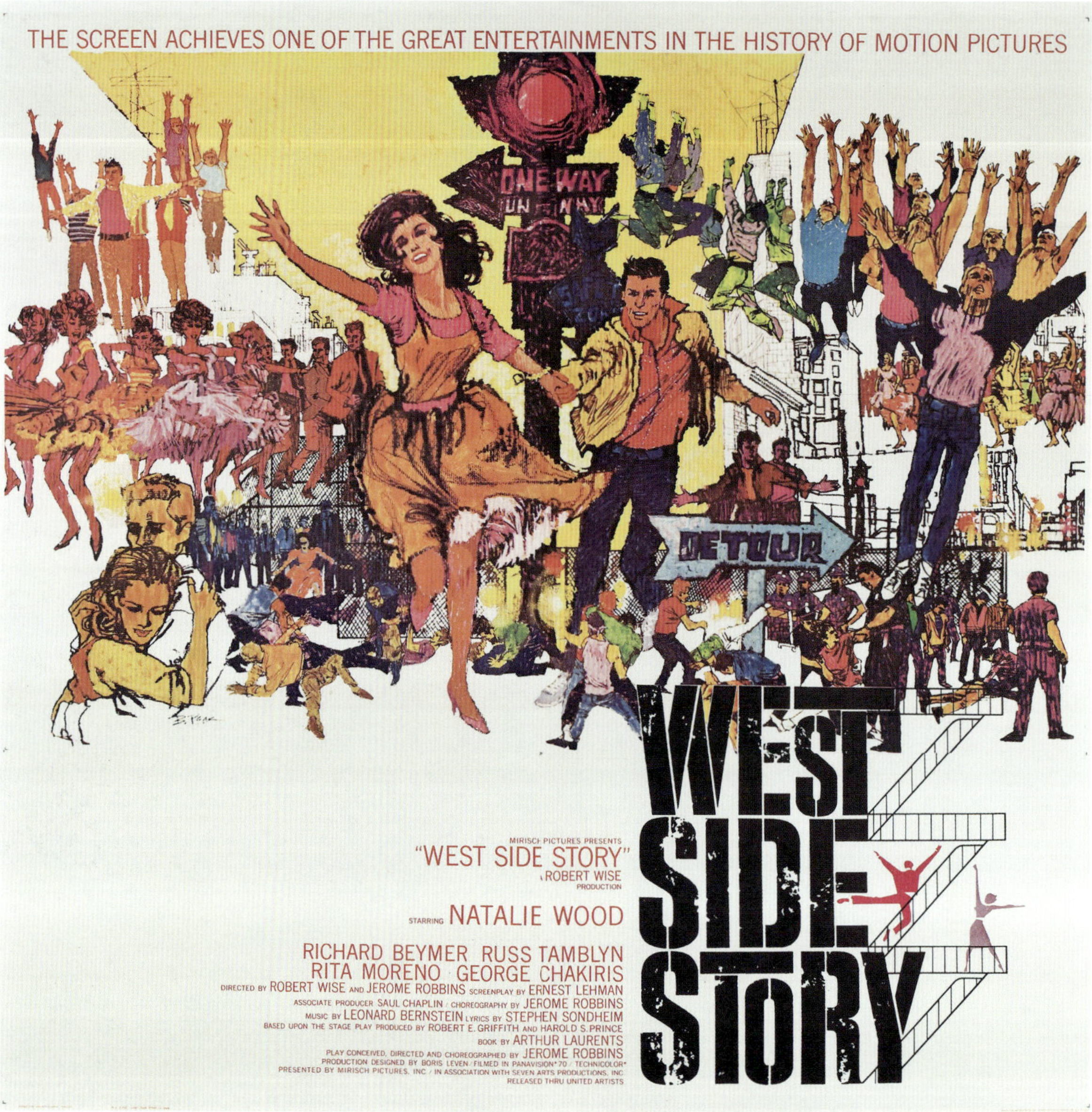

Richard Attenborough compèred the stage show and took pleasure in announcing the proceeds from the evening were well over £30,000. *West Side Story* went down a storm, with the audience applauding time and again at the musical numbers. It was reported that when the curtains came down, Princess Margaret had tears rolling down her cheeks. The *Daily Cinema* was not alone in calling this 'The greatest Royal Film night ever'. George Chakiris recalls:

> The Royal Film Performance of *West Side Story* was a very special evening.
>
> There was protocol that had to be followed when meeting the Queen. Do's and

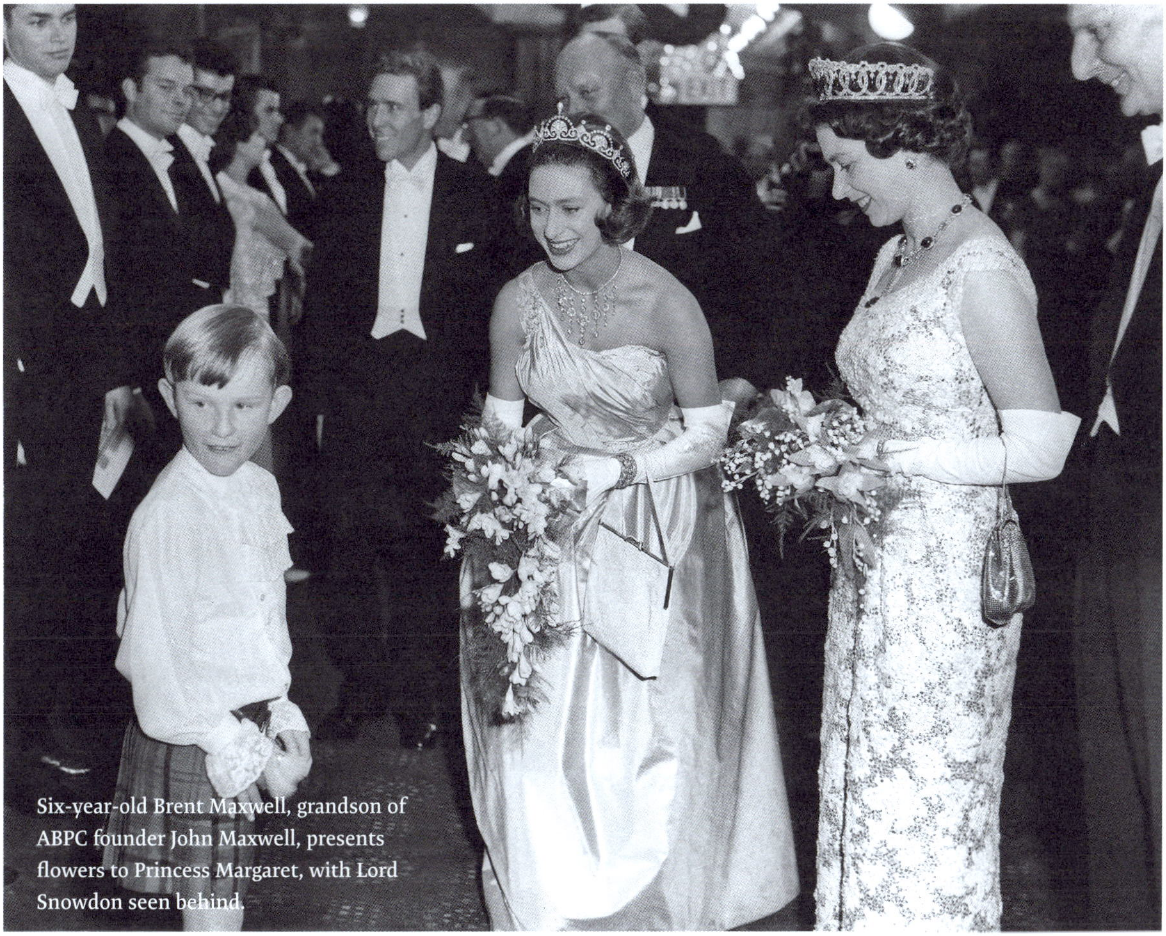

Six-year-old Brent Maxwell, grandson of ABPC founder John Maxwell, presents flowers to Princess Margaret, with Lord Snowdon seen behind.

don'ts. We had to wear 'tails'. Tuxedos were not quite up to par. It was all very exciting, and I loved every minute.

Queen Elizabeth was very gracious and very beautiful. I had met Princess Margaret in late 1958, and she too was very beautiful.

During the screening there was an intermission. It was during that intermission that Robert Wise learned that *West Side Story* had been nominated for 12 Academy Awards, one for me as Best Supporting Actor. So, it was a very memorable evening for me.

1963 *Sammy Going South*

This turned out to be quite the occasion for producer Sir Michael Balcon, best known for his leadership of Ealing Studios. Following *Scott of the Antarctic* in 1948 and *Where No Vultures Fly* in 1951, *Sammy Going South* was the third of his films to be chosen as a Royal Film Performance. And his 6-year-old granddaughter Deborah was also present to give a bouquet to Queen Elizabeth the Queen Mother. Also attending were Princess Margaret and the Earl of Snowdon.

Directed by Alexander Mackendrick, *Sammy Going South* tells the story of a 10-year-old English boy whose parents are killed by British

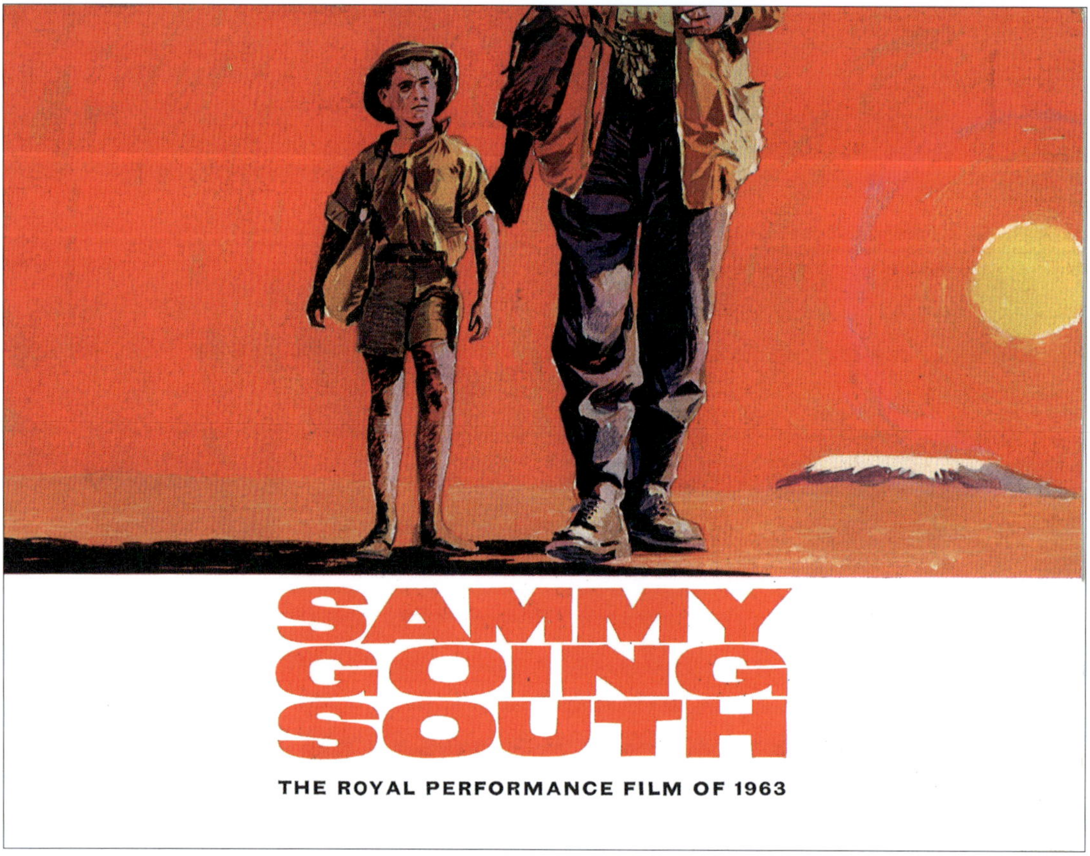

bombs in Egypt during the Suez Crisis of 1956 and makes his way across Africa to find his aunt. It was an unusually fraught production. Two members of the crew were bitten by snakes and star Edward G. Robinson suffered a heart attack on location that kept him off the film for several weeks.

Robinson turned out to be the hit of the evening. In the line-up the Queen Mother asked the veteran Hollywood actor how he was feeling after his health scare. 'Great,' he replied. 'It was like kicking a pebble out of your path and going right on.' And then in the stage presentation, he stepped forward to pay a sincere tribute to the industry to which he had belonged for so many years. 'And tonight, for me, is the crowning achievement in a long and rather varied career.' He ended by asking the royal party's indulgence as he said to them what had so often been said to him, 'You look just like you do in the pictures!'

Other stars warmly received by the audience were Jessie Matthews, who sang snippets of her most dearly loved songs, and Norman Wisdom, who clowned around with the aid of Geraldo and his orchestra. The stage show had now largely become a procession of stars making a personal appearance on the stage, rather than the big productions of previous years. It was compèred by John Mills, who brought his daughter Hayley along for the evening. Also making an appearance were Claire Bloom, James Robertson Justice, Sarah Miles, Terence Stamp, Richard Todd and Rita Tushingham.

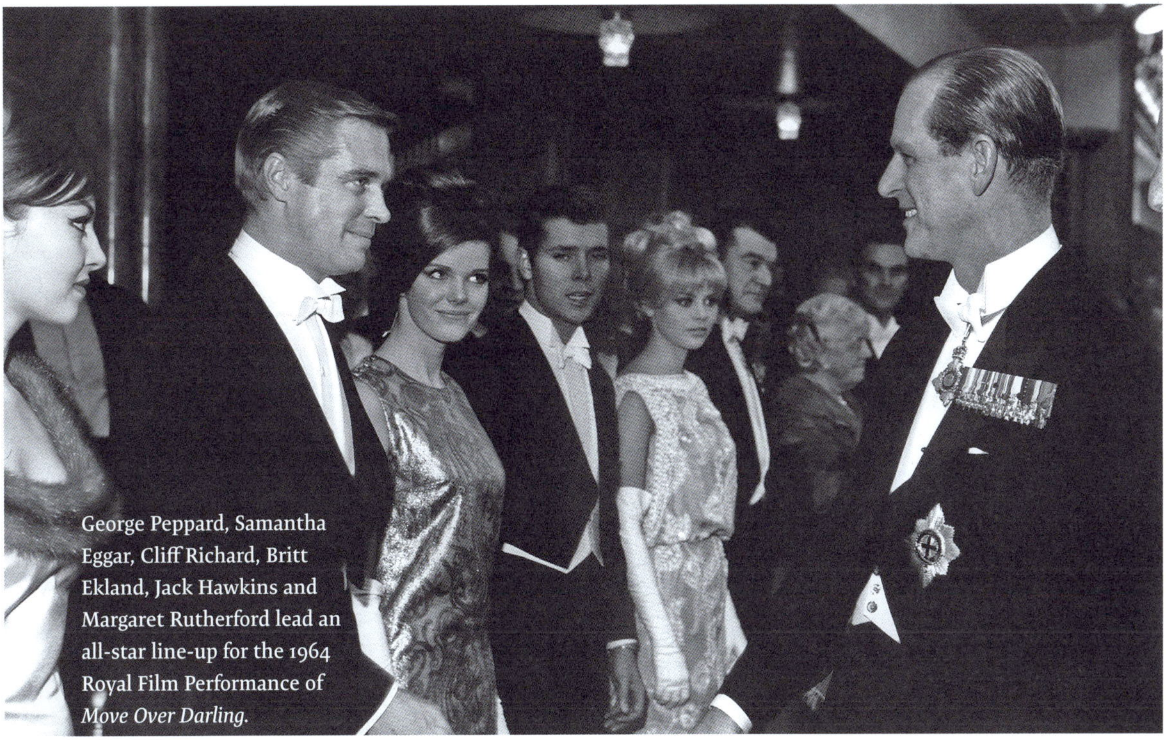
George Peppard, Samantha Eggar, Cliff Richard, Britt Ekland, Jack Hawkins and Margaret Rutherford lead an all-star line-up for the 1964 Royal Film Performance of *Move Over Darling*.

1964 *Move Over, Darling*

The picture chosen for this year's Royal Film Performance was an enjoyable if lightweight romantic comedy that had an unusual history. Originally, it was a vehicle for Marilyn Monroe. Going under the title of 'Something's Got to Give', Marilyn worked on it for several weeks before being fired by 20th Century Fox – the studio said, for erratic behaviour. Co-star Dean Martin quit the production in protest and the film was shelved. Less than two months later, Marilyn was dead.

Keeping many of the same sets, the project was resurrected less than a year later with Doris Day and James Garner and retitled *Move Over, Darling*.

With the Queen unable to attend due to pregnancy, Prince Philip took on the honours by himself and was happily presented to a host of stars including Stanley Baker, Honor Blackman, Samantha Eggar, Britt Ekland, George Peppard, Leslie Phillips, Cliff Richard and Margaret Rutherford. And there was the star of *Move Over, Darling*, James Garner, who had been allowed time off from filming in Hollywood to fly to London.

From the stage of the Odeon, Richard Attenborough made the announcement that since the first Royal Film Performance in 1946, the charity had raised £500,000 from the events. He then introduced the stage show, where fourteen stars appeared, with amusing introductions given by Millicent Martin. By far the biggest ovation of the evening was for Margaret Rutherford.

The screening of *Move Over, Darling* was met with roars of laughter from the audience and

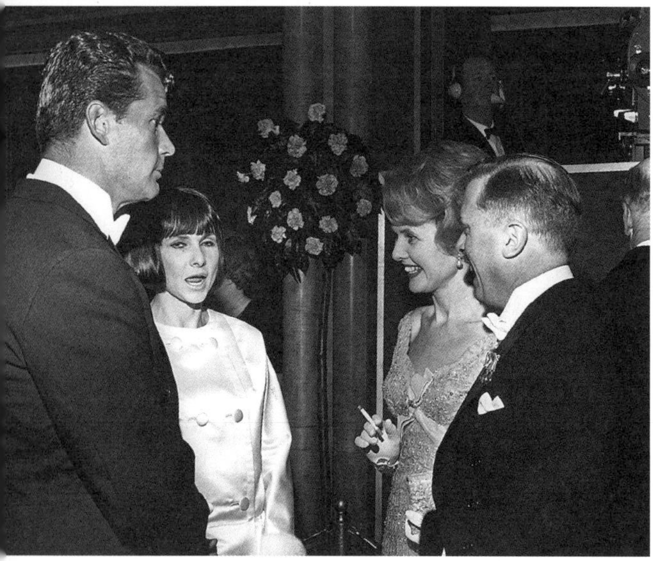

James Garner and his wife Lois Clarke share a laugh with Richard Attenborough and his wife Sheila Sim.

proved a big success. Perhaps the most unexpected outcome of the evening was the Royal Film Performance's role in saving a little piece of James Bond history. The third 007 movie, *Goldfinger*, was due for release later that year. However, the stuffy American censor was bristling over the name of the character Pussy Galore, played by Honor Blackman.

The threat to ban the use of the name was very real, and the Bond makers even had an alternative lined up just in case, Kitty Galore. But the publicity team devised a plan. Honor was sent along to the Royal Film Performance, where she was photographed with Prince Philip. The image appeared in newspapers around the world the following day. One headline read, 'The Prince and the Pussy.'

After the publicity coup, Bond producer Cubby Broccoli flew to America armed with a file of newspaper clippings and the censors reluctantly agreed to let the name stand. After all, if it was acceptable in connection with a royal function, who were they to argue? The Royal Film Performance had helped to save the day.

1965 *Lord Jim*

Despite a bitterly cold evening, an enthusiastic crowd gathered early to watch the arrival of the stars and the royal party. The Queen Mother, wearing the Greville tiara, arrived with Princess Margaret and the Earl of Snowdon. Inside the foyer, they were introduced as usual to leading chiefs of the film industry and then to a host of stars including Diane Cilento, Sean Connery, Françoise Dorléac, Peter Finch, Sid James, Maximilian Schell, Jean Simmons, Susannah York and then the stars of the chosen film, Jack Hawkins, Curt Jurgens, Daliah Lavi, James Mason and Peter O'Toole. Broadcaster Bernard Braden interviewed the various guests for a highlights programme to be transmitted later that evening on ITV.

O'Toole was seen chatting to the Queen Mother about horses. 'Her horse runs in the National quite soon,' the star revealed. 'I was hoping to get a hot tip.' O'Toole's father used to be a bookmaker.

This year's film was a spectacular epic, *Lord Jim*, filmed at great expense on location in Cambodia and Hong Kong. Based on the Joseph Conrad novel, Peter O'Toole played a nineteenth-century seaman guilty of cowardice who carries on living for the sole purpose of one day redeeming himself. Anticipating perhaps another *Lawrence of Arabia*, tickets for what was the world premiere of *Lord Jim*

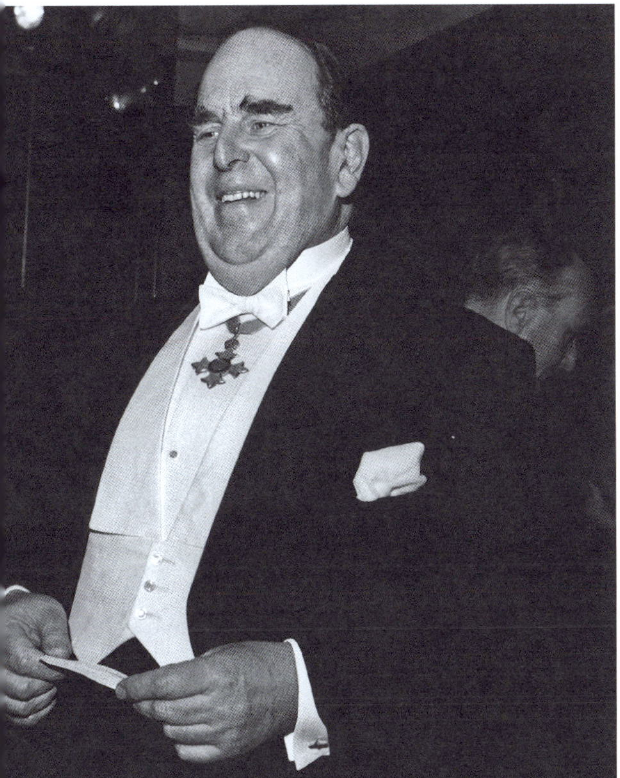

Robert Morley arrives at the *Lord Jim* premiere in full evening attire and proudly wearing his CBE medal. 'Tails and medals' were encouraged to be worn at Royal Film Performances.

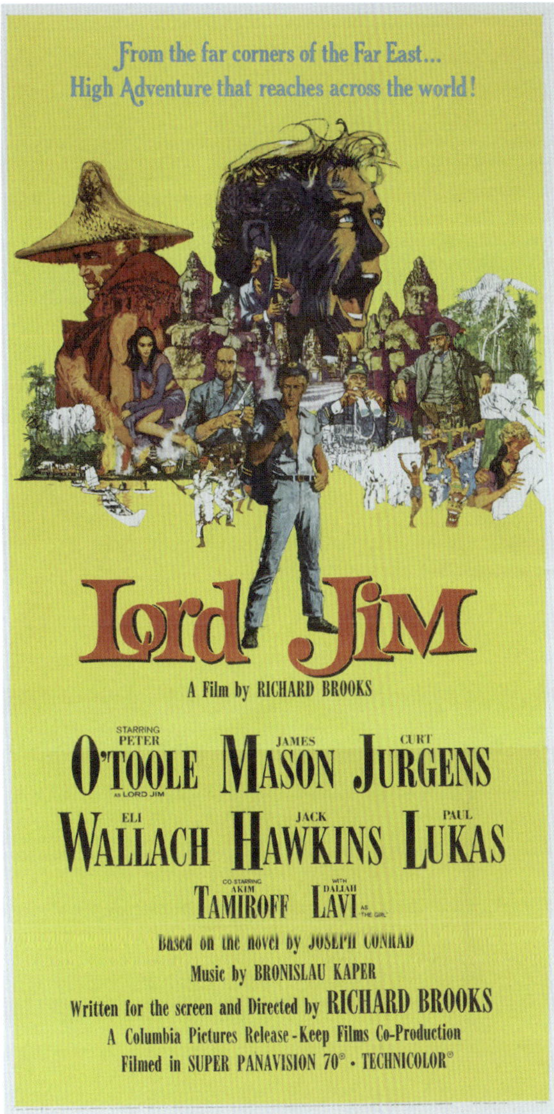

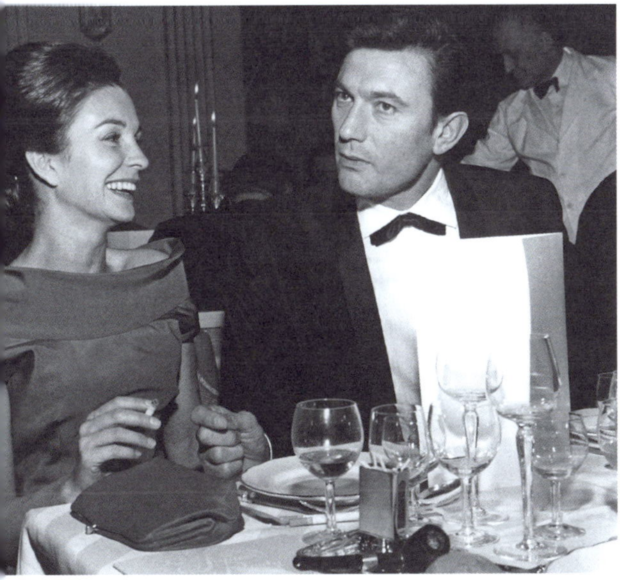

Jean Simmons and Laurence Harvey enjoy some post-premiere hospitality.

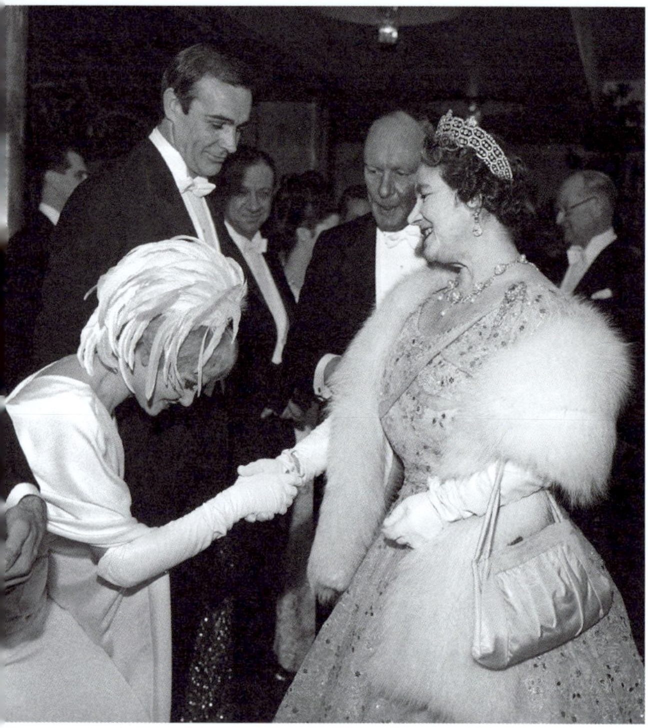

Husband and wife Sean Conney and Diane Cilento join the line-up of *Lord Jim* with old mate Sid James to meet the Queen Mother.

sold out quicker than any previous Royal Film Performance, resulting in the biggest amount of money yet raised. It helped that there was now an accepted arrangement that important charity premieres within a few weeks either side of the Royal Film Performance were to be avoided so that the charity benefited to the maximum financially.

Vivian Cox again provided a simple but elegant stage presentation of the stars, introduced by Robert Morley. The audience also enjoyed newsreel footage of the recent tour of Ethiopia and Sudan by the Queen and Prince Philip. In Ethiopia, the Queen was met by the ruler Haile Selassie and at the imperial palace she observed his 'pet' lions in the gardens.

1966 *Born Free*

This year marked the twentieth anniversary of the Royal Film Performance, and it was a special occasion in many ways, not least because it was the first attended by the Queen since 1962. She arrived with the Duke and Duchess of Kent, looking resplendent in a frock of pale green lace embroidered with peridots, pale emeralds and iridescent jewels.

Born Free turned out to be the perfect film choice and went down extremely well with the audience on the night. Based on Joy Adamson's best-selling book, this well-loved family film tells the extraordinary story of how she and her husband George raised Elsa, an orphaned lion cub, before releasing her into the wilderness of Kenya. The stars of the film, real-life husband and wife team, Virginia McKenna and Bill Travers, were on hand for what was the film's world premiere, and Joy Adamson flew to London especially for the occasion. Other stars attending included Woody Allen, Ursula Andress, Warren Beatty, Leslie Caron, Julie Christie, Catherine Deneuve, James Fox, Rex Harrison, Deborah Kerr, Christopher Lee and Raquel Welch.

The state trumpeters of the Life Guards sounded a fanfare as the royal party took their seats inside the Odeon, Leicester Square. The national anthem was played by the theatre orchestra under the direction of John Barry, who composed the music for *Born Free*. He

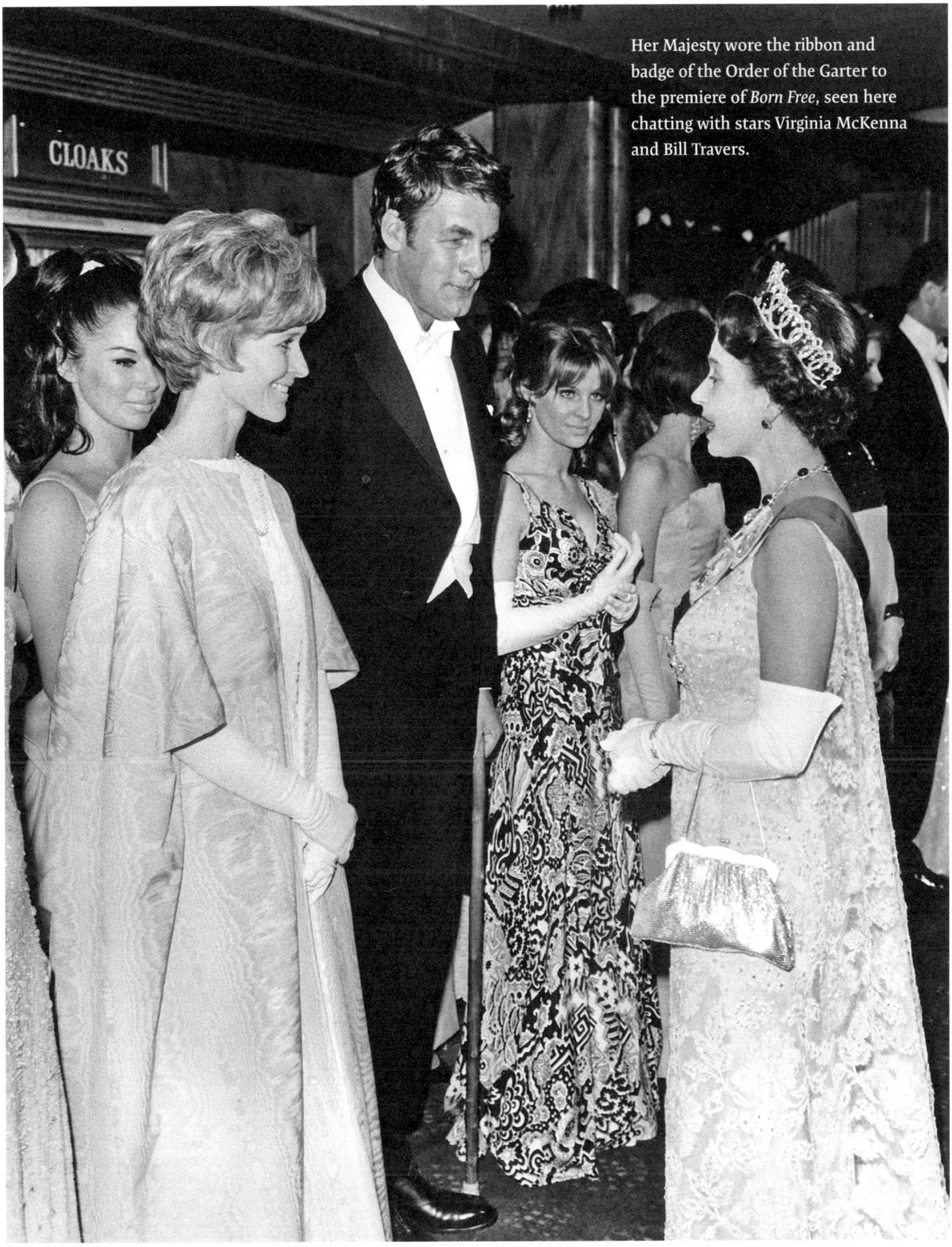

Her Majesty wore the ribbon and badge of the Order of the Garter to the premiere of *Born Free*, seen here chatting with stars Virginia McKenna and Bill Travers.

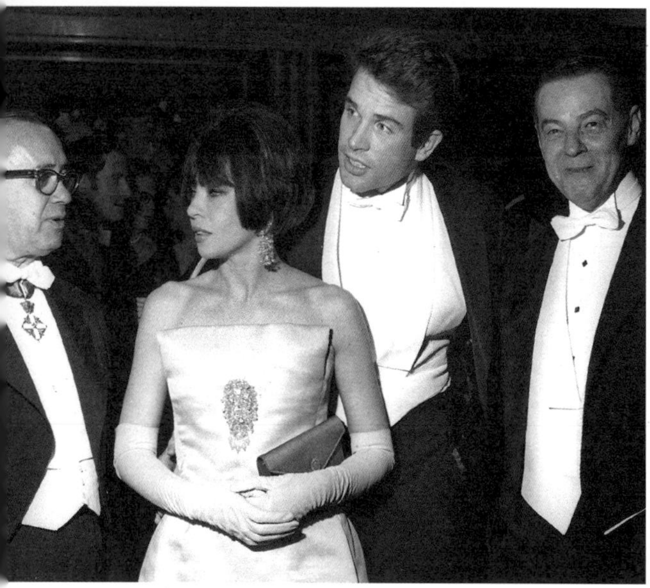

Columbia Pictures executive Leo Jaffe joins Lesley Caron, Warren Beatty and Marion Jordan, with composer John Barry in the background.

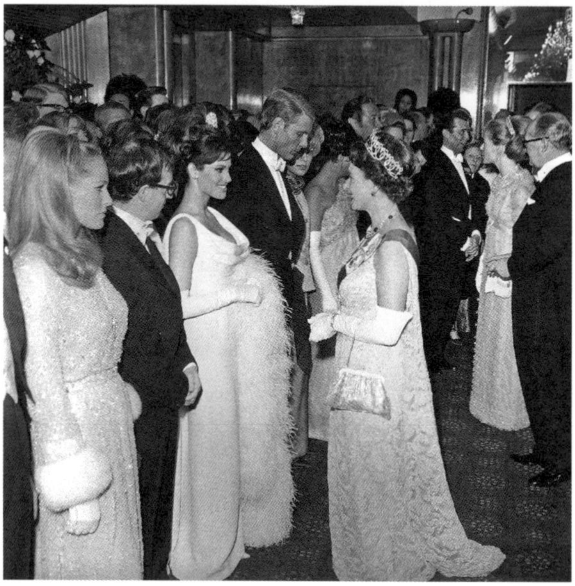

The *Born Free* Royal Film Performance attracted many of the cast from *Casino Royale*, which was filming at the time. Here with Ursula Andress and Woody Allen are Raquel Welch and James Fox.

became the first film composer to receive that honour.

The curtains opened and the first item was a Pathé news film of the highlights of the royal tour of the Caribbean, plus the latest film of Prince Philip in America. After a Disney cartoon film, *Winnie the Pooh and the Honey Tree*, came the stage presentation hosted by Dirk Bogarde. Seventeen stars were introduced onto the stage and there was a surprise guest at the end.

Jack Hawkins made his first public appearance after leaving hospital following an operation for throat cancer. His appearance elicited the biggest ovation of the evening. Still unable to speak (sadly, he never regained his speech and was dubbed in subsequent films), he bowed graciously and waved to the audience. It was a touching moment for a man who was a regular attendee of Royal Film Performances.

Virginia McKenna DBE recalls:

My memories of the Royal Premiere of *Born Free* are as vivid as if it was only a few days ago. Bill and I were extremely nervous, and I remember worrying that I might fall over as I curtseyed to Her Majesty, but she put us all at ease and was her warm and charming self.

I have many enduring recollections of that life-changing film, which led to Bill and I dedicating much of our time to helping wild animals in need through our charity, the Born Free Foundation, but the Royal Premiere is one I treasure beyond words.

1967 *The Taming of the Shrew*

This year marked the twenty-first anniversary of the Royal Film Performance and it was perhaps fitting that the film chosen was suitably distinguished – a spectacular version of Shakespeare's *The Taming of the Shrew*, starring the couple of the decade, Richard Burton and Elizabeth Taylor. Filmed in Rome under the direction of Franco Zeffirelli, the Burtons waived their usually exorbitant salaries to get the film made.

In London, the star couple took over the Royal Film Performance in grand fashion. Burton brought virtually his entire Welsh clan down by train from Port Talbot in South Wales. His six brothers and three remaining sisters, along with assorted spouses, children, aunts and uncles took up fourteen suites at the Dorchester Hotel. A fleet of chauffeured Daimlers escorted them to the Odeon, Leicester Square, where Burton had paid for 150 Dress Circle seats for family and friends. It really was the Burton and Taylor show.

Making an impression with the crowds outside, who had gathered despite torrential rain and strong blustery winds, was Princess Margaret, dressed in a long, slim dress of silver and wearing the Persian Turquoise tiara. She entered the theatre foyer, which was beautifully decorated with mimosa that had been specially flown in from the south of France, to meet with leading chiefs of the film industry and a plethora of stars – Stanley Baker, Tom Courtenay, Richard Johnson, Mia Farrow, Laurence Harvey, Gina Lollobrigida, John Mills, Zero Mostel, Christopher Plummer, Charlotte Rampling, Sir

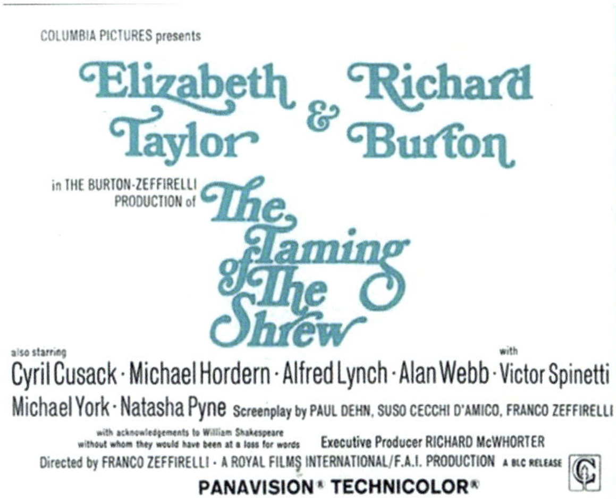

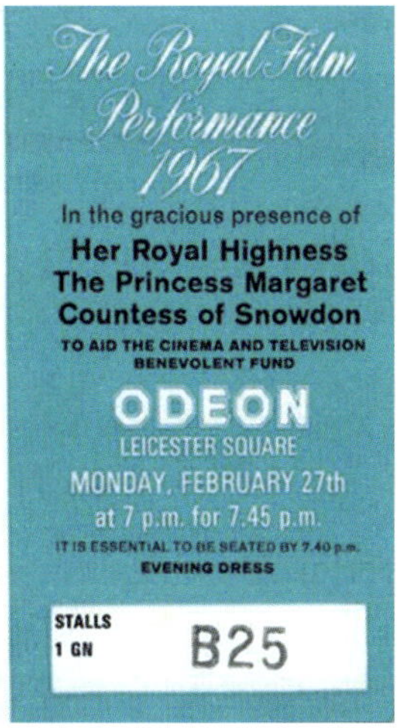

Michael Redgrave and Jean Seberg. The princess paused for a few words with many of them but spent several minutes talking with Elizabeth Taylor and Richard Burton.

The evening began with a tribute to Walt Disney, who had recently passed away, with the inclusion of a Mickey Mouse cartoon, which evoked the applause of the audience. With film composer Ron Goodwin conducting the orchestra, the stage presentation took on a celebratory feel, including a nostalgic newsreel flashback to the very first Royal Film Performance back in 1946.

A further link to that very first Royal Film was the introduction on stage of Raymond Massey, one of the stars of the picture shown that night, *A Matter of Life and Death*. Stepping out from the star-studded line-up, Richard Burton made a short speech, finishing with:

> My name is really Richard Jenkins; therefore, my wife is Liz Jenkins. And up there is a young lady whose real name is Maggie Jones [a reference to Princess Margaret]. When we took over the Dorchester, it was only a desperate attempt to try to keep up with the Joneses.

As was now tradition, a thirty-minute programme of highlights from the evening was shown later that evening on ITV.

1968 *Romeo and Juliet*

Not only was this the second screen adaptation of a William Shakespeare play to be chosen as a Royal Film Performance in quick succession, but also the second to be directed by Franco Zeffirelli. It was chosen without the selection committee viewing a frame of film. Chairman Philip Warter flew to Rome to see a rough cut while the picture was still in production and thought it 'a beautiful film'.

This choice also broke with the tradition that nothing suggestive should be shown at a Royal Film Performance. Zeffirelli feared that a love scene featuring Olivia Hussey as Juliet, naked from the waist up, and Leonard Whiting's Romeo nude on a bed would fall foul of the British censor. Concerns were voiced, too, of the Queen viewing partial nudity on the screen. In the end, the chief censor, John Trevelyan, passed the film uncut, declaring the scene in question to have been done 'with impeccable taste' and there was nothing to cause concern for Her Majesty.

For the very first time, the Prince of Wales, then a 19-year-old freshman at Cambridge University, accompanied his mother and father. People observed how Charles took longer to go along the line-up, straggling behind his parents and evidently enjoying chatting to the stars. An official asked the Queen if the usual precise timings of the occasion should be halted for the prince to catch

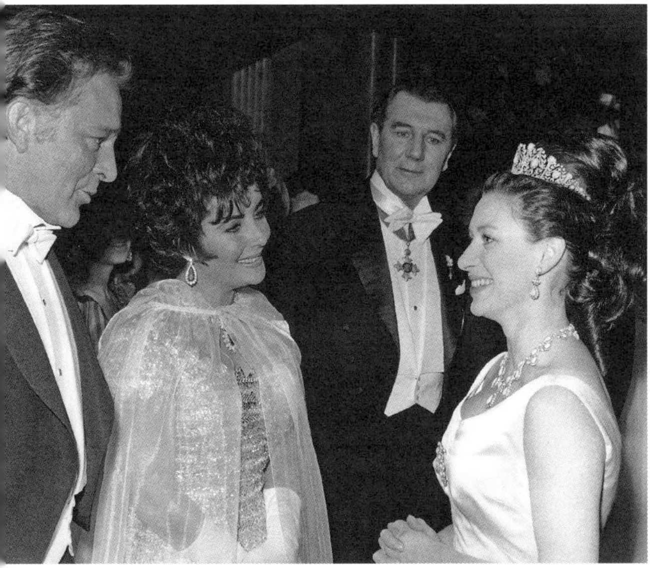

The Taming of the Shrew (1967): Richard Burton, Elizabeth Taylor and Sir Michael Redgrave meet Princess Margaret.

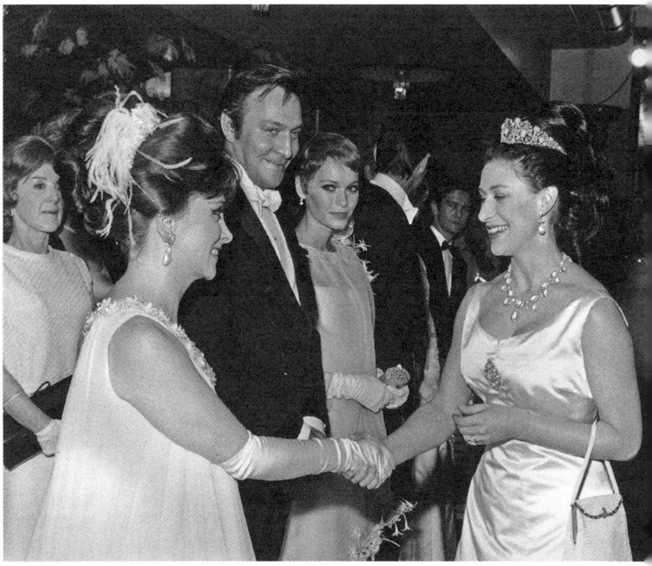

Before Princess Margaret meets Gina Lollobrigida, Christopher Plummer and Mia Farrow, who are also in the line-up.

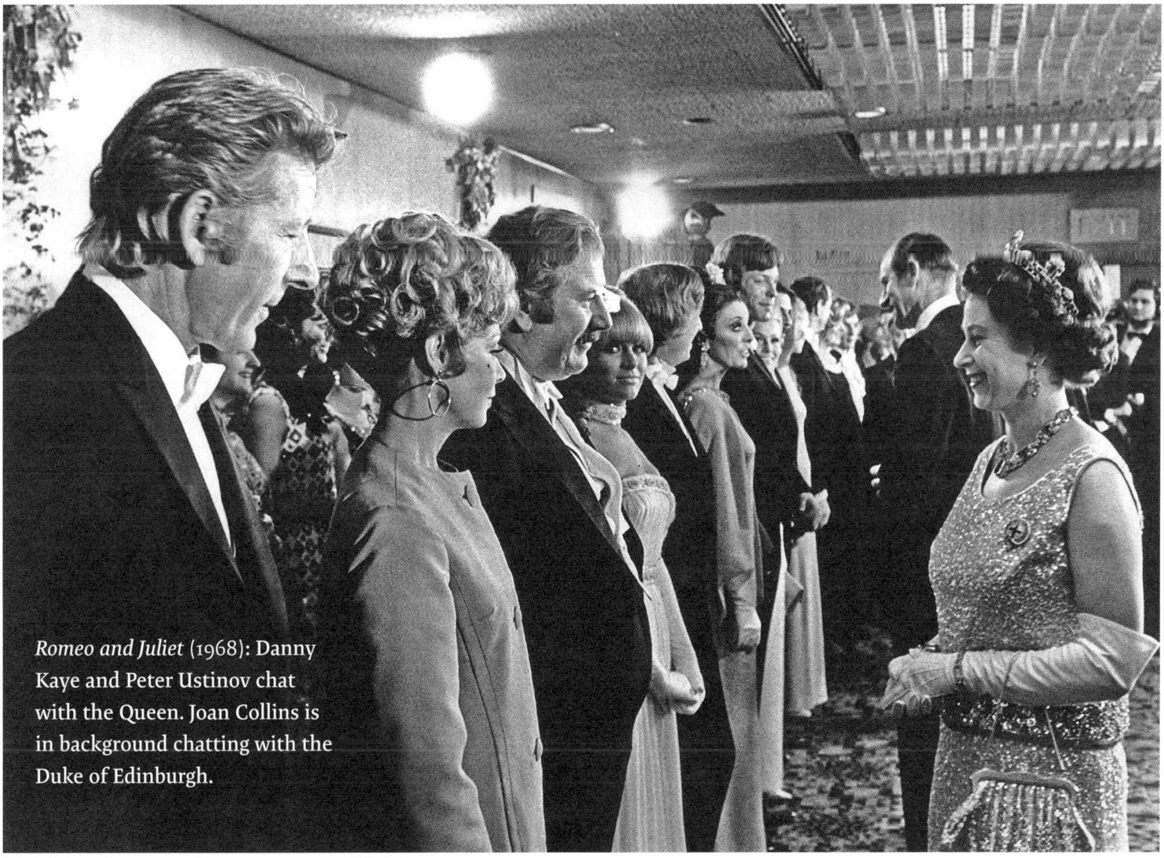

Romeo and Juliet (1968): Danny Kaye and Peter Ustinov chat with the Queen. Joan Collins is in background chatting with the Duke of Edinburgh.

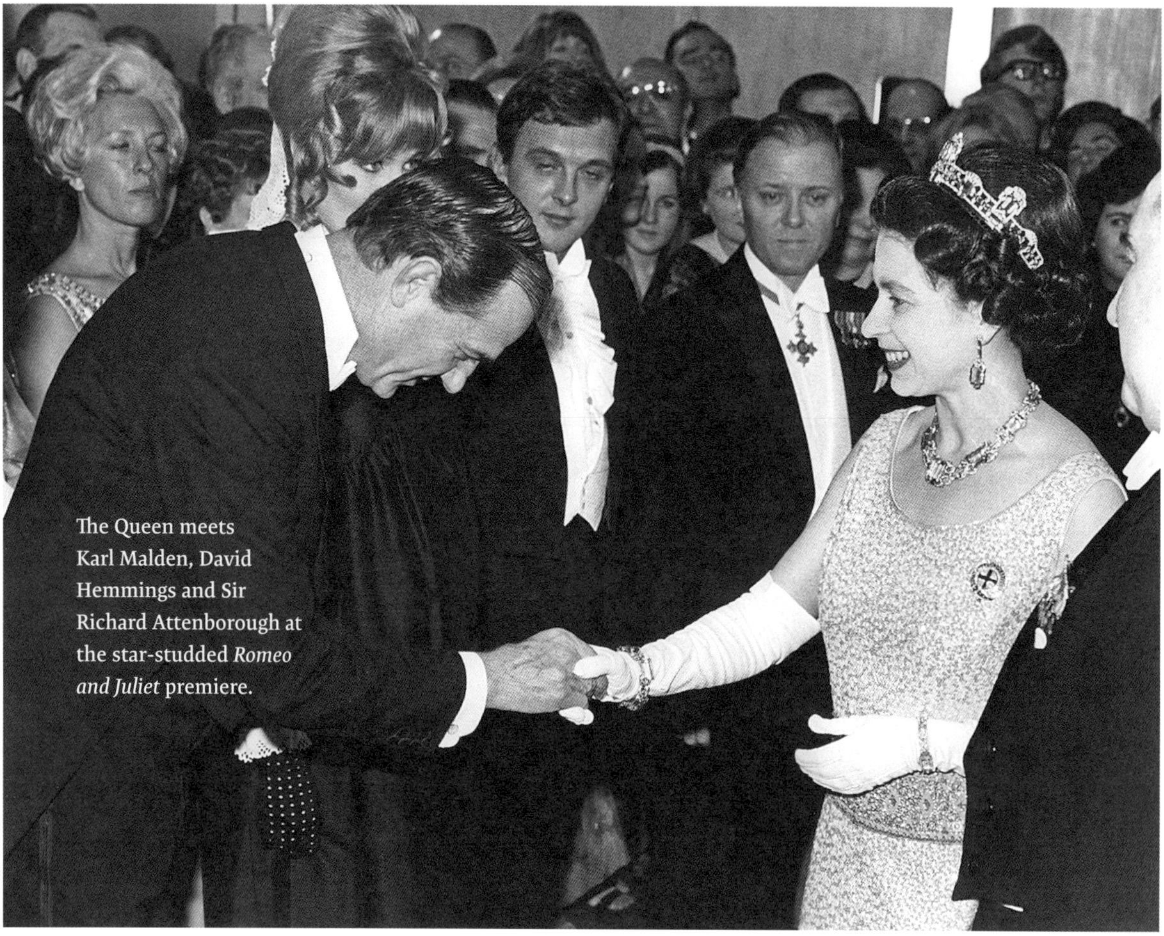

The Queen meets Karl Malden, David Hemmings and Sir Richard Attenborough at the star-studded *Romeo and Juliet* premiere.

up. The Queen smiled and said, 'It's no use waiting for him – he'll be hours yet.'

The stars on show included Richard Chamberlain, Joan Collins, David Hemmings, Danny Kaye, Roger Moore, Tommy Steele, Topol, Carol White and Peter Ustinov. During the stage presentation there was a nice touch when the established stars allowed the young Olivia Hussey and Leonard Whiting to take centre stage and the limelight. Then Sir Richard Attenborough stepped forward to announce that a record sum had been raised. This had much to do with the generosity of the head of Paramount, Charles Bluhdorn, who, when told earlier that the event was within £900 of beating the previous record, without hesitation agreed to donate £1,000.

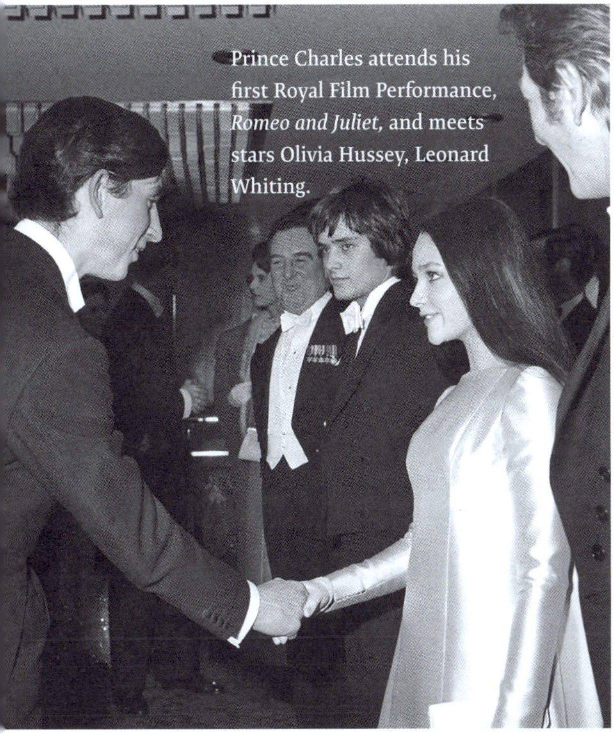

Prince Charles attends his first Royal Film Performance, *Romeo and Juliet*, and meets stars Olivia Hussey, Leonard Whiting.

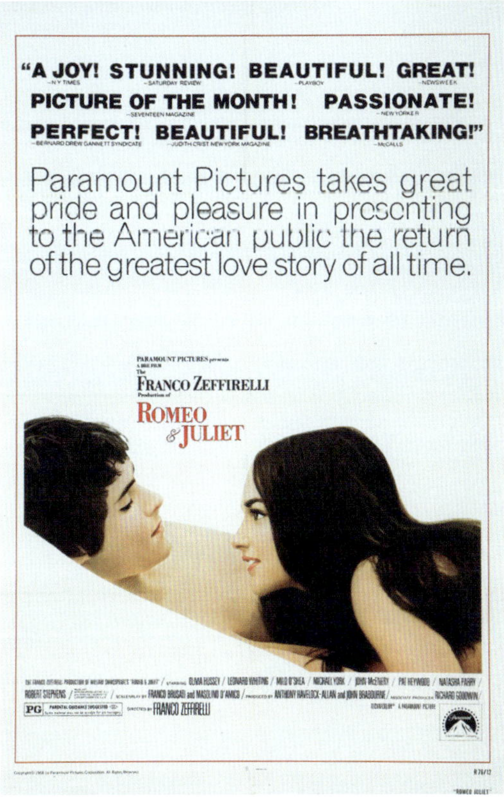

1969 *The Prime of Miss Jean Brodie*

This year's choice for the Royal Film Performance made history as the first to carry an 'X' rating from the British censor. Based on Muriel Spark's novel and starring Maggie Smith, *The Prime of Miss Jean Brodie* was set in 1930s Edinburgh and introduced us to Miss Brodie, a charismatic, free-thinking and unorthodox teacher at an all-girls school. As she famously proclaims, 'Give me a girl at an impressionable age, and she is mine for life.'

The picture was selected prior to certification. Both the film's director, Ronald Neame, and 20th Century Fox protested and asked the Board to reconsider to allow a wider audience to appreciate the film. But the censor stuck to its guns. Rather than any graphic or adult content, the X certificate was given due to the general philosophy espoused by Miss Brodie towards her charges.

However, ten seconds of the film was cut out of the version to be presented in front of the Queen Mother. This marked the first occasion the charity's committee had censored a Royal Film to meet imagined royal sensibilities. The charity did not take this action lightly. Indeed, they sought the advice of Ronald Neame, relaying to him the thought that they might perhaps be acting too square in their reaction and so left the final decision to him. Neame agreed to the cut, which

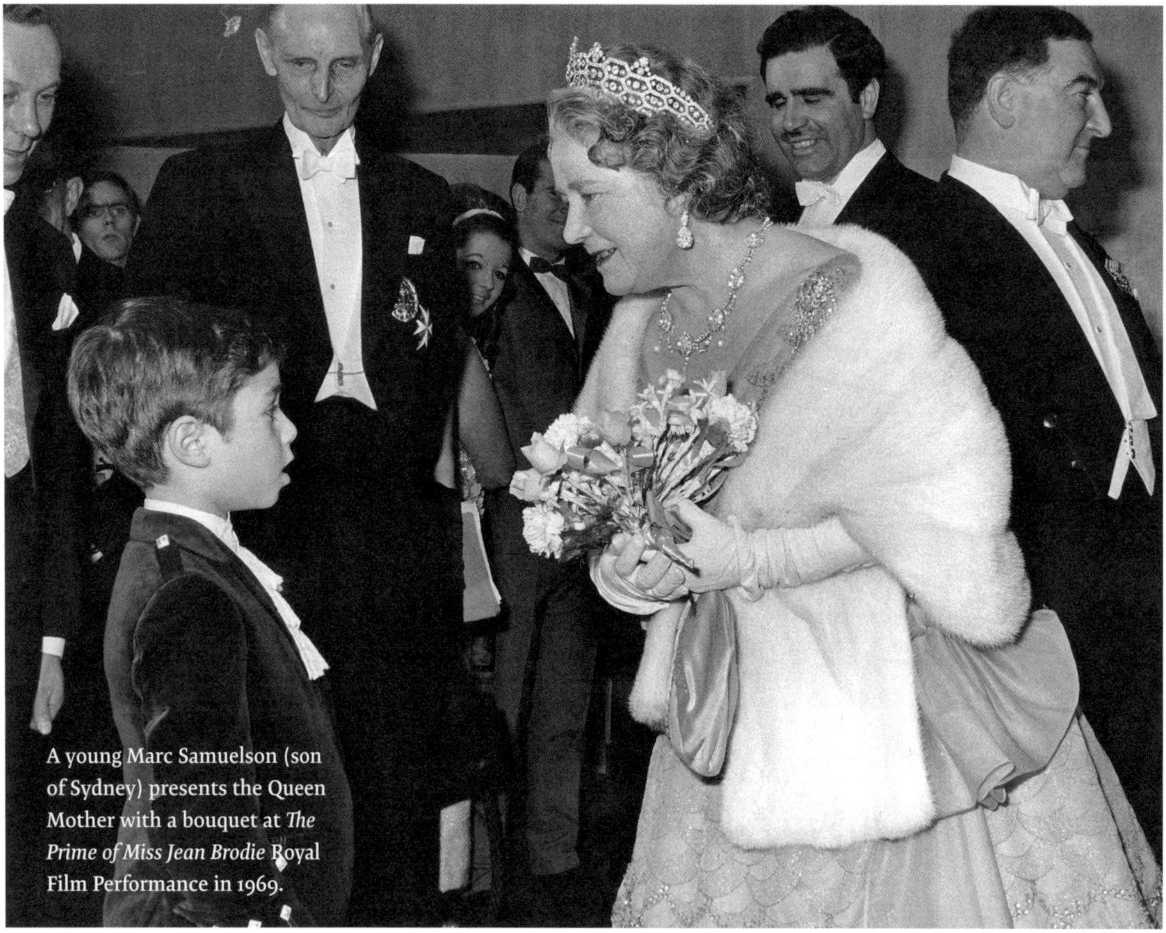

A young Marc Samuelson (son of Sydney) presents the Queen Mother with a bouquet at *The Prime of Miss Jean Brodie* Royal Film Performance in 1969.

featured the schoolgirls looking at a drawing of a male nude and giggling at a joke.

Ironically, the committee chose *The Prime of Miss Jean Brodie* over what may have been an even more controversial choice, the musical *Sweet Charity*. In the end, that film's subject matter, Shirley MacLaine playing the hostess at a clip joint, was deemed to be far too risqué for royalty. The film's director, Bob Fosse, thought it was because of a two-word remark Charity makes – 'Up yours!'

To reflect the Scottish flavour of the film, the pipes and drums of the Scots Guards marched through the West End to form a greeting party at the Odeon, Leicester Square, for the Queen Mother, Princess Margaret and the Earl of Snowdon. The stars presented to the royal party included Ava Gardner, Rex Harrison, Ron Moody, Roger Moore, Nyree Dawn Porter, Sir Michael Redgrave, Peter Sellers, Robert Vaughn and the stars of the film, Maggie Smith and Robert Stephens, who were both given standing ovations when they entered the auditorium. Flowers were presented to the Queen Mother by Marc Samuelson, son of Sir Sydney Samuelson, later president of CTBF and involved in the 'Filmharmonic' concerts.

Helped by its launch at the Royal Film Performance, *The Prime of Miss Jean Brodie* went on to win critical favour and commercial

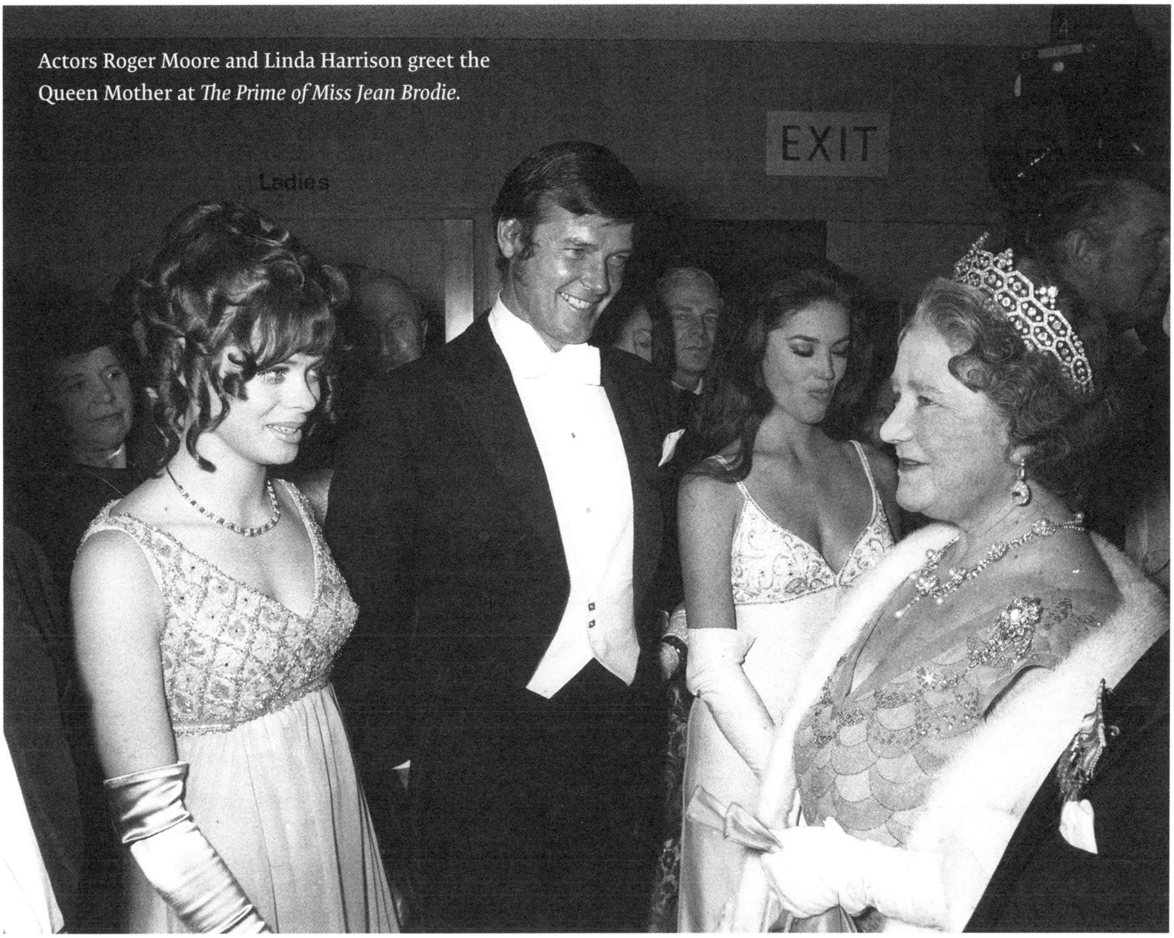

Actors Roger Moore and Linda Harrison greet the Queen Mother at *The Prime of Miss Jean Brodie*.

success. Maggie Smith won an Oscar for her performance.

The evening concluded at a gala ball at Claridge's, where there was a huge police presence due to the arrival of President Nixon at the hotel and the fear of anti-Vietnam War demonstrations. Inside, plain-clothes security men mingled with the guests.

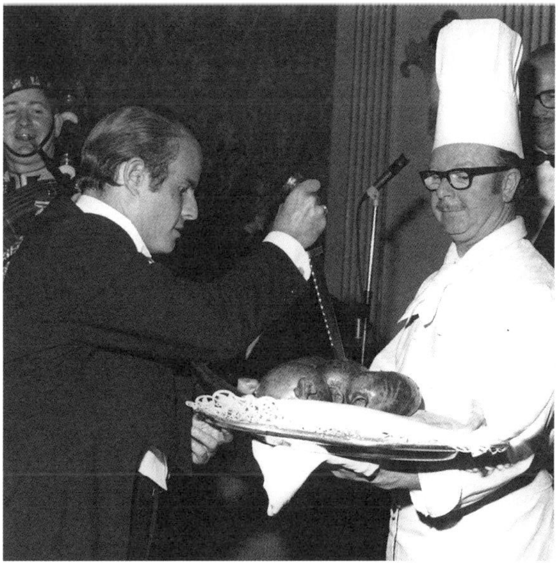

Richard Zanuck (head of 20th Century Fox, the studio behind *The Prime of Miss Jean Brodie*) cuts the haggis at the Scottish-themed post-premiere party at Claridge's Hotel.

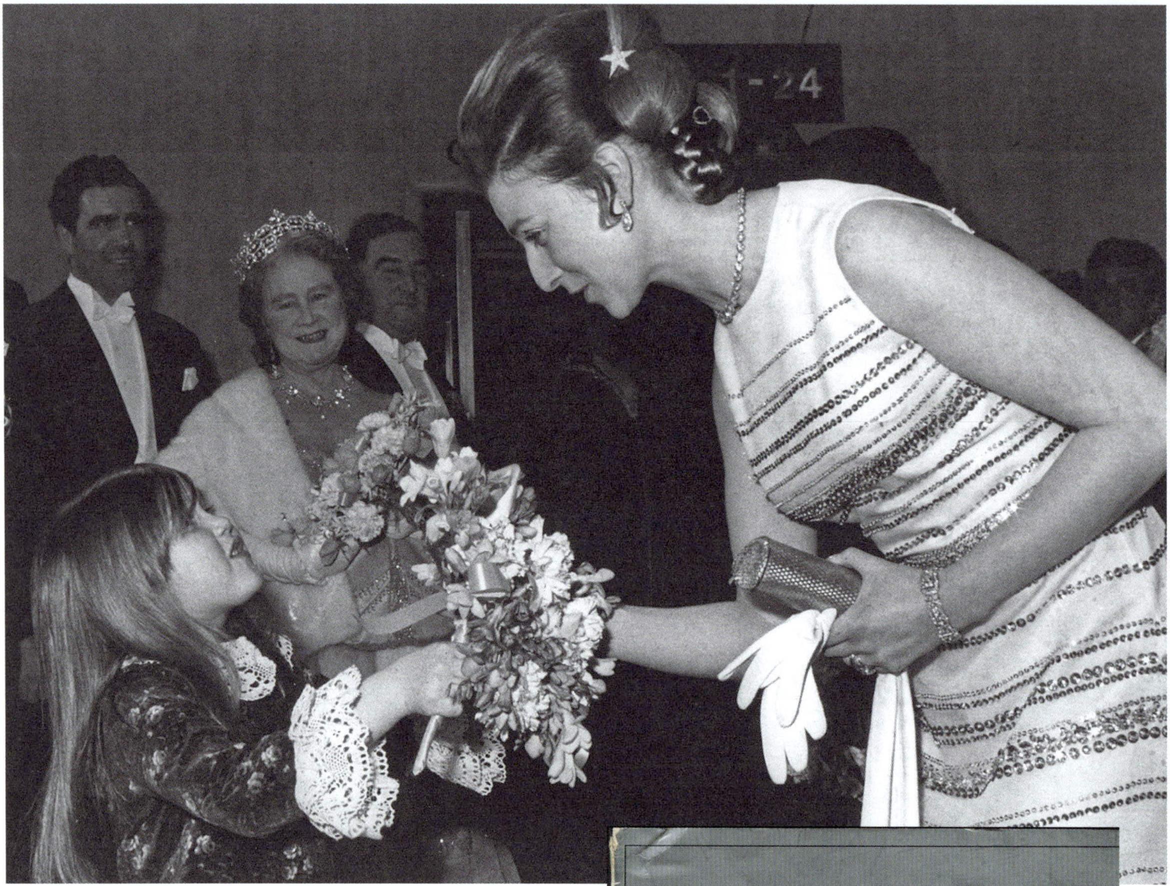

Young Samantha Perkins presents a bouquet to Princess Alexandra as the Queen Mother and Vivian Cox look on.

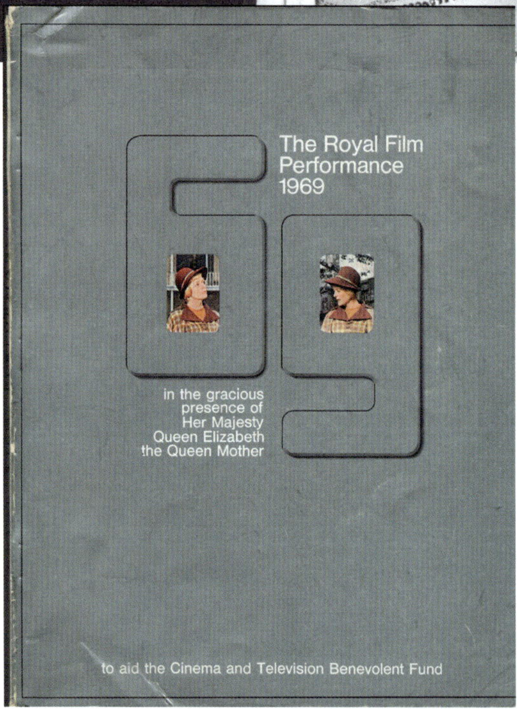

1970 ***Anne of the Thousand Days***

After winning all the headlines in 1967, Richard Burton was forced to cancel plans to attend this Royal Film Performance after being struck down by pneumonia. In *Anne of the Thousand Days*, Burton gave a memorable performance as King Henry VIII in the famous story of how he discarded one wife, Catherine of Aragon, who had failed to produce a male heir, in favour of the younger and more beautiful Anne Boleyn. It was during the dress rehearsal of the presentation of the stars that the film's producer, Hal B. Wallis, received a telegram from Burton from his home in Puerto Vallarta, Mexico. It read, 'What I thought was a bad cold has turned into viral pneumonia which is rampant at the moment.' Both Burton and Elizabeth Taylor were 'profoundly disappointed' not to be there.

In Burton's absence, it was his co-star Geneviève Bujold who took the limelight. She certainly won the fashion stakes, thanks to a snow-white dress with high Victorian neck and cape. And it was a case of two queens coming face to face as Queen Elizabeth was presented to Miss Bujold, who played Anne Boleyn in the film. Accompanying the Queen was Princess Anne.

When introduced to the film's producer, Hal B. Wallis, in a story the Hollywood veteran enjoyed telling, the Queen whispered in his ear as she shook his hand, 'Thank you, Mr Wallis. We're learning about English history from your films.' Wallis was also responsible for the historical drama *Becket*, which starred Richard Burton and Peter O'Toole.

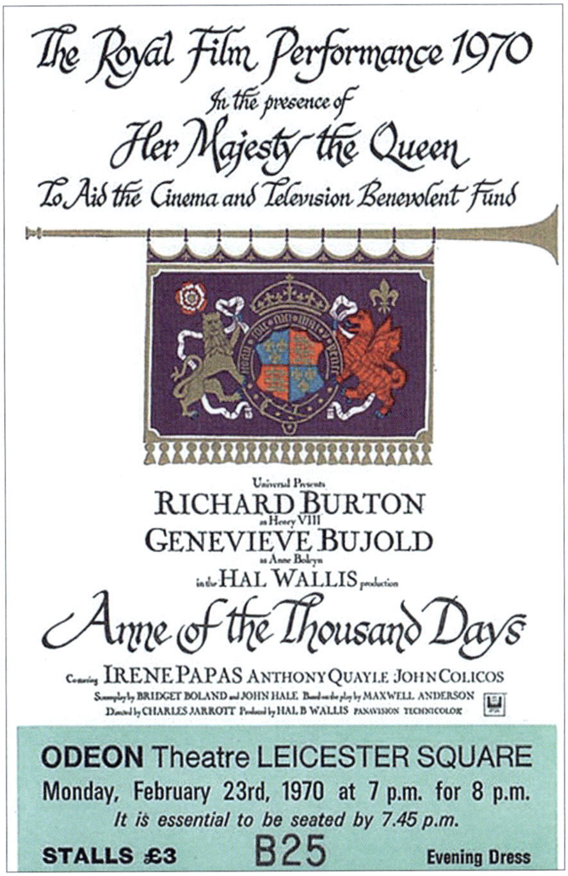

Bandleader and film composer Stanley Black wielded the baton in the orchestra pit as host David Frost introduced the stars on stage, this time within a Tudor-style setting with extras dressed in historical costume. These included Richard Attenborough, Hywel Bennett, Michael Caine, Michael Crawford, Britt Ekland, Judy Geeson, Susan Hampshire, Michael Hordern and Franco Nero. Harry Secombe sang 'Rose of England' and, to a fanfare of trumpeters, Miss Bujold made her entrance.

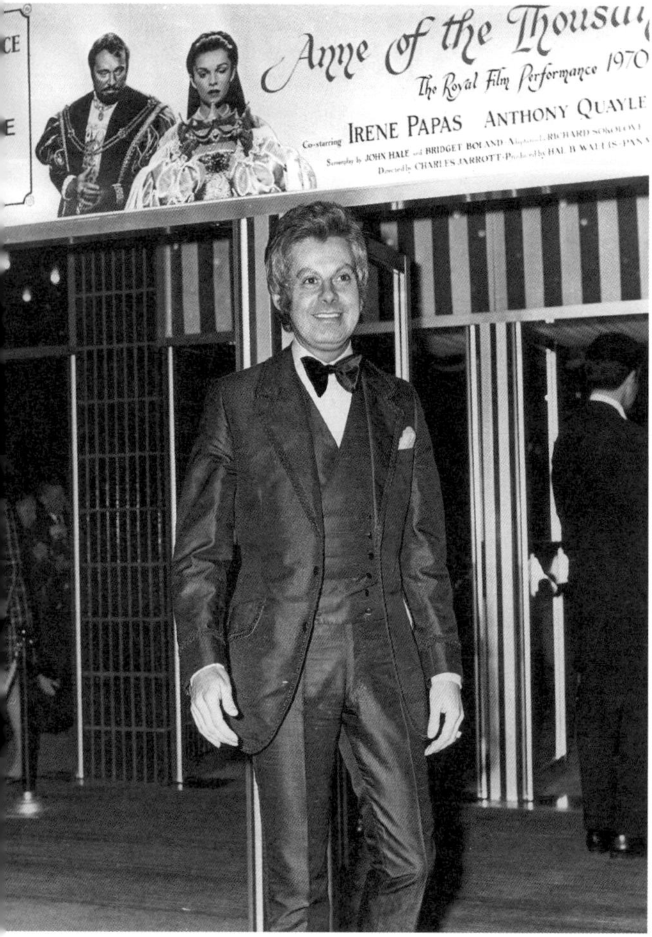

Danny La Rue, who had just been named Theatre Personality of the Year, arrives the Odeon.

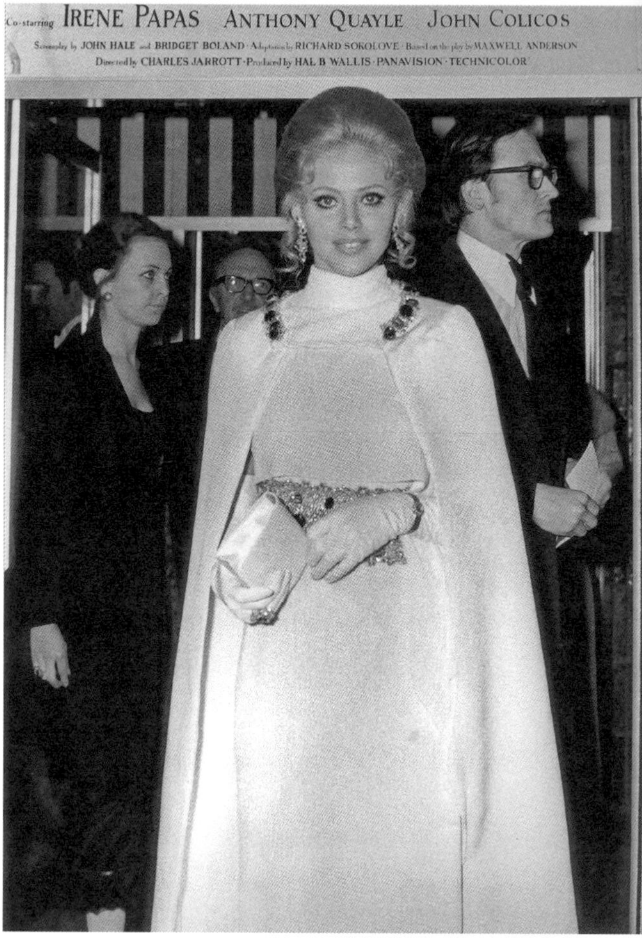

Britt Ekland arrives for *Anne of a Thousand Days* (1970).

It was another record-breaking evening and there were TV crews from Australia, Canada and New Zealand covering the event. But there was a note of sadness because this was to be the very last Pathé newsreel. This one looked at the forthcoming royal visit to New Zealand and Australia. Pathé had stopped producing the cinema newsreel that month as it could no longer compete with television. When the newsreel finished there was thunderous applause of thanks and gratitude to an iconic institution now gone.

The evening concluded in a supper party hosted by Universal, in the distinguished environs of Banqueting House in Whitehall with its splendid Rubens paintings on the ceiling.

1971 ***Love Story***

This year marked the Silver Jubilee of the Royal Film Performance, and it was a particularly special occasion for the Queen Mother and Princess Margaret, both of whom had been present at that very first Royal Film night back in 1946. The charity had selected a film that was already a box-office smash in America, earning back its modest production costs in its first three days. Destined to become one of the all-time great weepies, *Love Story* was about two young people from different backgrounds who fall in love, only for tragedy to stifle any future they may have had.

Again, Leicester Square was completely closed to traffic save for cars bringing guests to the Odeon, and huge crowds gathered to catch a glimpse of the stars and the royals. In the line-up to meet the Queen Mother were the film's two young performers, Ali MacGraw and Ryan O'Neal. 'I've brought my hankie,' the Queen Mother confessed to O'Neal.

'I hope you need it,' he replied.

In America, some cinemas were giving patrons packets of tissues along with their tickets.

Other stars in the line-up were Jenny Agutter, Tony Curtis, Olivia de Havilland, Dustin Hoffman, John Hurt, Sid James, Glynis Johns, John Mills and Roger Moore. Michael Parkinson was on hand for the television coverage interviewing the stars.

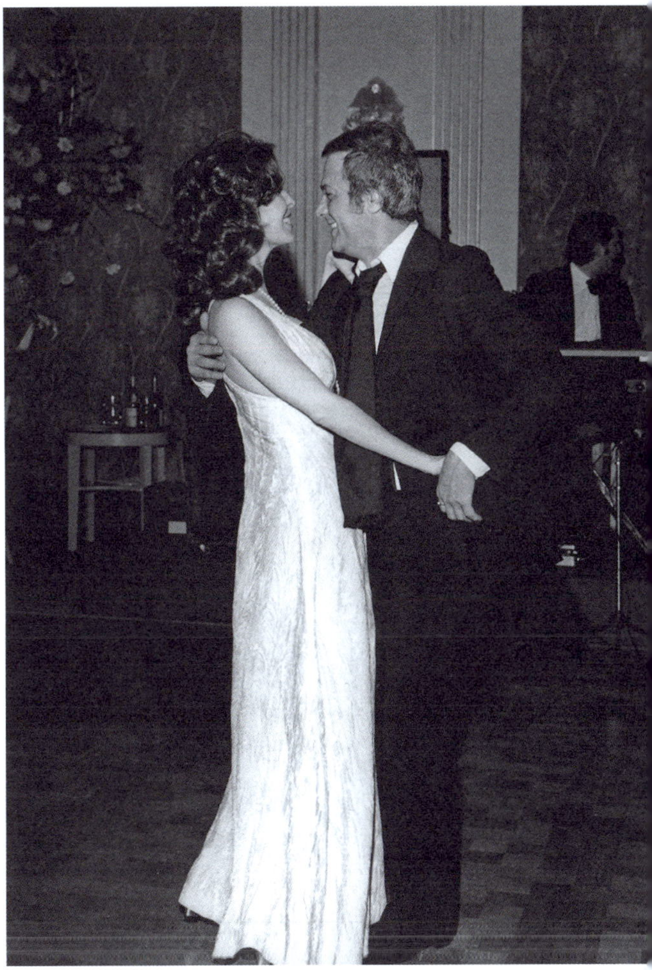

Tony Curtis with his wife Leslie Allen at the post-premiere party for *Love Story* at The Savoy.

Poor Ali MacGraw suffered a wardrobe malfunction. The American actress had recently given birth, and the fashion designer Halston had made a special dress to accentuate her new temporary curves. But when she put it on it barely covered her modesty. 'Great for a stripper,' said her husband, film executive Robert Evans, in his 1994 autobiography, *The Kid Stays in the Picture*. 'But not suitable for the royals.' The couple had just forty-five minutes to find a replacement. Ali ended up with a brown pantsuit with white and yellow flowers.

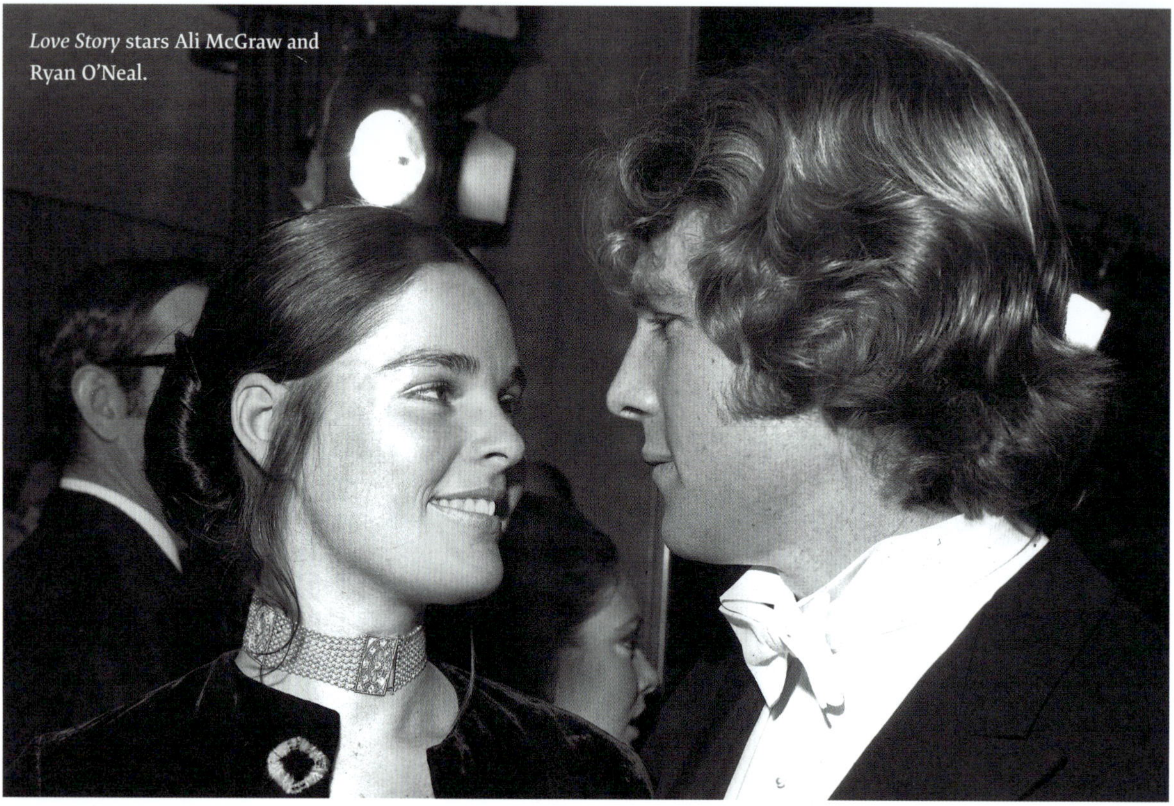

Love Story stars Ali McGraw and Ryan O'Neal.

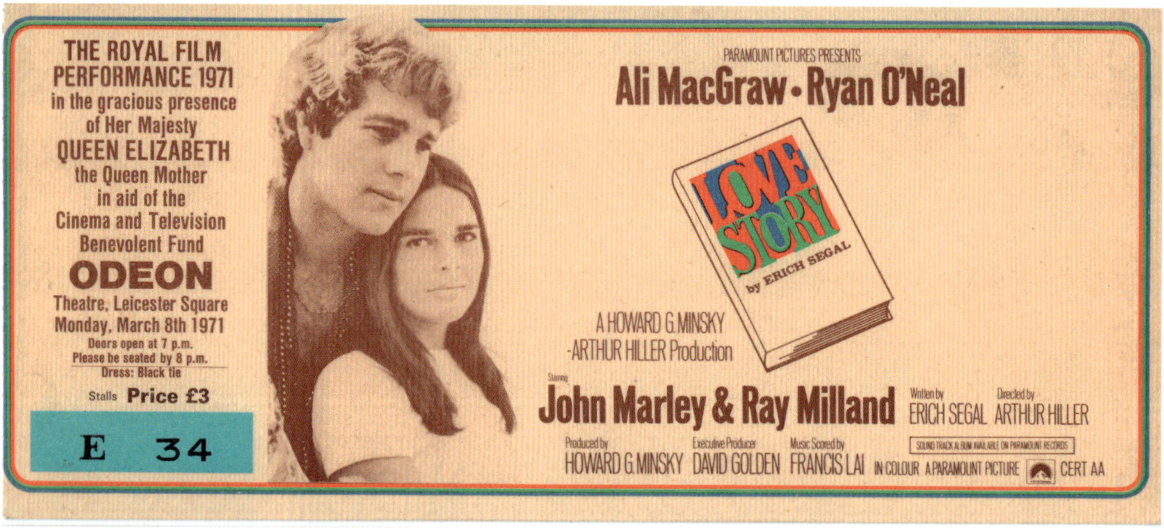

Back in Hollywood, Evans angrily confronted Halston for ruining Ali's big night. The designer explained that she had put the dress on backwards.

Later that evening, Ali and Evans returned to the Odeon, Leicester Square, along with Sid James and a few others who had attended the film performance to watch the first satellite telecast of a heavyweight championship boxing match, Muhammad Ali versus Joe Frazier.

There had been some controversy over the selection of *Love Story* due to Ali MacGraw's character's repeated use of the word 'bullshit'. The press reported that the court officials at Buckingham Palace were shocked to hear the news. After worrying about the situation, the charity in the end decided to show the film uncut. The censor had given the film an AA certificate, meaning over-14s could see it.

The stage presentation took place against a backdrop of the sky at dawn with the Young Generation dance group performing as the stars made their entrances. Shirley Bassey performed the film's title song, 'Where Do I Begin', live on the stage.

1972 *Mary, Queen of Scots*

For the second time in three years, the choice for the Royal Film Performance was another historical production from Hal B. Wallis. In his 1980 autobiography, *Starmaker*, Wallis said he was 'thrilled and very honoured'. This was a slice of British history that had always fascinated Wallis, the story of the Catholic Mary, Queen of Scots' fight for the English crown against her cousin, the Protestant Elizabeth I.

For his two queens, Wallis knew that he had to pick from the very top of the acting tree and brought in Vanessa Redgrave to play Mary and Glenda Jackson as Elizabeth. Jackson had only recently played the monarch in a BBC drama serial and at first refused to play the role again. The personal intervention of Wallis and a large fee changed her mind. Glenda happily attended the Royal Film Performance, but Miss Redgrave stayed at home, inciting a backlash from some sections of the press.

By now, the importance of a picture being chosen for the Royal Film Performance, both in terms of prestige and publicity value, was such that it was used as part of the publicity campaign. In the case of *Mary, Queen of Scots*, some of the newspaper adverts highlighted the fact it had been chosen for the Royal Film Performance above the fact that it had been nominated for five Oscars.

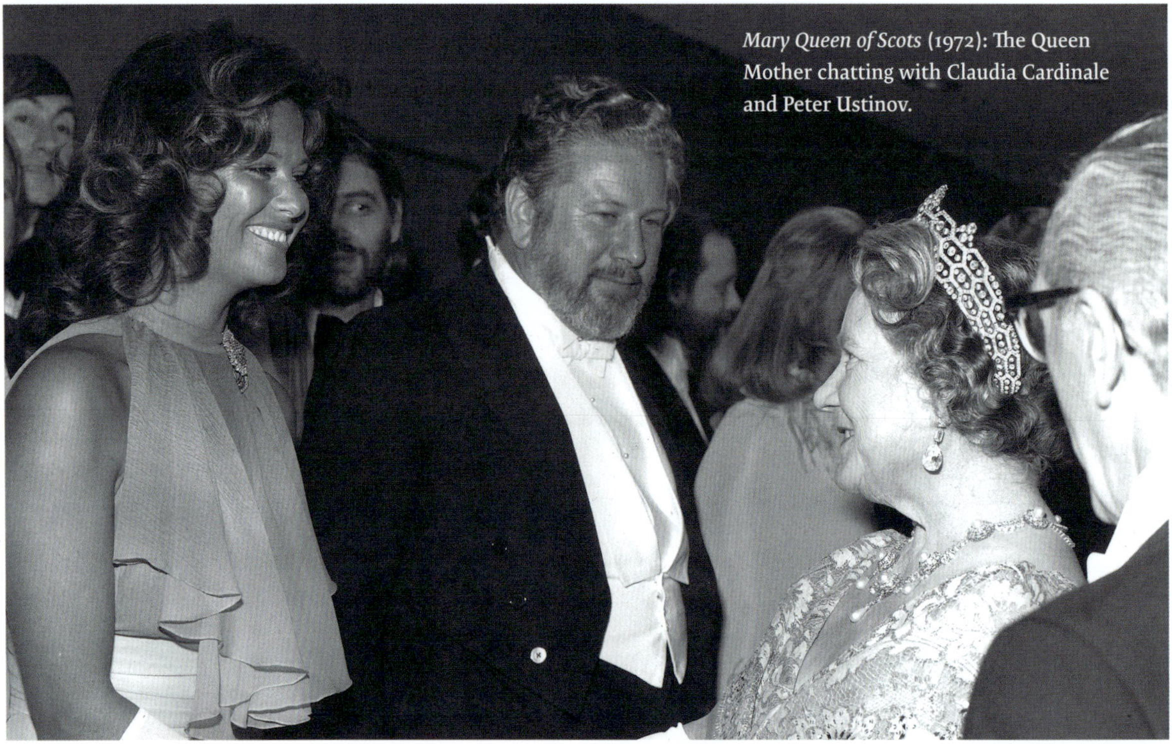

Mary Queen of Scots (1972): The Queen Mother chatting with Claudia Cardinale and Peter Ustinov.

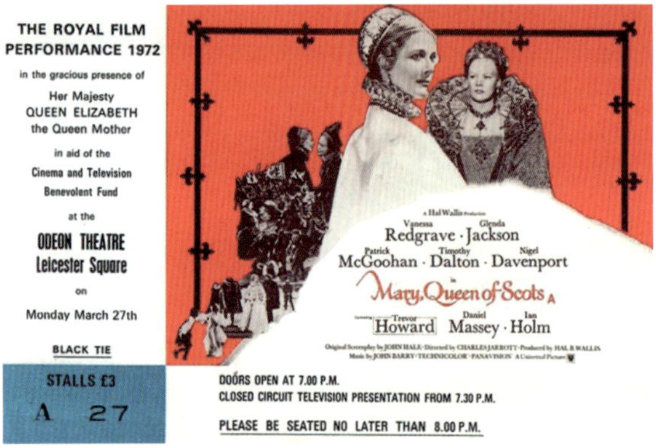

THE ROYAL FILM PERFORMANCE 1972

in the gracious presence of

Her Majesty QUEEN ELIZABETH the Queen Mother

in aid of the Cinema and Television Benevolent Fund

at the

ODEON THEATRE Leicester Square

on

Monday March 27th

BLACK TIE

STALLS £3

A 27

A Hal Wallis Production

Vanessa Redgrave · Glenda Jackson

Patrick McGoohan · Timothy Dalton · Nigel Davenport

in

Mary, Queen of Scots A

Trevor Howard Daniel Massey · Ian Holm

Original Screenplay by JOHN HALE · Directed by CHARLES JARROTT · Produced by HAL B WALLIS

Music by JOHN BARRY · TECHNICOLOR · PANAVISION · A Universal Picture

DOORS OPEN AT 7.00 P.M.

CLOSED CIRCUIT TELEVISION PRESENTATION FROM 7.30 P.M.

PLEASE BE SEATED NO LATER THAN 8.00 P.M.

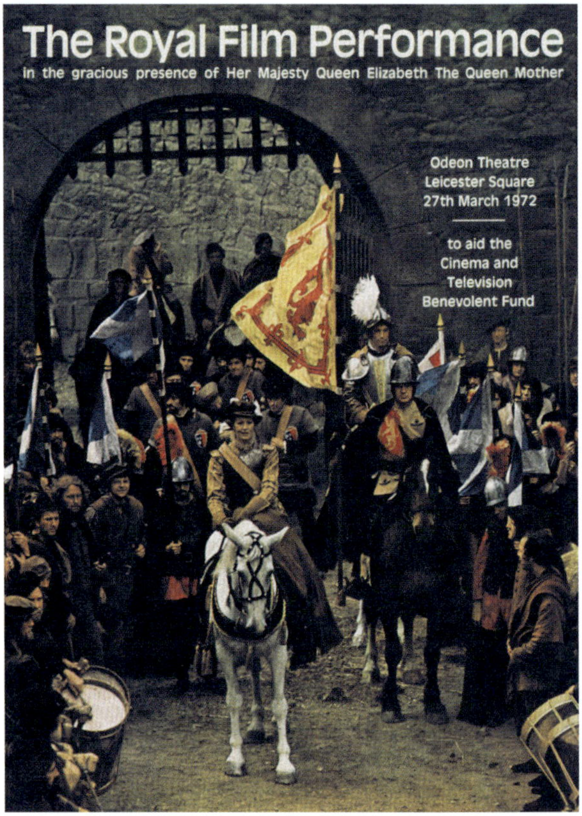

Once again, the evening was a starry affair. In the line-up to meet the Queen Mother, Princess Margaret and the Earl of Snowdon were Stanley Baker, Alan Bates, Claudia Cardinale, James Mason, Hayley Mills, Janet Suzman, Reg Varney and Michael York, along with stars from the film, Nigel Davenport and Glenda Jackson. Susan George, the star of the recently released and very controversial movie *Straw Dogs*, caused a few gasps in the crowd by wearing a clinging jersey dress. Later, Susan couldn't recall what the Queen Mother said to her except to ask if she felt a little hot.

When introduced to Hal B. Wallis, the Queen Mother asked the Hollywood veteran what he was doing next. 'The story of Lord Nelson,' he said.

'Oh, he's my hero,' replied the Queen Mother.

David Frost again hosted the stage presentation, which included a live performance by country and western star Glen Campbell. Frost announced that the charity had raised a record profit that evening and since the first Royal Film Performance in 1946, over £825,000 had been raised.

1973 *Lost Horizon*

For the third time in four years, a film directed by Charles Jarrott was chosen as the Royal Film Performance, following *Anne of the Thousand Days* and *Mary, Queen of Scots*. It was a remarkable achievement for this unassuming London-born director and places him alongside no less a figure than Steven Spielberg as the director with the most Royal Film Performances.

Alas, *Lost Horizon* was not to be a credit that sat well on Mr Jarrott's CV. It turned out to be an expensive flop and critically reviled. Dubbed 'Lost Investment', it was a big-budget musical remake of Frank Capra's *Lost Horizon* (1937) about a group of people who discover the Tibetan utopia Shangri-La, and featured an all-star cast. Producer Ross Hunter had waited to make the film for ten years and brought in the supreme songwriting team of Burt Bacharach and Hal David to provide the score. Its calamitous reception meant that Hunter never produced another feature film.

John Gielgud saw the writing on the wall very early on in the production and in a letter wrote, 'The part is an idiotic walkabout, and I feel a bit ashamed of the bribery that makes me accept it. But I had a bad income tax disaster three years ago and this should help to put me straight again.'

The stars of *Lost Horizon* were presented to the Queen, including Peter Finch, Sally

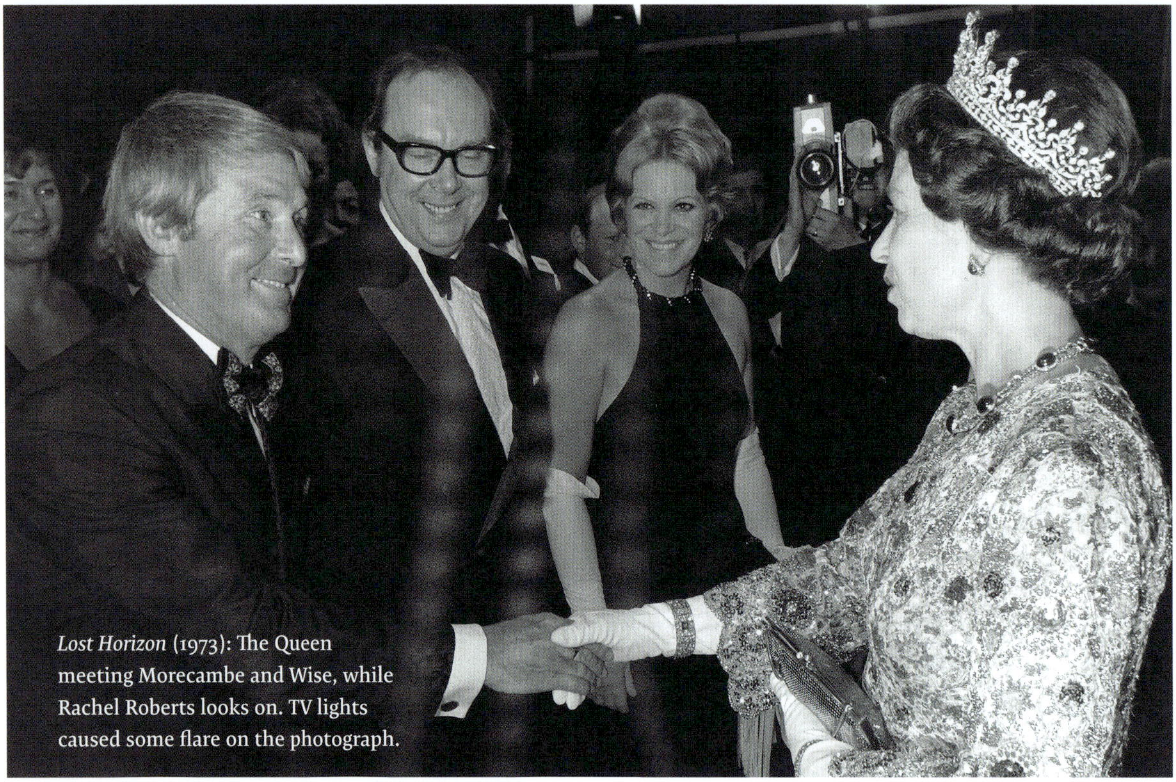

Lost Horizon (1973): The Queen meeting Morecambe and Wise, while Rachel Roberts looks on. TV lights caused some flare on the photograph.

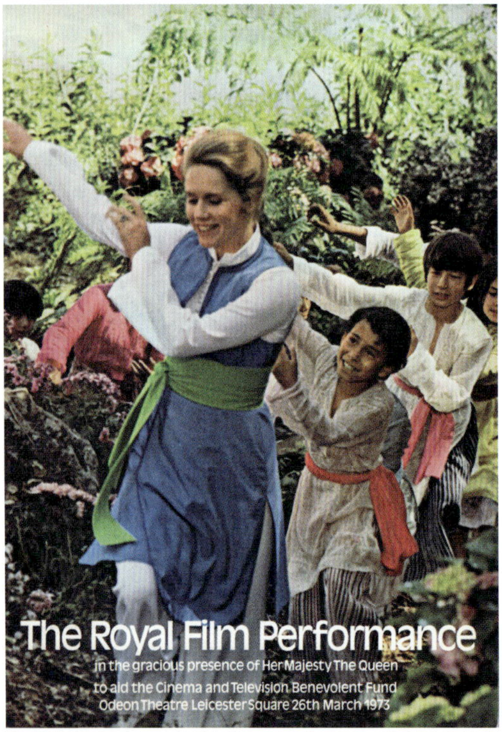

Kellerman, George Kennedy and the dutiful John Gielgud, along with a smattering of other stars like Rachel Roberts, Robert Vaughn and Simon Ward. One nice touch was the presence of L.H. Heath in the line-up to meet Her Majesty. Heath was head gardener at Glebelands, supervising the 40-acre site. With him was his wife, who also worked at the home.

Without doubt the biggest reception was for Eric Morecambe and Ernie Wise, who cracked jokes with the Queen and elicited laughs from everyone nearby. It was interesting to note how the Queen did not speak to them individually in the line-up, rather as a pair.

In the foyer, Pete Murray was doing the honours for the TV highlights show, interviewing the stars, and he grabbed the comedy duo for a chat, asking Morecambe, 'You're on tour at the moment, aren't you, Eric?'

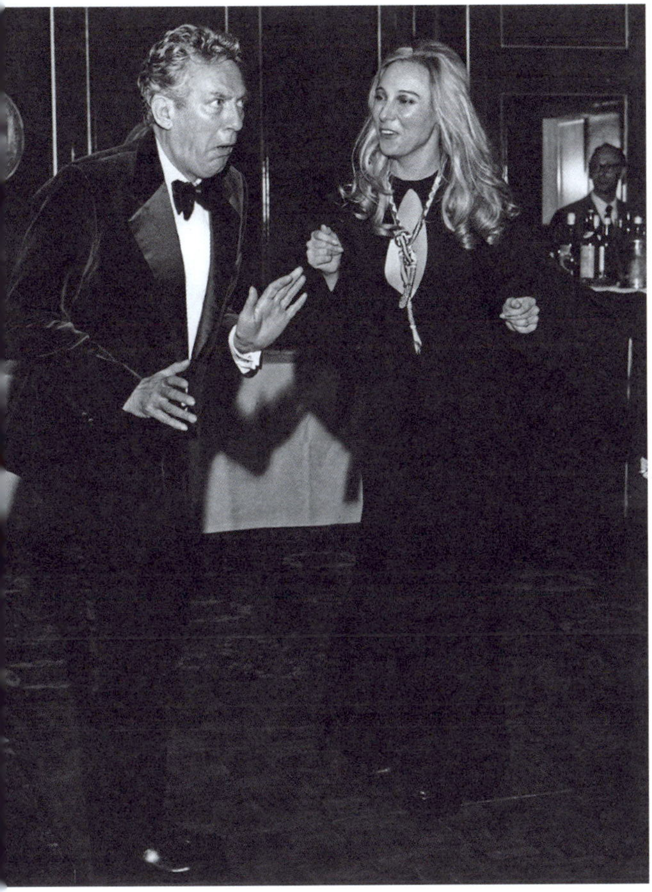

Peter Finch takes to the dance floor with Jill Saint Amant at Les Ambassadeurs after the premiere of *Lost Horizon*.

'No, I'm here,' Morecambe answered.

Once again, the power of being chosen for the Royal Film Performance was in evidence as the evening proved to be a launchpad for *Lost Horizon* to perform well at the UK box office, while it pretty much flopped everywhere else.

1974 *The Three Musketeers*

This Royal Film Performance took place at the height of the 'three-day week' energy crisis then blighting the country and the Odeon, Leicester Square, was lit up specially for the occasion and the appearance of the Queen Mother for the only time in three months. The Queen Mother also showed concern for the current state of the UK film industry, as she went down the line chatting to industry chiefs. Then in something of a downturn, with fewer films being made in the UK and dwindling audiences, the Queen Mother tried to sound hopeful. 'It's coming back, isn't it? And it's very good news because it's such a wonderful entertainment for the people. And it's always a treat for us.' The Queen Mother revealed that Buckingham Palace was regularly supplied with films for private showings.

Perhaps never have so many stars of one Royal Film turned up for the event. There was Jean-Pierre Cassel; Geraldine Chaplin; Frank Finlay, wearing dark glasses, not for affectation, but because he sported two black eyes after a visit to his dentist; Roy Kinnear; Christopher Lee; Spike Milligan; Oliver Reed; Simon Ward; Raquel Welch; and Michael York. Other stars joining the line-up included Jane Seymour and Jacqueline Bisset. Roger Moore compèred the stage presentation and apologised for the absence of Charlton Heston, who played the villainous Cardinal Richelieu in the film, 'He

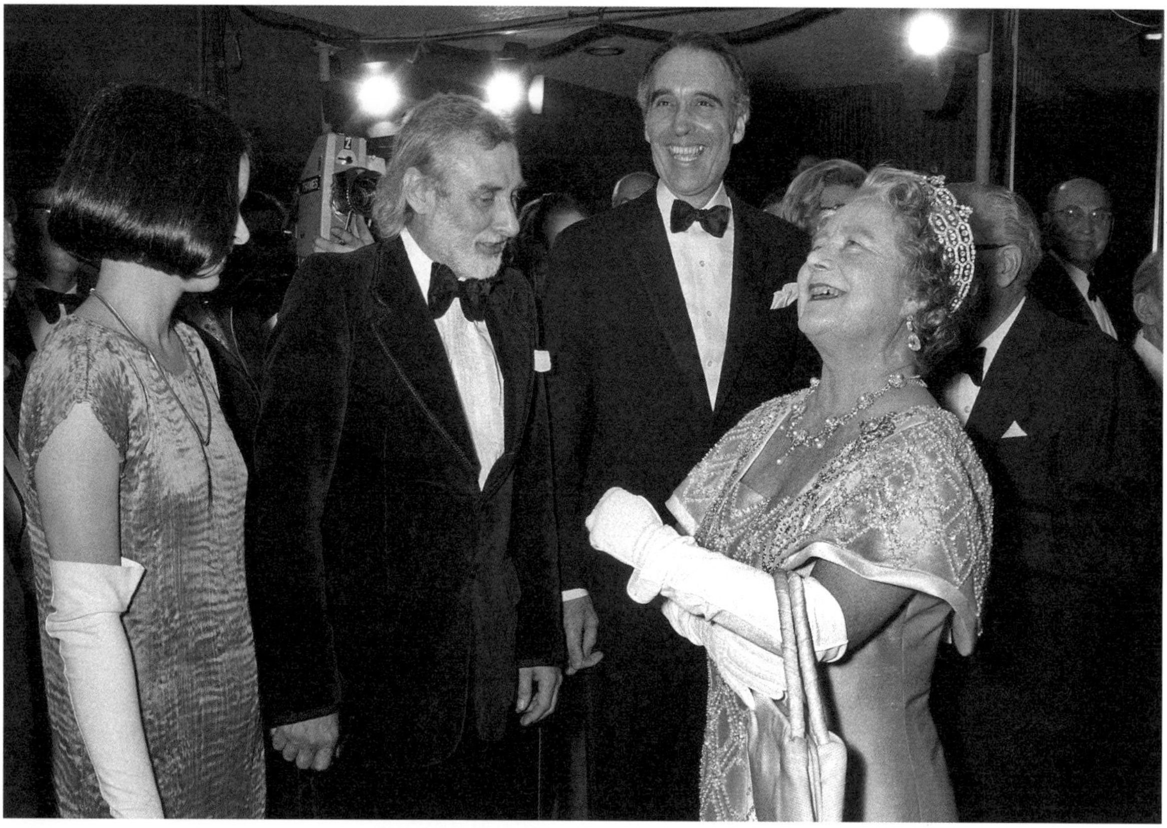

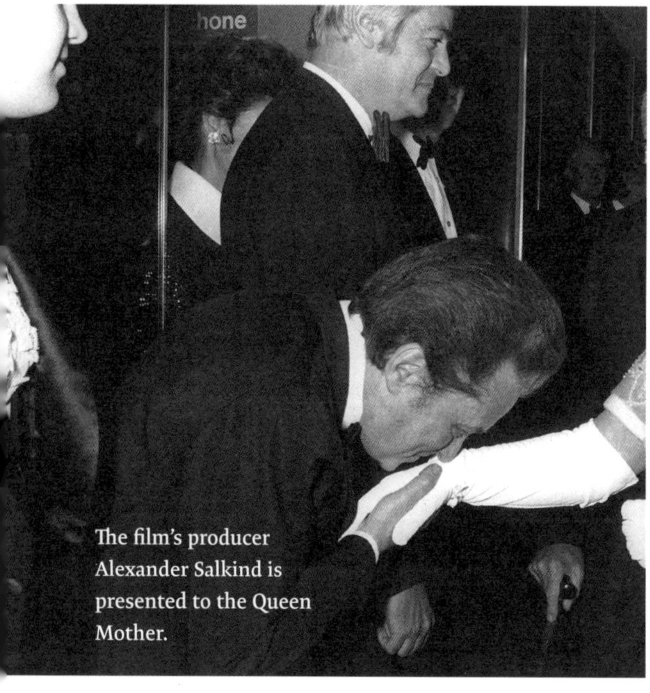

The film's producer Alexander Salkind is presented to the Queen Mother.

Spike Milligan amuses the Queen Mother as Christopher Lee looks on, in the line-up for *The Three Musketeers.*

must have had to go up the mountain again either to see Cecil B. DeMille or his dentist.'

In the foyer, Spike Milligan was asked about playing Raquel Welch's husband in the film. 'I've been under a course of electric shock treatment since I did this film and I'm alright now, and all the measurements are back to normal.'

Before opening, *The Three Musketeers* had already caused controversy when the producers decided to cut the film into two halves, rather than releasing it as a three-hour epic as originally intended. The problem was that not all the actors knew about the decision. They were further incensed at having only been paid for just the one film and their

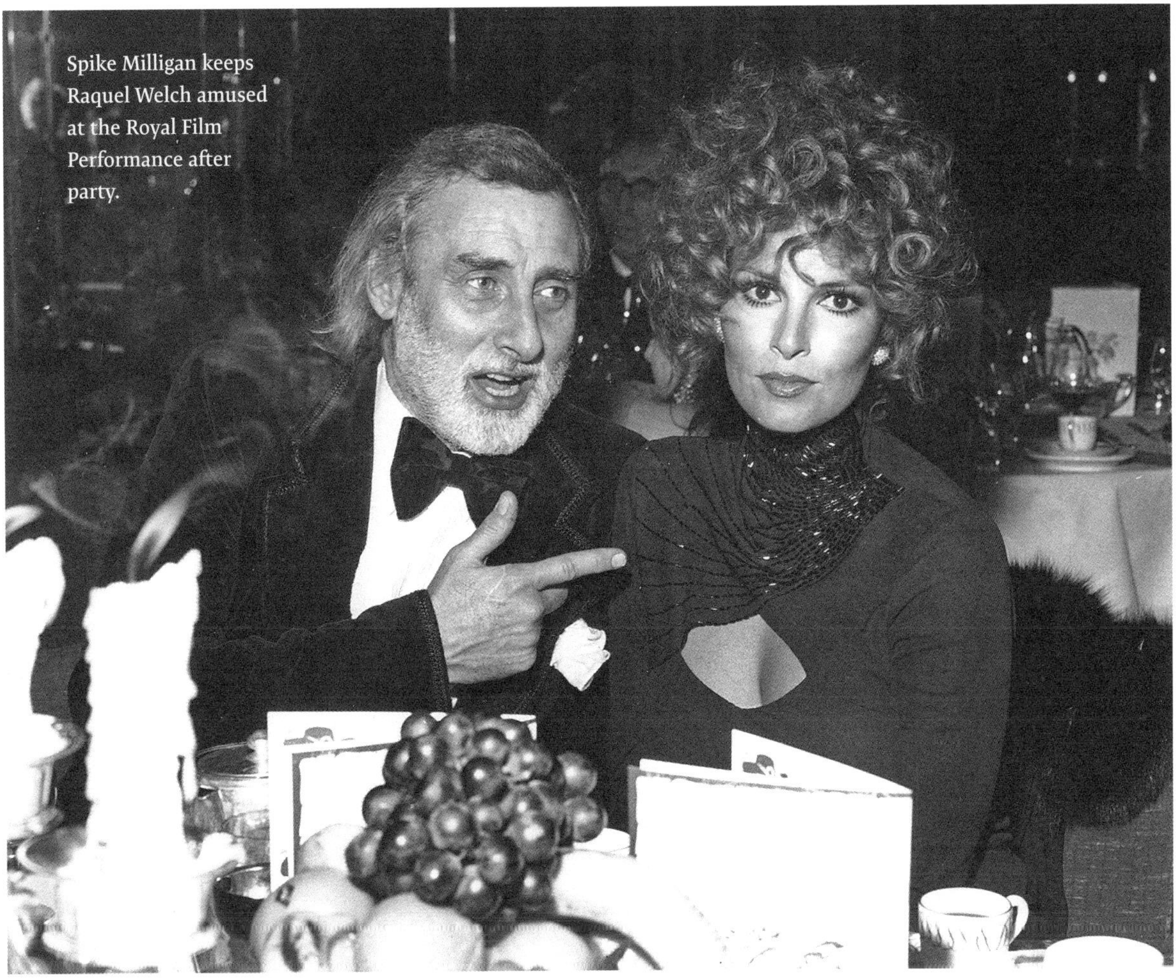

Spike Milligan keeps Raquel Welch amused at the Royal Film Performance after party.

original contracts made no mention of a sequel. This resulted in lawsuits being filed for compensation when *The Four Musketeers* was released later.

As the Queen Mother left the auditorium, she went over to the usherettes to ask them if they had seen the film yet. They said they hadn't. 'You must – it really is the most enormous fun. I thoroughly enjoyed it.'

Producer Ilya Salkind says:

The Royal Film Performance of *The Three Musketeers* was a very special evening. It was the beginning of a very special run for the film.

I met the Queen Mother and still have a photograph of myself with her hanging in my living room.

It was such an honour and to this day it brings back fond and proud memories.

1975 *Funny Lady*

Following her success as a recording artist, Barbra Streisand made her film debut in the critically acclaimed *Funny Girl* (1968), for which she won the Academy Award for Best Actress, sharing it with Katharine Hepburn (*The Lion in Winter*), the only time there has been a tie in this Oscar category. The film was loosely based on the comedienne Fanny Brice.

A sequel was inevitable, although Barbra Streisand needed to be persuaded to do it. *Funny Lady* was a fictionalised account of the later life and career of Fanny Brice and her marriage to songwriter and impresario Billy Rose, played by James Caan. It seemed an ideal choice for the Royal Film Performance, a big colourful musical with the star presence of the indomitable Miss Streisand.

The singer and actress made the trip to London for the event but was less than amused, and a little mystified, to be told that she would have to wear gloves to meet the Queen, as all women were obliged to do. This bugged her, along with the fact that her boyfriend, Jon Peters, was not allowed to be presented to the Queen. Instead, like the friends and family of those being presented, he stood in a crowd of people behind.

On the evening of the Royal Film Performance, and last in the line-up to meet the Queen, Miss Streisand, dressed in a velvet cloak and hood, broke protocol, which dictates

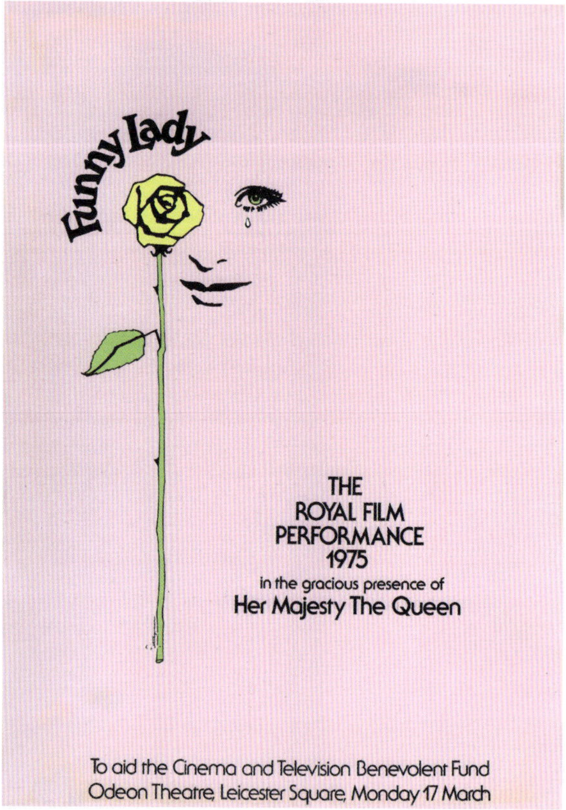

that one waits for the Queen to speak first, and came right out and asked, 'Your Majesty, why do women have to wear gloves and the men don't?'

The Queen was a little taken aback but remained composed and replied, 'Well, I don't really know. It's tradition, I suppose.'

The encounter made headlines round the world. When the Queen had left, Barbra turned to Jon Peters standing behind her and said, 'Well, I guess I still don't know.'

John Mills compèred the stage show and as a veteran of the business and regular attendee of such occasions, he was the perfect choice to make a personal speech to the Queen. 'We thank you and your family for the wonderful help and encouragement you have given us year after year by gracing this royal occasion.

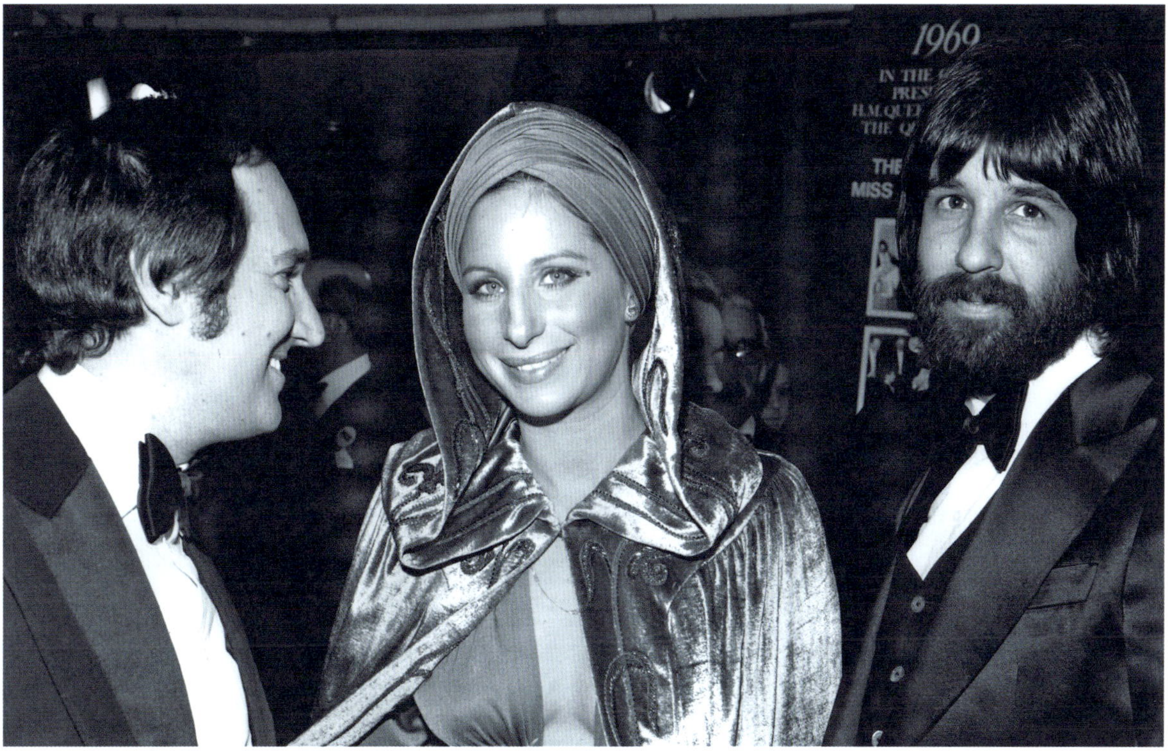

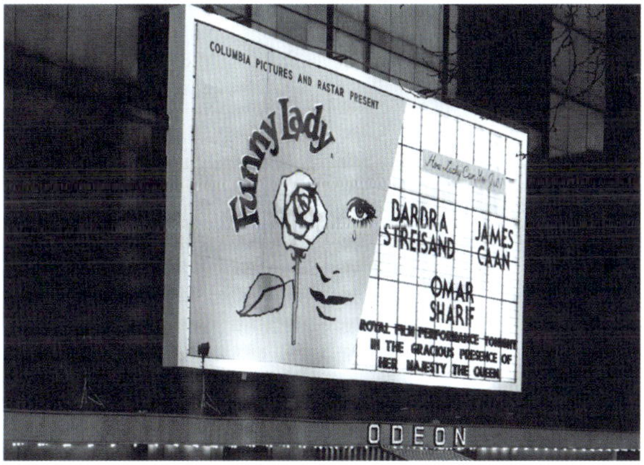

The funny lady herself, Barbra Streisand, flanked by singer Neil Sedeka and producer Jon Peters.

1975's Royal Film Performance *Funny Lady* gracing the front of the Odeon Leicester Square.

Your presence ensures success and the almost astonishing sum that goes to the fund. I was told just before I came on stage that tonight's figure is the highest yet.'

Other stars in attendance included comedian Stanley Baxter, James Caan, Deborah Raffin, Lee Remick, Elke Sommer, James Stewart and Peter Ustinov.

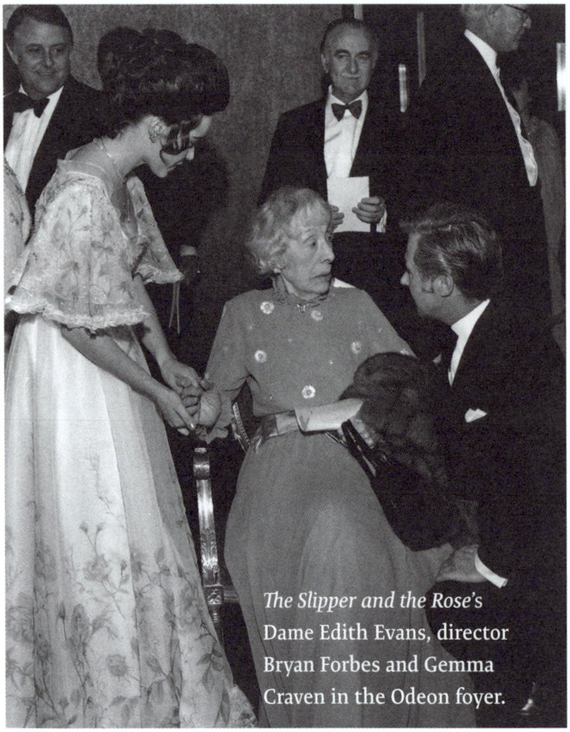

The Slipper and the Rose's Dame Edith Evans, director Bryan Forbes and Gemma Craven in the Odeon foyer.

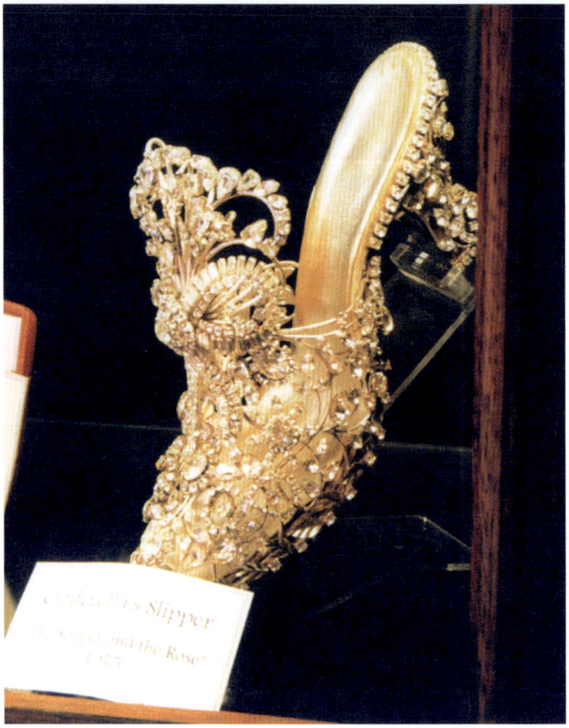

The glass slipper was on display at Pinewood Studios for many decades after filming.

1976 *The Slipper and the Rose*

This musical retelling of the classic fairy tale 'Cinderella' was brought to the screen by actor/director Bryan Forbes. As a friend of the royals, during production the Queen Mother and Princess Margaret visited the set to watch one of the musical numbers being filmed. Afterwards, they joined the main cast for lunch. Playing the prince, Richard Chamberlain was in full costume, knee breeches and long stockings. Beguiled by the Queen Mother, Forbes later told the actor that she thought he had great legs. 'That remains my favourite compliment ever,' Chamberlain wrote in his autobiography.

How fitting, then, that it was the Queen Mother, accompanied by Princess Alexandra, who attended the Royal Film Performance of *The Slipper and the Rose*, arriving swathed in furs and wearing a glittering gown. Presented once again to Richard Chamberlain, the Queen Mother also met the other stars of the film, Gemma Craven, chosen from over 800 other girls considered for the part of Cinderella; Annette Crosbie, who had just portrayed Queen Victoria in a television drama; and Dame Edith Evans. Other stars included Ronnie Barker, Candy Clark, Susan George, David Hemmings and Nanette Newman. In the foyer hosting the television coverage were Judith Chalmers and Chris Kelly.

Before entering the auditorium, the Queen Mother was handed a bouquet by Emma Forbes, the 10-year-old daughter of Bryan Forbes and Nanette Newman. Earlier that day, she had fallen off a pony and Nanette stood by

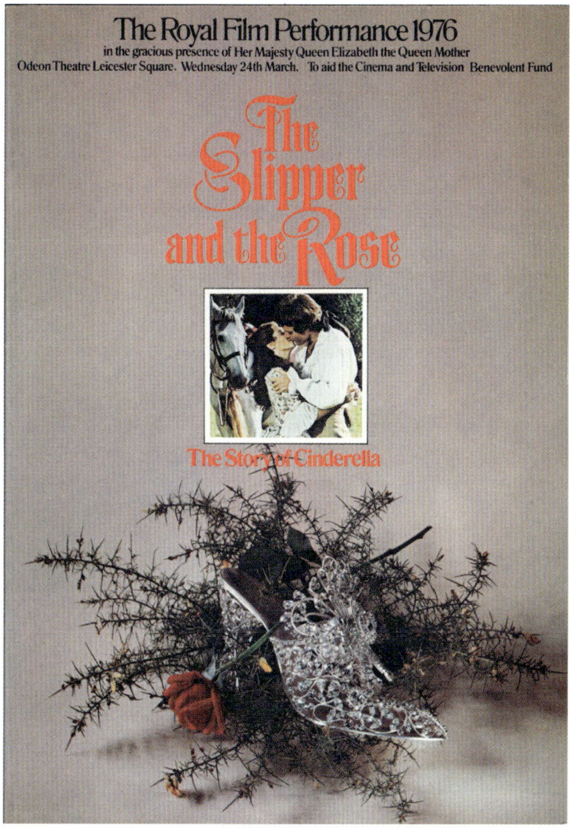

with an eye patch just in case she sprouted a black eye.

The old-fashioned nature of the film certainly appealed to the Queen Mother. The songs had been written by the brothers Richard M. and Robert B. Sherman, who were famous for their collaboration on numerous Disney pictures, including *Mary Poppins*. When the Queen Mother left the cinema, she commended the musicians on an excellent score, commenting that the waltz they wrote for the ballroom scene was the most beautiful song she had ever heard.

1977 *Silver Streak*

In this, the Queen's Silver Jubilee year, the picture chosen for the Royal Film Performance was, suitably enough, *Silver Streak*, a romantic comedy thriller that saw the very first pairing of what became one of cinema's greatest comedy double acts, Gene Wilder and Richard Pryor. The pair reteamed a further three times. Wilder couldn't make the premiere due to filming commitments in the United States, but Pryor attended and was presented to Queen Elizabeth the Queen Mother, Princess Margaret and Princess Alexandra.

In the film Wilder played a meek book publisher who stumbles onto a murder plot on a cross-country train journey and meets a mysterious woman, played by Jill Clayburgh. Pryor plays an escaped thief, a role that was originally much smaller but was enlarged by the studio when it became clear that he was stealing the film.

Silver Streak was a big box-office hit and made Pryor, formerly known largely for his stand-up act, into a mainstream star. The film is famous for its brilliantly staged train crash climax at the Chicago railway terminal, which was filmed in an aircraft hangar in Burbank using a full-sized mock-up of a locomotive.

The film is problematic today for the scene where Pryor makes up Wilder to look like a black man to evade the police by using shoe polish and a floppy hat. It's uncomfortable to

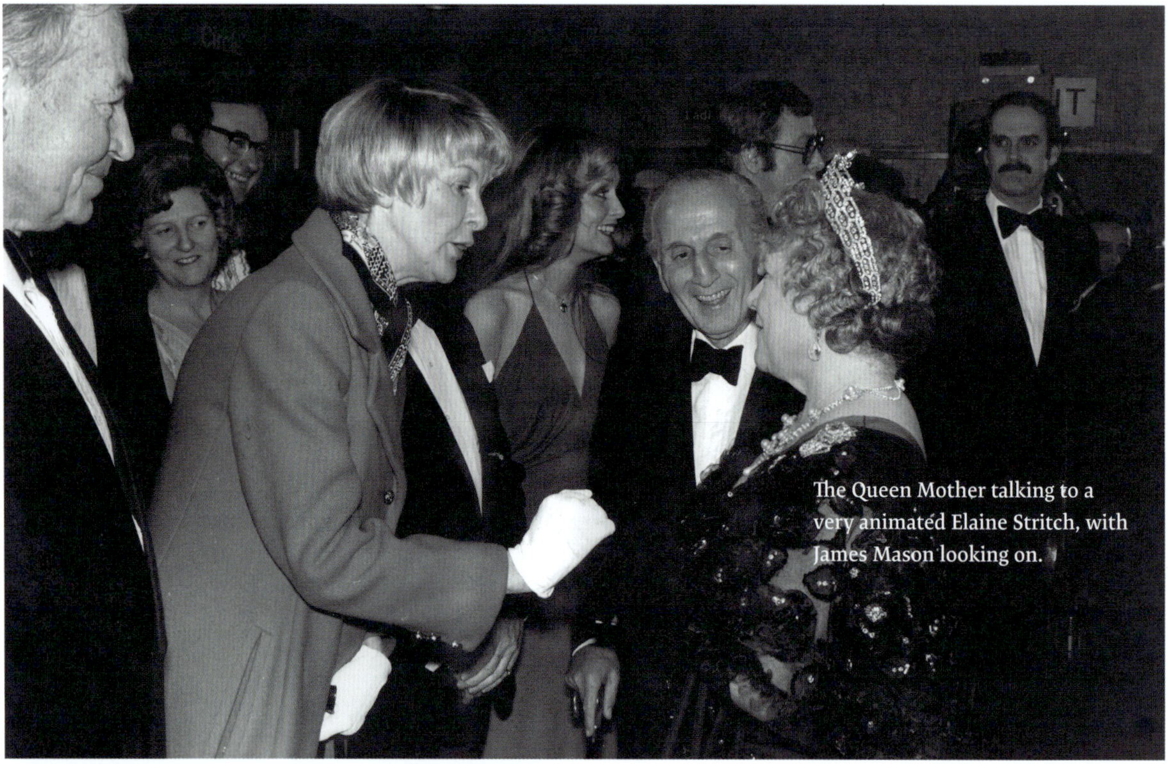

The Queen Mother talking to a very animated Elaine Stritch, with James Mason looking on.

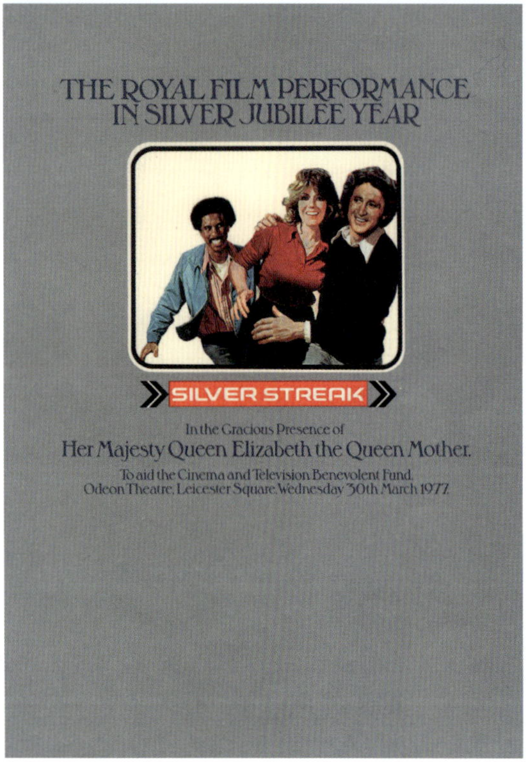

THE ROYAL FILM PERFORMANCE IN SILVER JUBILEE YEAR

SILVER STREAK

In the Gracious Presence of

Her Majesty Queen Elizabeth the Queen Mother.

To aid the Cinema and Television Benevolent Fund.

Odeon Theatre, Leicester Square. Wednesday 30th March 1977.

watch and, at the time, uncomfortable for the actors to play. In the film, Wilder doesn't think anyone will buy the disguise. Pryor reassures him, 'Al Jolson made a million dollars doing that shit.'

Along with Pryor, the line-up consisted of Michael Caine, James Mason, Kenneth More,

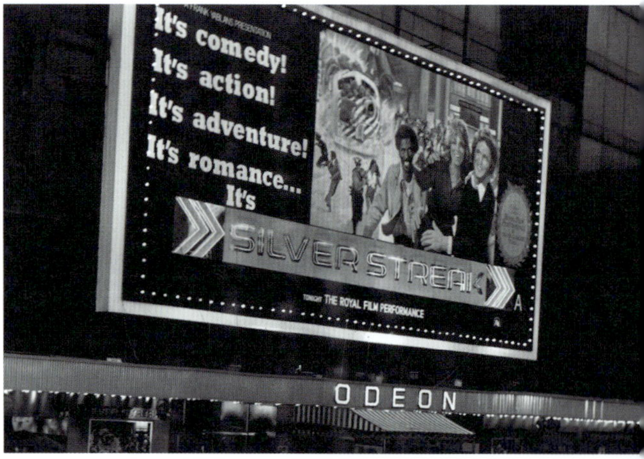

Roger Moore, Susan Penhaligon, Gareth Hunt and Joanna Lumley, then the stars of TV's *The New Avengers*. Roger Moore recalled in his memoirs standing close to Broadway veteran Elaine Stritch, who was getting very excited about the arrival of the royal party, 'This is so thrilling. Oh my God!' And each announcement of how close the Queen Mother was would set her off again. 'As Her Majesty started climbing the stairs,' wrote Moore, 'I thought Stritch would quiet down. Oh no! Suddenly there was a screech. "Oh my God! Look at that coronet. Oh my God. Look at that darling hairdo. Oh, what a darling dress. Isn't she a darling."'

Standing right next to her was James Mason, who tried to shush her, with no effect. Out of the corner of his mouth, Mason asked Moore if he could have a try. 'I can't,' said Moore. 'You tell her.'

Finally, the Queen Mother was face to face with Stritch. The actress clasped her hands with both of hers. 'You are a darling. You really are a darling.' The Queen Mother looked a trifle bemused, even more so when Stritch announced that she had a song in the presentation, and she was going to sing it to Her Majesty there and then. 'She started singing this damn song,' recalled Moore. 'And the Queen Mother was trying very hard to pull her hand away. Oh, the embarrassment.'

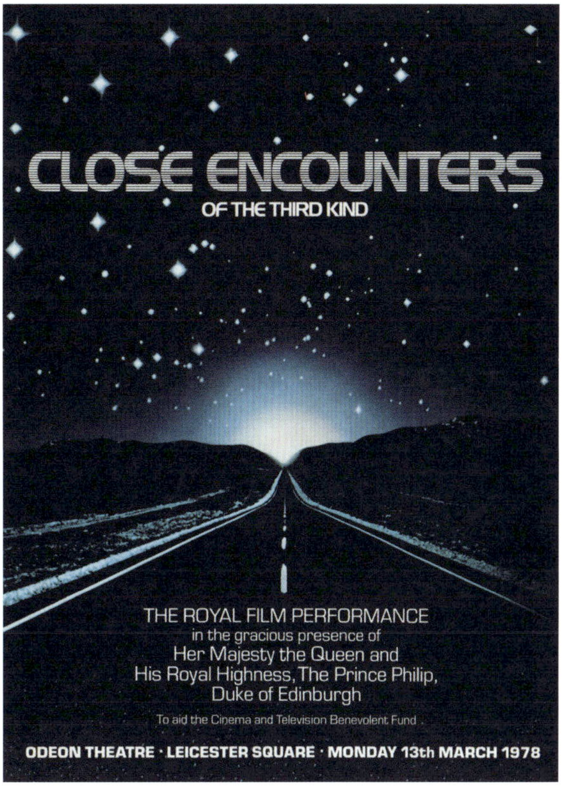

1978 *Close Encounters of the Third Kind*

Steven Spielberg's groundbreaking science-fiction drama was the film everyone was talking about in 1978. Already a smash hit in the United States, Spielberg brought to London many of the film's key creative talents – effects maestro Douglas Trumbull, composer John Williams and cast members Richard Dreyfuss, François Truffaut and 5-year-old Cary Guffey, who presented a bouquet to the Queen, telling reporters afterwards that meeting the Queen had been more exciting than making the movie.

It turned into a busy visit for Spielberg. A few days after the Royal Film Performance, he stepped on the stage at the National Film Theatre to inaugurate a short season of his work. He also spent a day with one of his film

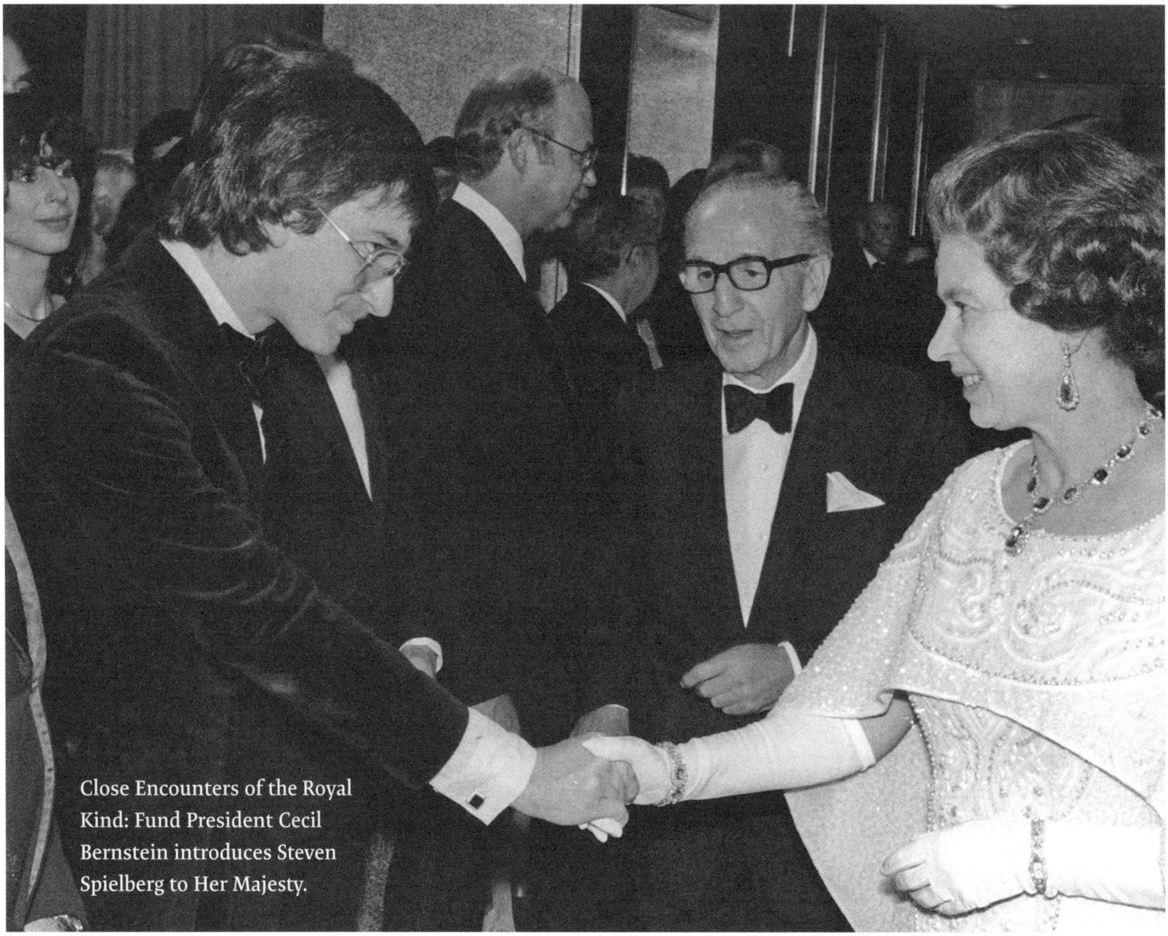

Close Encounters of the Royal Kind: Fund President Cecil Bernstein introduces Steven Spielberg to Her Majesty.

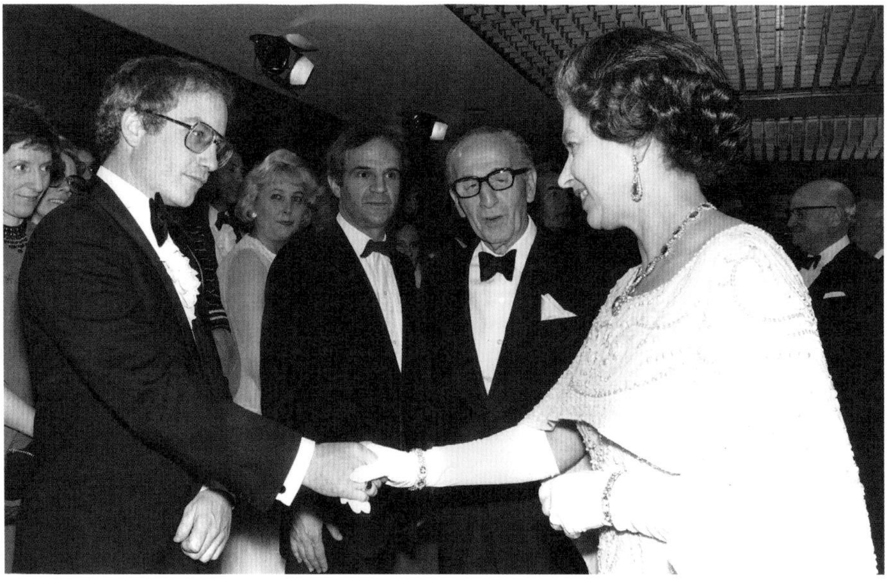

The Queen greeting Richard Dreyfuss, the star of *Close Encounters*.

heroes, Stanley Kubrick, who was prepping *The Shining* at Elstree Studios. Spielberg admitted that the main reason for coming to London was to meet Kubrick rather than Her Majesty.

Close Encounters grew out of Spielberg's fascination for UFOs, which began when he was a child at elementary school. He had planned to ask the Queen whether she believed in UFOs herself but admitted later that he froze when the monarch reached him in the line-up.

Richard Dreyfuss, staying at the Dorchester, found himself met by the hotel staff and measured for a suit resplendent enough to meet the Queen. He was then visited in his suite by someone from Buckingham Palace to go through the do's and don'ts about meeting royalty – namely, never to turn your back on the Queen, never speak before she does (unless you're Barbra Streisand) and on presentation to the Queen, the correct formal address is 'Your Majesty' and subsequently 'Ma'am', pronounced with a short 'a', as in 'jam'.

Once again, Chris Kelly and Judith Chalmers did the honours interviewing the stars in the foyer of the Odeon, Leicester Square, for television. Spielberg revealed his hopes to make a sequel to *Close Encounters*, one not necessarily set in space, although this never in fact materialised. Other stars attending that evening included Jenny Agutter; Shirley Bassey, who confessed to being a big sci-fi fan; Dyan Cannon; Harrison Ford; James Mason; Michael Parkinson; and Katharine Ross.

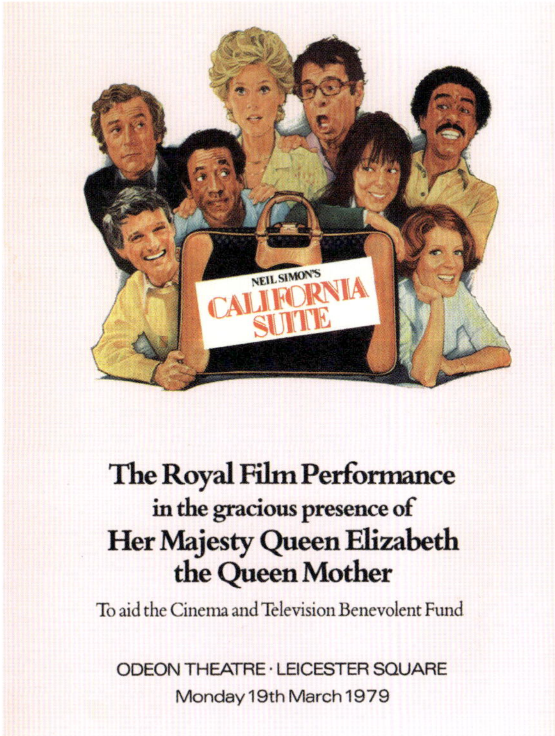

1979 *California Suite*

The name of playwright Neil Simon was synonymous with Broadway comedy and commercial success in the theatre for many years. Most of his plays were translated successfully into movies, and *California Suite* was one of his most popular.

Like his previous play *Plaza Suite*, which comprised three stories involving different characters all staying at the same New York hotel, *California Suite* featured a collection of different couples staying at the famous Beverly Hills Hotel. Jane Fonda plays a magazine editor duelling with her ex, played by Alan Alda; Bill Cosby and Richard Pryor are competitive doctors holidaying with their wives; Walter Matthau is a married man lumbered by his brother with a prostitute in his room; and, best of all, Maggie Smith is a waspish, yet

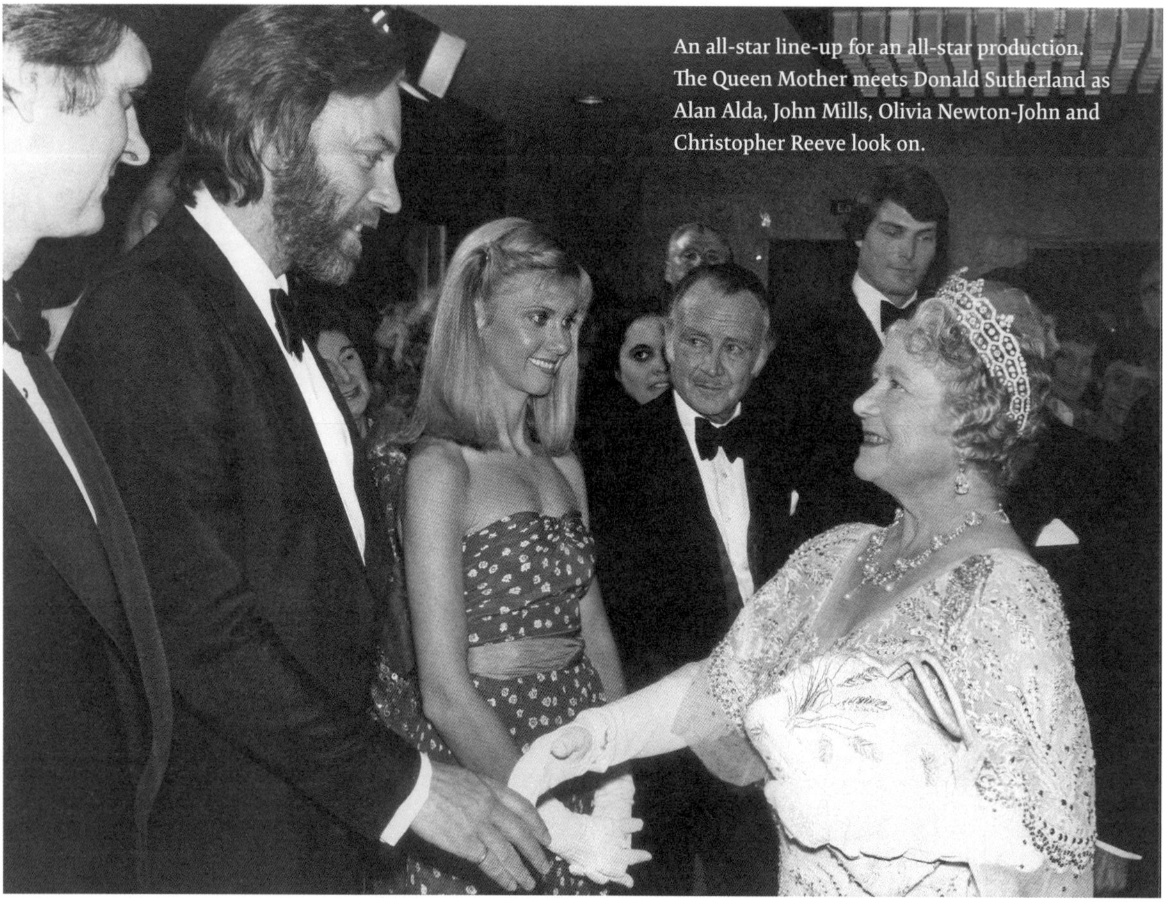

An all-star line-up for an all-star production. The Queen Mother meets Donald Sutherland as Alan Alda, John Mills, Olivia Newton-John and Christopher Reeve look on.

vulnerable actress in town for the Oscars with her homosexual husband, played by Michael Caine. Ironically, in the film, Maggie Smith's character loses out on the Oscar, while in real life the actress won hers. Although uneven, the star power of the players makes *California Suite* just about work.

Neil Simon flew to London for the Royal Film Performance along with his wife, Marsha Mason, and star, Alan Alda. Maggie Smith also attended. They were presented to the Queen Mother; Princess Margaret, sporting a suntan after a holiday in the Caribbean; Princess Anne; and Captain Mark Phillips. Other stars in the line-up were Anthony Andrews, Olivia Newton-John, John Mills, Ian Ogilvy, Christopher Reeve, Donald Sutherland and Michael York.

This year, the cinematographer and producer Sydney Samuelson took over the duties of organising the stage presentation from Vivian Cox, which he was to do for the next five years. Samuelson had long been an avid supporter and member of the charity and a fervent fundraiser. He was the brains behind the successful 'Filmharmonic' concerts between 1970 and 1980 and became president of the CTBF in 1983. For his first show, Samuelson organised a special stage and screen presentation to commemorate the Queen Mother's seventeenth attendance at a Royal Film Performance.

1980 *Kramer vs. Kramer*

As happened in 1978 with *Close Encounters of the Third Kind*, the charity managed to choose a film that was currently one of the most talked about movies of the year and had recently picked up nine Academy Award nominations. *Kramer vs. Kramer* would win five, including Best Picture and Oscars for Dustin Hoffman and Meryl Streep. They play a divorced couple fighting for the custody of their child. The film won plaudits for the adult way it dramatised a difficult situation and for not picking a side. It also addressed a cultural shift in the traditional roles of motherhood and fatherhood.

Streep and Hoffman both flew to London for the event, but it was 8-year-old Justin Henry, who played their son in the film, who captured the headlines. In the line-up, the Queen asked if this was his first acting job. He said it was. She then asked if he thought the movie would make her cry. 'You might,' he said. 'It made my mom cry four times.' It was a response that made the Queen laugh. The young actor almost didn't make it. Arriving in London, he was told he had tonsillitis, but after treatment was well enough to attend the performance.

This wasn't the first Royal Film Performance for Hoffman. He recalled being in the line-up back in 1971 for *Love Story* and was presented to the Queen Mother. At the time, he observed how someone at the Queen Mother's side informed her about the person she was about to be introduced to. It seemed a lot of effort, and so when the Queen Mother got to Hoffman, the actor said that she didn't have to talk to him and that he could see she was tired. She insisted, however, on asking what he was doing in London. Stood nearby was Tony Curtis, so Hoffman said he was there to try and collect some money off the actor and that he had been chasing him all over the world. The Queen Mother looked bemused. 'I didn't get any laughs out of her.'

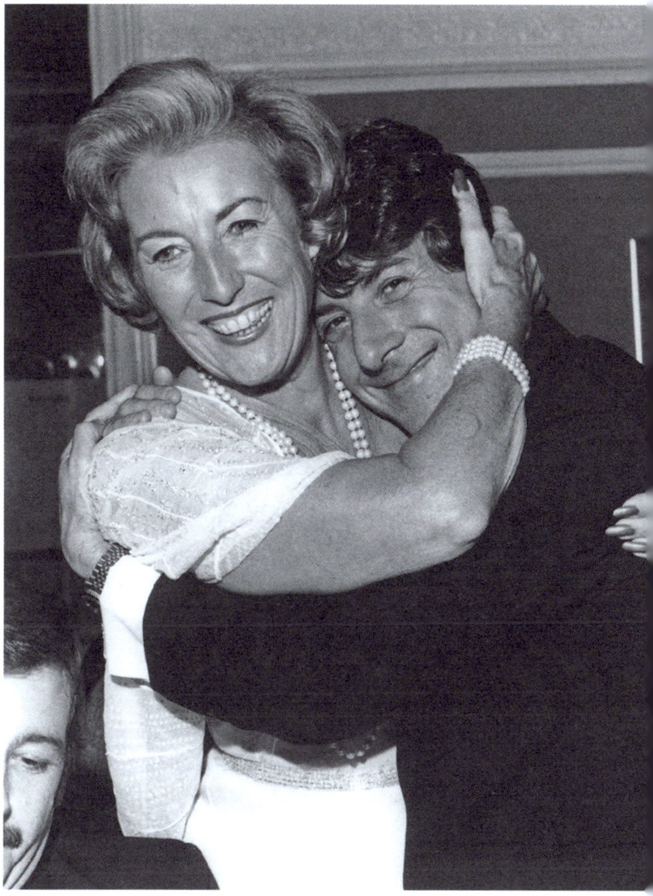

Dustin Hoffman warmly hugging Dame Vera Lynn at the *Kramer vs. Kramer* post premiere party, where Hoffman played the drums at The White Elephant.

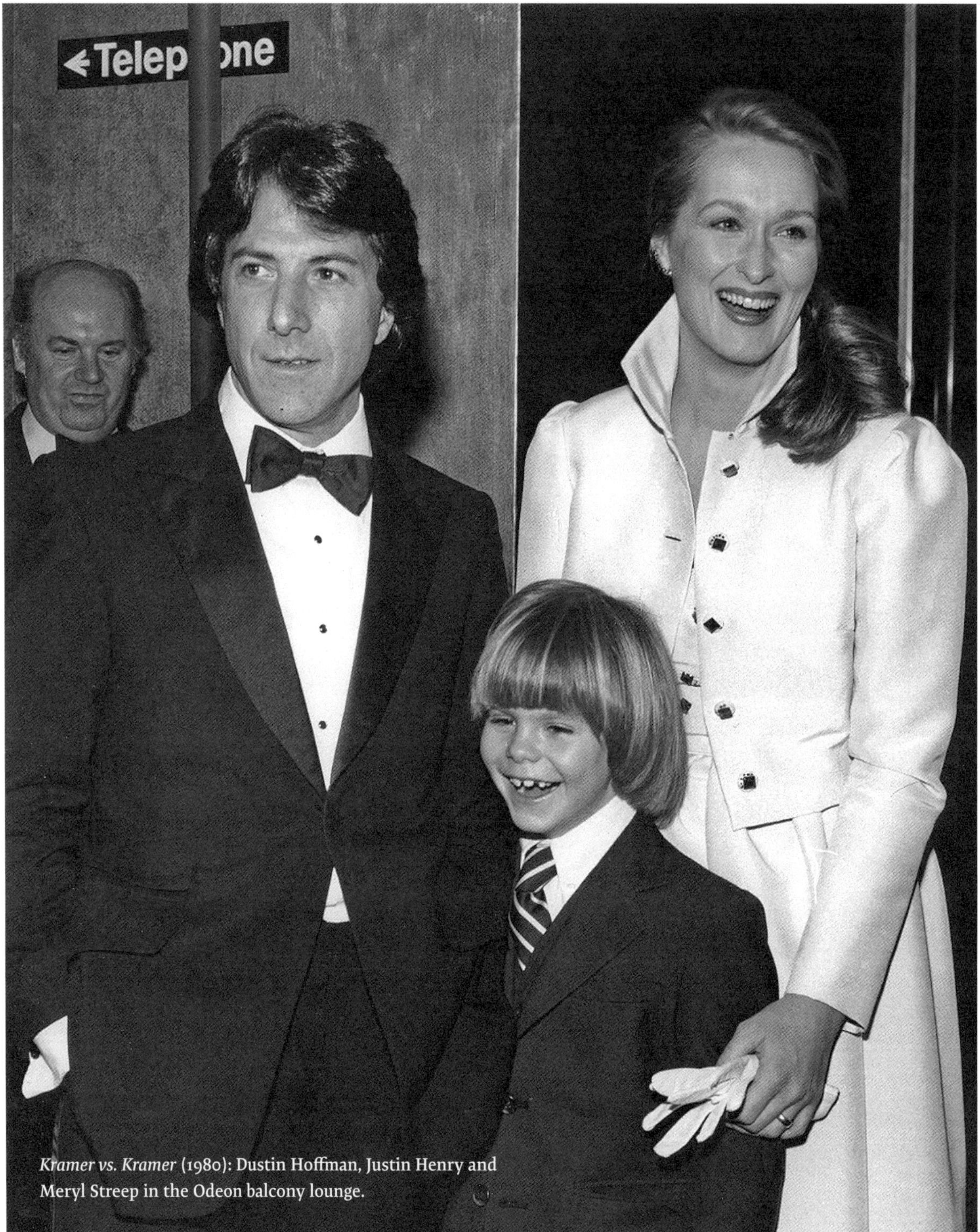

Kramer vs. Kramer (1980): Dustin Hoffman, Justin Henry and Meryl Streep in the Odeon balcony lounge.

Other stars attending included Dirk Bogarde, Stewart Granger, Penelope Keith, Deborah Kerr, Jessie Matthews, Peter Sellers and Liv Ullmann. Prior to the film, there was a screen presentation produced by Sydney Samuelson and introduced by David Jacobs. The theme was British musicals and at one point there was a clip of a wartime film with Vera Lynn in her uniform singing to the troops. As it went into the second chorus, Dame Vera Lynn herself walked on the stage, singing live and accompanied by the orchestra. It was quite a moment.

1981 *Chariots of Fire*

This royal screening turned out to be the start of an incredible journey for producer David Puttnam's much-loved film. It went on to win the Oscar for Best Picture, launched several careers, including Nigel Havers', and aided the rejuvenation of British cinema in the 1980s.

Once the film was in the can, David Puttnam mentioned to Nigel Havers that he hadn't properly been introduced to his father. Nigel organised a dinner at his home:

> David arrived with two bottles of Dom Pérignon, which I thought was very generous, but I couldn't work out really why he wanted to see mum and dad. And then during dinner I heard him say to my father, 'I think you know the man who chooses the Royal Film Performance.' Because my father was then in government. He was Attorney General. And my dad said, 'Do you know something, I think I do.' And David said, 'I wonder if you could do me a favour and put in a word for our film.' And dad said, 'I think I should do that. Absolutely.' And dad did put in a word. That goes to show how clever David Puttnam is. And, of course, my father would do anything to support the film, his son was in it.

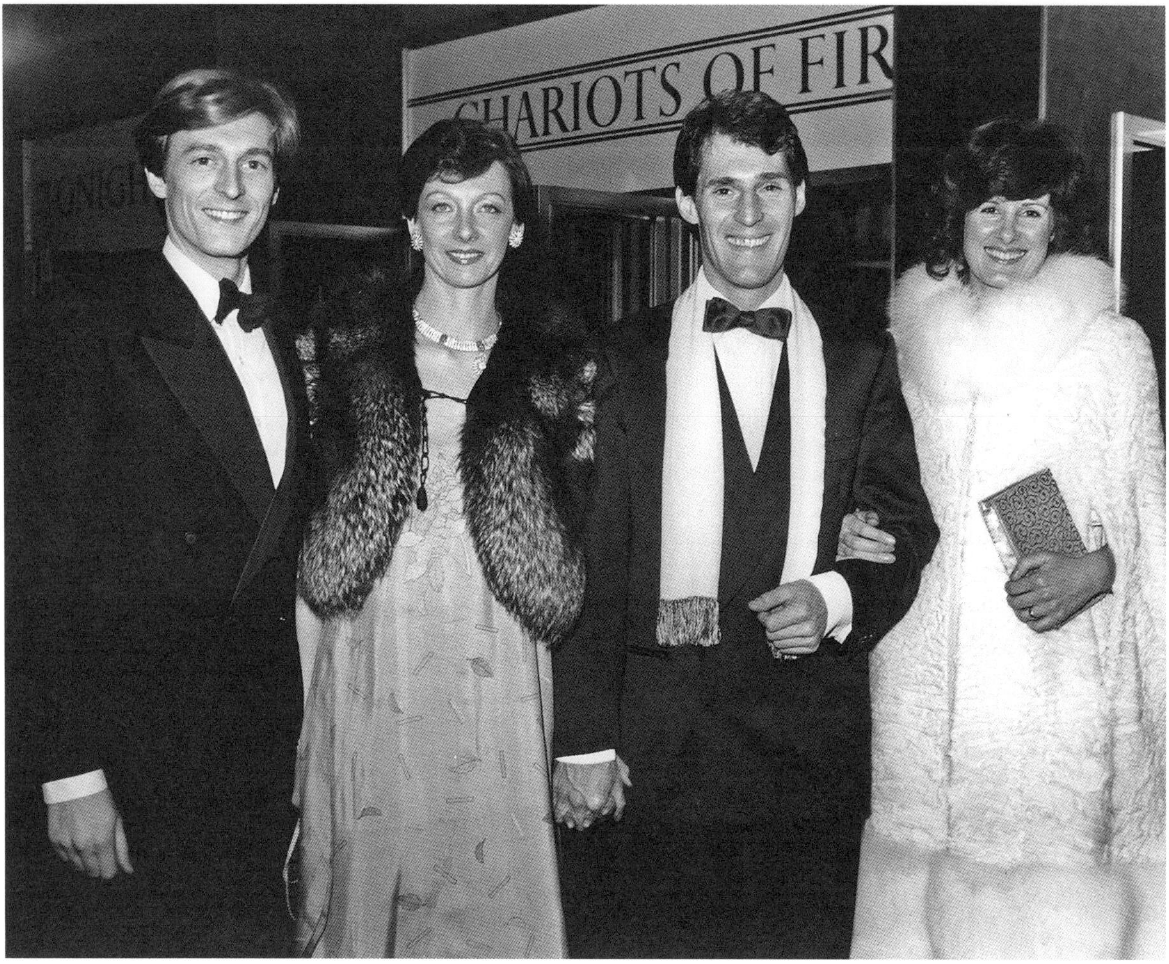

Chariots of Fire (1981): Stars Nigel Havers and Ben Cross arrive with their wives. The Queen Mother asked Havers, 'Do you have double glazing?', leaving him somewhat lost for words.

The consequence of being chosen as the Royal Film was felt immediately. 'Our distributors, 20th Century Fox, suddenly were prepared to spend some serious money on promotion,' recalls Lord Puttnam. 'And they printed a new poster. On all the posters on the London Underground we did promote heavily the fact it was the Royal Film.'

The evening itself was a memorable occasion and a deeply moving one for Puttnam. 'My mum and dad were there. My father died just a few months later. It was the first time he'd seen the film. He didn't live to see the BAFTA win or the Oscar win, so in that sense it was very special.' Nigel's parents attended, too. 'So, it was a big night for us all. And the whole audience cheered at the end. Amazing.'

In the line-up, Nigel was introduced to the Queen Mother, 'I might have mentioned to her the fact that she'd had a winner at Cheltenham, and I said, "You must have won a bob or two." And she looked at me and said, "I never gamble," and gave me a wink.'

David Puttnam sat next to the Queen Mother throughout the screening:

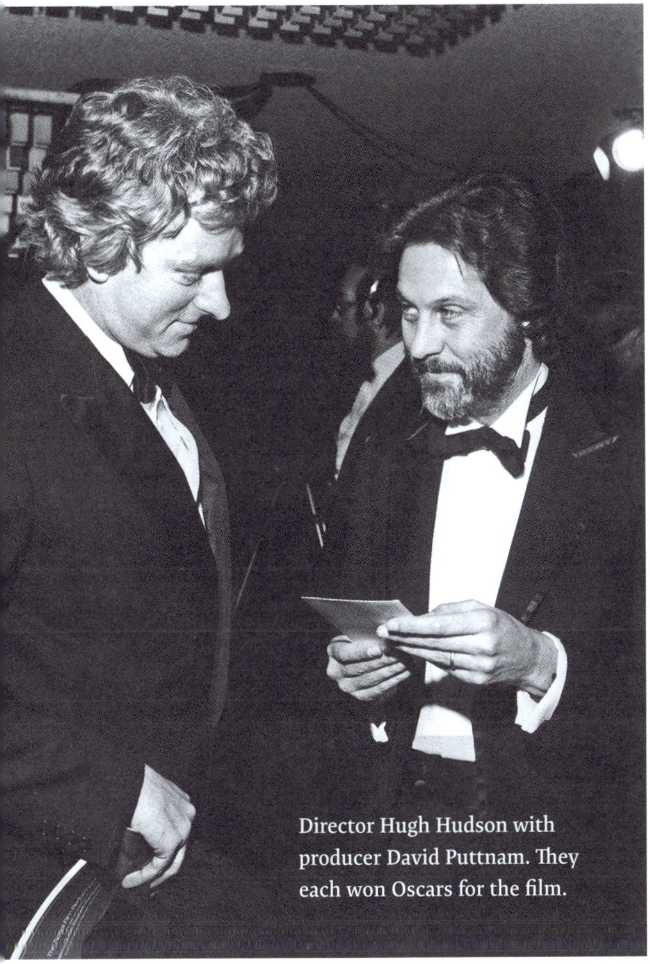

Director Hugh Hudson with producer David Puttnam. They each won Oscars for the film.

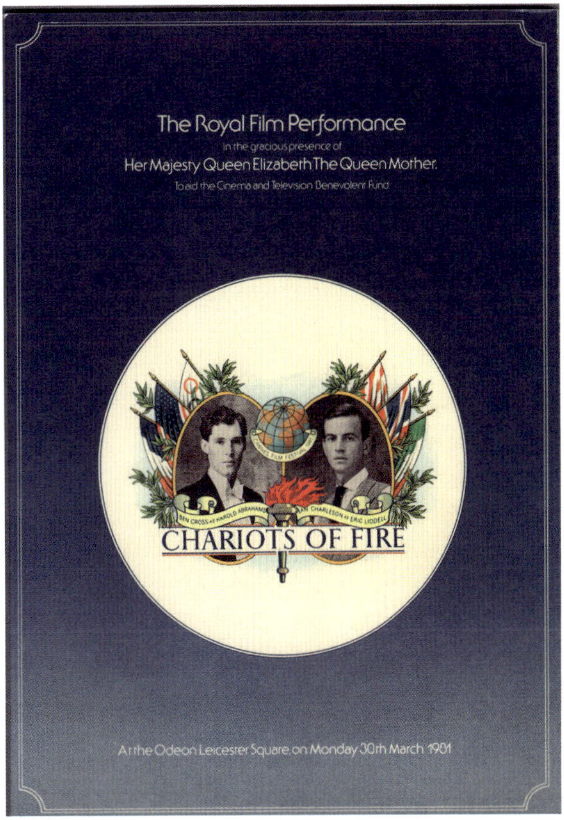

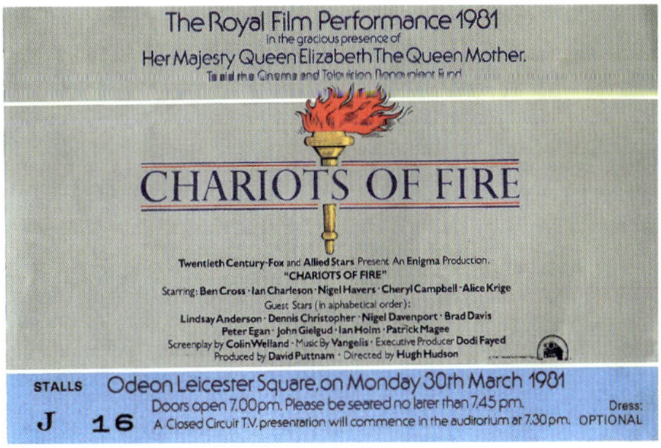

The Royal Film Performance 1981
in the gracious presence of
Her Majesty Queen Elizabeth The Queen Mother.
To aid the Cinema and Television Benevolent Fund

CHARIOTS OF FIRE

Twentieth Century-Fox and Allied Stars Present An Enigma Production.
"CHARIOTS OF FIRE"
Starring: Ben Cross · Ian Charleson · Nigel Havers · Cheryl Campbell · Alice Krige
Guest Stars (in alphabetical order):
Lindsay Anderson · Dennis Christopher · Nigel Davenport · Brad Davis
Peter Egan · John Gielgud · Ian Holm · Patrick Magee
Screenplay by Colin Welland · Music By Vangelis · Executive Producer Dodi Fayed
Produced by David Puttnam · Directed by Hugh Hudson

STALLS Odeon Leicester Square, on Monday 30th March 1981
Doors open 7.00pm. Please be seated no later than 7.45 pm.
J 16 A Closed Circuit T.V. presentation will commence in the auditorium at 7.30pm. Dress: OPTIONAL

> And the then Prince of Wales appears in the movie, and as his character was introduced into the film, she did this enormous kind of snort. Clearly, she'd never forgiven him and loathed him. It was a very audible and physical snort. That was quite funny.

Prior to the event, the Queen Mother was asked to select her three favourites from all the Royal Film Performances she had attended over the years, so the orchestra on the night could play a medley of music from them. She chose *The Prime of Miss Jean Brodie*, *Love Story* and *The Three Musketeers*. Barry Gray, composer of the *Thunderbirds* TV theme, was conductor and did the arrangement.

Following the success of *Chariots of Fire*, David Puttnam made the decision to allocate 5 per cent of the film's profits to the CTBF in perpetuity. This is also the case with some of his other films, such as *Local Hero*. Puttnam was always aware of the importance of those working behind the scenes, but this decision was taken due to a change he saw coming within the film business:

> When I came into the industry it was 90 per cent permanent staff and 10 per cent freelance. I saw that the industry was becoming a freelance industry. And because I'd been chairman of the union, I was very conscious of hardship and the insecurity of freelance work, so it was absolutely a natural choice to make.

It's a shame that most of Lord Puttnam's fellow filmmakers never followed his example.

1982 *Evil Under the Sun*

For some, the showing of the latest screen adaptation of a classic Agatha Christie mystery played second fiddle to a piece of cinema history. Film historian Kevin Brownlow had recently won kudos for restoring the classic 1927 silent film *Napoleon*. Someone thought it would be a good idea to start the screening off by showing the last twenty minutes of it, including the famous battle scene.

The battle sequence had been filmed in an early form of Cinerama and required three projectors. The Odeon, Leicester Square, did indeed have three projectors, but they weren't lined up. Dave Norris had recently been taken on as a trainee projectionist at the cinema. He ended up working there for twenty-five years. He and his fellow projectionists took a very scientific approach to the problem and simply kicked the projectors until they all synced up on the screen. A full orchestra was also going to play live, with Carl Davis conducting, who had written a new score for the film.

As usual, rehearsals took place on the morning before the performance. Everyone turned up, including the musicians. As Dave Norris recalls, 'Sydney Samuelson sent somebody over to the café across the road and they came back with something like 60 bacon rolls so everyone could have something to eat.' At the end of the battle sequence, someone had the idea of replicating the French flag on the

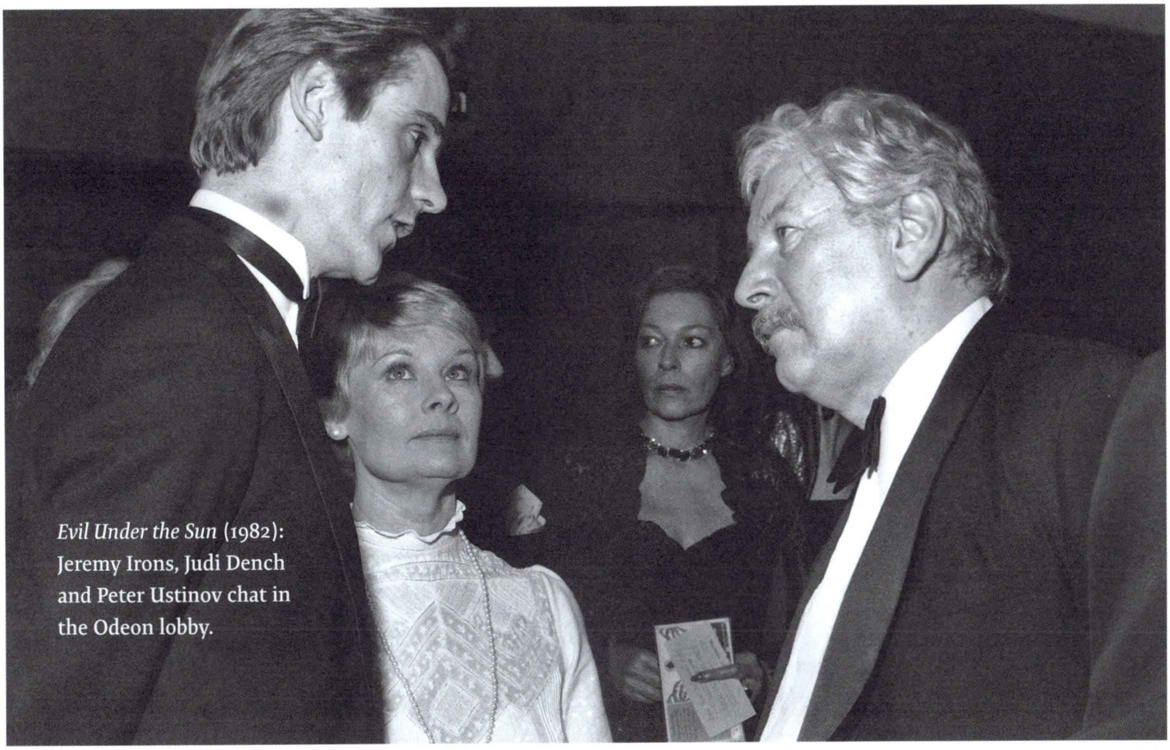

Evil Under the Sun (1982): Jeremy Irons, Judi Dench and Peter Ustinov chat in the Odeon lobby.

screen. Dave recalls how this was achieved from the projection booth:

> I ran the right-hand projector, so the guy on the left had to hold a blue gelatine up, the guy in the middle didn't have to do anything, and I had to hold the red up, so on the screen it did the blue, white and red of the French flag.

Very hi-tech.

Peter Ustinov, who played Poirot in *Evil Under the Sun*, was asked to introduce the *Napoleon* film. 'And the first time we did a test run of it, it was before the orchestra turned up,' recalls Dave:

> We started playing it and of course there was no music and when the battle started Ustinov got on the mic and was doing all

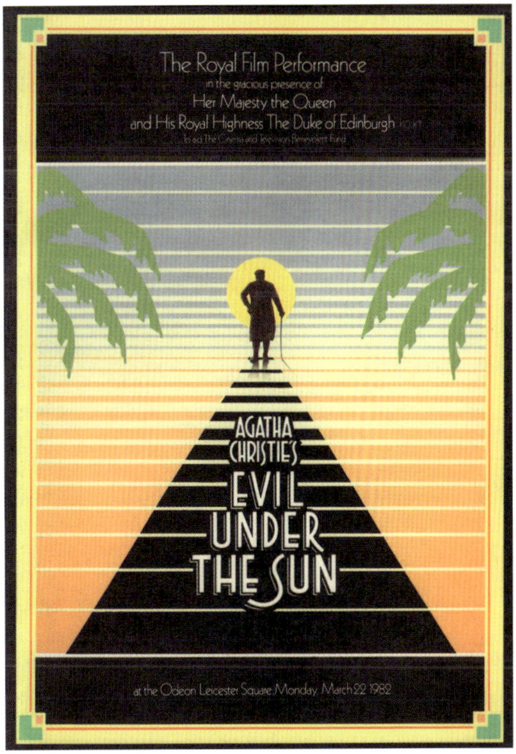

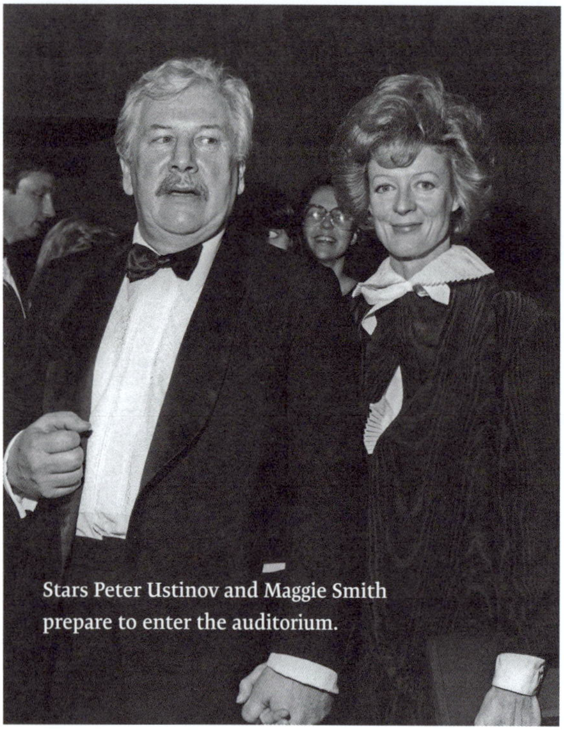

Stars Peter Ustinov and Maggie Smith prepare to enter the auditorium.

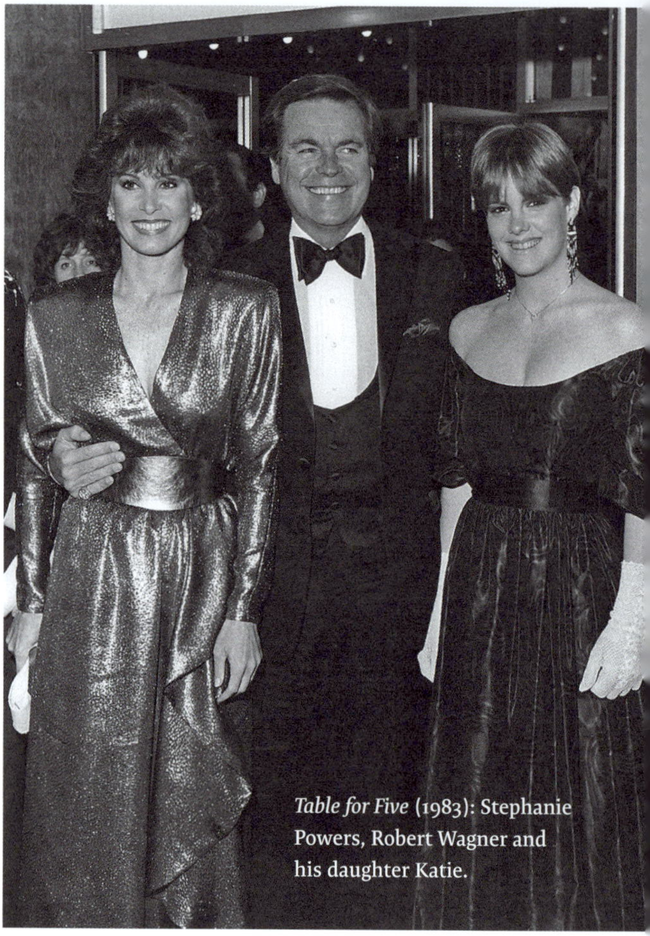

Table for Five (1983): Stephanie Powers, Robert Wagner and his daughter Katie.

> the sound effects, the trumpets, horses galloping, and cannons going off. He did this for about five minutes. He just carried on. It would have been better if he'd done that on the night.

Another complication was that once *Napoleon* was shown, the projectors had to be put back to their original position, all within five minutes, to present *Evil Under the Sun*. This was again achieved by Dave and his colleagues kicking the machines back to a chalk marking they'd made on the floor. It all worked, and the evening passed off successfully. The Queen and the Duke of Edinburgh were in attendance and met the stars of the film, including Peter Ustinov, Jane Birkin, Nicholas Clay, James Mason and Maggie Smith.

1983 *Table for Five*

One of the problems of finding the right film to show the royal guests was always the need to present not only something that was suitable, but something that was deemed to be suitable. There was nothing very controversial about *Table for Five* – nothing very interesting either, although its heart was in the right place. It traded on the success of *Kramer vs. Kramer*, the Royal Film just two years before, in that it dealt with issues of divorce and an absent parent, this time an errant father, played by Jon Voight, who takes his three children on an ocean voyage to close the gap that's grown between them. Voight claimed he did the film because he thought it was an important statement to make. 'It was made for an audience of people who had come from broken families,' he said. In one of his earliest screen roles, Kevin Costner appears briefly as a passenger aboard a cruise liner.

From the tradition of big weepies, the *Hollywood Reporter* warned, 'The Queen of England is in for a good cry. They are going to have to mop up the London Odeon afterwards.' In fact, it was the Queen Mother who attended, along with Princess Margaret. Jon Voight flew into London to make an appearance and was joined in the line-up to meet the royal party by the likes of Julie Walters, and Stephanie Powers and Robert Wagner, then the stars of the popular television drama series *Hart to Hart*. Wendy Craig gave the Loyal Address. The evening raised over £68,000 for the charity.

It was still tradition, one that eventually faded away, to have a Royal Box. The night before the Royal Film Performance, several regular seats were taken out of the Odeon Circle and gold-painted chairs were brought over from Buckingham Palace. The box was kept backstage and decorated with a red carpet and flowers. 'The old Queen Mum especially liked the box,' recalls projectionist Dave Norris:

> I remember we did a Royal premiere of *Champions* and the Queen mum came to that. She asked about the Royal box and was told, we only put that in for the Royal Film Performance. But the Queen mum insisted, so they had to put in the box, take the seats out and put them back in. And then a couple of weeks later they had to do it all again for the Royal Film Performance.

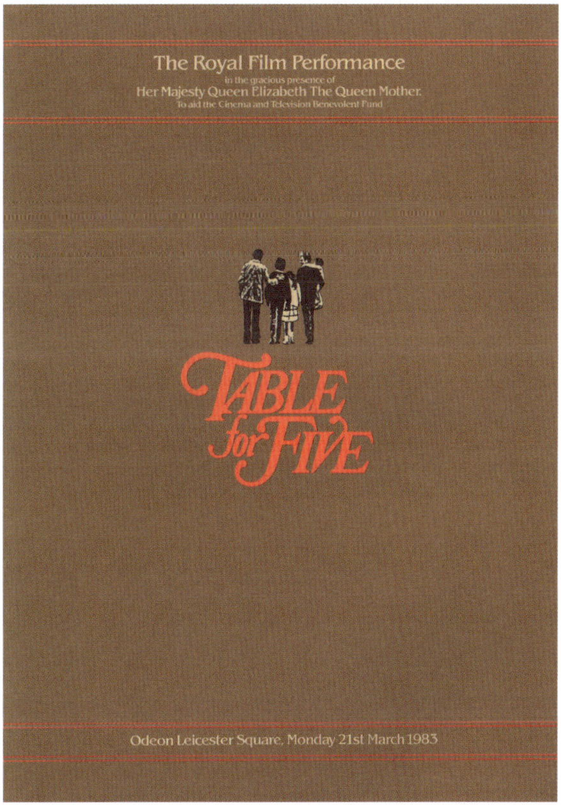

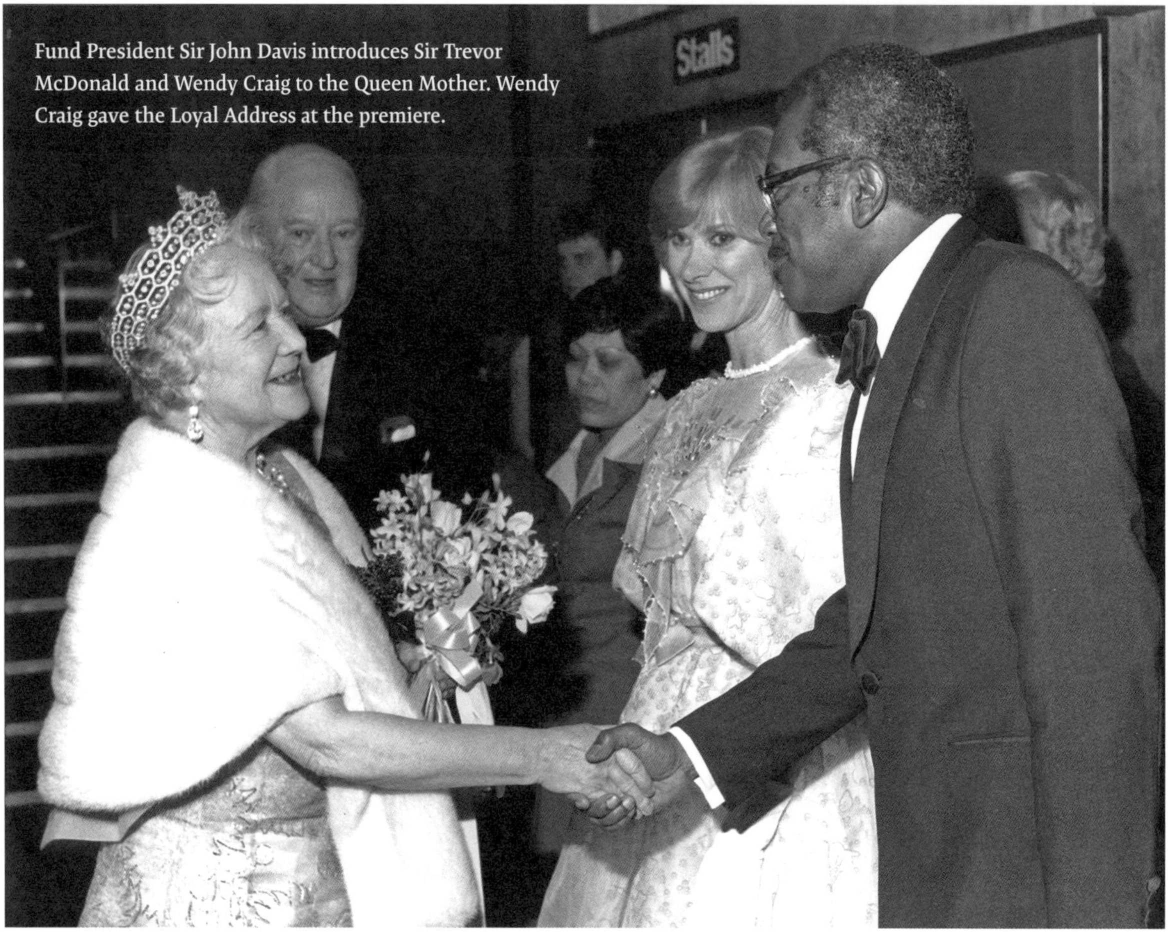
Fund President Sir John Davis introduces Sir Trevor McDonald and Wendy Craig to the Queen Mother. Wendy Craig gave the Loyal Address at the premiere.

Another tradition was several minutes of orchestral music played while the royal party was greeting the line-up of VIPs. President Sydney Samuelson suggested they ask the Queen Mother whether there was any item of music she would like. When he was told that he couldn't possibly ask such a question – 'It just isn't done!' – Samuelson took it upon himself to write to the Queen Mother, explaining that he was going to have the pleasure of escorting her that evening and whether there was any special piece of music she would like the orchestra to play.

Samuelson received a letter back with an emphatic 'yes'. Expecting something ceremonial, he was surprised when the request was for 'My Blue Heaven'. Stanley Black arranged a special version for the orchestra and when Samuelson presented the conductor to the Queen Mother, she said, 'I so much enjoyed My Blue Heaven because that song meant so much to me when King George and I were first married.'

1984 *The Dresser*

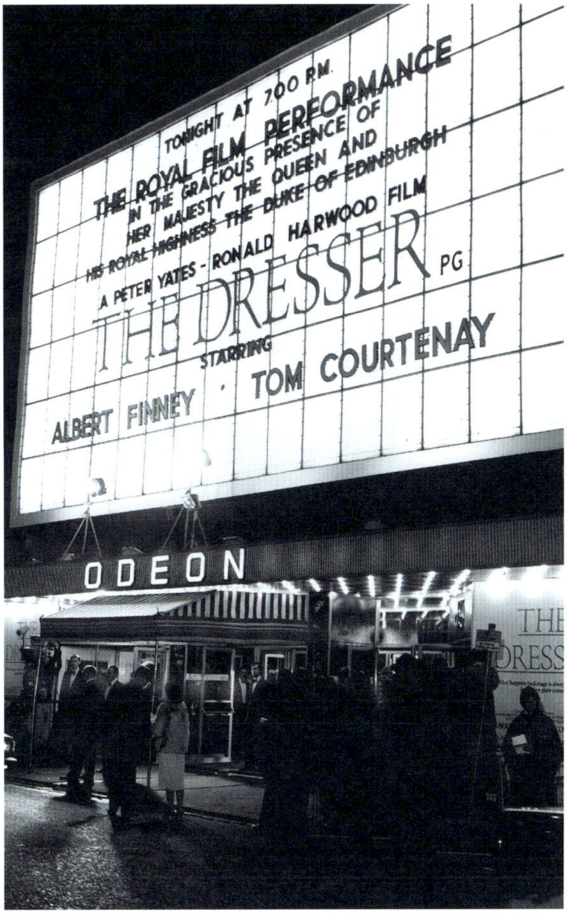

This year's Royal Film Performance featured a pair of tour de force performances from Albert Finney and Tom Courtenay, both of whom would earn Oscar nominations for Best Actor. Finney plays the tyrannical head of a touring Shakespearean theatre company in the days of the London Blitz. Courtenay played his devoted backstage assistant. Both actors graced the event and were introduced to the Queen and Prince Philip. Tom Courtenay recalls:

> I can remember the hordes of Hollywood celebs who had been flown in so that they could meet Her Majesty. They had absolutely nothing to do with the making of the film and would go on the publicity costs of the film thereby ensuring that it would never be in profit. I was standing between Edward Fox and Albert Finney when I bowed to Her Majesty and was horrified to see that my shoes looked very out of keeping beside the elegant evening pumps sported by Albert and Edward.

Her Majesty was also introduced to 86-year-old Dolly Curtis, who had been working as an usherette in London for seventy-two years. Dolly revealed that it was her intention to carry on with the job until she was 100 and then retire.

Prior to the screening of *The Dresser*, there was a short archival film from 1924, the year of the charity's foundation, introduced by Ben Kingsley and with a specially composed score by Stanley Black, who also conducted the orchestra. The Loyal Address was given by Gloria Hunniford. A print of *The Dresser* was also made available and shown on the same evening for the residents at Glebelands.

One of the traditions of the Royal Film Performance was that at the end of the line-up, a child, usually the son, daughter, niece or granddaughter of somebody at the charity, presented a bouquet to the royal lady. If Prince Philip or Prince Charles was also attending, they received a leatherbound copy of the

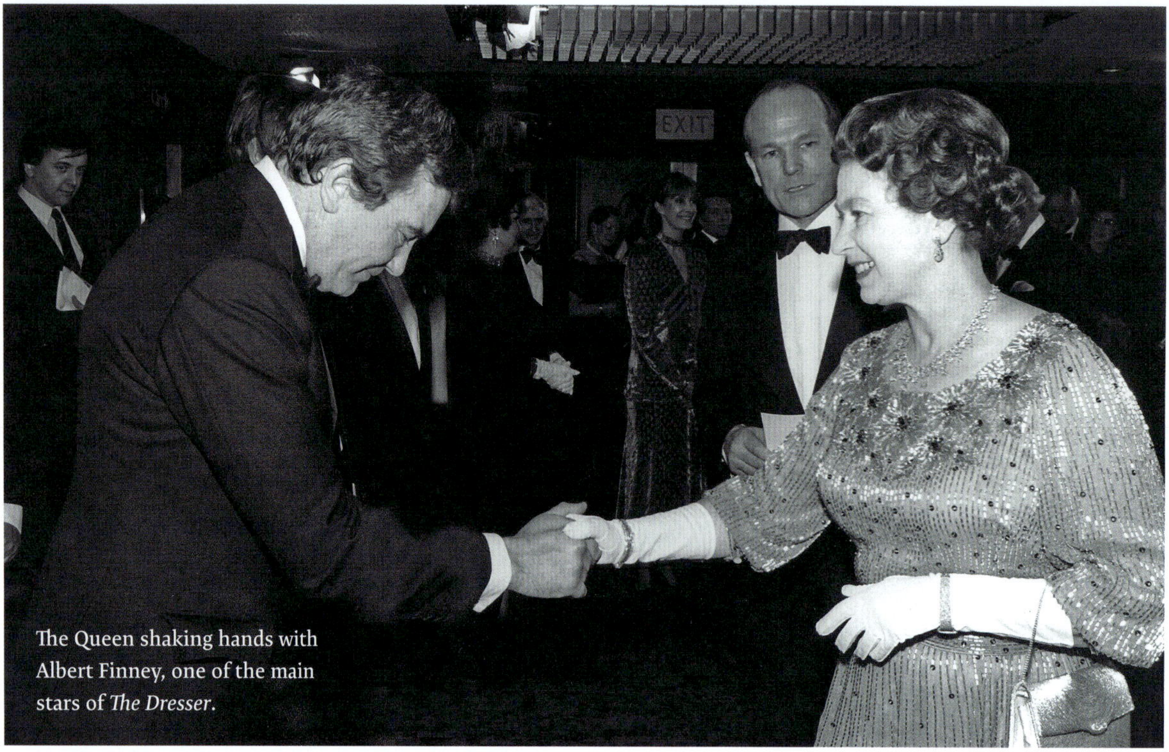

The Queen shaking hands with Albert Finney, one of the main stars of *The Dresser*.

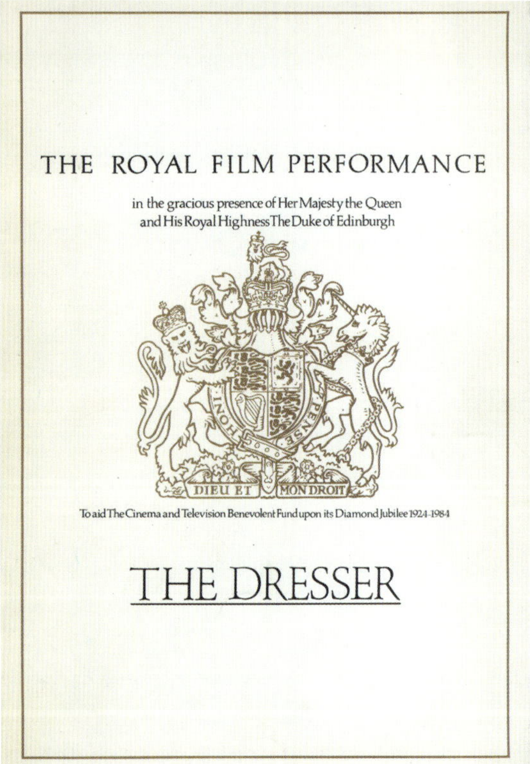

THE ROYAL FILM PERFORMANCE

in the gracious presence of Her Majesty the Queen and His Royal Highness The Duke of Edinburgh

DIEU ET MON DROIT

To aid The Cinema and Television Benevolent Fund upon its Diamond Jubilee 1924-1984

THE DRESSER

programme. This brochure, with all the advertising in it, was and remains one of the most important fundraising elements of the evening. Sydney Samuelson recalled an amusing conversation he had with Prince Philip regarding the brochure. 'I don't know how many of these you people have given to me,' the prince explained to Samuelson. 'But you are amazing because you go to all this expense and I sit down with it in the theatre and you put the lights out.'

Apparently, the Duke of Edinburgh enjoyed telling that same joke at most of the Royal Film Performances. Indeed, he was still grumbling about only getting to see the programme as the lights dimmed to charity president Peter Hore at the 2006 Royal Film, *Casino Royale*.

1985 *A Passage to India*

This year was declared to be British Film Year and its stated aim was to coerce more people to go to the cinema and to boost and promote British filmmaking. The charity certainly played its part, choosing the high-profile British film *A Passage to India* as that year's Royal Film Performance and sprinkling the evening with some high-wattage royalty, with the Queen Mother, the Prince and Princess of Wales, Princess Anne and Captain Mark Phillips all in attendance.

A Passage to India was certainly an event. It was the first film directed by master filmmaker David Lean since *Ryan's Daughter* in 1970. Nigel Havers numbered among the cast and on the first day of shooting confesses to have been extremely nervous, and he wasn't the only one, 'David Lean said to me, "How are you doing?" I said, "I didn't sleep very well." He said, "Nor did I. I didn't catch a wink."' Sadly, *A Passage to India* turned out to be Lean's final film.

Nigel got the part quite out of the blue:

> David rang me up and said, 'It's David Lean, would you like to be in a film,' and I said, 'Now, who's taking the piss here.' But it was David and he said, 'Are you free next week to have a chat about this part, see if you fancy it.' I knew the book. I did it for A level. And I met E.M. Forster because my English tutor took me to Cambridge to meet him. So, it was an extraordinary thing. I had tea with David and he said to me, 'I tend to cast my films with people I think I can have dinner with.' And we did have lots of dinners in India and I got to know him very well.

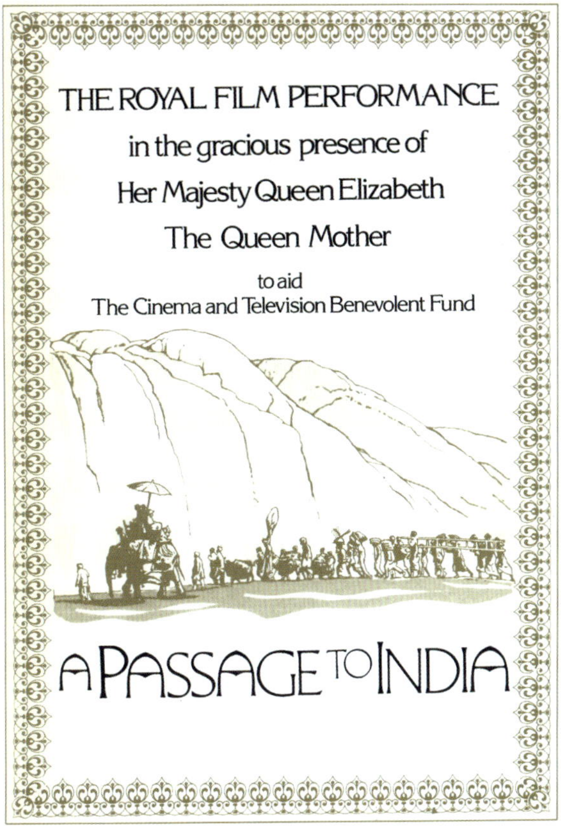

On his days off, Nigel asked Lean if he minded him coming to the set. Lean was fine with it, and Nigel sat behind the director observing for the best part of the shoot. 'I learnt everything from him.'

Lean had put together an excellent cast, which included Alec Guinness, Peggy Ashcroft, Judy Davis, James Fox and newcomer Victor Banerjee. When Peggy Ashcroft arrived in India, she said to Lean, 'We must have a read-through.' Lean looked bemused, 'What

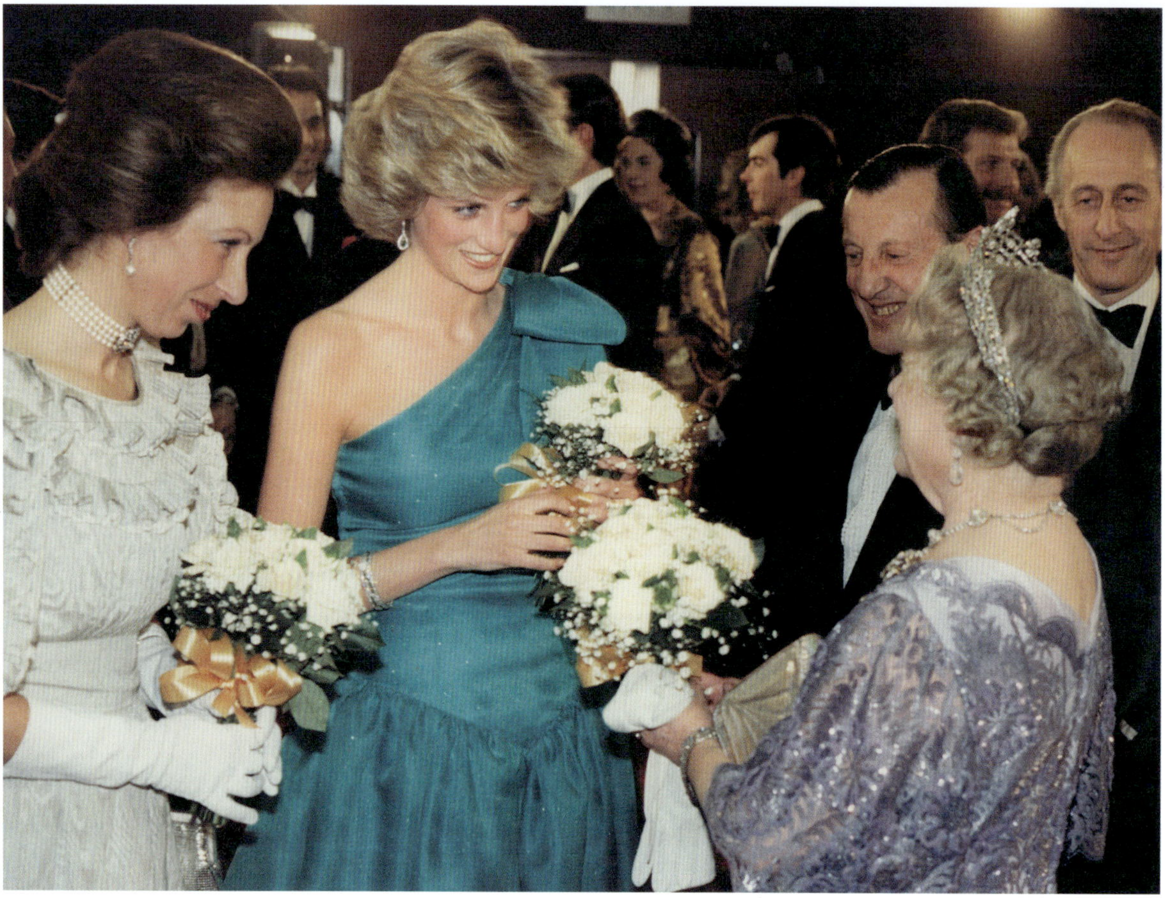

is a read through?' he asked. It was explained to him that it was when the whole cast read through the script together. 'Oh God,' he said, but acceded to Peggy's request. 'So, on the Sunday off we spent the day having a read through,' Nigel recalls, 'which was, as it turned out, fascinating because between each scene David said, 'Now in this scene the camera is here, such and such comes in, he walks here ...' He'd already shot the whole film in his head. I saw the whole film.'

Lean's perfectionism extended to doing what very few other directors did, and that was to attend the rehearsal for the Royal Film Performance the day before, when the film was run through to check the print was fine. 'He was sitting in the auditorium with us,' recalls projectionist Dave Norris. 'And he talked all the way through it. He was going, oh, you see that location, it was an awful place. I've always said that David Lean invented director's commentary something like 20 years before it was actually a thing because he sat and did it live.'

A Passage to India (1985): Princess Anne, Princess Diana and Lord Brabourne chat with the Queen Mother.

1986 ***White Nights***

This year marked the fortieth Royal Film Performance and Dame Peggy Ashcroft, celebrating sixty years in the business, gave the Loyal Address in which she congratulated the Queen on her forthcoming sixtieth birthday. The film chosen was *White Nights*, directed by Taylor Hackford, who had come to prominence with *An Officer and a Gentleman*. Hackford and his cast, including Mikhail Baryshnikov and Gregory Hines, flew over to London. 'And we were thrilled,' says Taylor:

> And it was an extraordinary experience for me because being American and not being part of the British culture, the idea of a King and Queen is a little anathema to our system. And so, yes, I thought it was terrific, that we were going to have this honour, but on the other hand I kind of went, this is just like meeting the President or something like that. And only as the process evolved did I realise how special it was.

Hackford was introduced to Prince Philip first and found him charming. But when it came to being presented to the Queen, the director found himself shocked by his reaction:

> She didn't have much to say, she was very kind, and offered her congratulations, and I thought, my goodness Taylor, you walked into this full of confidence and you were intimidated. It's funny because I started as a reporter covering politics, I've met a lot of important people, and to be intimidated to shake somebody's hand I found to be very unusual.

After the line-up, Taylor, Baryshnikov and Hines all compared notes. 'And we all spoke about the extraordinary intimidation factor,' says Taylor:

> She wasn't trying to intimidate me at all, she was perfectly nice. What was going on was a lot of gravitas and history. But I think it was the woman herself. It's not the reputation. It's how one wears it. How you carry it. And that's what I marvelled over, that she had this presence that was embodied in her being.

This was Taylor's first introduction to the royal family. His wife, Helen Mirren, of course, would go on to play the Queen to great acclaim and Taylor would proudly accompany her to her investiture at Buckingham Palace.

It was Taylor's idea to do a dance film, but one with a dramatic story, something that wasn't just an excuse for dance numbers. And it proved to be a winning idea to bring

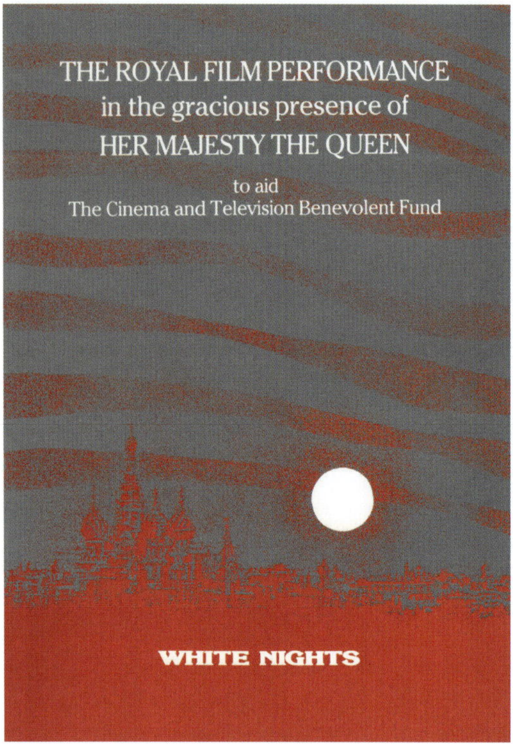

together two dancers who were the best of the era in their individual disciplines, Baryshnikov in ballet and Hines in tap, each of whom were enormous admirers of the other.

The launch of *White Nights* at the Royal Film Performance certainly helped it at the UK box office but there was a bonus waiting for Taylor as he prepared to fly back to the United States from Heathrow Airport:

> A person from British Airways came out and said, 'I saw you last night on the TV highlights of the Royal Film Performance and we're upgrading you from business class to first class, and we're putting you down in the British Airways files as a very important person.' That happens all the time for movie stars but for filmmakers that doesn't usually happen. And I was on that VIP list for many years after.

1987 *84 Charing Cross Road*

This charming film was based on a real-life transatlantic literary love affair that lasted twenty years between a feisty New Yorker, the writer Helene Hanff, and a mild-mannered antiquarian bookseller, Frank Doel. From his small bookshop on the famous London street, Doel posted out-of-print British classics to Helene across the Atlantic. The pair never met, and when Helene finally visited London in 1971, Doel had already passed away. Helene wrote about her experiences in an autobiographical book that was turned into a play and then the film, with Anthony Hopkins as Doel and Anne Bancroft as Helene.

It must have been a special moment for Helene Hanff to be present at the Royal Film Performance of *84 Charing Cross Road* and to be introduced to the Queen Mother and Prince and Princess of Wales. Anne Bancroft also attended, along with Judi Dench, who also appeared in the film. The line-up was boosted by other stars, including Jane Asher, Helena Bonham Carter, Joan Collins, George Peppard and Dennis Waterman. Sir John Gielgud gave the Loyal Address.

The presence of Princess Diana meant there was a larger than usual press contingent. 'I had never seen so many photographers outside the Odeon,' recalled the cinema manager, Chris Hilton. 'She was totally charming and always made full eye contact with anyone she was

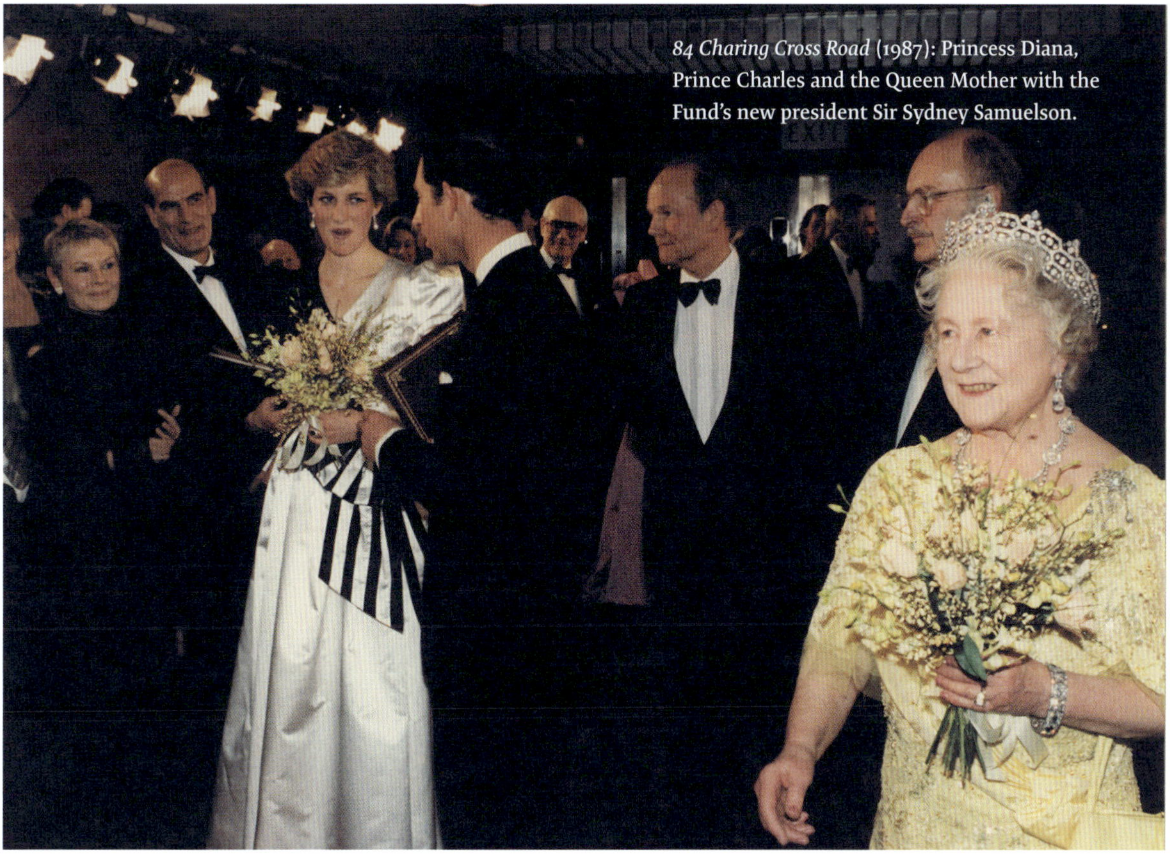

84 Charing Cross Road (1987): Princess Diana, Prince Charles and the Queen Mother with the Fund's new president Sir Sydney Samuelson.

speaking with – myself included – and had a very warm and natural personality.'

Sydney Samuelson, president of the CTBF, had the job of escorting Princess Diana to the Royal Circle. As usual, the royal party met film-industry people prior to being introduced to the stars. 'And if you're sensible, you know you've got that double flight of stairs to walk up with your royal guest, you've worked out something to say.'*

As they set off, Samuelson mentioned, 'I'm afraid the line-up is four people longer than we were expecting.'

'Oh, why's that?' asked Diana.

'Well, it's a funny reason but Columbia, whose film it is, has just been purchased by the Coca-Cola Company and would you believe it, four executives who know all about making fizzy drinks but not too much about cinema have found it essential that they come from Atlanta representing the Coca-Cola Company. So, I shall be introducing you to them.'

'Coca-Cola, that's disgusting,' said Diana. 'I won't even let my children drink it!'

'I don't think we'll say that to the four executives will we?'

Diana replied, 'Well, I suppose not.'

* Sydney Samuelson, quoted from his interview with the British Entertainment History Project, May 2002.

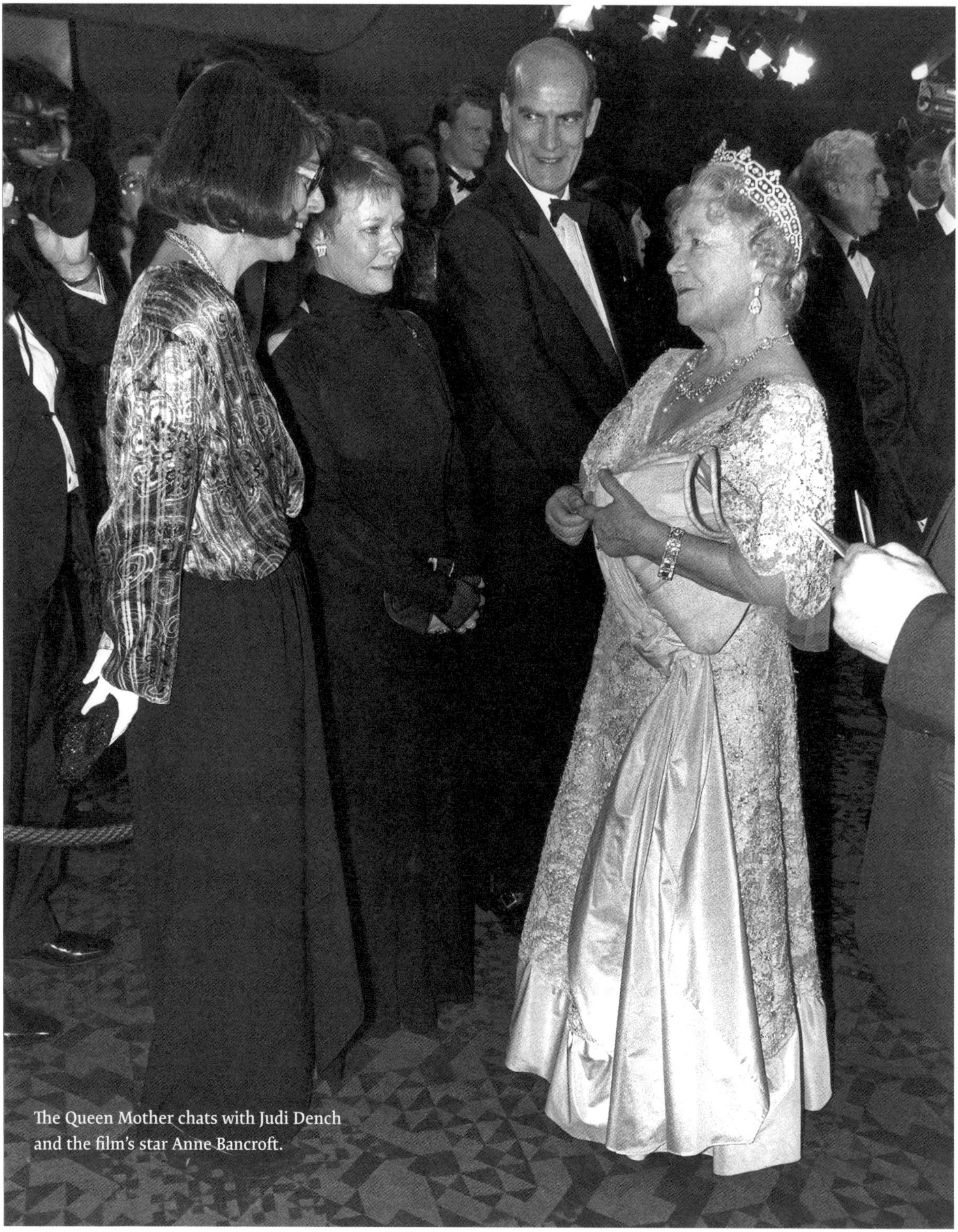

The Queen Mother chats with Judi Dench and the film's star Anne Bancroft.

1988 *Empire of the Sun*

Following the Royal Film Performance of *A Passage to India*, there was a celebration dinner at the Savoy Hotel. Nigel Havers recalls being sat at the same table as David Lean:

> And he was in very good form because he genuinely felt that everyone liked the film. And up came a man who whispered in his ear and then went away. And David said to me, 'Do you know who that was.'
>
> And I said, 'I know exactly who that was. That was Steven Spielberg.'
>
> David said, 'Yes. He's just said to me that he will produce any film I want to direct.'
>
> I said, 'Wow, have you got something?'
>
> He said, 'Yes I have.'
>
> I asked what it was.
>
> 'It's called *Empire of the Sun*.'

Nigel had read the J.G. Ballard novel, which was a semi-autobiographical story about the author's experiences growing up in China and of the Japanese occupation of Shanghai during the Second World War. It was obvious to him that Lean was very keen to make it but was having difficulty obtaining the rights. 'Eventually Steven Spielberg bought the rights,' recalls Nigel:

> … and said to David, 'I've got them.' And David said, 'You know, I've sort of gone off the idea of it.' And Steven said, 'Oh my God, it's cost me a fortune.' And David said, 'No, no, don't get upset because you should direct this film. It's absolutely what you should do. And I'll give you three key moments that you must have in the film.' And Steven used them. He was in awe of David Lean.

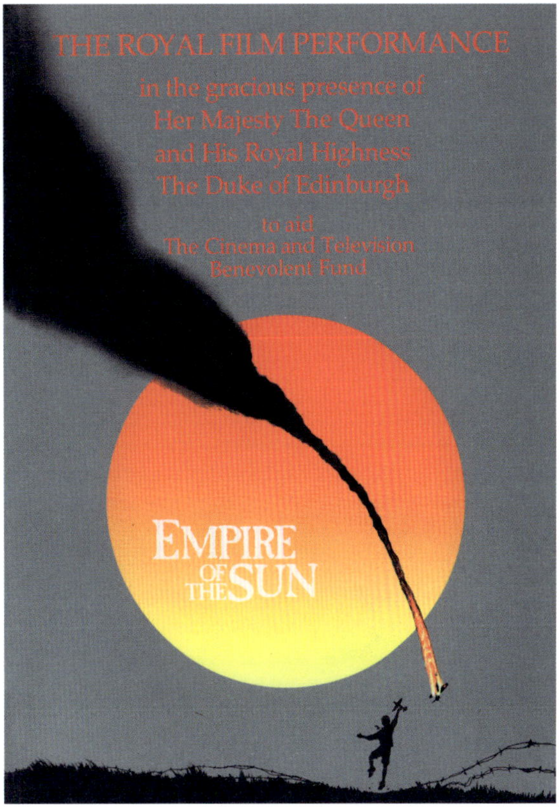

Nigel also landed a role in the film, playing a doctor in the internment camp operated by the Japanese army. He enjoyed working with Spielberg and with his young co-star Christian Bale, who he remembers as:

> … totally focused. At the party after the Royal Film Performance Christian sat there and everybody was being sweet to

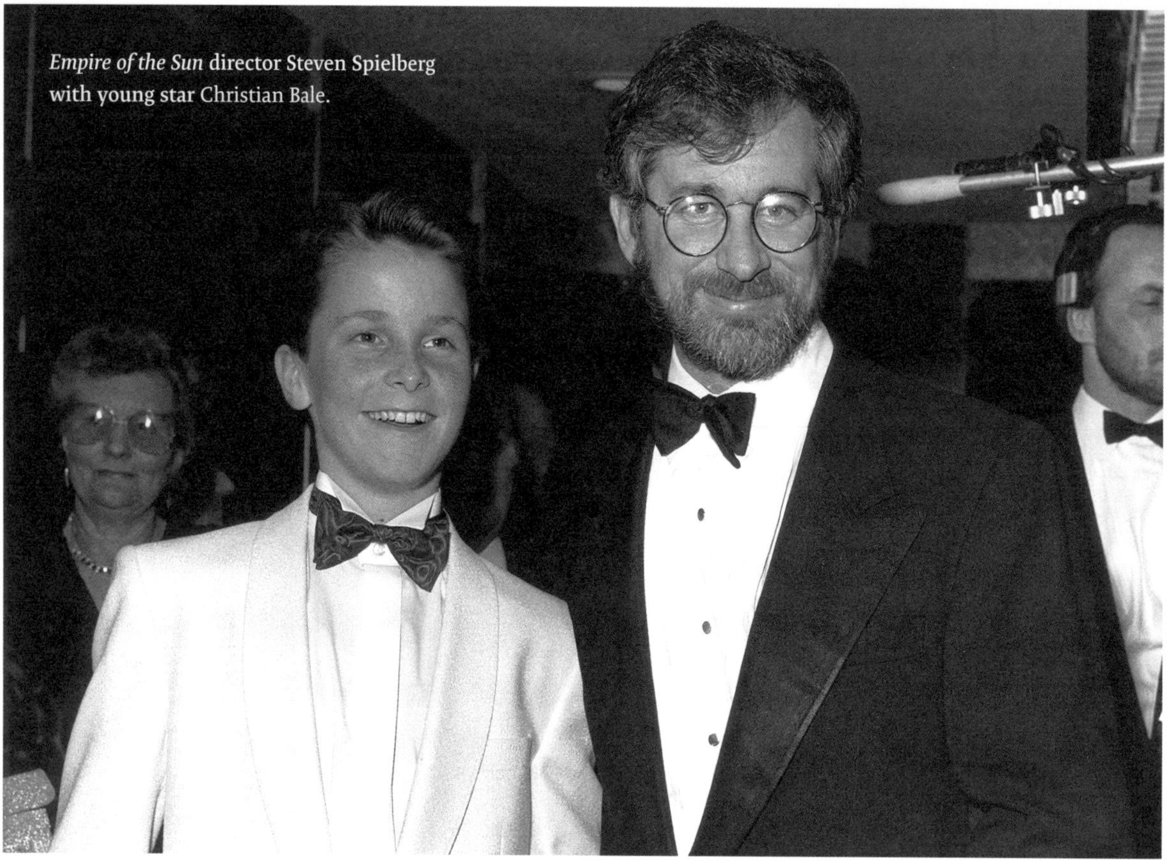

Empire of the Sun director Steven Spielberg with young star Christian Bale.

> him and I think the producer Kathleen Kennedy said to him, 'So, what are you going to do?' He said, 'I'm going to be a movie star.' And I thought, you probably will. He's fantastic in the film. But Steven was great with kids. He knows how to deal with them.

At the time Bale was just 12 years old and making his first major film. 'He was a kid,' says Nigel. 'But on the set, he was treated like an adult, which he liked.'

Nigel, along with other stars from *Empire of the Sun*, Christian Bale, Leslie Phillips and Miranda Richardson, was introduced to the Queen. 'She was everything you expected – and a little bit more.' Unfortunately, the Duke of Edinburgh was indisposed on the evening. Walking up the stairs with the Queen, Sydney Samuelson remarked, 'I am very sorry Ma'am that Prince Philip is not with us tonight.'

She replied, 'Well, you know, it's probably just as well, because Prince Philip is a terrible man to watch a film with. If anybody on screen asks a question, he will probably be so bored that he will answer the question out loud before the other actor has a chance to say anything.'

Spielberg flew in from the United States to be present. And it was another star-laden affair, with the likes of Cher, Twiggy and Fiona Fullerton also in the line-up. Dame Wendy Hiller gave a most eloquent Loyal Address and was introduced on stage by Robert Powell.

1989 *Madame Sousatzka*

This Royal Film had an especially long path to the screen. Robin Dalton was a literary and theatrical agent with a legendary client list that included John Osborne, Edna O'Brien, Iris Murdoch and Arthur Miller. She very badly wanted to see one book made into a movie, *Madame Sousatzka*, which no one was taking up. It told the story of the relationship between an unorthodox piano teacher (Sousatzka) and a child prodigy. 'I believed in it so much I thought, I'm bloody well going to buy this myself,' Robin said in *The Oldie* in July 2022.

Robin turned film producer, but it still took her years to find the financing. She finally managed to get noted director John Schlesinger interested and in turn, it was Schlesinger who brought in Shirley MacLaine to play Sousatzka.

The film was distributed in the UK by Curzon. George Biggs, then director of Curzon Film Distributors, recalls the preparations that took place before the big night itself:

> We had to go to the Odeon for a rehearsal to make sure the print was in first class condition. And we had to check the sound levels, so we all had to sit in the dress circle where the royal party was going to be and watch and listen to the film. And then the manager of the Odeon ran through what was going to happen on the evening, where we stood for the presentation.

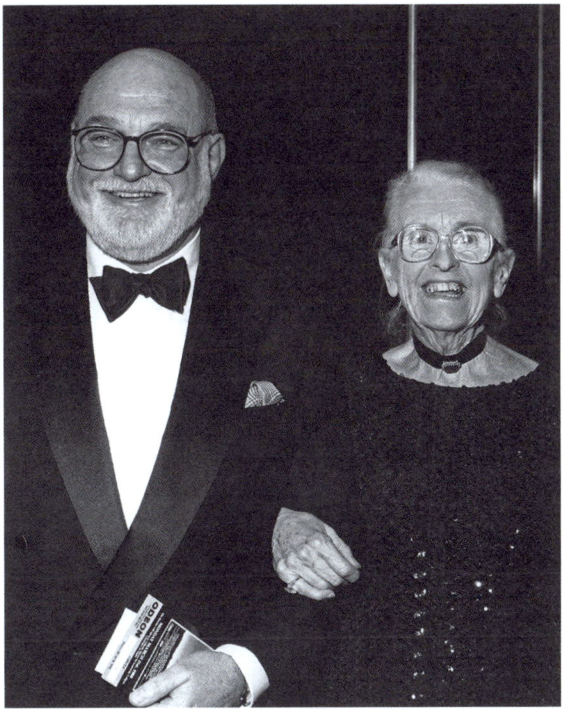

Famed director John Schlesinger attends the Royal Film Performance in 1989 with his mother.

Robin Dalton invited Shirley MacLaine to come over from the United States for the premiere. 'I got her a suite at the Savoy,' says George Biggs:

> ... which I thought would be fine and she was quite happy when she went there. After the first night we had a phone call the following morning to say that she couldn't stay there because of the bin men who woke her up too early. So, I had to move her to the Athenaeum Hotel.

Other stars of the film attended, including newcomer Navin Chowdhry, Leigh Lawson

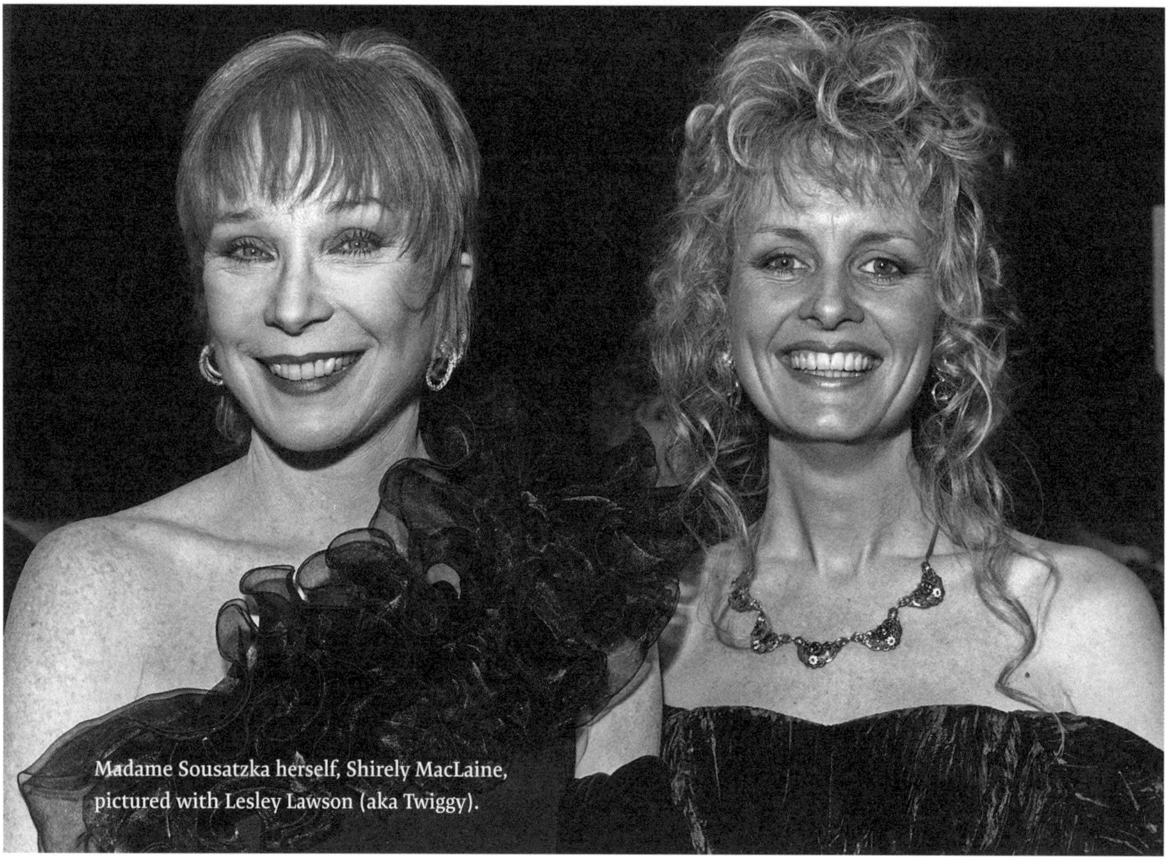

Madame Sousatzka herself, Shirely MacLaine, pictured with Lesley Lawson (aka Twiggy).

and Twiggy, along with John Schlesinger. Adding extra star lustre to the line-up were Peter Bowles, Amy Irving, Jeremy Irons and Elizabeth Welch.

It turned out to be a very significant evening because this was the final Royal Film Performance ever to be attended by the Queen Mother, who of course attended the very first one and many more afterwards. 'You could see she loved going to them when you met her,' says George Biggs:

> She was very chatty. I got introduced to her several times. She was an extraordinary lady. But she didn't take much nonsense. And she always referred to George VI as the King, but never her husband. She always used to say, the King used to do this or the King used to do that.

After the show, there was a reception at the Savoy for 250 people to finish off what had been another successful Royal Film Performance. 'The Odeon Leicester Square, was so used to doing premieres and royal premieres that the thing ran like clockwork,' confirms George. 'Not a single thing went wrong. Everything was done totally correctly. The national anthem was played, we had the royal trumpeters, the Queen Mother made her entrance and all that. It was all beautifully done, beautifully choreographed.'

1990 *Always*

This marked the third occasion a film directed by Steven Spielberg had been chosen for the Royal Film Performance. *Always* is a romantic fantasy drama about daredevil flyers battling runaway forest fires. Richard Dreyfuss, making his third film for Spielberg, plays a pilot who is killed but returns as a spirit to mentor a rookie pilot, played by newcomer Brad Johnson, and he watches as he falls in love with the girlfriend he left behind, played by Holly Hunter.

This year the selection committee had an especially difficult task because many films were submitted for their consideration. Famous film critic Barry Norman was a member of the committee and saw as its first function choosing a film that the Queen was going to enjoy and then to avoid anything political or controversial, 'so that the tabloid press can't go, good lord, fancy putting this in front of the Queen'.*

Unfortunately, Spielberg was unable to come to London for the event, nor did most of the cast attend. Instead, there was just Brad Johnson to be introduced to the Queen and Prince Philip. 'I can remember the Odeon manager saying to us,' recalls projectionist Dave Norris:

* Barry Norman from Thames TV coverage, 21 March 1989.

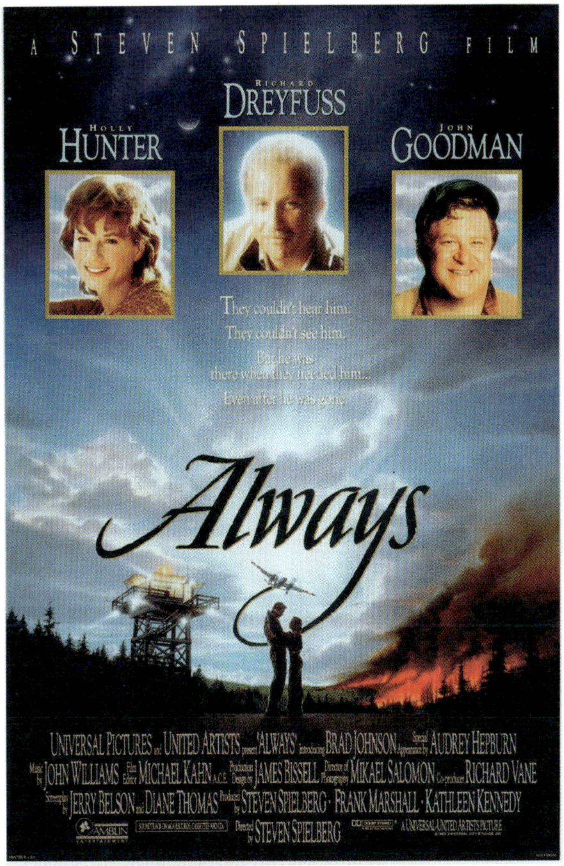

> … the Queen was walking down the line-up and she kept saying, 'Are you in the film?' And everyone kept saying, 'no'. And finally, she got to Brad Johnson and she said, 'Oh, you're in the film.' When you've got a line-up of maybe fifteen to twenty people and there's only one person there that's actually connected with the movie, it sticks out like a sore thumb.

Following this disappointing turnout, a communique was sent out to all the film distributors and companies to remind them that there should always be a good turnout of stars from the chosen film.

The Loyal Address was given by Sir Richard Attenborough, who was introduced by Pauline

Collins, who just the previous evening had received the BAFTA award for Best Actress for *Shirley Valentine*. Music for the evening was provided by the band and trumpeters of the Welsh Guards.

While festivities were going on at the Odeon, Leicester Square, a print of the film was made available at Glebelands, so the residents were able to watch it at the same time. A short segment about Glebelands featured during the TV highlights programme that had become very much part of the tradition of the Royal Film Performance. This programme was crucially important, not just as a means of entertainment but it was the one TV airing each year when the charity had a link to the public, who may otherwise be unaware of their activities. The programme was also a vital contact for people the charity needed to target. Proof of this came following that year's transmission when the charity received numerous enquiries from people within the industry requiring help and assistance.

1991 *Hot Shots!*

Without doubt, this ranks as the most outlandish comedy ever chosen as a Royal Film Performance. Described as a parody of fighter pilot movies, with particular attention being paid to *Top Gun*, it was directed by Jim Abrahams, the co-writer and co-director of the hugely popular *Airplane!* Its stars all

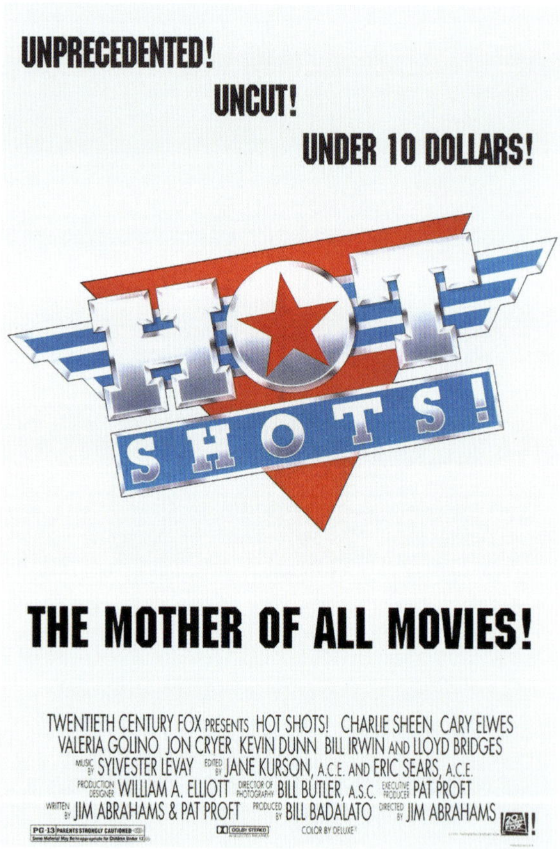

attended the event, Charlie Sheen, Lloyd Bridges and Valeria Golino, who admitted to being extremely nervous about meeting the royals. Other star guests included Susan George, Catherine Zeta-Jones and Simon MacCorkindale.

This was indeed a special occasion. Held in the presence of the Prince and Princess of Wales, it marked the first time the couple had been the principal royals at the Royal Film Performance. Diana looked stunning in a red chiffon dress embroidered in a tartan design in silver lamé, designed by Bruce Oldfield.

In the summer of 1997, not long before her death, Diana put seventy-nine of her dresses up for auction with Christie's in New York, the proceeds of which were to be spread between multiple charities. These included some of the most famous of her life. The auction brought in $3.25 million for charity. The red dress from that Royal Film Performance raised $34,500.

Hot Shots! went down extremely well with the audience on the night, as did a short film screened beforehand, *Mr Bean Goes to a Première*, in which Rowan Atkinson's iconic comic creation causes chaos while waiting in line at a movie premiere attended by a royal guest. Atkinson was to appear in a cameo role in the sequel to *Hot Shots!* in 1993, *Hot Shots! Part Deux*.

1992 *Chaplin*

When Richard Attenborough was 9, his father took him to see a rerelease of *The Gold Rush* (1925) and Charles Chaplin became an idol of his ever since. After directing film biographies of Winston Churchill, Gandhi and Steve Biko, Attenborough wanted to make a movie about his film hero, but Chaplin's widow Oona had always steadfastly refused all requests from

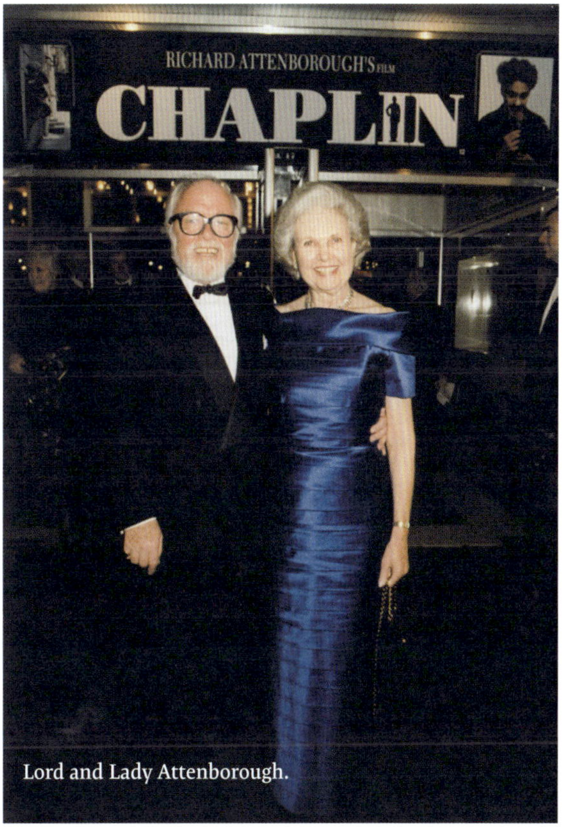

Lord and Lady Attenborough.

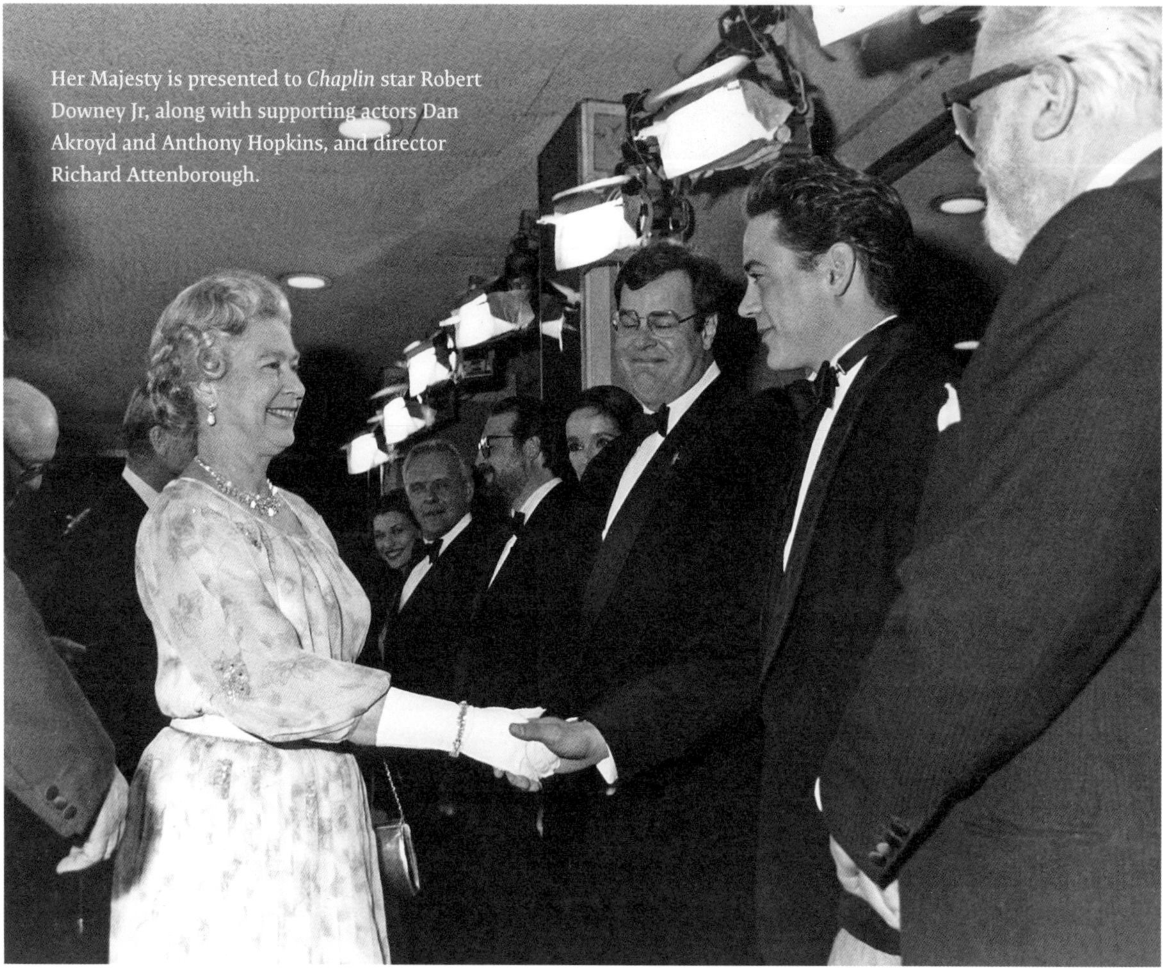

Her Majesty is presented to *Chaplin* star Robert Downey Jr, along with supporting actors Dan Akroyd and Anthony Hopkins, and director Richard Attenborough.

filmmakers wanting to dramatise the life of her late husband. Finally, she put her faith in Attenborough, only to sadly pass away herself two weeks before production began.

Following a wide search, Attenborough cast Robert Downey Jr, then just 25 and relatively unknown, as Chaplin. Then calamity hit, when Universal withdrew funding from the film just days before shooting was due to start – a decision largely attributed to doubts about Downey's suitability and box-office appeal. When Attenborough refused to reconsider his casting choice, alternative financing was arranged from elsewhere.

Downey spent almost a year preparing for the role, including watching Chaplin's films endlessly to master the comic postures and pratfalls of his screen persona. The work paid off, and while the film itself received mixed reviews and performed poorly commercially, Downey viewed it as an important step in his career.

The evening was a special one for Attenborough, who had many times been a guest at a Royal Film Performance, but this was the first and only film of his to receive the royal honour. In attendance were the Queen and Prince Philip, and they were presented to

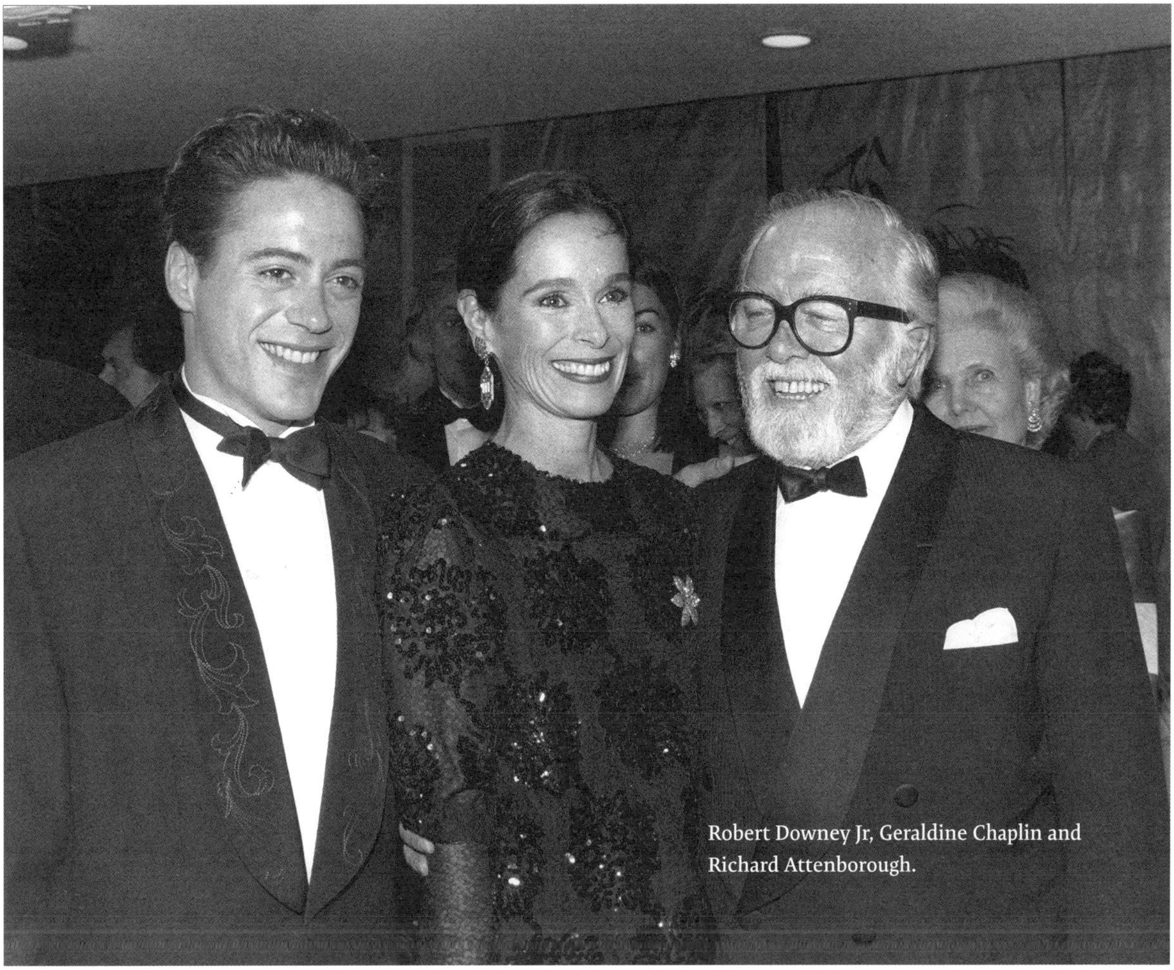

Robert Downey Jr, Geraldine Chaplin and Richard Attenborough.

numerous stars of the film, including Downey, Dan Aykroyd, Anthony Hopkins and John Thaw. Fittingly, Geraldine Chaplin, who played her own grandmother in the film, was also there.

Once the royal party were sat in the auditorium, Michael Grade presented *Precious Images*, an eight-minute film that featured many memorable movie moments from the history of cinema. Then Sir Richard Attenborough gave the Loyal Address before introducing his film. After the screening, he brought Downey up onto the stage where the young actor received a standing ovation.

As was becoming tradition, a print of Chaplin was sent to Glebelands for the residents and convalescents to enjoy at the same time as those at the Odeon, Leicester Square. Alas, the residents of Glebelands were unable to attend the post-premiere party held at the Park Lane Hotel, which was enjoyed by some 500 guests.

1993 *The Man Without a Face*

History was made this year by Mel Gibson, who became the first director to have his directorial debut selected as the Royal Film Performance. Made by Gibson's own production company, Icon, the actor plays McLeod, a former teacher whose face and body are horribly burned from a car accident. To play the role, Gibson had to endure three hours in make-up every day.

McLeod lives like a recluse in a big house on an island off Maine and is shunned and mocked by the local inhabitants. One day, a young adolescent named Chuck (Nick Stahl) arrives and asks McLeod to be his tutor. What begins as a distant relationship grows into friendship.

Still sporting western-style sideburns from shooting the action-adventure film *Maverick* in Hollywood, Gibson flew to London to attend the event and was presented to the Prince of Wales. Others in the line-up included Helena Bonham Carter, Ralph Fiennes and Ian McShane. Stephen Fry performed the Loyal Address with his own inimitable humour and style.

When the royal party, in this case Prince Charles, entered the auditorium to take their seats, this was the cue for the trumpeters to walk onto the stage to play a fanfare. They would usually come in during the afternoon to rehearse, as the length of fanfare had to be just long enough for the royal to reach their seat, at which point the cinema manager pressed a button which illuminated a light to prompt the playing of the National Anthem by the trumpeters and the mighty Compton organ.

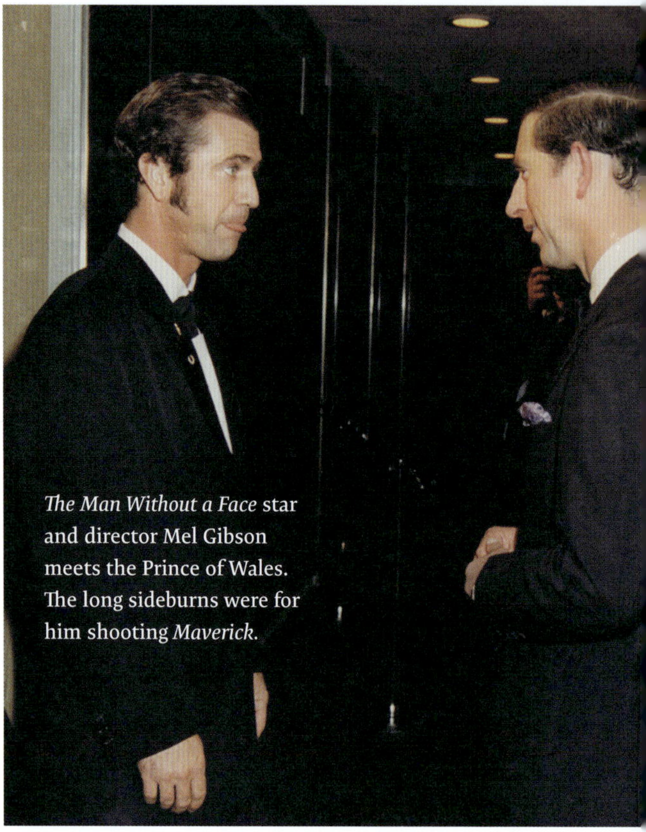

The Man Without a Face star and director Mel Gibson meets the Prince of Wales. The long sideburns were for him shooting *Maverick*.

Following the performance, there was a post-premiere party at the Planet Hollywood Restaurant for some 350 guests. The whole evening was seen to have been a great success and raised over £106,000 for the CTBF.

The TV highlights programme of the event, essentially a forty-minute free advert for the chosen film, remained a traditional fixture on ITV, and proof of its popularity was that it won a respectable 4.8 million viewers. One innovation this year was to advertise the fact that *The Man Without a Face* had been chosen for the Royal Film Performance in the movie's UK trailer, 300 of which were played around the country.

1994 *Miracle on 34th Street*

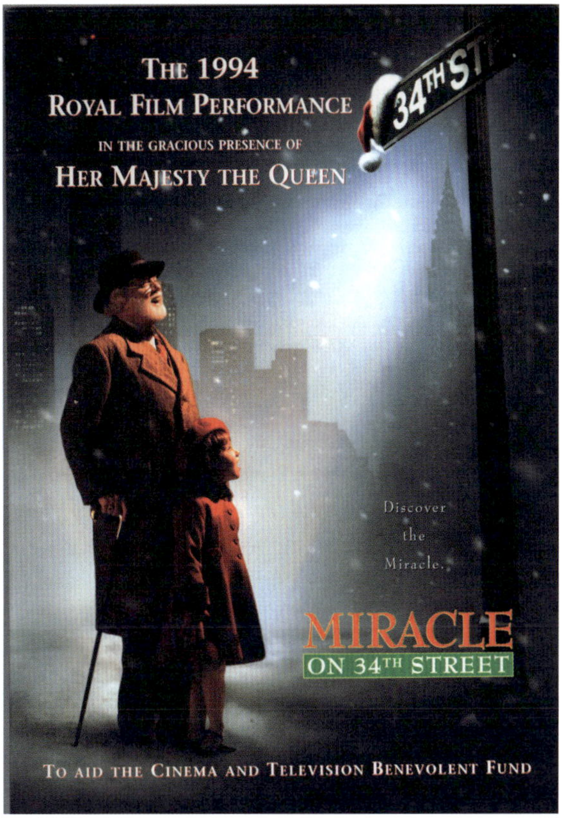

Richard Attenborough started his film career as an actor before moving into producing (with partner Bryan Forbes) in the early 1960s, after becoming frustrated by the type of films being made, and eventually turned to directing with *Oh! What A Lovely War* in 1969. Other directorial projects followed in the 1970s, which he punctuated with occasional acting jobs such as in *10 Rillington Place* (1971) and *Brannigan* (1974), but after appearing in Otto Preminger's version of *The Human Factor* (1979), he retired from acting to concentrate solely on directing and getting his long-cherished biopic *Gandhi* (1993) off the ground. The sweep of Oscars he subsequently won led to him becoming the toast of Hollywood and being able to take his pick of directorial assignments in the 1980s.

But it was Steven Spielberg who persuaded him to step in front of the camera again as John Hammond in *Jurassic Park* (1993). In a 1993 interview, Attenborough said the director had 'the charm of the devil' and was solely responsible for him coming out of acting retirement. With it, a whole new generation of studio executives realised just what a charismatic actor he was, and other offers swiftly came his way – not least the 1994 remake of *Miracle On 34th Street*.

Written and produced by the late John Hughes (of *Home Alone* fame) and directed by relative newcomer Les Mayfield, it was the fourth remake of the 1947 original. When asked about his casting wishlist at the premiere, producer Hughes revealed, 'It was a shortlist of one – Richard Attenborough. We sent him the script; he liked it and flew to Chicago to meet us for lunch, and it ended with him asking, "What hotel should I stay at during the production?"

Filmed in Chicago and New York City, the production necessitated closing nine blocks around Central Park West for the fictional Cole's Department Store annual parade. 'We had to shut off the areas for a week,' Mayfield revealed, much to the annoyance of yellow cab drivers. But was he wary of having such a famous director in his cast? 'Richard put his arm around me on the first day and said, "I'm very happy to be the actor in this movie" – he'd not long finished directing *Shadowlands* (1993) – and he proved to be a very generous man to work with.'

Cast and crew arrived at the Odeon, Leicester Square, for the Royal Film Performance and were met by general manager, Bill Weir, and fund president, Sir Paul Fox, while the St Martin-in-the-Fields Church Choir sang Christmas songs at the entrance to the theatre. The Queen and Duke of Edinburgh arrived for the festive film treat. Along with being introduced to stars Dylan McDermott, Elizabeth Perkins, Richard Attenborough and scene-stealing 7-year-old Mara Wilson and some of the 20th Century Fox executives (who greenlit the movie), there was an interesting royal line-up consisting of Sylvester Stallone (in town filming 1995's *Judge Dredd*), Barbara Knox and Kevin Kennedy from TV's *Coronation Street* and actor Joss Ackland. What a movie those names together would have made!

Richard Attenborough, who plays Santa Claus in the movie, declared just ahead of curtain up, 'This film has given me the greatest possibility to legitimise my role with my grandchildren,' before adding, 'someone asked if I'd rehearsed a lot for the part – I said yes, for about forty-five years!'

1995 ***French Kiss***

British production company Working Title Films was founded by Tim Bevan and Sarah Radclyffe in 1983, before Eric Fellner later replaced the departing Radclyffe. A newly created UK broadcaster, Channel 4, commissioned the company to make *My Beautiful Laundrette* (1985), directed by Stephen Frears. The film was an enormous success at the Edinburgh Film Festival and was thereby guaranteed a theatrical release. The company's follow-up productions, *Wish You Were Here* (1987) and *Sammy and Rosie Get Laid* (1988) preceded *A World Apart* (1988), which was entered in the 1988 Cannes Film Festival and won the Special Grand Prize, while *The Tall Guy* (1989) marked the feature debuts of screenwriter Richard Curtis and director Mel Smith. But it was a quirky little British comedy called *Four Weddings and a Funeral* in 1994 that skyrocketed the company into the big league.

Following *Four Weddings*' worldwide success, Bevan and his team were in a development meeting in Wimbledon after he'd recently and fortuitously met Meg Ryan on a trip to LA. Being the 'queen of romantic comedies', the producer chanced his luck by saying, 'It'd be brilliant if we could make a film together', and Ryan suggested he send her a script. Bevan related his encounter to one of the American executives in attendance, who in turn helped get the thumbs-up.

Writer Adam Brooks was quickly approached to develop a treatment he'd penned into a full script. He'd had the idea of setting a love story in the French capital, but purposely set out to offer anything but a picture-postcard-perfect Parisian romance; it was instead a story about everything going wrong.

The script was couriered to Meg Ryan who, in turn, sent it to director Lawrence Kasdan, asking him to come on board. 'There are certain perceptions of Americans about France, and of French people's view of Americans and those differences in attitude intrigued me,' Tim Bevan said at the performance:

> Meg then sent it to Kevin Kline, who was on a bit of a roll after his Oscar winning turn in A Fish Called Wanda (1988), and between Lawrence and Meg they persuaded Kevin to come on board. Within just a few months it all moved into production – the quickest of any Working Title movie.

At the premiere, the producer stated the significance of the movie being chosen for the Royal Film Performance, 'It gives the film a great kick-off in the UK which is obviously a particularly important market for this picture. We have never had a royal premiere before and it's a special thing, making everyone involved

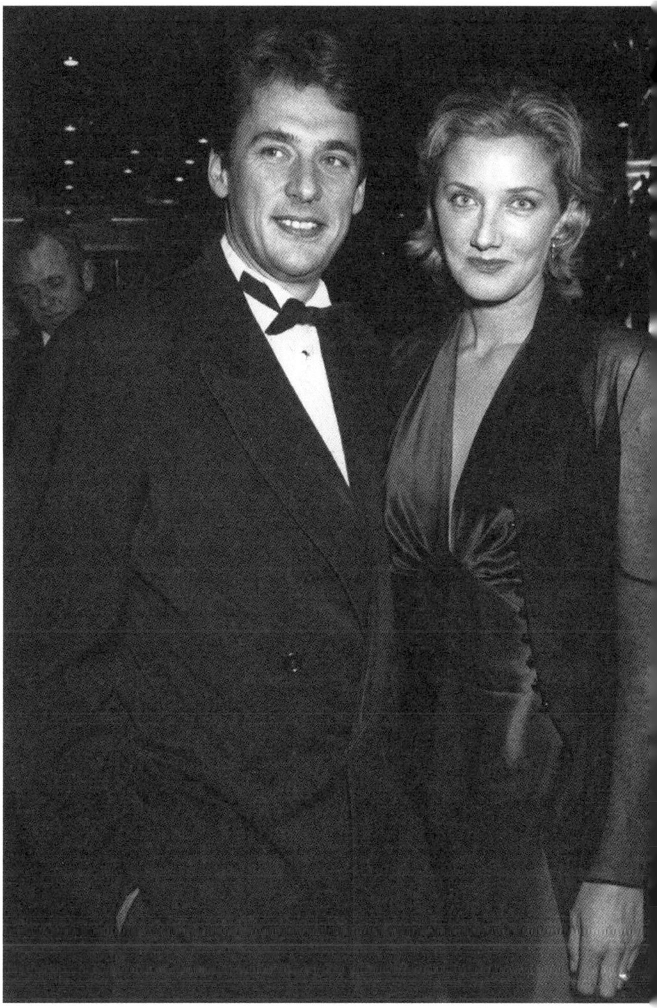

French Kiss producer Tim Bevan with his (then) wife Joely Richardson.

feel very special. The icing on the cake!' On its international release, the film generated over $60 million in box-office receipts (compared to $39 million in the USA) demonstrating the all-important launchpad offered by the Royal Film Performance.

On the evening itself, Fred Turner, president of the CTBF (and managing director of Rank Film Distributors), welcomed Prince Charles to the Empire, Leicester Square, and introduced him to studio executives ahead of Uma Thurman (then partner of the star, Timothy Hutton) and Joely Richardson (former wife of Tim Bevan), along with the writer Adam Brooks. Sadly, neither Meg Ryan nor Kevin Kline was available to attend, both citing filming commitments.

The afterparty at London's Hyde Park Hotel featured an extravagant French-themed garden complete with a model of the Eiffel Tower carved out of ice in a nod to filming locations in Paris and the glamorous Côte d'Azur.

1996 *True Blue*

Alan Parker's biopic *Evita* was to be the Royal Film Performance fiftieth-anniversary screening, but post-production delays meant the film was not ready in time for the November event (it was in fact released in January 1997). Charity president Fred Turner reached out to producers Davina Belling and Clive Parsons with their Film 4 and National Lottery-funded adventure set on the River Thames, dramatising the 1987 University Boat Race mutiny.

After Oxford lost in 1986, they suggested recruiting some of their American Olympic rower friends, several of whom came over. But trouble soon ensued when they did not agree with the legendary Dan Topolski's coaching methods and walked off. Three weeks before the race, the Oxford crew who had been jettisoned for the Americans were brought back in and against all odds they won. The Cambridge crew in the film, incidentally, were played by members of the rowing squad from Imperial College, London, including several members of the British international squad.

The film was shot across the same locations as the actual race, during one of the most bitter winters in a decade. It marked Dominic West's first major film role.

The producers had initially met at Warner Bros UK, where Clive Parsons became head of business and where Davina Belling was assistant to the head of production. They quickly

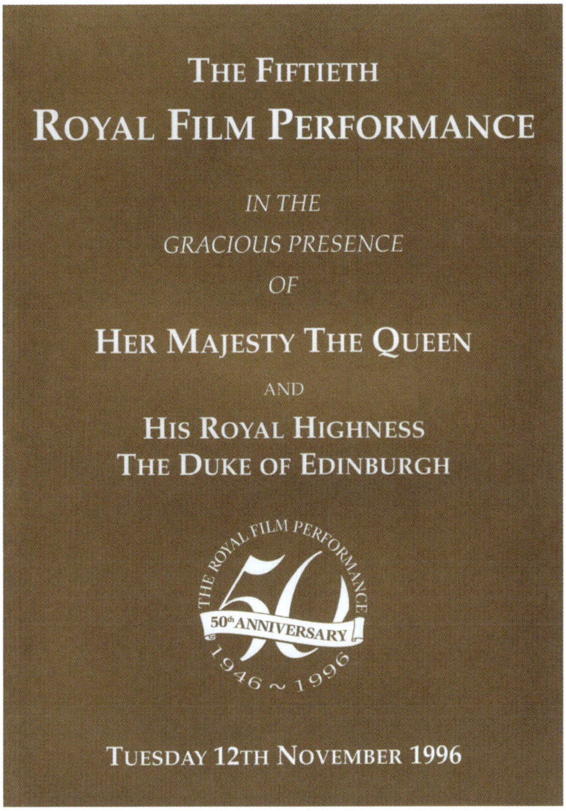

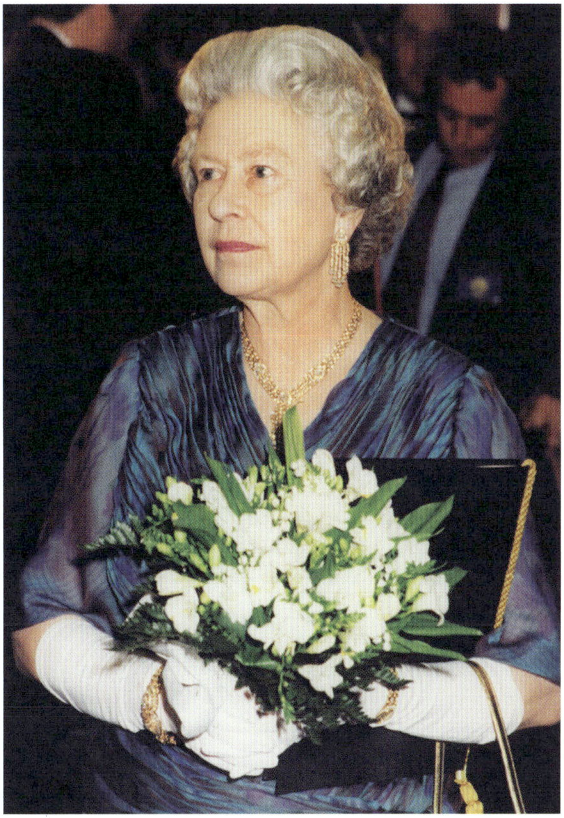

Her Majesty the Queen attends the 50th Royal Film Performance *True Blue*. It was to be *Evita*, but the film was not completed in time.

realised they shared the same vision and ethics on how business should be conducted and in 1971 formed their own company, Film & General Productions, initially to provide money for producers developing feature films, but a few years later, it led to the duo embarking on their own productions, which included the triumph of *Gregory's Girl* (1981) and the satirical *Britannia Hospital* (1982), among others.

'Of course, we were delighted and flattered to be approached at the time but, as you probably know, the film was a disappointment at the box office partly, I think, because it came across as too elitist,' says Davina Belling on being approached by the charity about becoming the Royal Film Performance.

As to the premiere itself at the Odeon, Leicester Square, Belling adds:

Before the royal party arrived everyone had been joking around in the foyer, somewhat mocking the formality of the occasion, but the minute Her Majesty's grey coiffed head appeared, coming up the stairs, all the formally dressed imposingly looking group transformed instantly into one of full awe!

I remember Prince Philip asking Ferdy Fairfax [the director], 'Did these two treat you properly?', nodding to Clive and myself. I responded, 'Do we look as if we didn't?!'

Ferdy's 5 yr old daughter presented the programme with strict instructions

> to simply curtsey and not say anything but when her big moment came and Her Majesty said, 'Thank you', Tallulah replied, 'My pleasure entirely'!

On the night, long-time resident of Glebelands Robert Burns introduced 'Reflections', a compilation of films made by BAFTA in celebration of 100 years of British cinema, followed by a short film looking back on Royal Film Performances from the previous forty-nine years, together with interviews with some of the CTBF's residents and convalescents at Glebelands. Don Hunsley, incoming executive director of the fund, stepped in at the last moment to give the Loyal Address after Lord Attenborough had fallen ill on the day, compounded by the loss of his voice. As Robert took his leave, it was revealed he was celebrating his 101st birthday that same day, which drew gasps and a massive round of applause from the audience.

1997 *Titanic*

Before it even opened, *Titanic* was making headlines around the world due to its mammoth budget, arduous shoot and predictions of disaster. Director James Cameron didn't want to hold the film's world premiere in Hollywood, so the studio opened it on 1 November 1997 at the Tokyo International Film Festival. Its next showing, a little over two weeks later, was the Royal Film Performance, taking place at the Empire Theatre for the first time in many years. *Titanic* didn't open in America until the middle of December and opened proper in the UK in late January.

Unsurprisingly, the evening quickly became a 'hot ticket' event and quickly sold out. James Cameron and Leonardo DiCaprio flew in from the United States to attend the performance and were presented to Prince Charles. Other members of the cast in attendance included Frances Fisher, Bernard Hill and Billy Zane. Kate Winslet was absent due to being struck down with illness. However, the press quickly spotted among the guests Tom and Laura Parker Bowles, son and daughter of Camilla Parker Bowles.

DiCaprio escorted both his mother and grandmother to the event and cheekily introduced his mother, who was standing behind him in the line-up, to Prince Charles. Later, at the glittering after-show party,

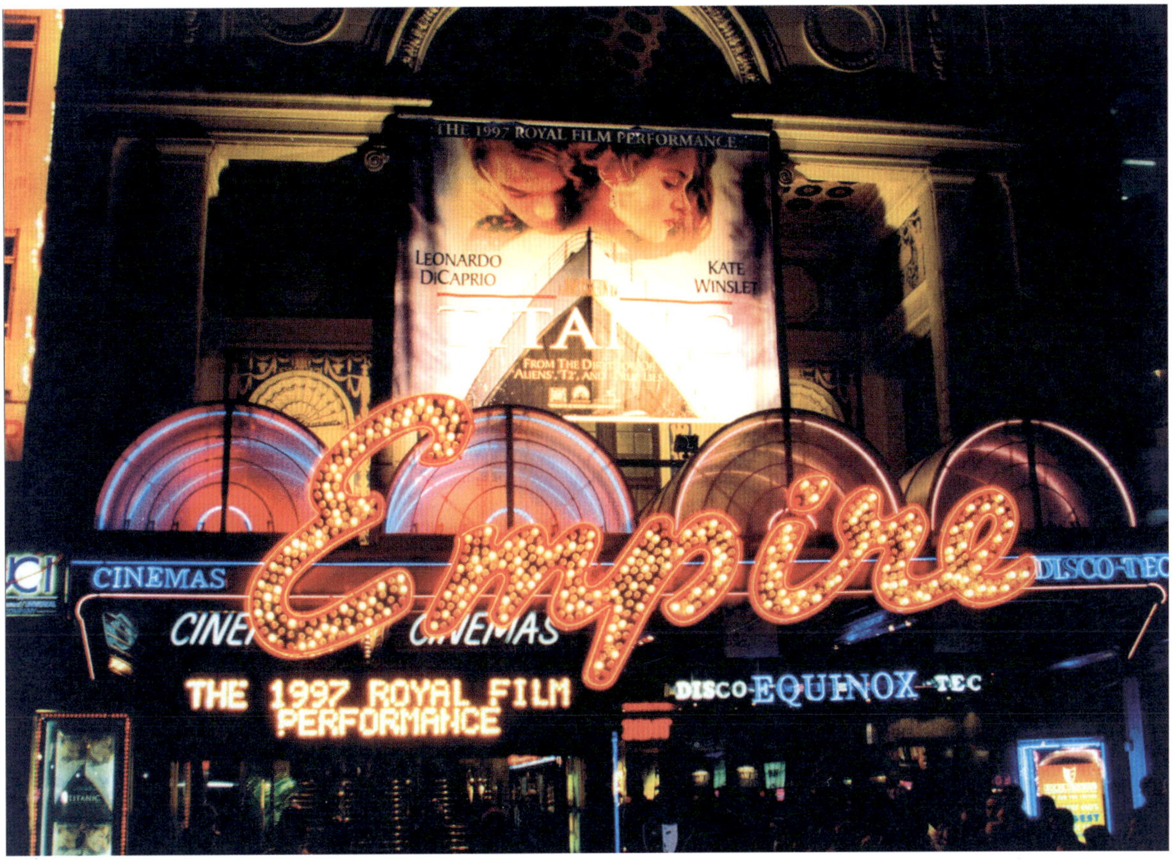

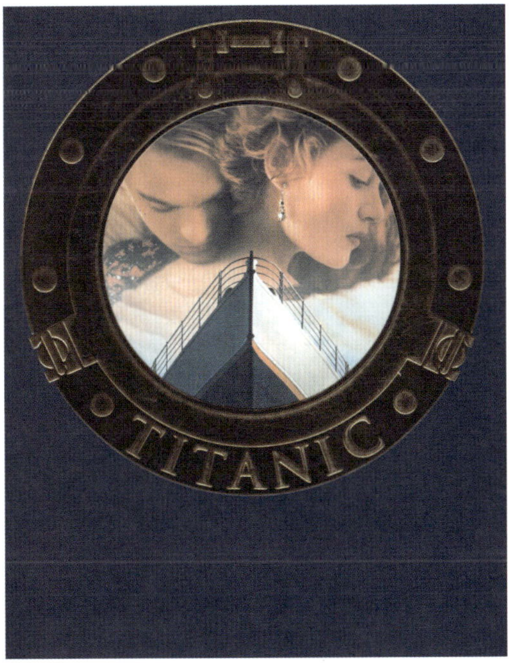

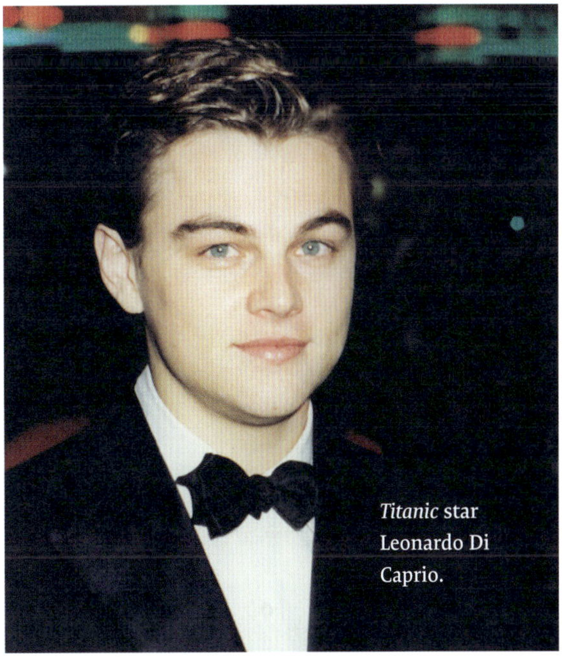

Titanic star Leonardo Di Caprio.

DiCaprio rubbed shoulders with models Elle Macpherson and Kate Moss.

In a demonstration of the celebrity status and prominence with which James Cameron was regarded, the director himself gave the Loyal Address. 'I've never actually made a speech in front of royalty,' he told the press. 'I much prefer being behind the camera than in the spotlight.'

During the screening, the audience broke out into applause on at least three occasions and gave the film rapturous applause at the end. Soon, the rest of the world was captivated by *Titanic* and it became the highest-grossing film of all time. It also remained number one at the US box office for a record fifteen consecutive weeks.

The evening was an unqualified success and raised £173,000 – a record for the charity. The souvenir brochure, another source of income for the charity, either through sales on the night or companies purchasing advertising space inside, proved to be more popular than ever, selling out its entire print run of 1,100 copies.

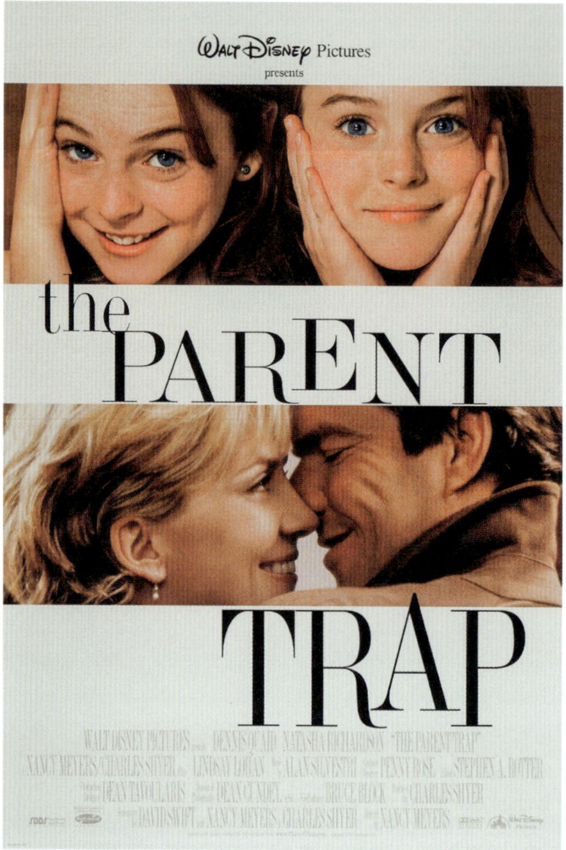

1998 *The Parent Trap*

A remake of Walt Disney Pictures' 1961 film of the same name (starring Hayley Mills) and based on Erich Kästner's original German book *Das Doppelte Lottchen*, director Nancy Meyers' movie starred Dennis Quaid, Natasha Richardson and 11-year-old Lindsay Lohan in her movie debut – on double duty, alternating between the roles of twin sisters Annie James and Hallie Parker.

Nancy Meyers said she was looking for 'a little Diane Keaton' to play the twins and auditioned 1,500 actors (including a young Scarlett Johansson, Mara Wilson and Michelle Trachtenberg) as part of an exhaustive casting search across Atlanta, Boston, Chicago,

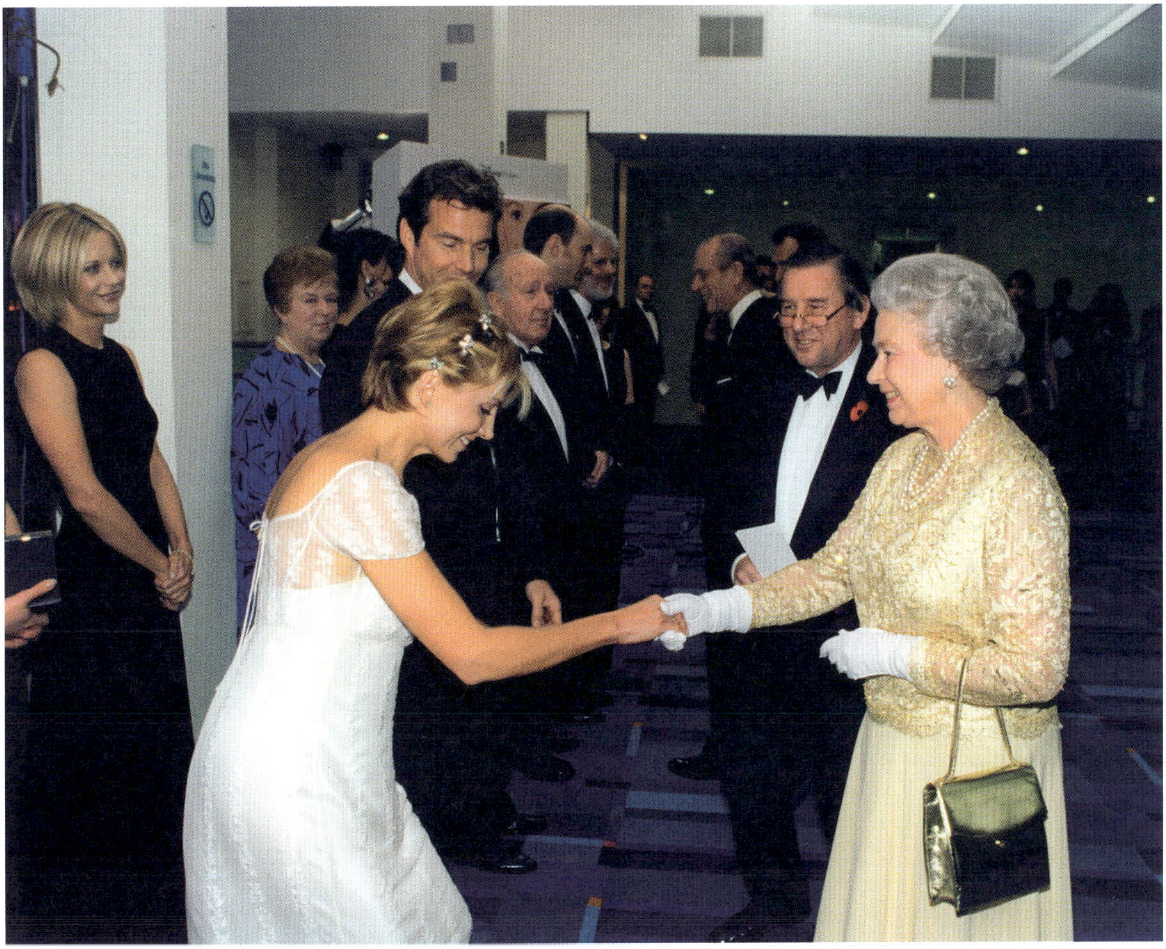

The Parent Trap (1998): Her Majesty meets stars Natasha Richardson and Dennis Quaid, and is introduced by Fund President David McCall.

London, Miami, Minneapolis, Toronto and Vancouver, with open calls in both LA and New York City. 'I saw Lindsay on a tape from New York,' Meyers revealed at the performance. 'I said, "There's something electric about this girl."'

The twins in the film were named after Meyers' and producer Charles Shyer's real-life daughters (who had small cameos in the film), but Lindsay Lohan had to employ camera trickery and split screens in order to play both parts, wearing an earpiece so that the other twin's lines could be fed to her.

The Queen and Duke of Edinburgh attended the premiere, although they were probably not aware that a scene in which Hallie met 'Queen Elizabeth' outside Buckingham Palace was filmed but ultimately wound up on the cutting room floor as the director felt it delayed the pacing of the movie. Had she known the film would be the Royal Film Performance, she might have thought twice!

Fund trustees David McCall and Fred Turner greeted the royal party with cinema manager Bill Weir at the newly refurbished and restored Odeon, Leicester Square, showing the theatre off to its former glory, including new sculptures of the four flying ladies (naked nymphs) adorning the walls either side of the proscenium arch as if leaping towards the screen. New leopard-skin-covered seats, in a nod to the cinema's original seating, were installed in both the Circle and Stalls, and a new light and airy central foyer with white ceramic floor lit from beneath. A grand central staircase made from green glass was added, complete with fibre-optic lighting.

Joining the line-up of executives and trustees at the premiere were director Nancy Meyers, producer Charles Shyer, actors Ronnie Stevens, Natasha Richardson and Dennis Quaid (with his wife, Meg Ryan, who had been unable to be at her own Royal Film Performance a few years earlier).

Perhaps the warmest reception came for Hayley Mills, star of the original movie, who accompanied her father, Sir John Mills – fifty years on from his Royal Film Performance – and gave the Loyal Address ahead of the screening. In an interview with the *Today Show* on US TV, Hayley Mills said, 'It was so like the one I did, and yet not. But I thought it was really good', praising Lindsay Lohan's performance as 'excellent'.

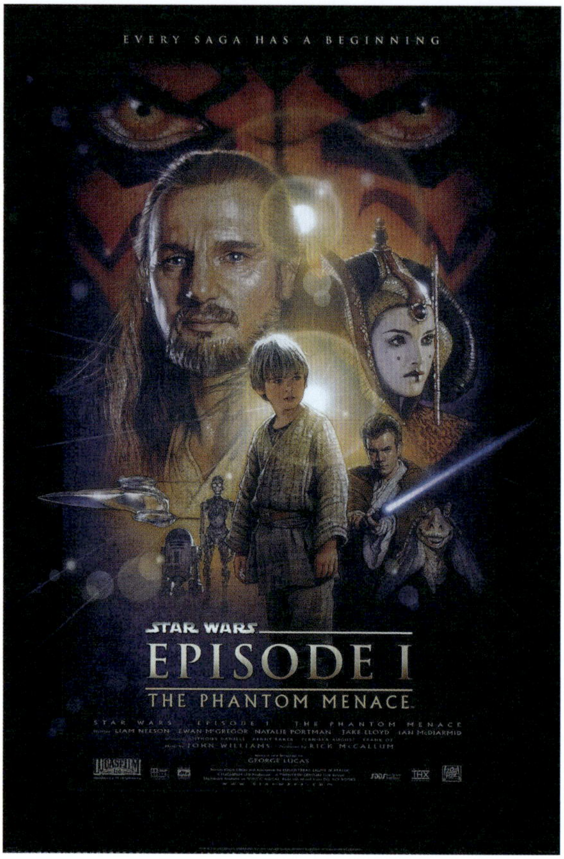

1999 ***Star Wars: Episode I – The Phantom Menace***

It seemed somehow fitting, given that the original *Star Wars* trilogy was made in the UK, that this newest adventure be chosen for the Royal Film Performance. George Lucas always had nothing but praise for British crews; it's why he based his *Indiana Jones* films in the UK too, along with other productions such as *Willow*. He saw being chosen as the Royal Film as validation for working in the country so many times, and the mogul flew in from the United States to attend the event. 'I am honoured that *Star Wars: Episode I – The Phantom Menace* has been selected as the 1999 Royal Film Performance,' he said. 'It has

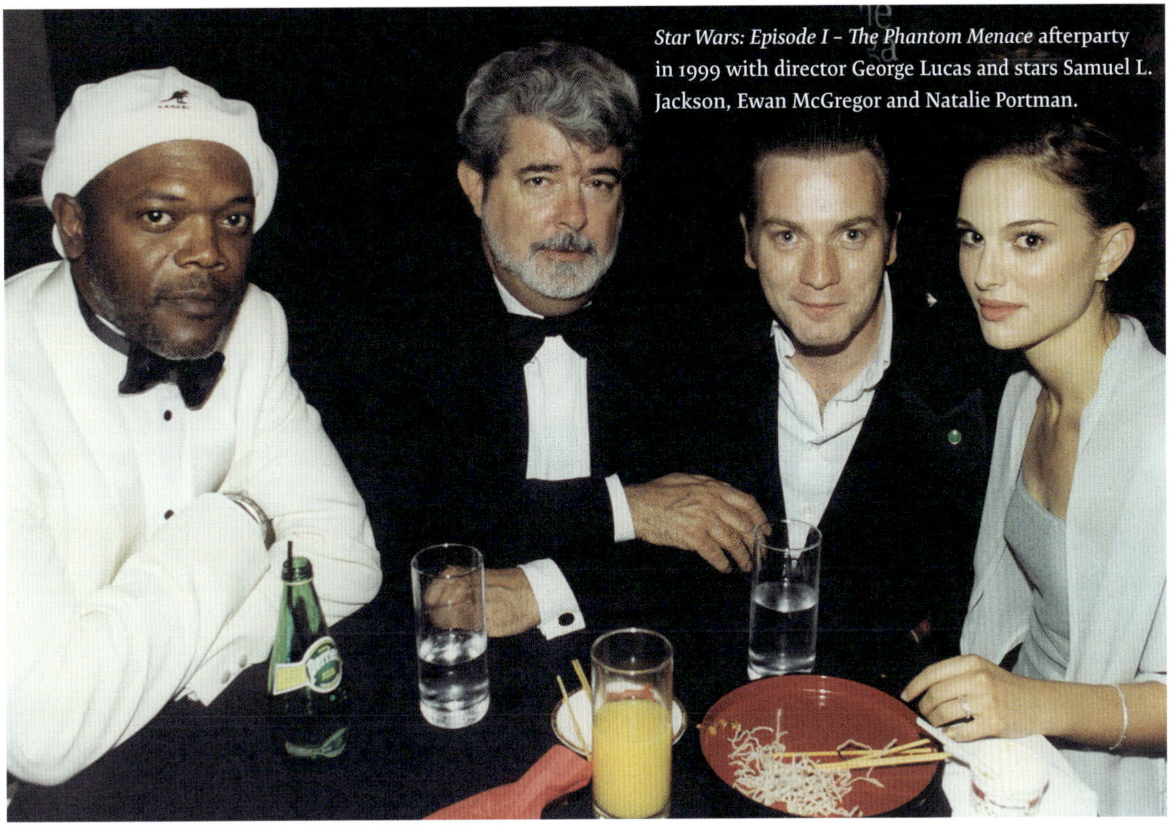

Star Wars: Episode I – The Phantom Menace afterparty in 1999 with director George Lucas and stars Samuel L. Jackson, Ewan McGregor and Natalie Portman.

been a privilege to work with British crews for twenty-three years on ten films.'

Lucas was joined by a cavalcade of stars from the film and the *Star Wars* universe – Ewan McGregor, resplendent in a kilt; Natalie Portman; Jake Lloyd, who played the young Anakin Skywalker; Ahmed Best, who played the controversial Jar Jar Binks character; Samuel L. Jackson; Anthony Daniels, better known as C-3PO; Peter Mayhew, who played Chewbacca; R2-D2 himself, Kenny Baker; and Warwick Davis. The red carpet also saw other celebrities including Jonathan Ross, Billie Piper, Sharleen Spiteri, Stephen Hawking, Dave Stewart and Brian May.

The premiere attracted a considerably larger crowd than previous years with *Star Wars* fans jostling for space to catch a glimpse of their favourites. A large marquee had been erected in Leicester Square Garden, where a full orchestra played musical highlights from *Star Wars*. A line of Stormtroopers stood menacingly at the front.

Prince Charles was the royal guest and entered the auditorium to a fanfare by the trumpeters of the Central Band of the Royal Air Force. The Loyal Address was given by broadcaster Sir Trevor McDonald, who then introduced the stars of the film onto the stage.

Earlier, Prince Charles made something of a boo-boo when introduced to Natalie Portman, asking if she had appeared in the original *Star Wars* trilogy. 'No, I'm 18,' she replied. Natalie was just 2 years old when *Return of the Jedi* was released in 1983.

2000 *How the Grinch Stole Christmas*

Dr Seuss refused all offers to sell the film rights to his books, but after his death at the age of 87 in 1991, his widow Audrey Geisel took control of the business empire and opened it up to licensing opportunities. 'I've never gone out looking for anything,' the 79-year-old told *Time Magazine* about the avalanche of adaptations and licensing. 'It all comes to me,' she added, in defence against the criticism she'd been experiencing about excessive profiteering. Nevertheless, in July 1998, an auction of the film rights of *How the Grinch Stole Christmas* was announced. Interested parties who pitched to the widow had to be willing to pay $5 million, plus 4 per cent of the box-office gross, 50 per cent of the merchandising revenue and music-related material, plus 70 per cent of the income from book tie-ins. Furthermore, it was stated, 'Any actor submitted for the Grinch must be of comparable stature to Jack Nicholson, Jim Carrey, Robin Williams and Dustin Hoffman.' Oh, and she would not consider a director or writer who had not earned at least $1 million on a previous picture.*

After several unsuccessful studio pitches, it was Universal that won the auction with a $9 million bid, after bringing in Ron Howard to further woo the widow. He signed on to direct

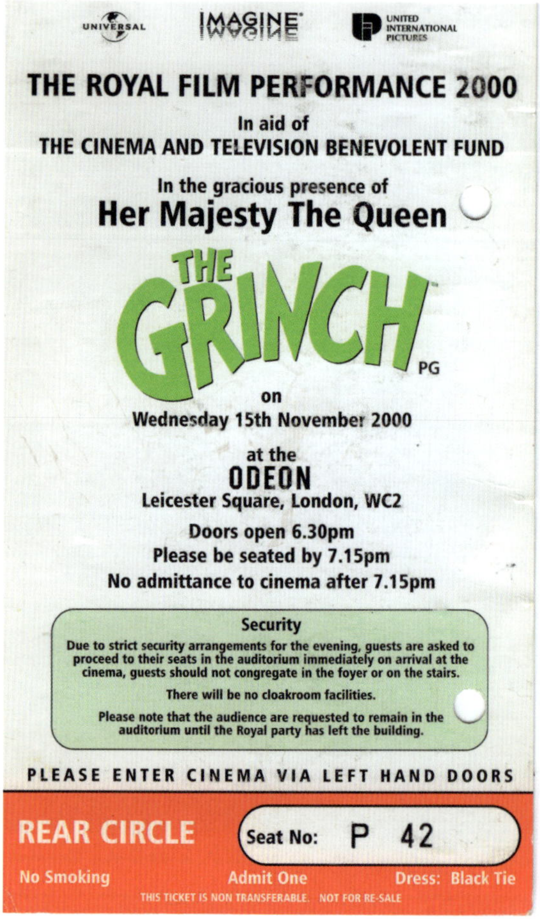

and co-produce the film, with Jim Carrey in the lead role.

Building across eleven sound stages and on the Universal Studios backlot, behind the Bates Motel set from *Psycho*, Rick Baker designed and created the prosthetic make-up for Carrey (winning an Oscar along the way). The Grinch suit was covered in yak hair, dyed green and sewn onto a spandex suit. Baker said at the Royal Film Performance:

> Ron [Howard] called me six months before production to figure out the look of the movie. It is a movie where everyone including the dog wears makeup, so

* *Los Angeles Times* report, 16 September 1998.

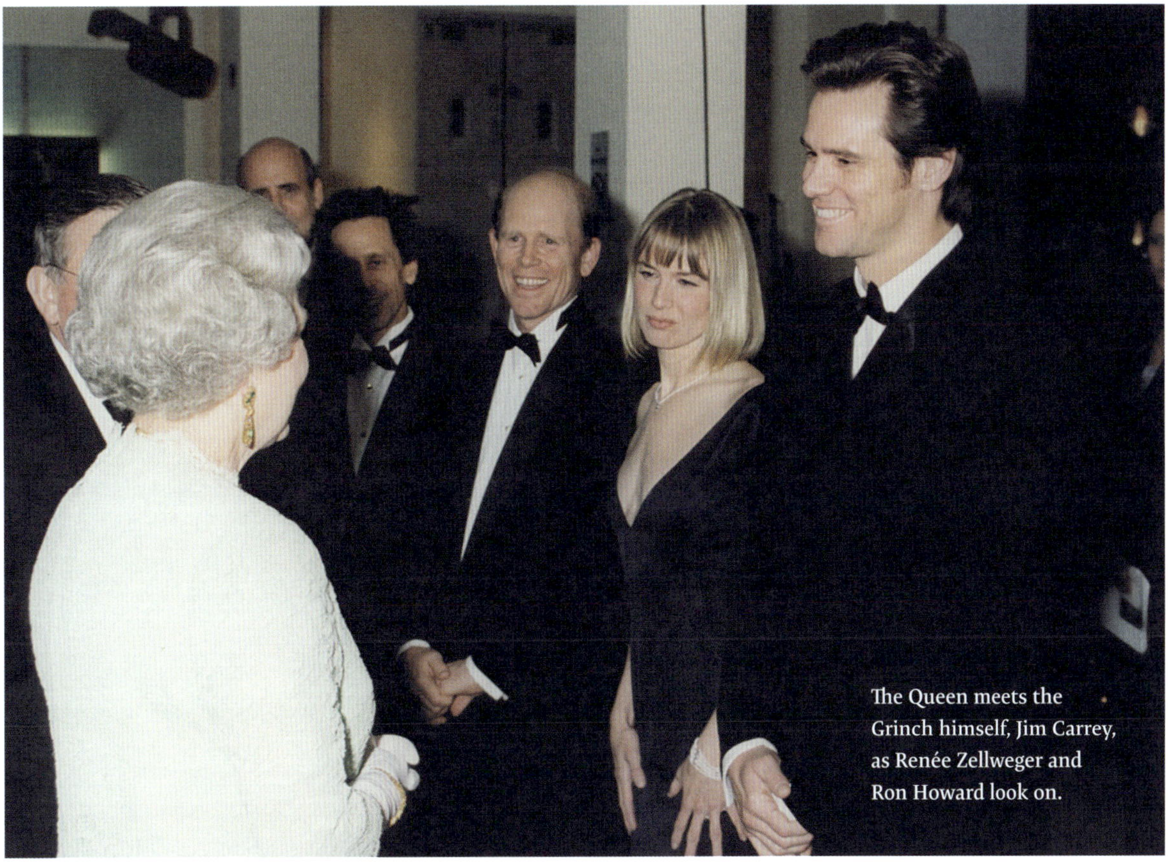

The Queen meets the Grinch himself, Jim Carrey, as Renée Zellweger and Ron Howard look on.

> I felt Grinch needed to be a particularly distinct and individual character, and not just Jim Carrey painted green, so he has a mask, prosthetics, and wig to make him look very individual. I redesigned the cartoon character that everyone is used to, so hope people like it!

At the Odeon, Leicester Square, premiere, a beaming Ron Howard stated, 'It's a great honour to have a screening like this and to even have a movie that would be considered for such an event. We have all been coached about meeting the Queen and hopefully we're not going to be too American!'

A usually chaotic Jim Carrey, meanwhile, grinned widely as he said, 'I'm trying to resist every impulse I have to avoid an international incident!'

Odeon manager Chris Hilton welcomed Her Majesty at what was his first Royal Film Performance at the helm, and introduced her to fund trustees, who in turn introduced the studio executives and cast members, Clint Howard (brother of Ron), Jeffrey Tambor, Jim Carrey, Renée Zellweger (then partner of Carrey), plus director Ron Howard and producer Brian Grazer.

Following fanfare trumpeters of the Central Band of the Royal Air Force, the National Anthem was played, accompanied by Donald MacKenzie on the Compton organ and the Loyal Address was given by Michael Parkinson.

2001: *Ali*

A biopic of the most famous and extraordinary sportsman of the twentieth century, Muhammad Ali, seemed to be a natural winner, but this project lay in 'development hell' for more than a decade. Several directors attempted to make the film, including Spike Lee and Oliver Stone, who wanted Denzel Washington to play Ali. Finally, Michael Mann took charge, overseeing a $105 million budget. Having earlier turned down the opportunity of playing the boxing legend, Will Smith relented after Ali called Smith personally to say the actor was the only one good-looking enough to play the role.

Ali had already opened in the United States to a largely favourable critical response but had lukewarm box-office receipts by the time it was chosen as the Royal Film. The event took place at the Empire, Leicester Square, the usual standby venue if the Odeon was unavailable. Crowds lined the routes into the Square to see the arrival of Prince Charles and Will Smith, who left his car to personally greet some of the fans whose cheers could be heard inside the cinema.

Among a host of celebrity guests such as Bob Geldof and Frank Skinner were several famous former boxers, Sir Henry Cooper, Barry McGuigan, Nigel Benn and Audley Harrison. Sir Henry Cooper, who famously fought against a young Ali, then known as Cassius Clay, back in 1963, introduced the film on the stage and there was a special message from Muhammad Ali himself screened to the audience.

The film went down well and after the performance, Will Smith joined 500 guests for a post-premiere party at the In & Out (Naval and Military Club) in Piccadilly. The evening was regarded as having been a huge success and raised a tremendous £150,000.

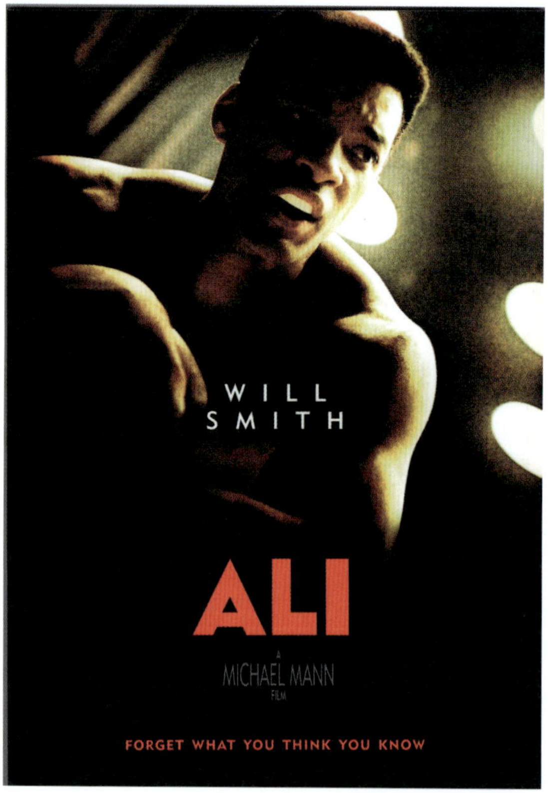

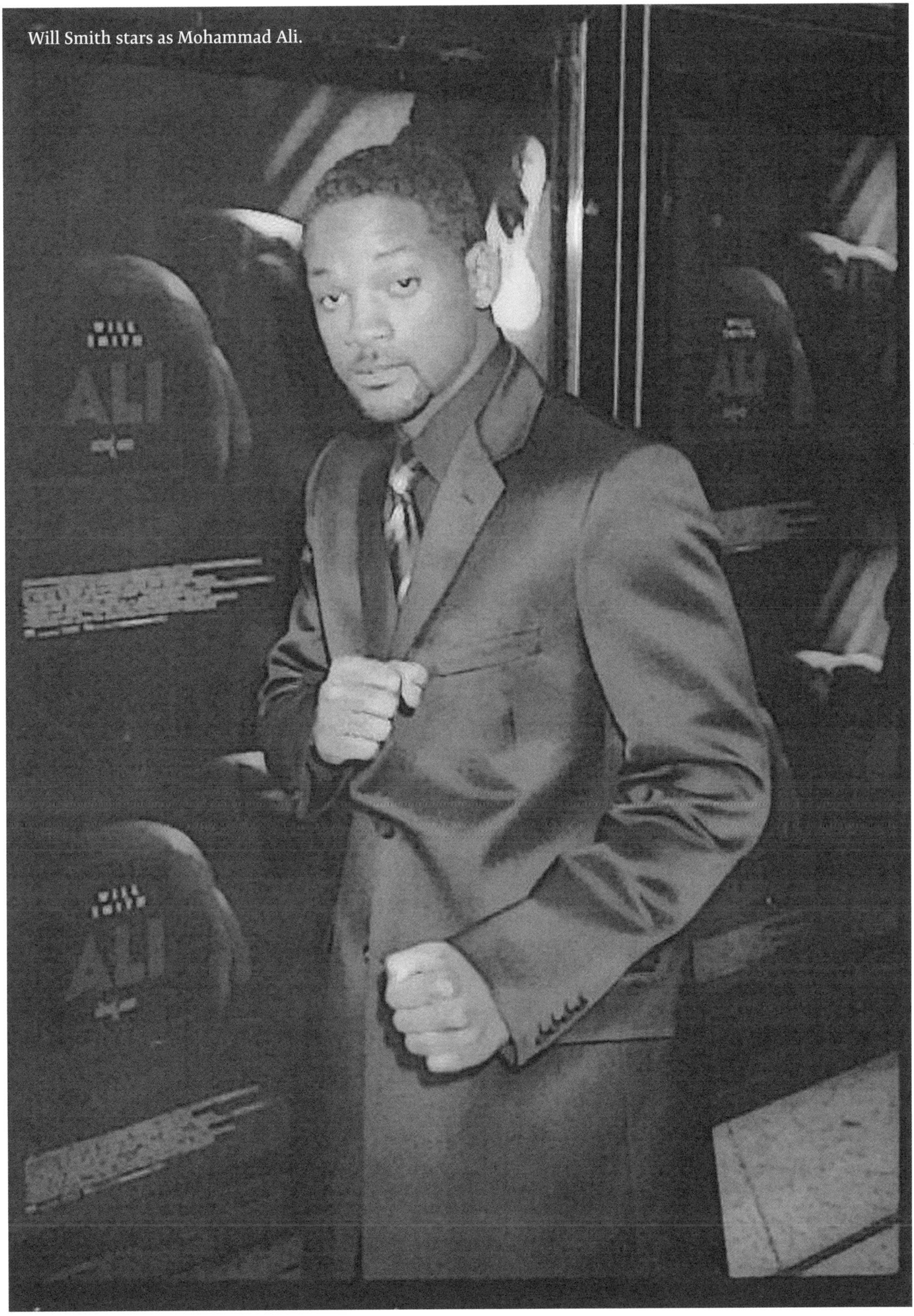

Will Smith stars as Mohammad Ali.

2002: *Die Another Day*

In the Queen's Golden Jubilee year and the ruby anniversary year of the James Bond film franchise, the twentieth 007 adventure premiered as the Royal Film Performance – the first for a Bond movie. It was only the second Bond premiere attended by the Queen, the previous being thirty-five years earlier for *You Only Live Twice* (1967).

For the first time in a generation, the Royal Film Performance was not held in Leicester Square because the scale and popularity of Pierce Brosnan's fourth (and final) outing as Commander Bond demanded a much larger venue and so it was relocated to the 5,000-seat Royal Albert Hall. Along with the film's cast and crew, the event was also attended by many other alumni from the series: Bond actors Roger Moore, George Lazenby and Timothy Dalton; leading ladies Maud Adams, Lois Chiles, Shirley Eaton, Eunice Gayson and Judi Dench; villains Richard Kiel, Julian Glover and Burt Kwouk; musicians John Barry, Monty Norman and Shirley Bassey, to name but a few.

The exterior of the venue was decorated with fifty-four giant icicles (imported from Germany), which surrounded the building, with the interior being dressed to resemble the 'ice palace' as seen in the film. Additionally, a huge 400m red carpet running the length of Kensington Gore greeted arriving guests,

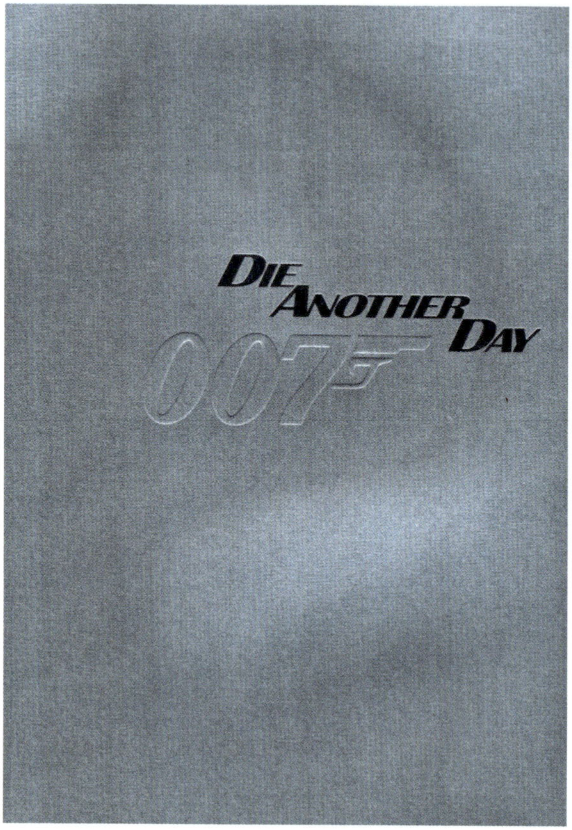

1,000m of electrical cables powered screens and cameras, along with 150 floodlights and a chase of pyrotechnics illuminated the whole length of the carpet when Pierce Brosnan arrived.

Brosnan, somewhat overawed at the spectacle of the event, said on arriving:

> You spend six or seven months of your life making a movie that is close to your heart, that is a big part of your life, part of your career and one in which you have a great respect for the franchise – so you want it to be the greatest, the biggest and the best. This is an outstanding evening – one for the history books.

Timothy Dalton echoed that sentiment, 'I think this is the greatest movie premiere, anywhere

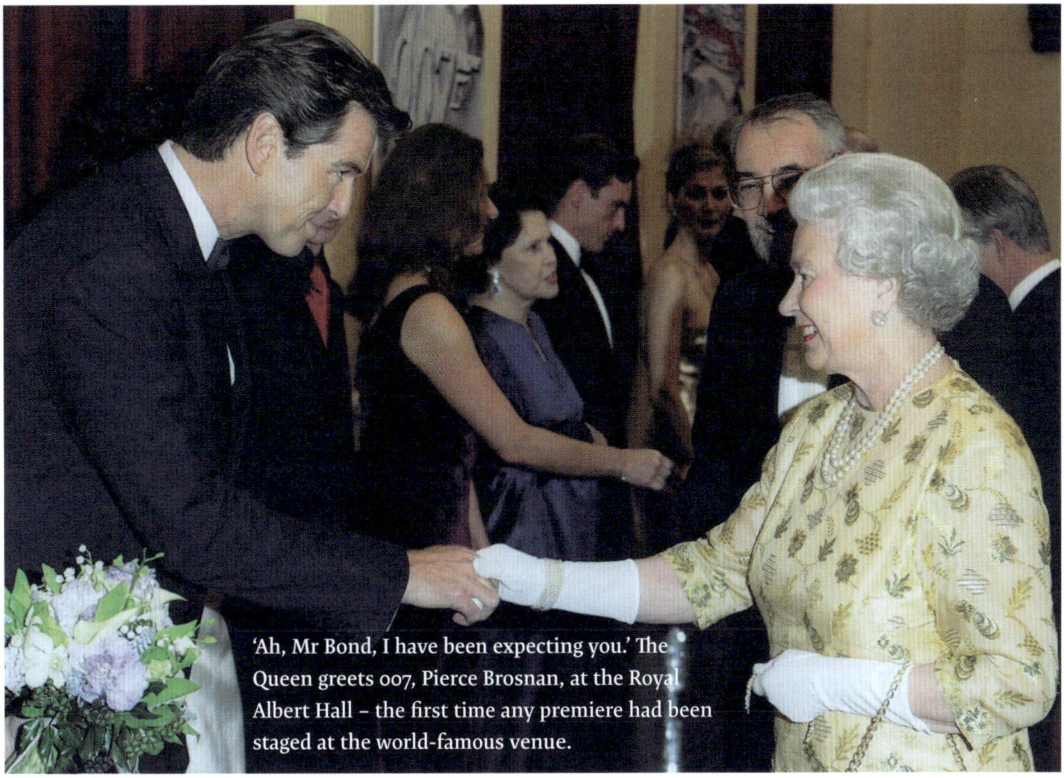

'Ah, Mr Bond, I have been expecting you.' The Queen greets 007, Pierce Brosnan, at the Royal Albert Hall – the first time any premiere had been staged at the world-famous venue.

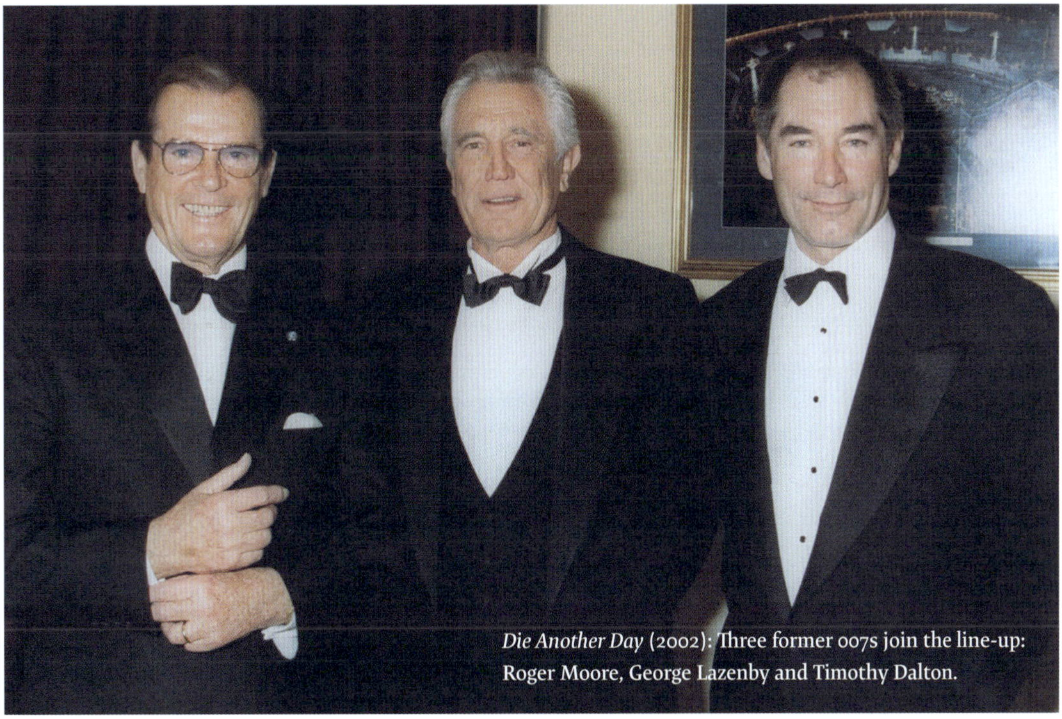

Die Another Day (2002): Three former 007s join the line-up: Roger Moore, George Lazenby and Timothy Dalton.

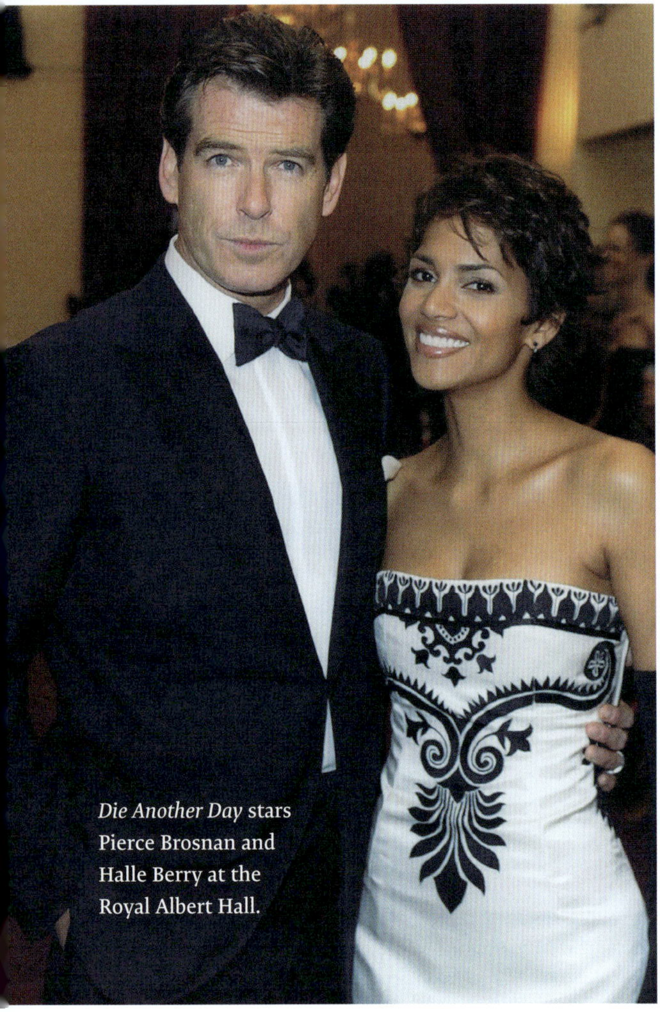

Die Another Day stars Pierce Brosnan and Halle Berry at the Royal Albert Hall.

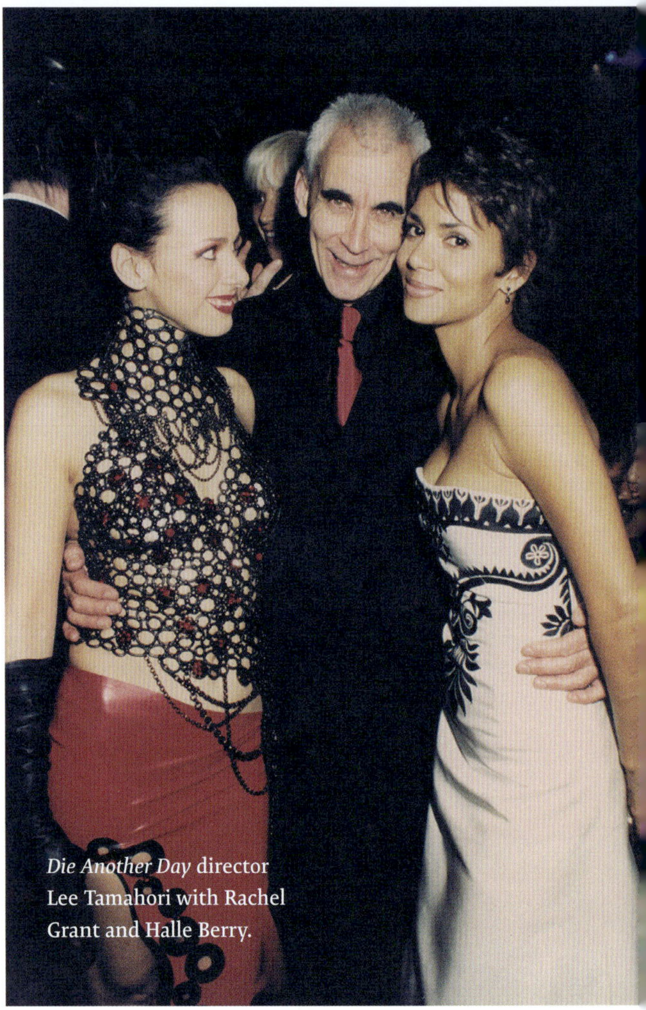

Die Another Day director Lee Tamahori with Rachel Grant and Halle Berry.

in the world, and it's even more special tonight because Her Majesty the Queen is coming.'

Producer Michael G. Wilson introduced Her Majesty and the Duke of Edinburgh to cast and crew, including Madonna (who performed the title song as well as playing a cameo role), Rick Yune, John Cleese, Rosamund Pike, Toby Stephens, Halle Berry, co-producer Barbara Broccoli, who was accompanied by the widow of Cubby Broccoli, and her mother, Dana Broccoli, plus director Lee Tamahori.

An earlier part of the line-up, hosted in an anteroom, included some of the studio executives and trustees of the CTBF, plus the three previous Bond actors who were not invited to join the main cast and crew of *Die Another Day* after Pierce Brosnan voiced a concern that they might detract from the focus on him being the current James Bond. Indeed, when the producers invited Lazenby, Moore and Dalton to join them and Brosnan on stage ahead of the film, the largest applause came for not the present incarnation of 007, but Roger Moore!

Twentieth Century Fox had just partnered with studio (and brand co-owner) MGM to distribute the Bond films, which caused potential friction leading up to the Royal Film Performance as Yvonne Dickens, former head of MGM Technical Services UK, recalls:

> It was the first Bond Royal premiere for Fox, and they wanted their logo to appear ahead of MGM's. I pointed out normal protocol was that distributor logos were not included in prints for screenings attended by Royals, but Fox replied they'd added their logo on Lucasfilm titles at royal premieres. I sent their response to our legal office in LA, and a compromise was reached: Fox could put their logo on the print, but the first sound had to be the lion roar from the MGM logo, which followed. At the premiere there was a bit of commotion when the Fox logo appeared without its usual fanfare music – people thought the sound was not on and there was a very brief moment of panic!

A parallel premiere was also held at Leicester Square's Empire UCI Theatre, along with regional premieres in Birmingham, Newcastle and Plymouth. In total, £500,000 was raised for the charity – the most financially successful to date.

2003 *Master and Commander: The Far Side of the World*

Despite heavy rain, crowds waited outside the Odeon for a glimpse of the celebrities arriving for this year's Royal Film Performance, including Honor Blackman, Timothy Dalton, accompanied by Barbara Broccoli, Richard E. Grant, Chrissie Hynde, Robert Lindsay, Emily Lloyd, Vanessa Mae and Sting.

With the chosen film having a nautical theme, it was apt that the royal guest was the Prince of Wales, then a vice admiral in the Royal Navy. He received a rousing reception from the crowd and inside the auditorium. As soon as the National Anthem finished and silence fell, a female guest called out, 'We love you, Charles!', much to the amusement of the audience.

The film's stars, Russell Crowe and Paul Bettany, were in attendance, as was the Australian director, Peter Weir, who the day before the event insisted on watching a run-through of the print. Much to Weir's bemusement, the run-through started at the ungodly hour of 4 a.m. This was because the Odeon was showing the Rugby World Cup Final between Australia and England live from Australia on the big screen. 'Can I stay afterwards and watch it?' asked Weir.

'So, we ran *Master and Commander*,' recalls projectionist Dave Norris, 'went for a coffee and came back and he watched the rugby final.'

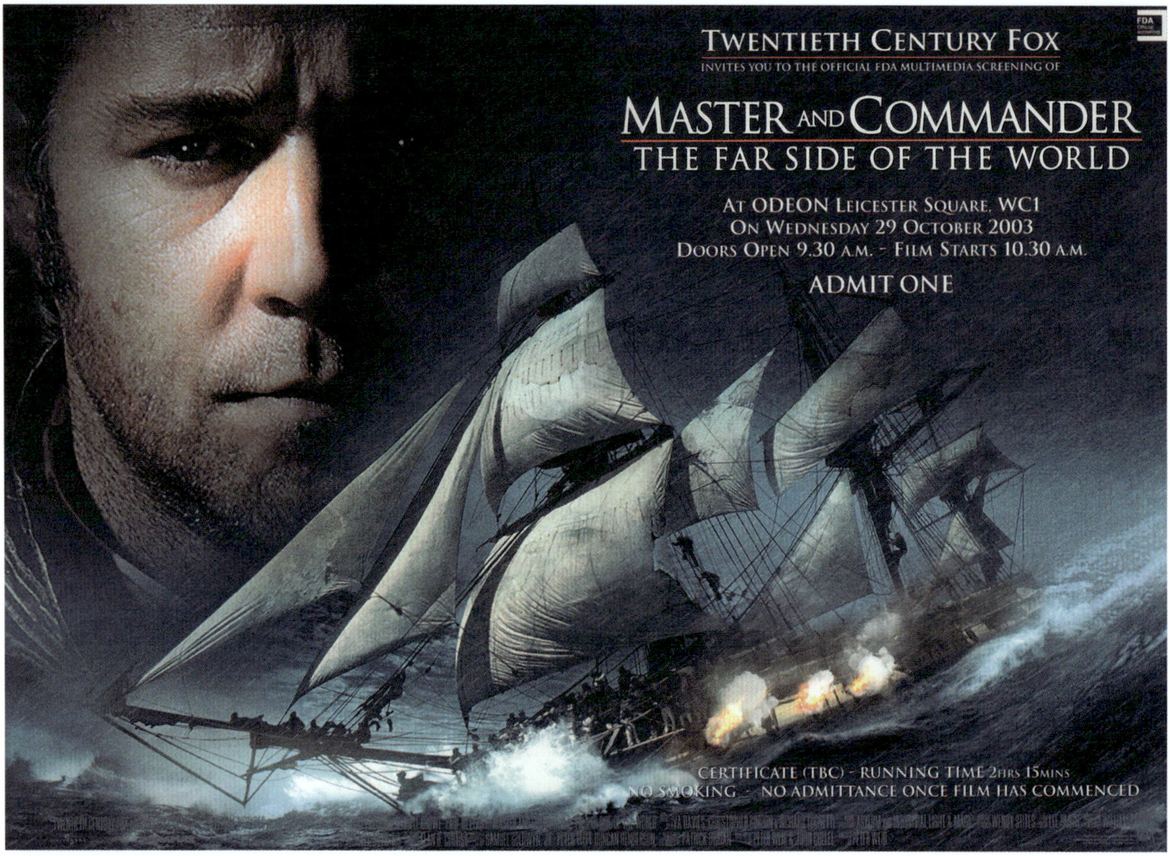

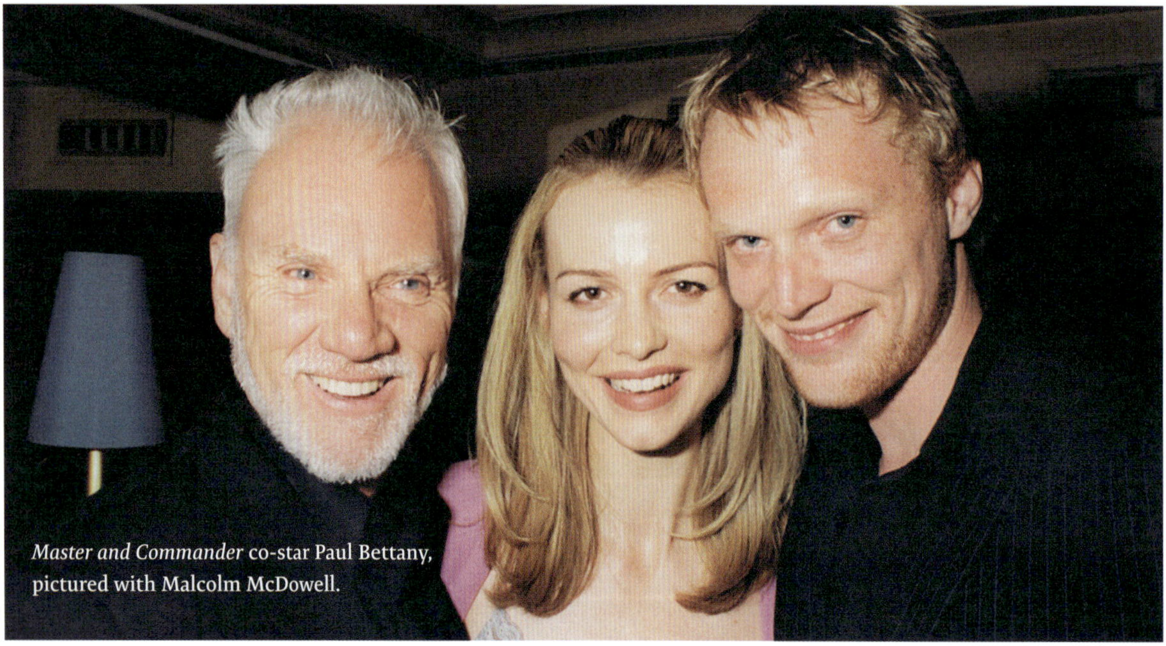

Master and Commander co-star Paul Bettany, pictured with Malcolm McDowell.

Master and Commander: The Far Side of the World is set during the Napoleonic Wars. Crowe plays a fearless British Naval captain who leads his ship and crew on a mission to seek out and destroy a formidable French vessel with a fearsome reputation for sinking British ships. During the screening, Chris Hilton, the manager of the Odeon, Leicester Square, noticed quite a few people leaving the auditorium for medical assistance with the St John Ambulance volunteers:

> I spoke with the royal security team and the police who thought there might be a problem with the air, so we all dashed up to the roof to check the inlets and air system – all was clear. It was then that one of the St John ambulance team said he was actually treating people for sea sickness!

Chris says he was fortunate to host several of the royal family at Royal Film Performances:

> But whenever the Queen attended, I found everyone behaved much better – that is to say when the actors were asked to form a line-up, they did so immediately without having to be reminded or herded. Her Majesty had an aura of authority that commanded total respect.

2004 *Ladies in Lavender*

This year, Charles Dance became only the second first-time director to have his directorial debut selected as the Royal Film Performance. Much better known as an actor, this was something of a pet project for Dance. He discovered the story when he was sitting on a film set one day, taking a break, surrounded by hundreds of prop books. He took one of them down. It was a collection of short stories by an author he had never heard of called William John Locke. One of the stories was *Ladies in Lavender*, about two spinster sisters who befriend a mysterious foreigner who washes up on the beach of their close-knit Cornish fishing village. Charles recalls:

> When I'd finished writing the screenplay, I had the nerve to ask Judi Dench to play one of the two principal characters. I was bowled over when she agreed to do it, and equally so when Maggie Smith also agreed. To have the two Great Dames grace my little film was humbling, flattering, and I have no doubt that without them I could never have made the film – it was hardly a blockbuster and had none of the essential ingredients to be one – no stunts, no car chases, and no sex!

On the day of the Royal Film Performance, Dance recalls arriving at the Odeon with the cast, well before the appointed hour, to be briefed on what to expect and what the protocol was:

> Judi and Maggie were 'old hands' as indeed was Miriam Margolyes, who regaled me about having been told off by Her Majesty for speaking out of turn in a previous royal line-up – knowing and adoring Miriam as I do, I was surprised it was only the once!

That evening, Dance was presented to the Queen and in turn introduced Her Majesty to the cast. 'As we moved along the line, I heard Miriam whisper (thankfully not a "stage whisper") that she hoped she wasn't going to regret having been to an Indian restaurant the night before.'

In the auditorium, a hush descended as the Queen and the cast entered, the lights went down and the film began. 'I was sat next to Her Majesty,' reveals Charles:

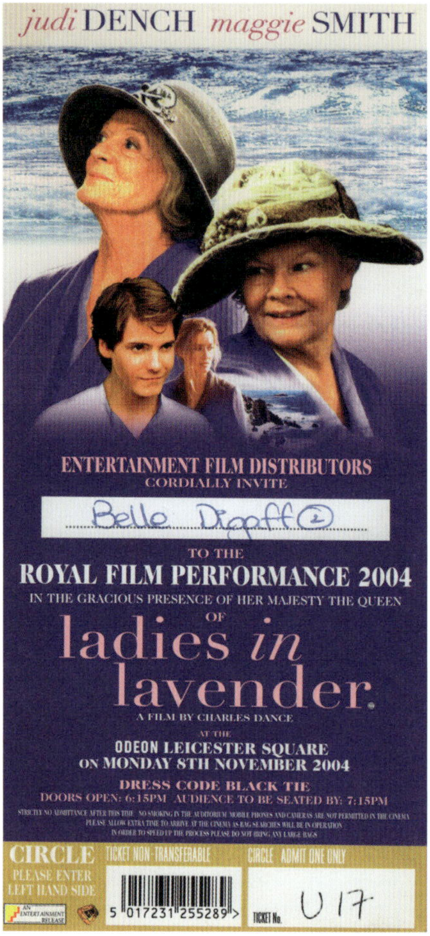

> … frightened to say a word. I was relieved to hear her laugh at the few comic moments there were in the film, and she at one point leaned in to ask where we had found all the wonderful old agricultural machinery that featured in the film's hay-making scene. I noticed that she sat with a small clutch bag on her lap that she moved gently from time to time – I did wonder at one point if perhaps she was concealing a small animal in there! Then as the end credits rolled, still in the darkness, she opened the bag, took out a lipstick, and without the aid of a mirror applied a quick touch-up to the Royal lips. When the lights went up, she thanked me, I thanked her for coming, and the Royal party left.

There was the obligatory after-show party, 'where I had more than one stiff drink', confesses Charles, 'and had a lot of hugging with cast and my family. I don't know whether being chosen to be the Royal Film had any effect on the film's success – I doubt it, but it certainly launched *Ladies in Lavender* in a wonderful way.'

2005 *The Chronicles of Narnia: The Lion, the Witch and the Wardrobe*

The Lion, the Witch and the Wardrobe is a fantasy novel for children by C.S. Lewis, first published in 1950, the first of a series titled 'The Chronicles of Narnia', which have sold 100 million copies worldwide and have been translated into more than three dozen languages.

Although there had been three TV adaptations of the book, plus numerous stage productions, C.S. Lewis never sold the film rights to the series during his lifetime as he was sceptical that any big-screen adaptation could tell the story realistically.

In the early 1990s, three decades after his death, producers Frank Marshall and Kathleen Kennedy entered negotiations for the film rights and proposed to set the story in modern-day Los Angeles. They proposed the Pevensie children would be sent to live there after younger brother Edmund shoplifted a CD. The late author's estate protested about the change in story and timelines and questioned whether film-effects technology was advanced enough to create realistic versions of Aslan and the other talking animals. (This being on the cusp of the release of *Jurassic Park*, which was the gamechanger.)

Kennedy and Marshall moved development of the story across to Walt Disney Studios from Paramount in 1995 but then let the rights lapse at the end of the decade when they moved to Universal Studios with a new eleven-year production deal, thus allowing newly formed Walden Media to step into negotiations with the C.S. Lewis estate in 2000.

Guillermo del Toro was approached to direct but his commitment to *Pan's Labyrinth* prevented his involvement, but then, following an Academy Award win for *Shrek*, director Andrew Adamson came into the frame. 'It was a book so dear to me, a story so dear to me and I couldn't handle the idea of not doing the film,' he said at the Royal Film Performance. Filmed in New Zealand on the back of the *Lord of the Rings* films, Adamson involved Peter Jackson's Weta Workshop to head up digital effects and Howard Berger took on the practical effects work, spending three months retooling designs for animatronics.

On 7 December 2005, the film had its world premiere in London as the fifty-ninth Royal Film Performance at the Royal Albert Hall attended by the Prince of Wales and Duchess of Cornwall. James McAvoy confessed he was 'feeling a bit overwhelmed by the turnout', with hundreds of fans lining the road outside.

The snow and ice themed hall also heralded a blue carpet instead of the traditional red. The royal party were introduced to cast members Tilda Swinton, James McAvoy, Ray Winstone, Jim Broadbent, Dawn French and the young

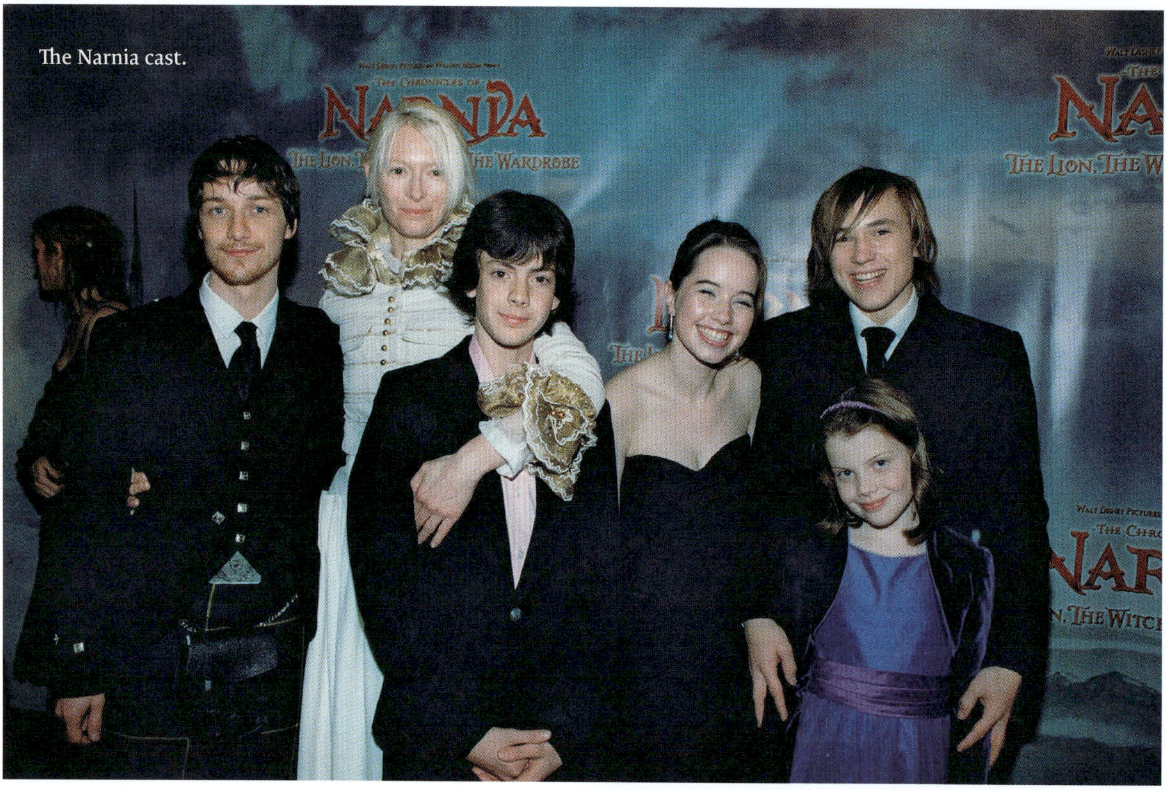

The Narnia cast.

stars, William Moseley (Peter Pevensie), Anna Popplewell (Susan Pevensie), Skandar Keynes (Edmund Pevensie) and Georgie Henley (Lucy Pevensie), along with the director and producers.

It marked the first of three 'Chronicles of Narnia' films. There had been more planned but diminishing box-office returns saw Walt Disney pull out after the second film, only for 20th Century Fox to sweep in to finance the third, but *The Magician's Nephew*, the proposed fourth feature film in the series never materialised after executor Douglas Gresham stated that Walden Media's contract with the C.S. Lewis estate had expired in October 2011, hinting it was due to internal conflicts over the direction of future films.

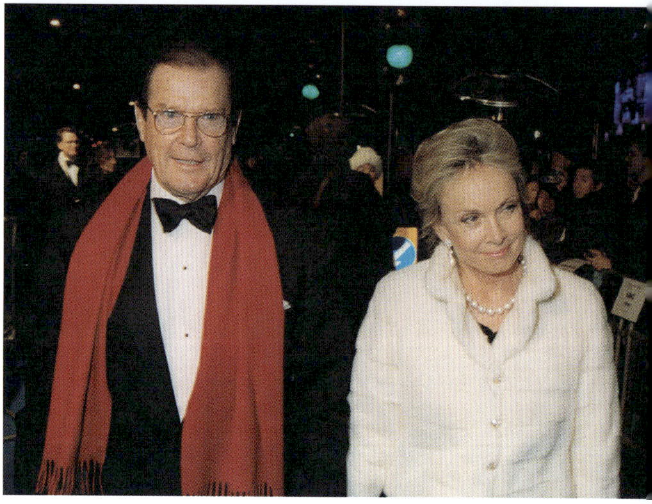

Sir Roger and Lady Moore arrive in Narnia.

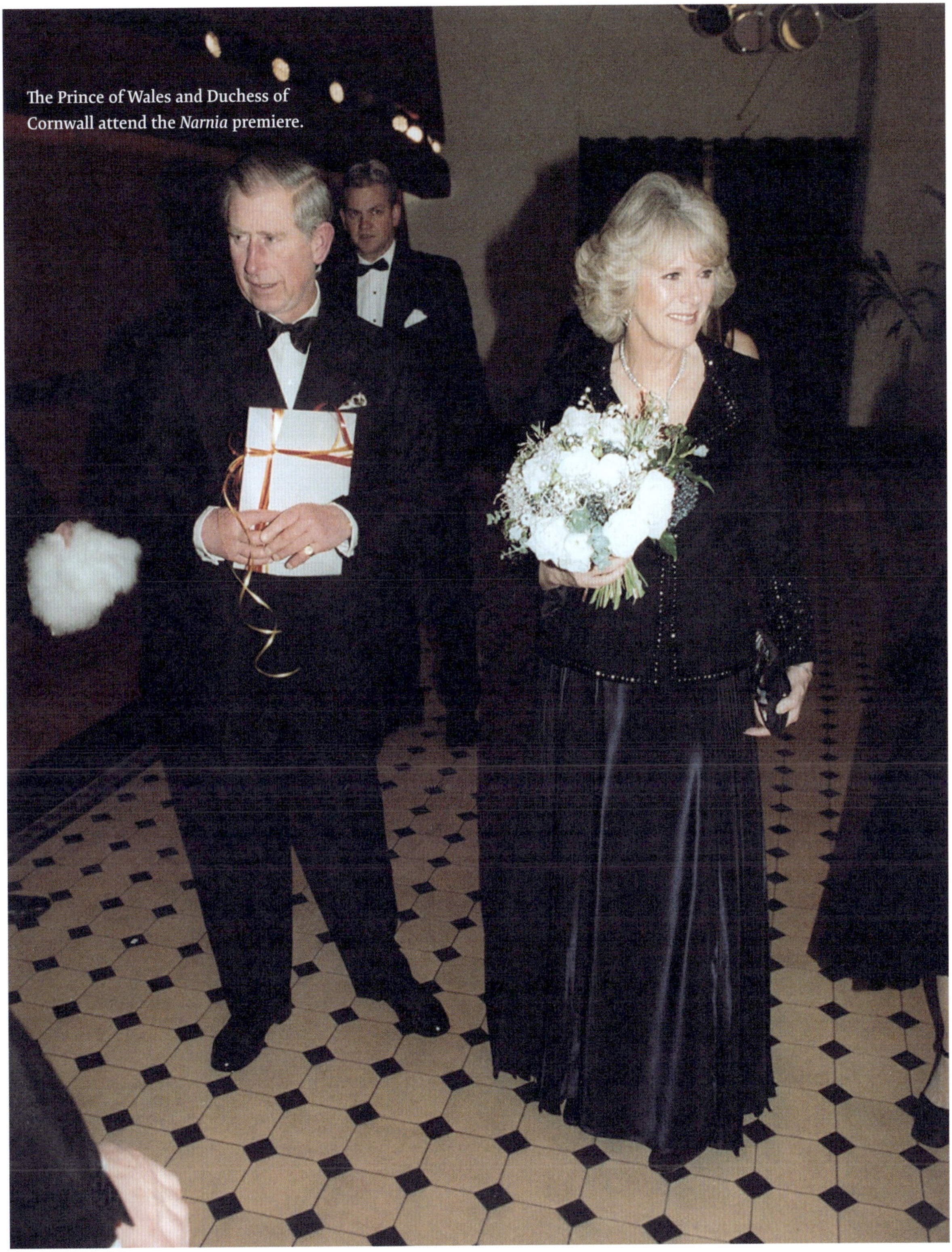

The Prince of Wales and Duchess of Cornwall attend the *Narnia* premiere.

2006 *Casino Royale*

After finally securing the film rights to Ian Fleming's first 007 book, the producers decided it was time to take Bond back to basics and as it made more sense to reboot the franchise, rather than try to rewrite the story to fit established and four-time Bond, Pierce Brosnan, a new actor was cast after many months of rumours and speculation. On 14 October 2005, Daniel Craig was unveiled as the sixth actor to take over the famed licence to kill.

Craig was initially given a rough ride by the media and fans as being too blonde and too short, even before filming had commenced. Just over a year later, most of the doubters were silenced when his debut was chosen for the Royal Film Performance in the presence of the Queen and Duke of Edinburgh. In fact, such was the demand that the whole of Leicester Square was taken over for the event with three cinemas, Odeon, Empire and Odeon West End, holding simultaneous screenings. Lord Attenborough, who gave the Loyal Address that evening, pointed out, 'It is the biggest ever premiere staged in Leicester Square with 4,200 cinemagoers across three theatres.'

'We managed to negotiate multiple prints of the film,' adds former head of development at the CTBF Gayle Gover, 'and actually had simultaneous premieres in Scotland and Ireland too. I introduced the film in Glasgow.'

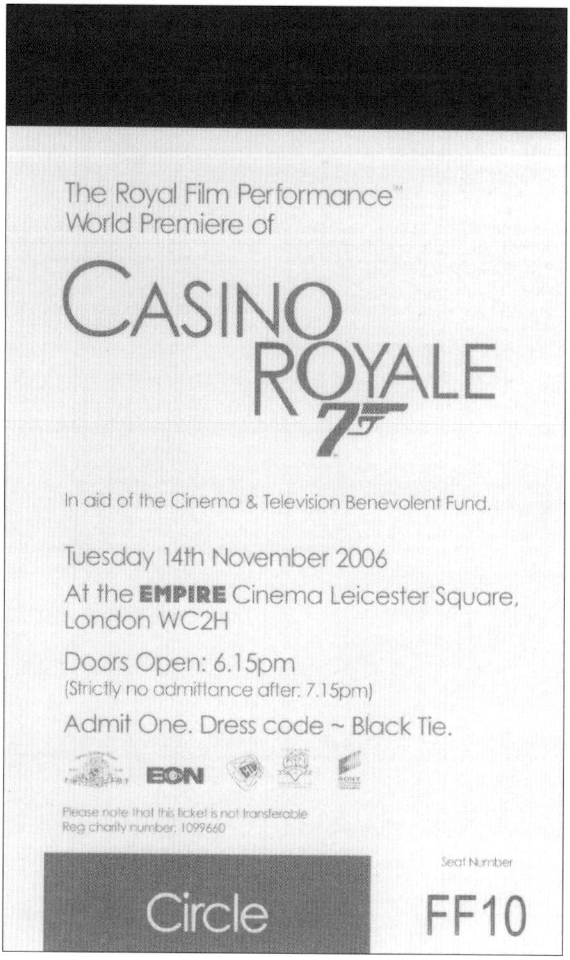
The Royal Film Performance™
World Premiere of

CASINO ROYALE 007

In aid of the Cinema & Television Benevolent Fund.

Tuesday 14th November 2006

At the **EMPIRE** Cinema Leicester Square, London WC2H

Doors Open: 6.15pm
(Strictly no admittance after: 7.15pm)

Admit One. Dress code ~ Black Tie.

Please note that this ticket is not transferable
Reg charity number: 1099660

Circle | Seat Number FF10

In the central area of the square, where an Aston Martin DBS took pride of place, premiere attendees trod one of three differently coloured carpets, each of which led to one of the three cinemas. Daniel Craig attended with former girlfriend Satsuki Mitchell, and leading lady Eva Green adopted a rather gothic-looking dress for the evening. Craig looked genuinely happy, shaking hands, signing autographs for fans and even taking photographs for them, holding the camera so both he and the camera owner were in the shot.

Earlier in the day, in the build-up to the premiere, the Changing of the Guard ceremony

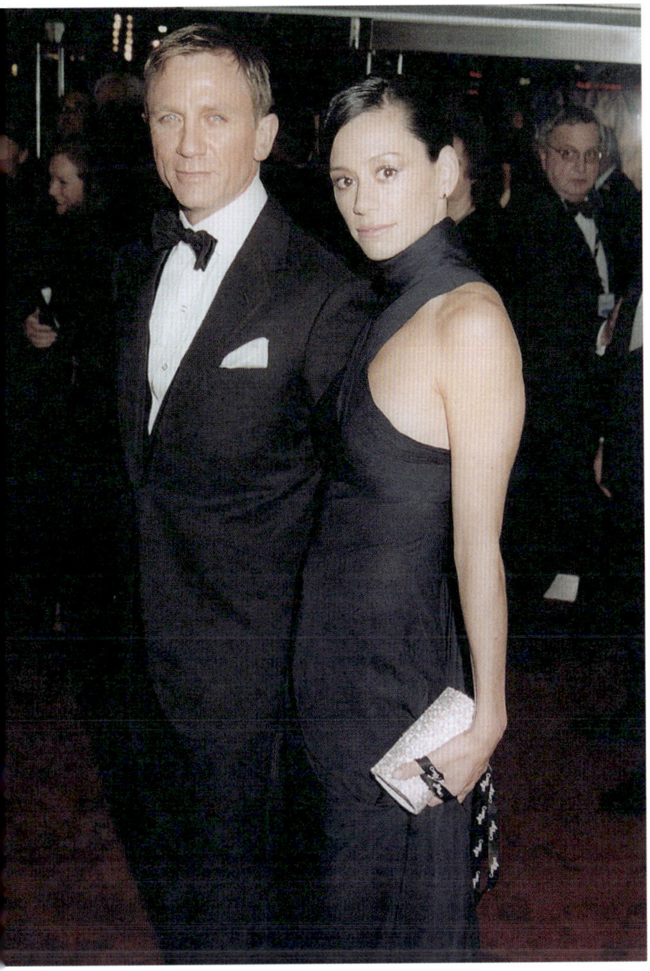

New 007 Daniel Craig arrives at the Odeon with (former) girlfriend Satsuki Mitchell.

was performed to a melody of Bond themes as the square was dressed for the event, with fans and media alike lining the surrounding area for the much-anticipated return of James Bond. 'Entrance to all three cinemas was via the north-west corner of Leicester Square itself', adds former CTBF CEO Peter Hore, 'where the only problem which we did not foresee, and which revealed itself on the night, was the disturbance to the birds roosting in the trees. Some guests were rather unpleasantly surprised!'

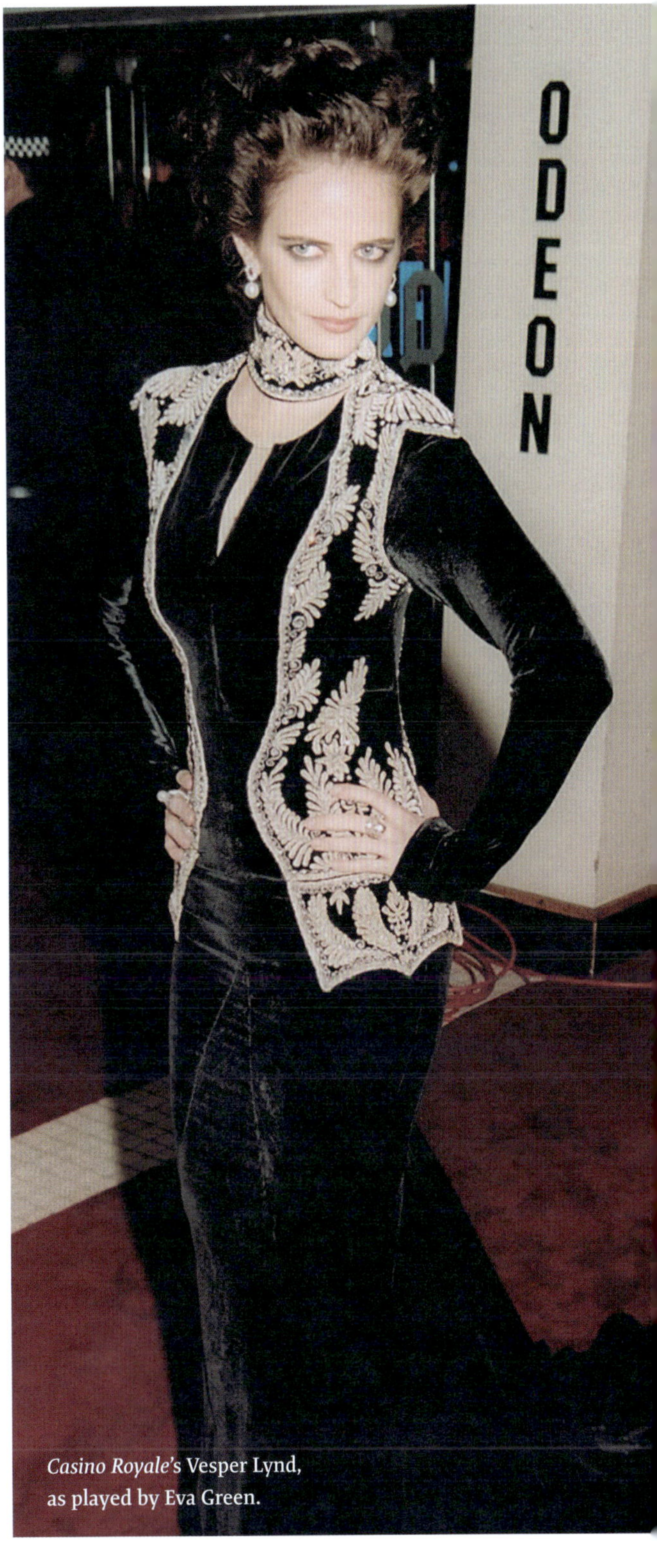

Casino Royale's Vesper Lynd, as played by Eva Green.

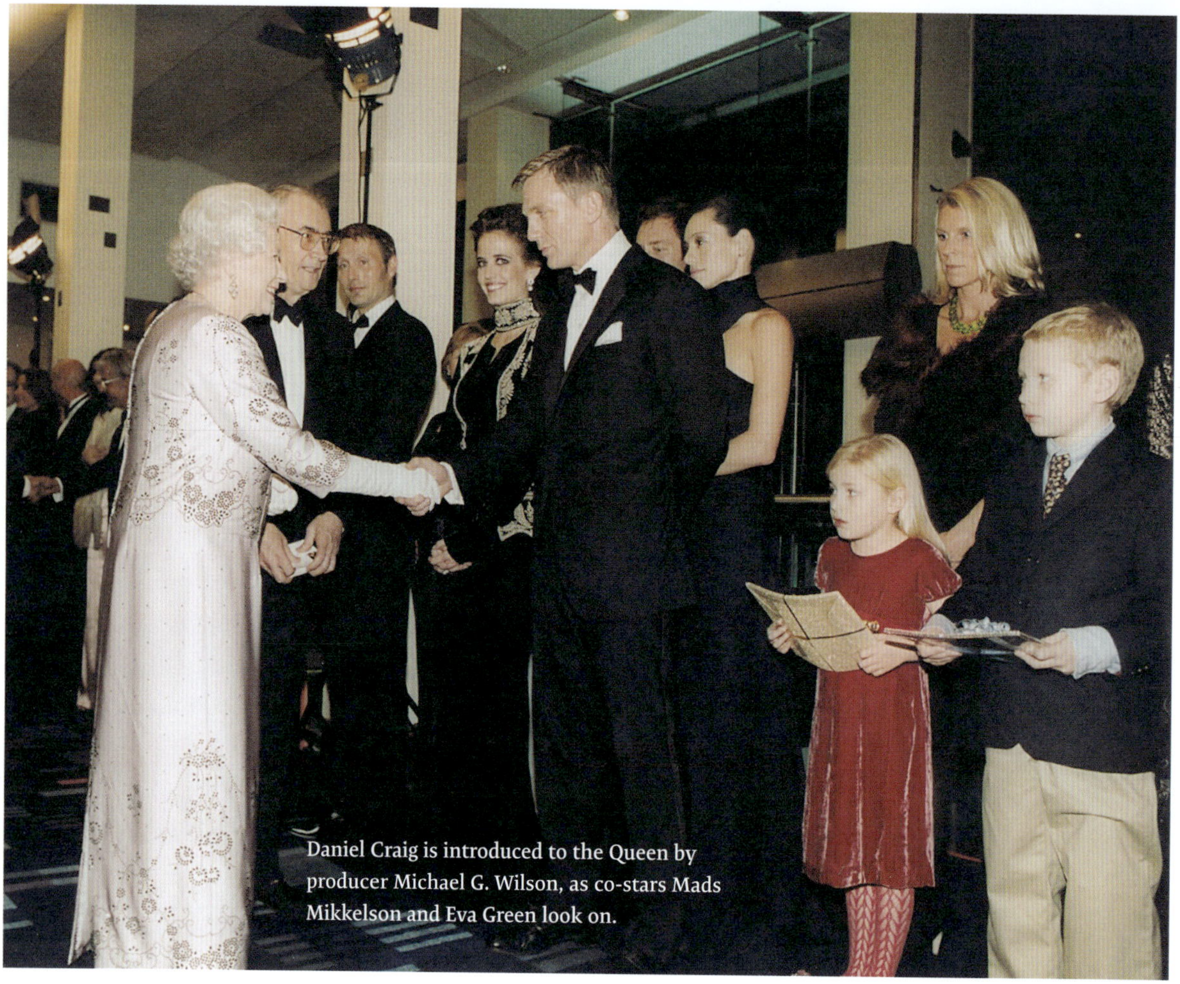

Daniel Craig is introduced to the Queen by producer Michael G. Wilson, as co-stars Mads Mikkelson and Eva Green look on.

While the film didn't feature regulars Q and Moneypenny, it did mark the return of Judi Dench as M and indeed the return of director Martin Campbell after he'd reinvigorated the series with Pierce Brosnan's debut film a decade earlier. Producer Michael G. Wilson introduced Her Majesty to an impressive line-up of key cast and crew, and the biggest premiere in Leicester Square history raised over £300,000 for the charity.

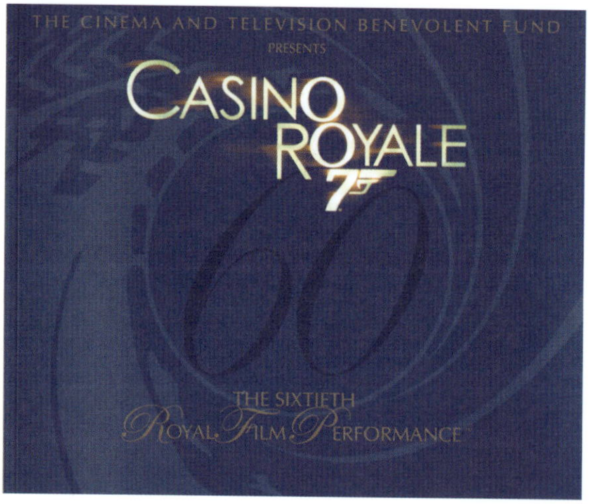

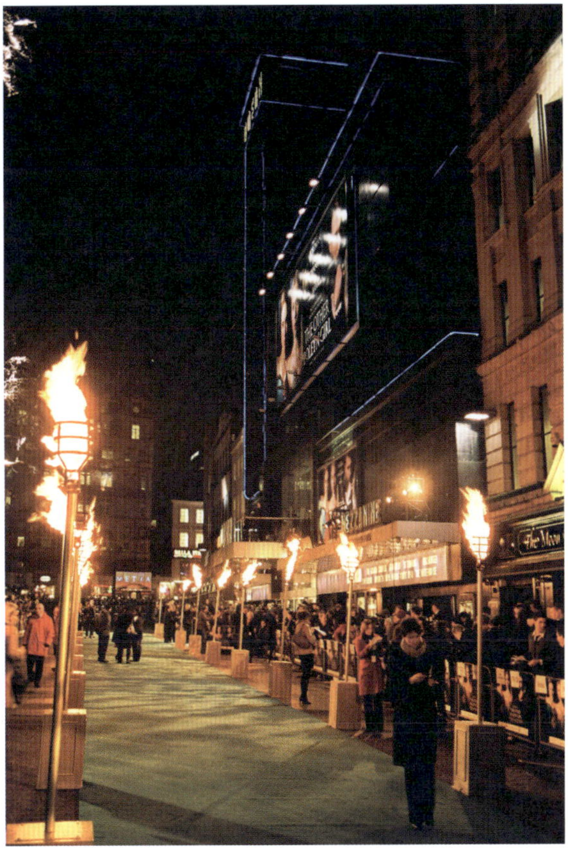

Exterior of the Odeon dressed for *The Other Boleyn Girl.*

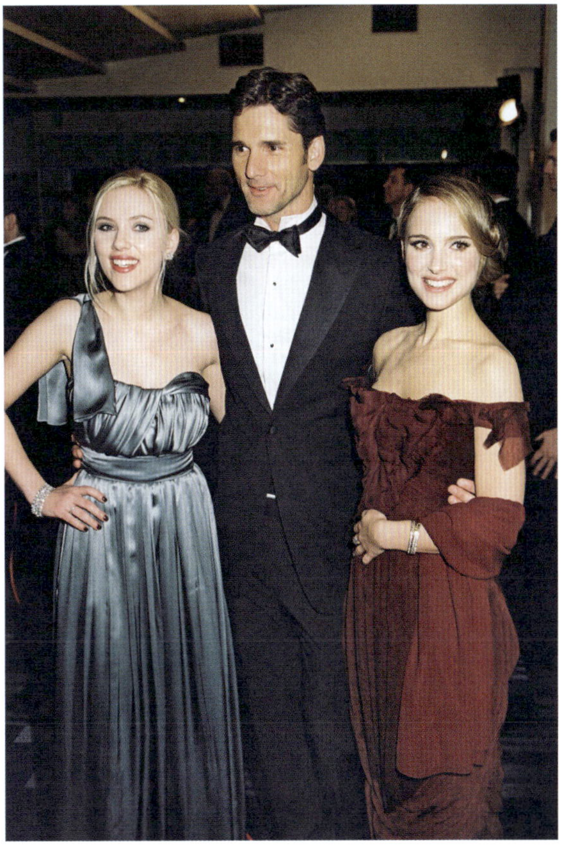

The leading players Scarlet Johansson, Eric Bana and Natalie Portman.

2008 *The Other Boleyn Girl*

The 2007 Royal Film Performance of *Brick Lane* had been cancelled due to 'scheduling issues with the Palace' and a decision was made to hold two Royal Film Performances the following year. However, media reports claimed the story, which centred on a young Bangladeshi woman struggling to adapt to her new life in London when she becomes part of an arranged marriage, might have caused protest after traders in Brick Lane, London's famed row of Bangladeshi restaurants, mounted a successful campaign to force production company Ruby Films to find an alternative location the previous summer, claiming it portrayed residents as 'uneducated'.

'The cancellation of the Royal Film Performance™ is a real shame,' the movie's director, Sarah Gavron, told trade newspaper *Variety*:

> The cast and crew of the film were excited at the recognition for their work and are now understandably disappointed. The clear message from audiences once they have seen the film is that it is absolutely not disrespectful or controversial in any

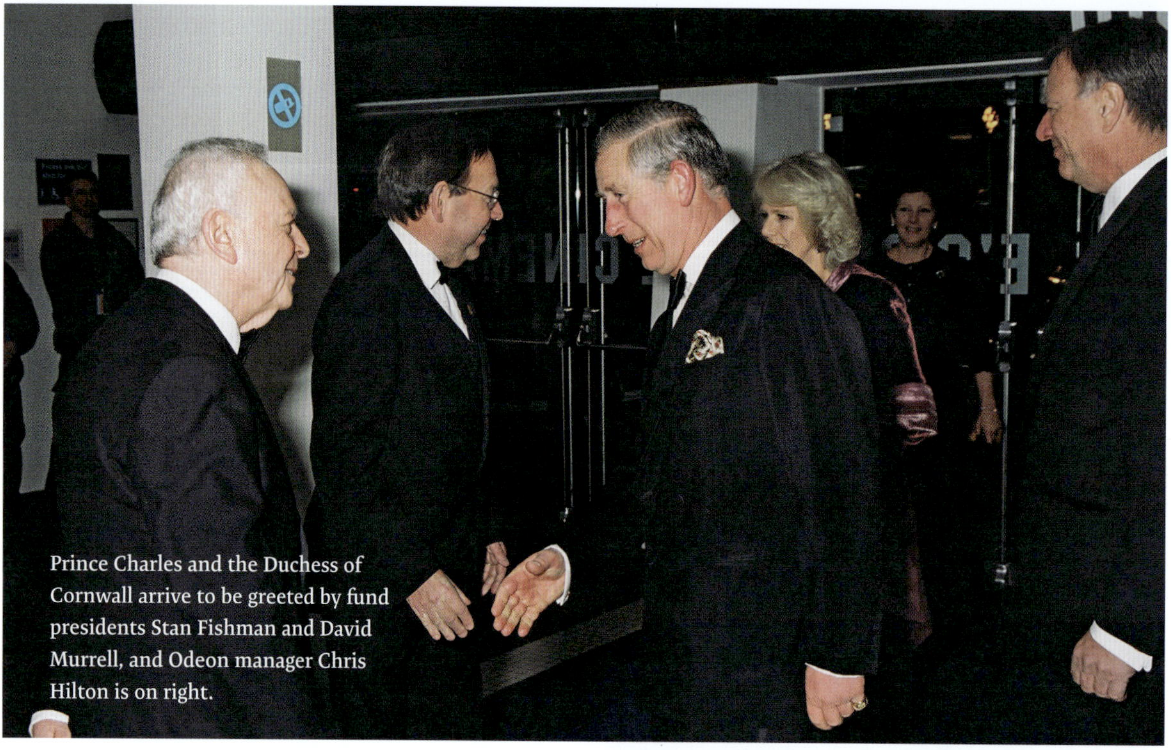

Prince Charles and the Duchess of Cornwall arrive to be greeted by fund presidents Stan Fishman and David Murrell, and Odeon manager Chris Hilton is on right.

way. None of those elements cited by the minority of protesters during the production period appear in the film.

Peter Hore, the charity's chief executive, stated, 'Brick Lane [is] a beautiful film and one of the best independent British productions of the season. For whatever reason it no longer works in the royal diary. The Prince's office has kindly offered to find a date in the new year.' Indeed, a new date for a spring Royal Film Performance was offered as 19 February 2008, and *The Other Boleyn Girl* was chosen, fresh from its premiere at the Berlin Film Festival.

Curiously, director Justin Chadwick has only made four films in his career to date and two of them have premiered as Royal Film Performances – not a bad average! Having been nominated for the Primetime Emmy

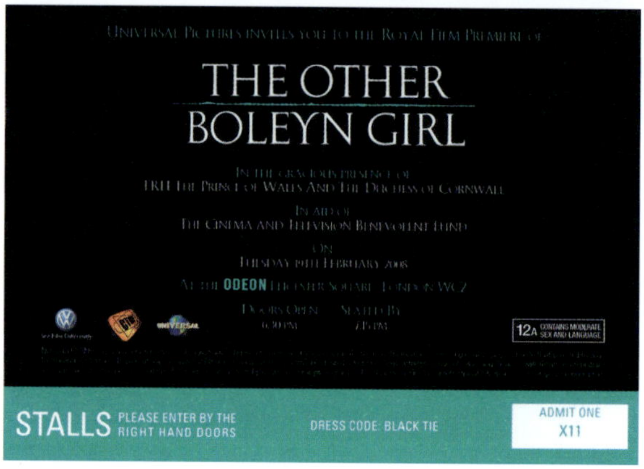

Award, the Royal Television Society Award and the BAFTA Award for Best Direction for BBC TV series *Bleak House*, it's easy to see why BBC Films recruited him to helm the film adaptation of the book that had sold 4 million copies. Author Philippa Gregory assured interviewers on the green-blue carpet, lined with medieval-style fire torches at the London premiere, that her novel was factually accurate, though she did hint that 'the film may take a few liberties!' Indeed, some critics claimed the movie played 'fast and loose' with British history.

'The film was a challenge and nerve wracking as I was playing a real-life character,' Eric Bana told press outside the Odeon about playing King Henry VIII, and when asked how it felt to be at the Royal Film Performance with the future King of England, he said, 'It's quite bizarre actually.'

Scarlett Johansson and Natalie Portman played the Boleyn sisters and were full of praise for one another at the Royal Film Performance: 'We really wanted to establish that sisterly bond and the sort of intimate relationship sisters would have so the audience would feel committed,' Johansson said. Natalie Portman concurred, 'Scarlett would be a great sister and I was lucky to have her as a team mate on this film. You know it's hard to find one great female role in the movie, but to have two is almost unheard of.'

Odeon, Leicester Square, manager Chris Hilton welcomed the Prince of Wales and Duchess of Cornwall to the line-up, which included actors Benedict Cumberbatch, Eddie Redmayne, Scarlett Johansson and Natalie Portman, along with writer Peter Morgan (before *The Crown*), producer Alison Owen and director Justin Chadwick.

2008 *A Bunch of Amateurs*

The second Royal Film Performance of 2008, held on 17 November at the Odeon, Leicester Square, in the presence of the Queen and the Duke of Edinburgh, was originally to have been *Harry Potter and the Half-Blood Prince*, but that film's release date was pushed back eight months to 17 July 2009 by the 2007–08 Writers Guild of America strike, in order 'to guarantee the studio a major summer blockbuster in 2009,' said Alan F. Horn of Warner Bros, as reported by Ben Child in *The Guardian* on 20 November 2008. The strike caused production on some previously scheduled summer film releases to be delayed – it was not the last time strikes would affect proposed Royal Film Performances either – so a 'plan B' was hastily needed.

That back-up came with David Parfitt's production of *A Bunch of Amateurs*, starring Burt Reynolds. 'He called it a "part of a lifetime", a role that reflected his own career to a certain degree,' says Parfitt, on his enthusiastic lead actor:

> Though it was a difficult film to make, not helped by the fact Burt was addicted to prescription painkillers and had trouble learning lines – and even moving. We cast a lookalike and through the miracle of editing were able to have Burt walk and move around – though anything wider than a mid-shot was not him but his double.

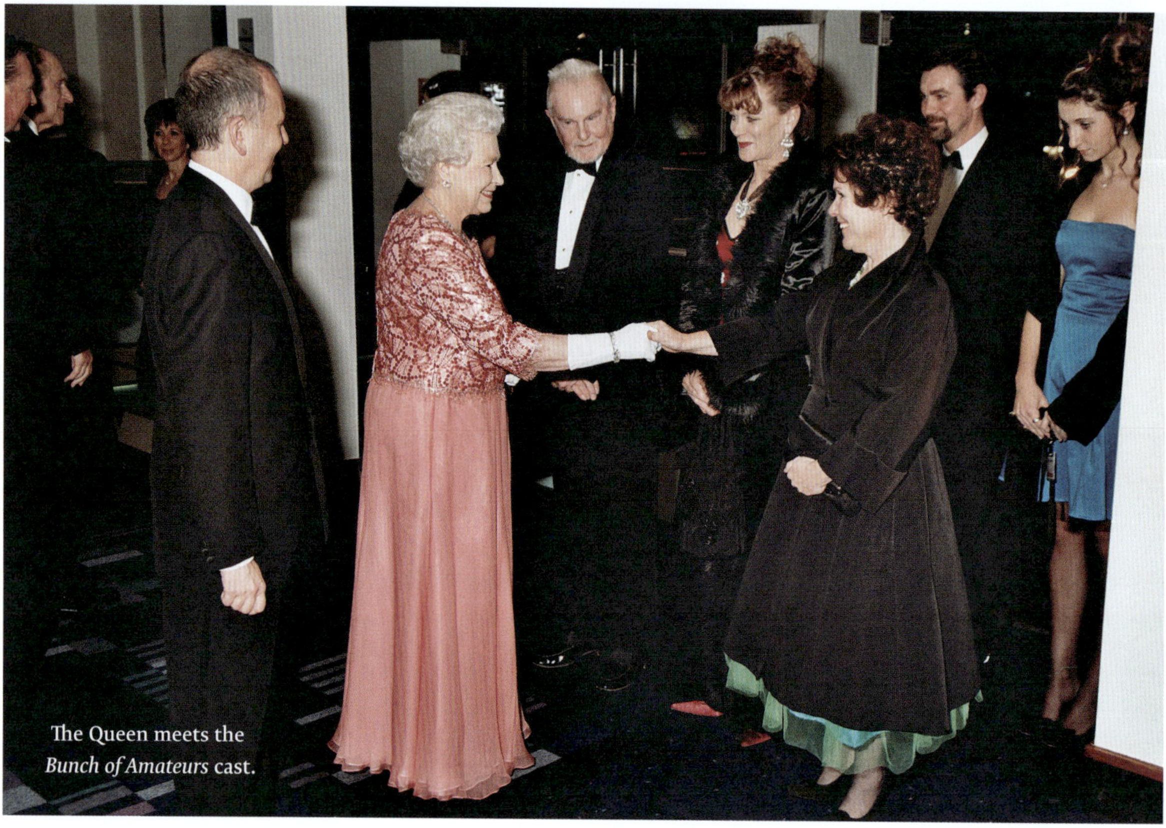

The Queen meets the *Bunch of Amateurs* cast.

His voice track came from a mix of production sound, ADR [additional dialogue recordings] and impressionist John Sessions helping replace missing words and even sounding the consonants in sentences, which Burt could no longer do.

It always amazes me to see the scene where Burt walks, talks and laughs – yet he wasn't even on set that day!

It was a fantastic launch for the film and so lovely for the cast and crew to have the project's profile raised so significantly, which delighted our distributor 'Entertainment' no end too, as it was a little film that no one had really seen or heard much about up until that point.

Burt Reynolds was unable to travel from the USA for the premiere, but main supporting cast members Derek Jacobi and Imelda Staunton were on hand to welcome the Queen and the Duke of Edinburgh to the Odeon, Leicester Square.

On the red carpet, co-star Samantha Bond enthused about the experience of working with Reynolds:

> It was completely awesome. When Burt tells stories about Frank Sinatra and the like, I kept thinking, in terms of a game of six degrees of separation, if I've kissed Burt (albeit in an affectionate way), does that mean that I have nearly kissed Sinatra? And thereby hangs a dream!

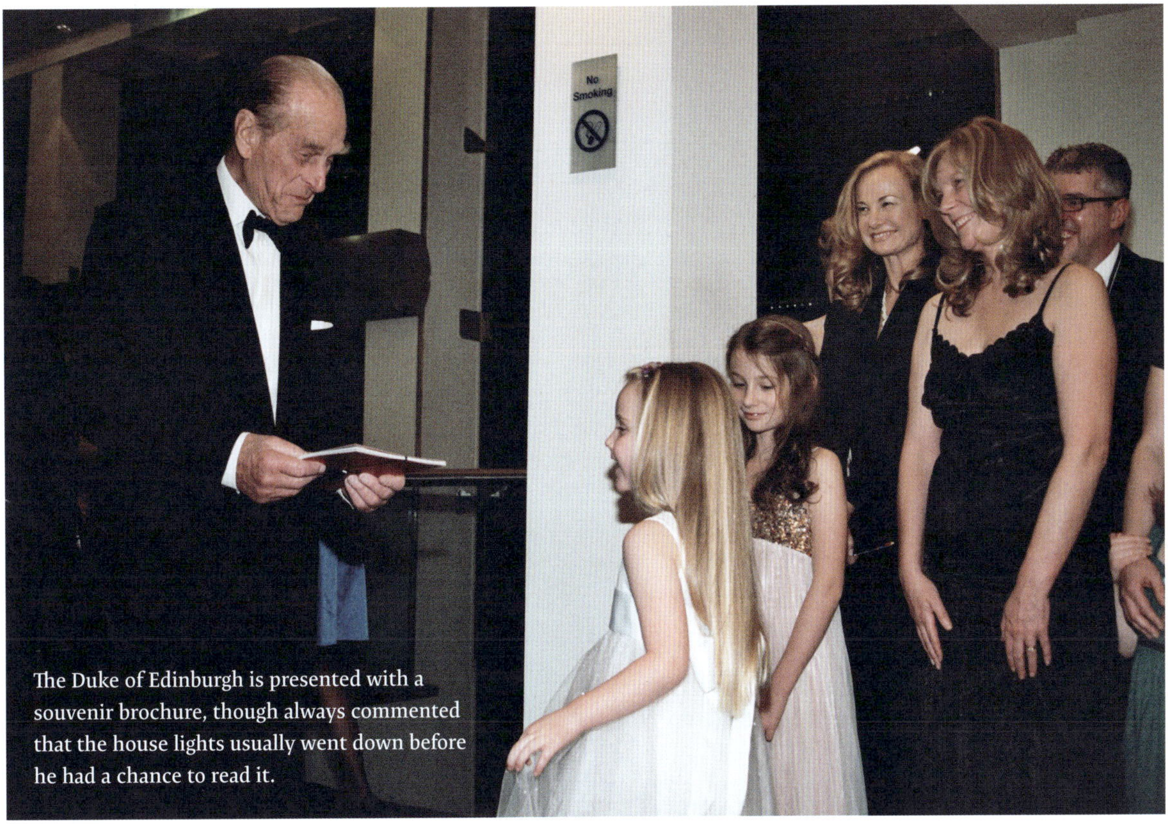

The Duke of Edinburgh is presented with a souvenir brochure, though always commented that the house lights usually went down before he had a chance to read it.

On the BBC News website, chief executive of the CTBF Peter Hore said the film was 'a feel-good movie that would be a classic movie after tonight'. Not all critics agreed with his enthusiasm; however, Her Majesty obviously enjoyed the movie more than some reviewers.

'I was seated quite near to the Queen and the Duke of Edinburgh and glanced over several times during the film only to see them genuinely laughing and enjoying it hugely,' said a proud David Parfitt.

The premiere marked manager Chris Hilton's last Royal Film Performance ahead of retirement. 'I asked the CTBF if my wife Sue might be allowed to meet the Queen and Duke as I escorted them out through the foyer,' reveals Hilton:

> The reply came back 'of course'. Her Majesty and His Royal Highness graciously shook hands with Sue and as I walked them out of the theatre the Duke paused, looked at me and, knowing I was about to retire, asked, 'So what are you going to do now?'
>
> 'Get a proper job, sir' was my reply, at which point the Duke laughed uproariously and stepped inside his awaiting car.

Chris Hilton was awarded an MBE for services to the film industry in the 2020 New Year Honours List.

Incidentally, it was reported in the press that Buckingham Palace later asked if *A Bunch of Amateurs* could be screened for Her Majesty and the royal family at Sandringham over Christmas. A royal approval if ever there was one!

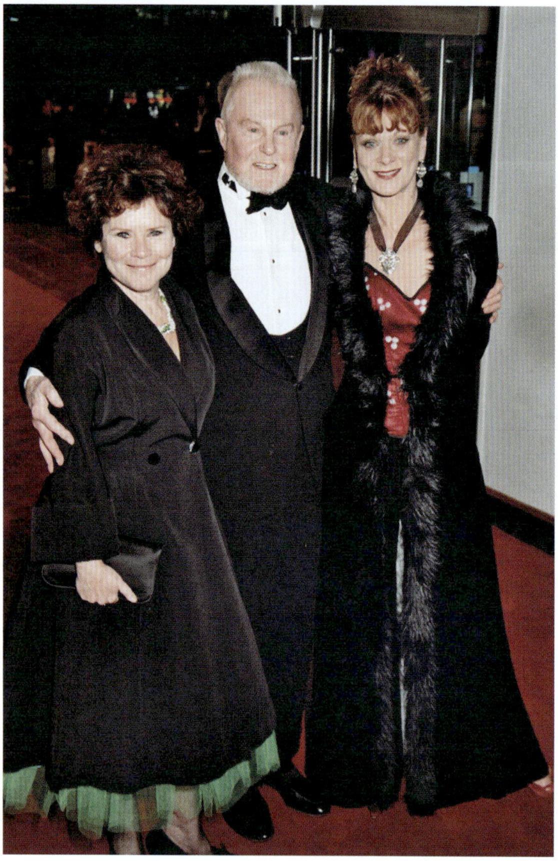

Derek Jacobi flanked by Imelda Staunton and Samantha Bond.

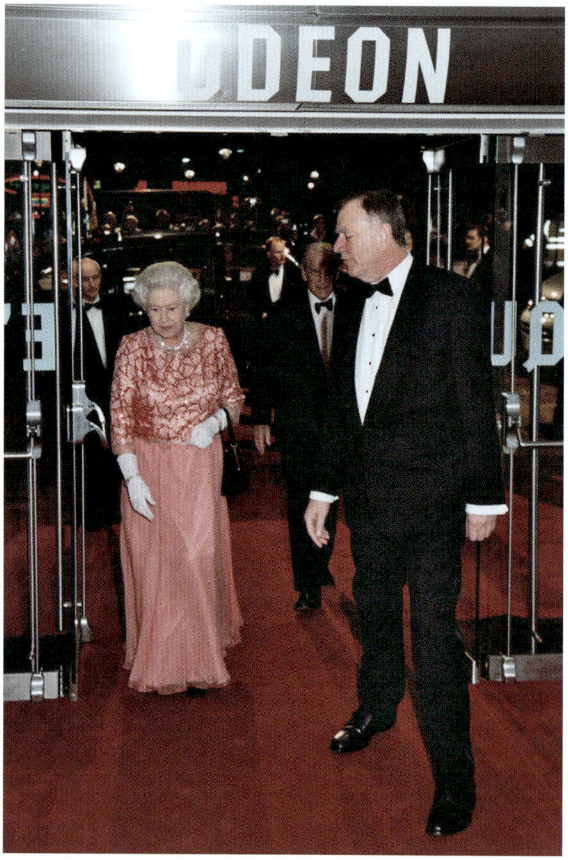

Manager Chris Hilton (at his last Royal Film Performance) welcome the royal party to the Odeon.

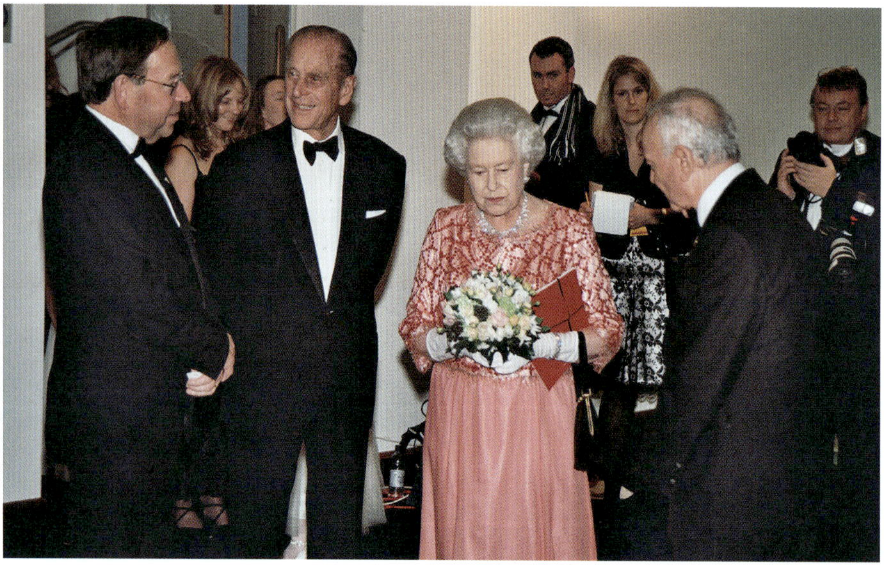

A Bunch of Amateurs (2008): David Murrell, the Duke of Edinburgh, the Queen and Stan Fishman.

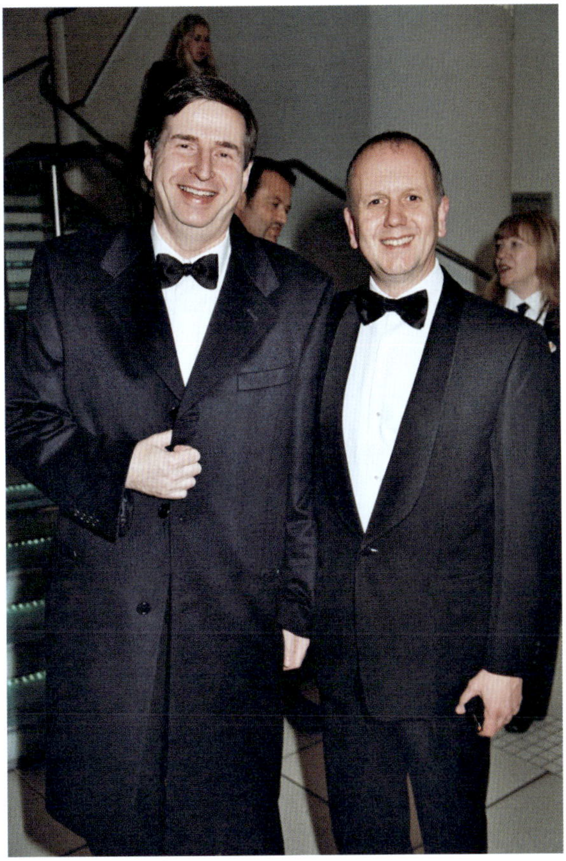

A Bunch of Amateurs producer David Parfitt with distributor Nigel Green.

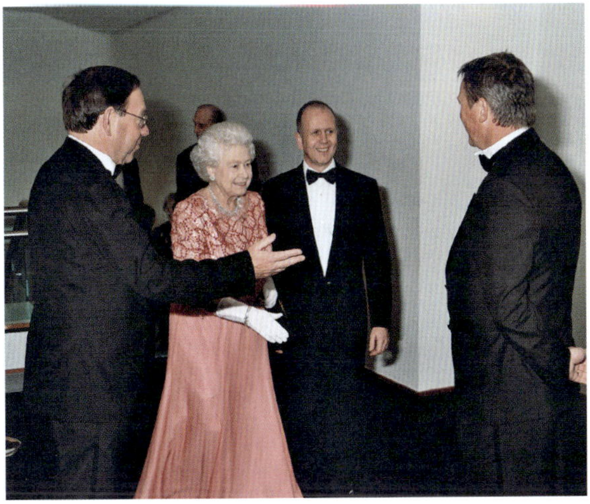

A Bunch of Amateurs (2008): David Murrell, the Queen, David Parfitt and Steve Christian.

2009 *The Lovely Bones*

Director Peter Jackson had no intention of making a film out of this acclaimed novel by Alice Sebold when his *Lord of the Rings* co-writers, Fran Walsh and Philippa Boyens, both ardent fans of the book, recommended it to him in 2002. As it was, Jackson was busy in post-production on *The Lord of the Rings: The Two Towers*. However, over time he found the story so affecting that it became something of a personal project for him and a welcome shift away from blockbuster filmmaking.

DreamWorks ended up backing the film with co-founder Steven Spielberg, a fan of both the novel and Jackson, coming in as executive producer. Featuring a stellar cast, including Stanley Tucci, Mark Wahlberg, Rachel Weisz and Susan Sarandon, *The Lovely Bones* tells the story of a 14-year-old girl who is murdered in 1970s Pennsylvania and watches from her personal heaven as her family struggle to come to terms with the loss.

Jackson decided to shoot on location in the United States, marking the first time he had directed outside of his native New Zealand. The director also makes his customary cameo appearance, *à la* Alfred Hitchcock, as a customer playing with a Super 8 camera in a store.

Mixing horror, psychological drama and fantasy, *The Lovely Bones* received mixed reviews and was a disappointment at the box office, especially given the credentials of

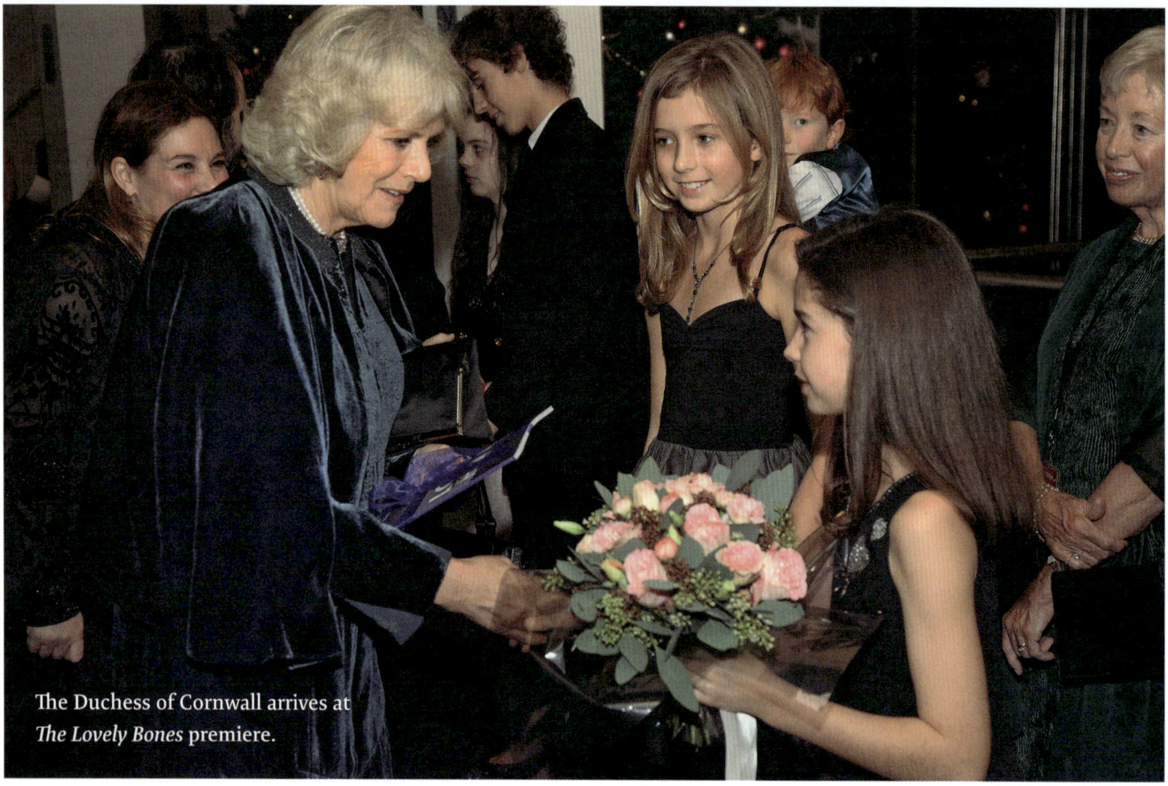

The Duchess of Cornwall arrives at *The Lovely Bones* premiere.

those involved. Some were disappointed that the more adult themes within the novel were diluted to appeal to the broadest audience. Given the dark subject matter, it was perhaps not best suited for a fun evening out at the pictures. 'I met the Prince of Wales and the Duchess of Cornwall as they left the cinema,' recalls Peter Hore, then the charity's CEO, 'and thought they both looked a bit shellshocked.' The charity's chief executive Brian Robertson remembers sensing a similar reaction from the royal couple. 'Charles came out with Camilla, and I always used to be in the reception for when they came out, and Charles went, "Well, that was interesting, wasn't it."'

Peter Jackson attended the event, along with one of the stars of the film, Susan Sarandon. Unfortunately for the waiting crowds and attendees, it was a filthy, wet and windswept evening. Dodging under umbrellas were other celebrity guests including Stephen Fry, Frank Skinner and Andy Serkis.

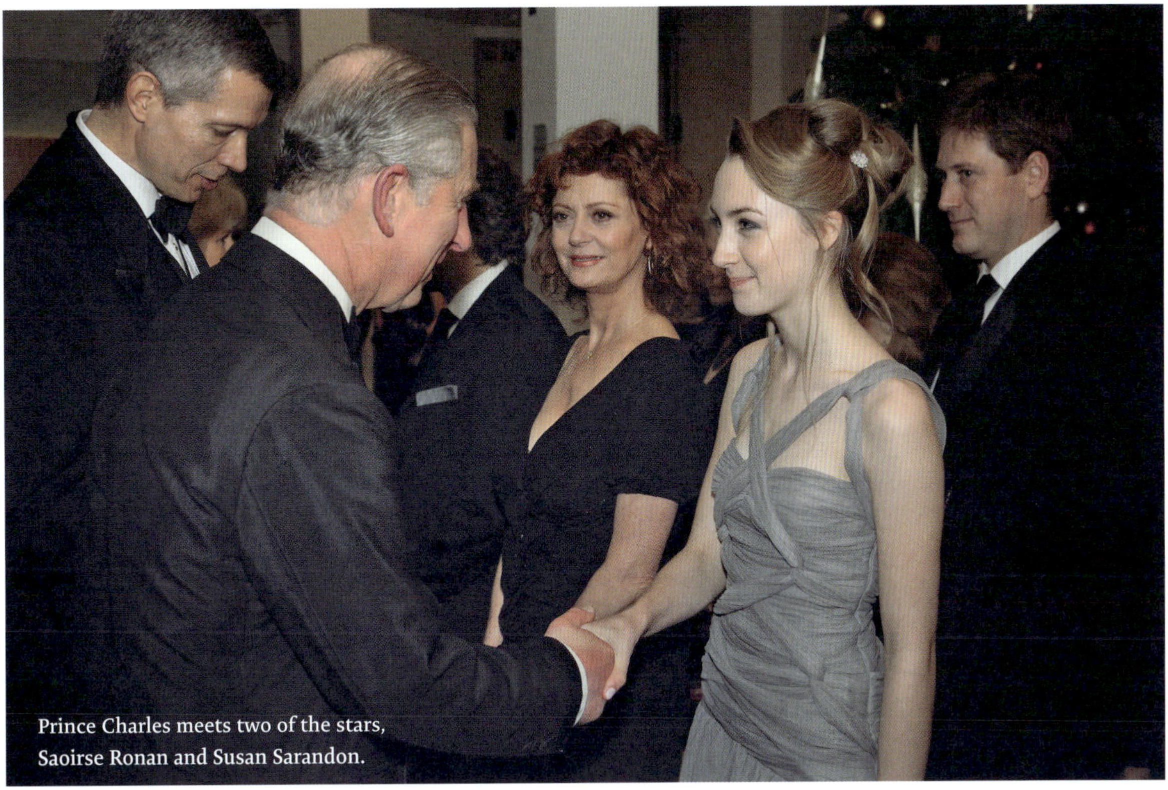

Prince Charles meets two of the stars, Saoirse Ronan and Susan Sarandon.

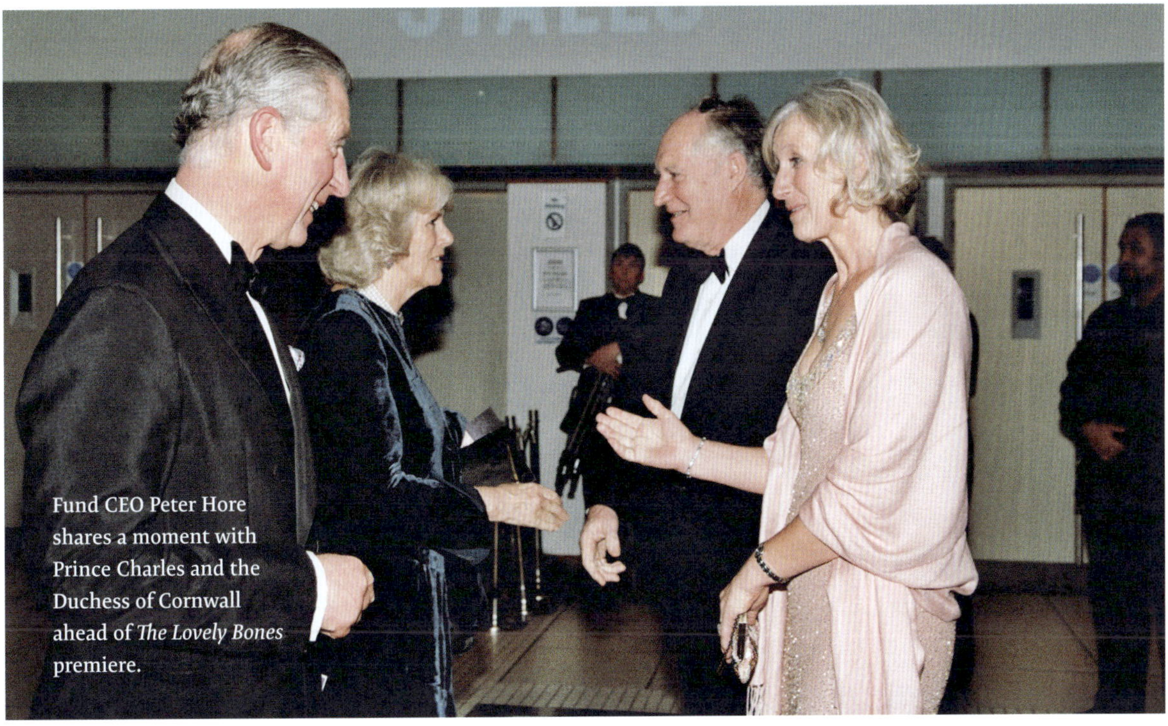

Fund CEO Peter Hore shares a moment with Prince Charles and the Duchess of Cornwall ahead of *The Lovely Bones* premiere.

2010 *The Chronicles of Narnia: Voyage of the Dawn Treader*

This third entry into the Narnia series was also the second to be chosen for a Royal Film Performance and one of only two 3D Royal Film Performances. On 30 November, Leicester Square was transformed into a winter wonderland as guests arrived at the Empire Cinema, with a fake snow machine giving the night a true Christmassy feel. Ironically, there was a huge snowfall in London during the film so, long after the fake snow had been cleared, guests emerged from the cinema to be greeted by a real winter wonderland!

Michael Apted had taken over from the director of the earlier instalments, Andrew Adamson, who remained on board as a producer. Filming had been due to commence in January 2008 for a 1 May 2009 release, but Disney announced that 'in consideration of the challenging schedules for the young actors', they were delaying the release date to 7 May 2010.

Financing partner and distributor Disney next announced on 24 December 2008 that it would no longer co-produce the film, having become concerned that their $100 million costs had grown to $140 million, with fears they would grow further during production. 'Creative differences' were cited, and film rights owner and producer Walden Media began searching for a new distributor for the film – 20th Century Fox stepped in.

Fox's Cameron Saunders was on hand to greet the Queen and the Duke of Edinburgh at the premiere and it marked the executive's first time hosting a royal line-up:

> It was remarkable seeing the Queen marching up the stairs, in quite quick fashion, all I could think of was, oh my god, you look just like you do on the money! She had remarkable hair, beautifully done, and her eyes were aquamarine. She wore a beautiful dress, sparkling, it was stunning and quite magical.
>
> It was nerve-wracking for me as I'd just become managing director and was suddenly introducing all the studio heads to the Queen! I had to memorise all the faces and the names, and the Queen listened very acutely ... 'Your Majesty may I present such and such,' and you could see she was really taking great interest in everything I was saying.
>
> Prince Philip was much more informal, laughing and joking with funny comments. Whilst the Queen was much more formal, very dedicated, and very respectful to people. She had a question for every third or fourth person. Obviously, she wanted to engage but couldn't talk to everyone.

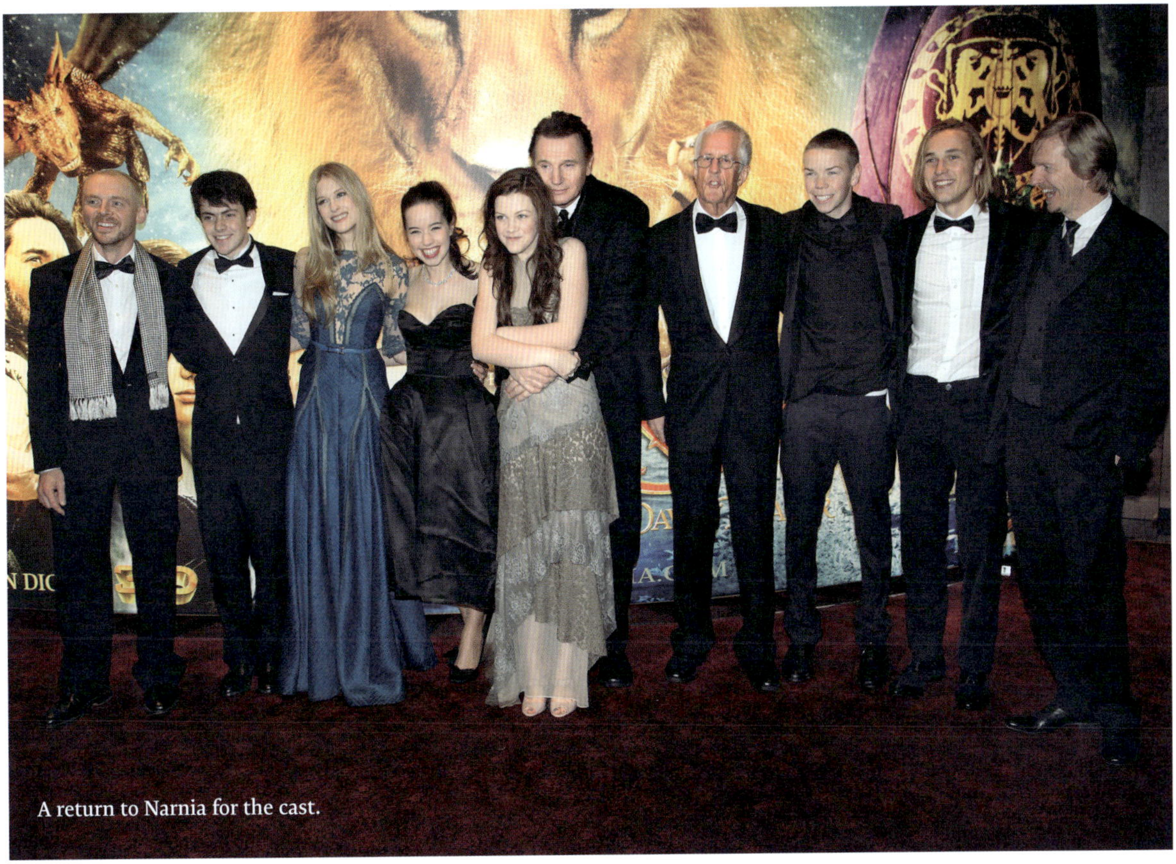

A return to Narnia for the cast.

Saunders continued, 'You're briefed, quite clearly, that you wait until you are spoken to, and you never lead the Queen – you always walk two steps behind.'

As the charity's patron met the cast and crew, Saunders revealed:

> Liam Neeson leant across and took both her hands. Obviously, you are supposed to present your hand, not grab hers, but she didn't seem particularly shocked by his enthusiasm. Joe McElderry, an *X Factor* winner, was there as he performed the song at the end of the film. I explained that he was a musician, and the Queen asked: 'You're a musician, what do you play?' He replied, in a heavy Geordie accent, 'I don't know if you've seen it, but I won the *X Factor*.' The Queen just said, 'Oh', and moved on.
>
> At the end of the line-up she asked me, 'Liam Neeson and Simon Pegg, they're not actually in the film, are they?'
>
> 'No, Your Majesty, they're voices,' I replied.
>
> 'Then, why are they here?' she asked quizzically.
>
> It was obvious the Queen had seen the other Narnia films because she talked at the end as I was escorting her out of the theatre about how interesting it was seeing the child actors all grown up. In the first film they were probably 8 or 9, and now they were teenagers.

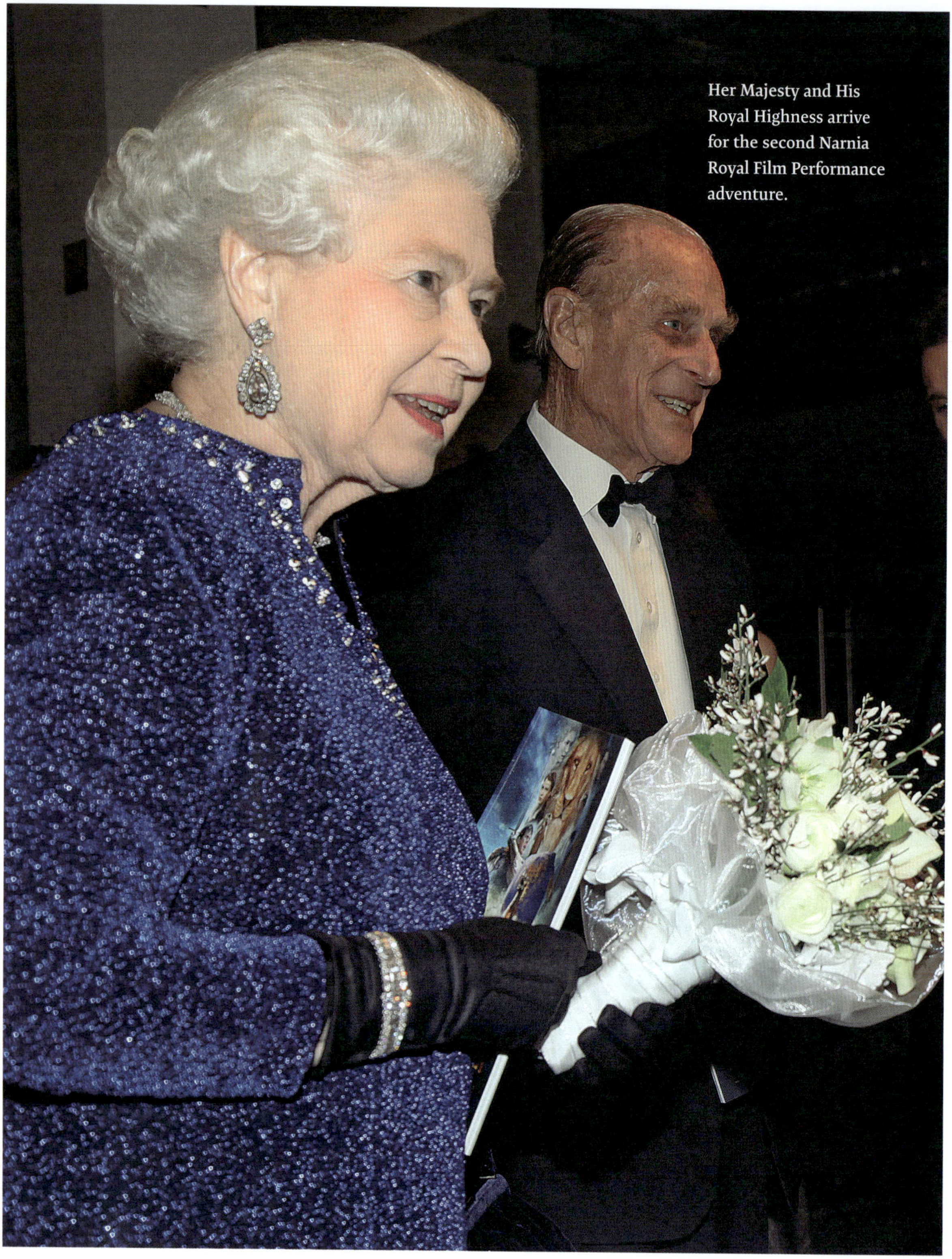

Her Majesty and His Royal Highness arrive for the second Narnia Royal Film Performance adventure.

2011 *Hugo*

This is a rare family film from Martin Scorsese, influenced by the fact that at the time he had a young daughter and perhaps now was the best time to make a piece of family entertainment. *Hugo* is an imaginative film that combines a heartfelt narrative with a celebration of cinema's early days. It tells the story of a young, orphaned boy living alone in a Paris railway station, the people he meets and befriends and the adventures he gets mixed up in. Scorsese employed extensive use of 3D technology for the first time in his career. This also marked the first time that any of his films had been the subject of a royal premiere. No surprise really, given the violent nature of most of his previous work. Scorsese attended the event and was introduced to the Prince of Wales and the Duchess of Cornwall, along with some of the film's stars, Ben Kingsley, Richard Griffiths, Helen McCrory and the two teenage stars of the film, Asa Butterfield and Chloë Grace Moretz.

Sometimes, unexpected problems can arise prior to any Royal Film Performance. For several weeks, there had been extensive building works in Leicester Square and up until the morning of the Royal Film Performance there was a large hole directly in front of the entrance to the Odeon. The cinema manager made urgent requests that the hole be filled in before the guests began arriving.

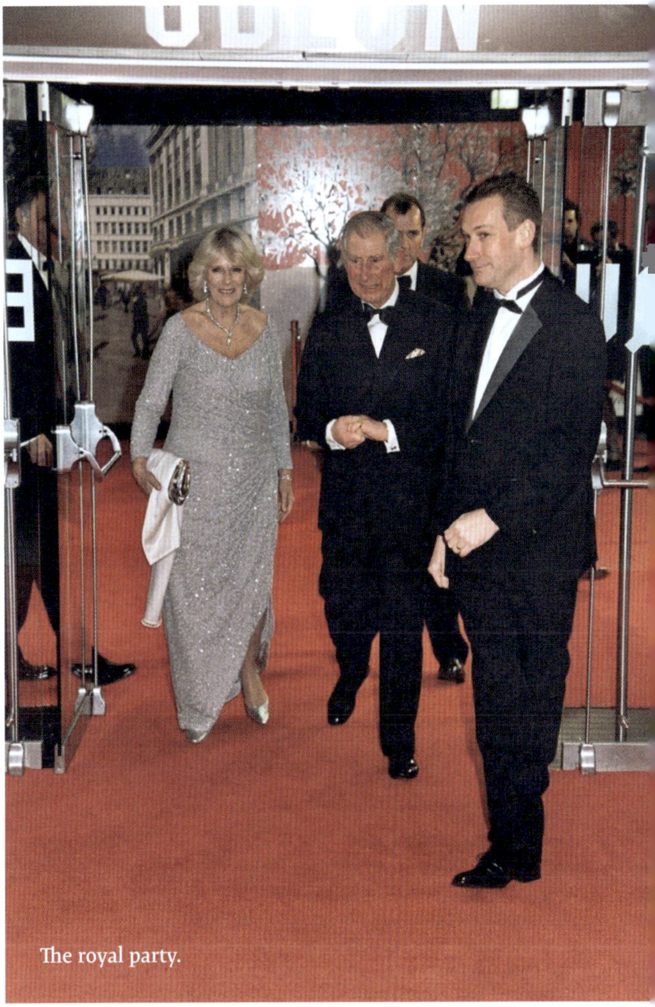

The royal party.

Chief executive of the CTBF at the time, Brian Robertson always got the impression that Prince Charles took much more of an interest in the films he was going to see and was more active in what he wanted to see than the Queen, who was generally happy to just turn up and go along with whatever was put on the screen. Brian also pays tribute to Trevor Green, who was a trustee of the charity and worked in film distribution with his brother Trevor, on some occasions providing suitable releases for showing at the Royal Film Performance. 'He was incredibly generous to the charity,' says Brian:

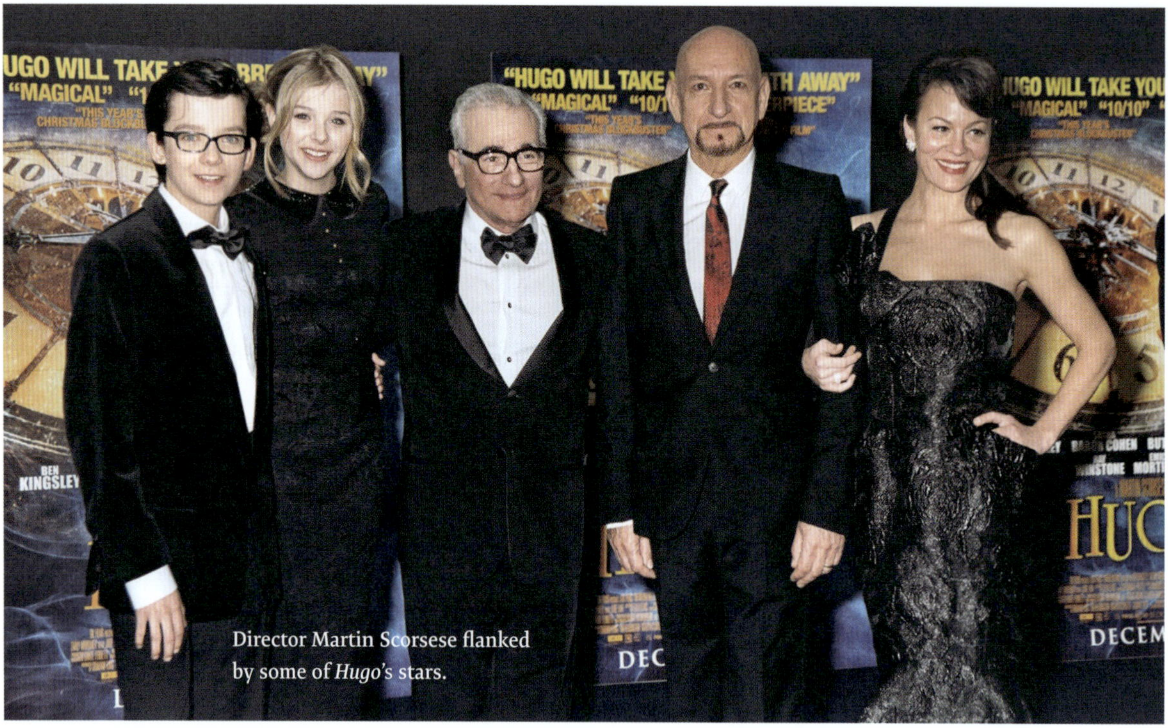

Director Martin Scorsese flanked by some of *Hugo*'s stars.

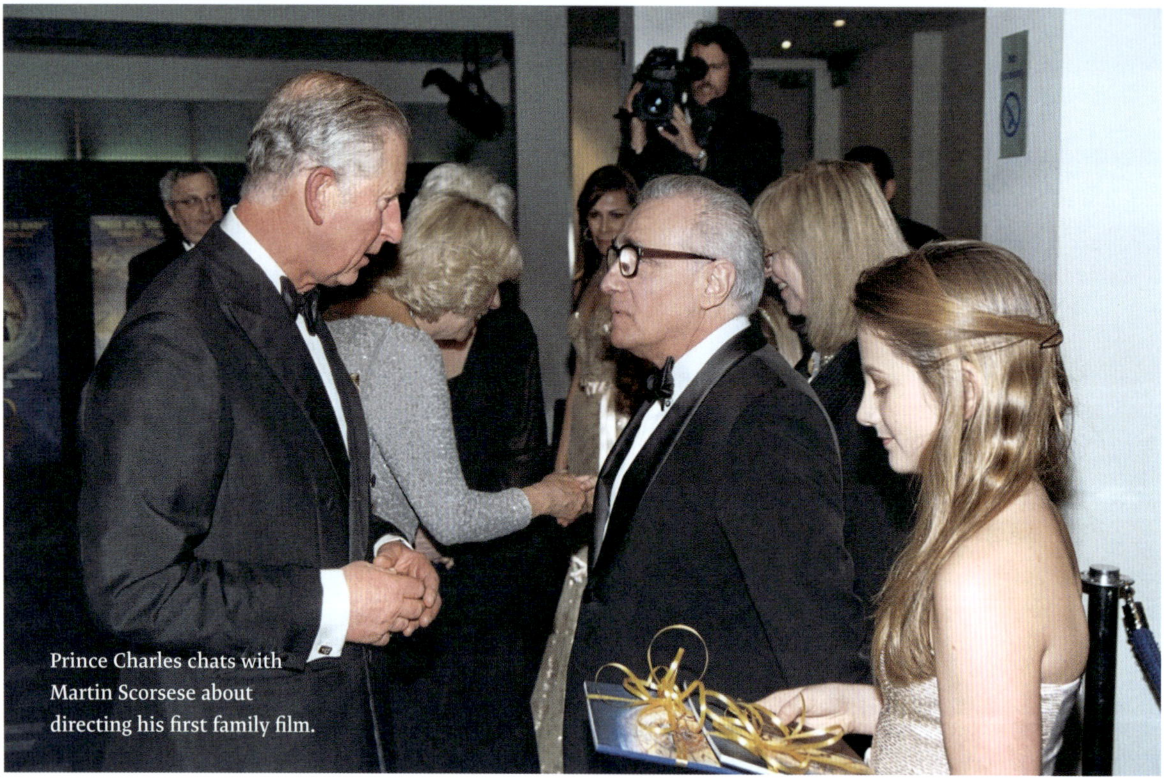

Prince Charles chats with Martin Scorsese about directing his first family film.

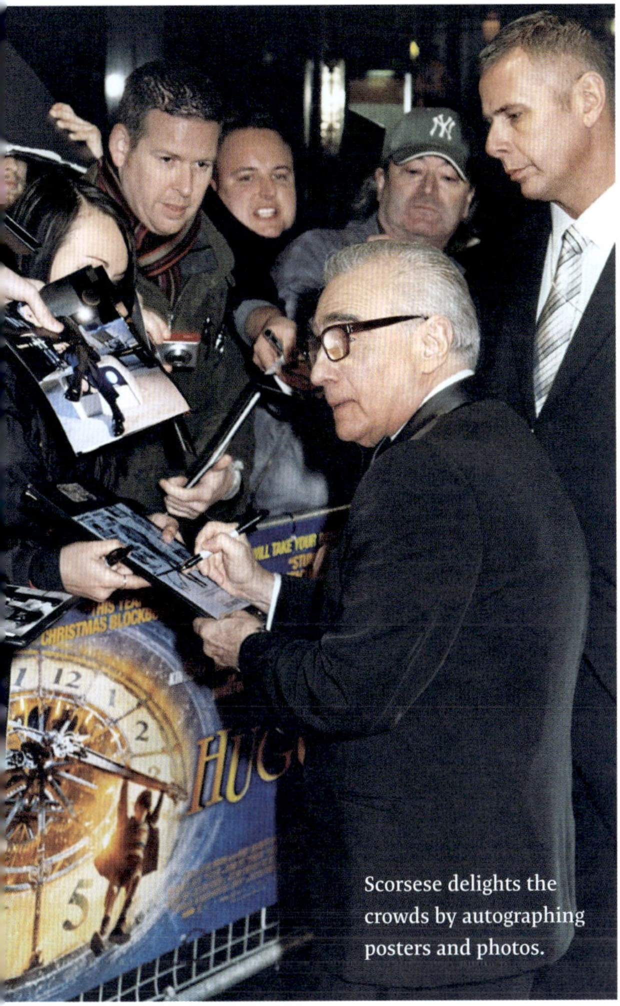

Scorsese delights the crowds by autographing posters and photos.

> After the *Hugo* premiere Trevor said to me, 'How much would you have expected to have made on this film,' and I told him the amount, and he asked, 'Well, how much have you made?' I told him the figure was below our expectations, and he took out a cheque book and just wrote a cheque for the difference.

One of the impressive automatons seen in the film was also donated by the production and auctioned off to raise extra money for the charity.

2012 *The Hobbit: An Unexpected Journey*

The first instalment of Peter Jackson's eagerly anticipated *Hobbit* trilogy made a fitting choice for the sixty-fifth Royal Film Performance. Many of the stars of the film were in attendance, including Martin Freeman, Sir Ian McKellen, Andy Serkis and Cate Blanchett, along with Peter Jackson himself. The December chill did not put off a vast crowd from packing out Leicester Square.

This was to have been the first royal premiere for Prince William and Catherine, Duchess of Cambridge. Sadly, William had to attend without his pregnant wife after she received hospital treatment for acute morning sickness, lamenting that Kate 'would have loved to have been here if she could'. As William met the cast, he was presented with a *Hobbit* goodie bag to take home to Kate.

Jackson and his production team returned to the same shooting location in New Zealand that they had used in the *Lord of the Rings* trilogy. For some of the returning cast members, it proved to be an emotional journey back. The land, part of a farm, had in the meantime been transformed into a tourism spot, offering guided tours. Some of the set was recreated in Leicester Square, a little piece of the Shire and a hobbit's home. The traditional red carpet was also changed to a green carpet.

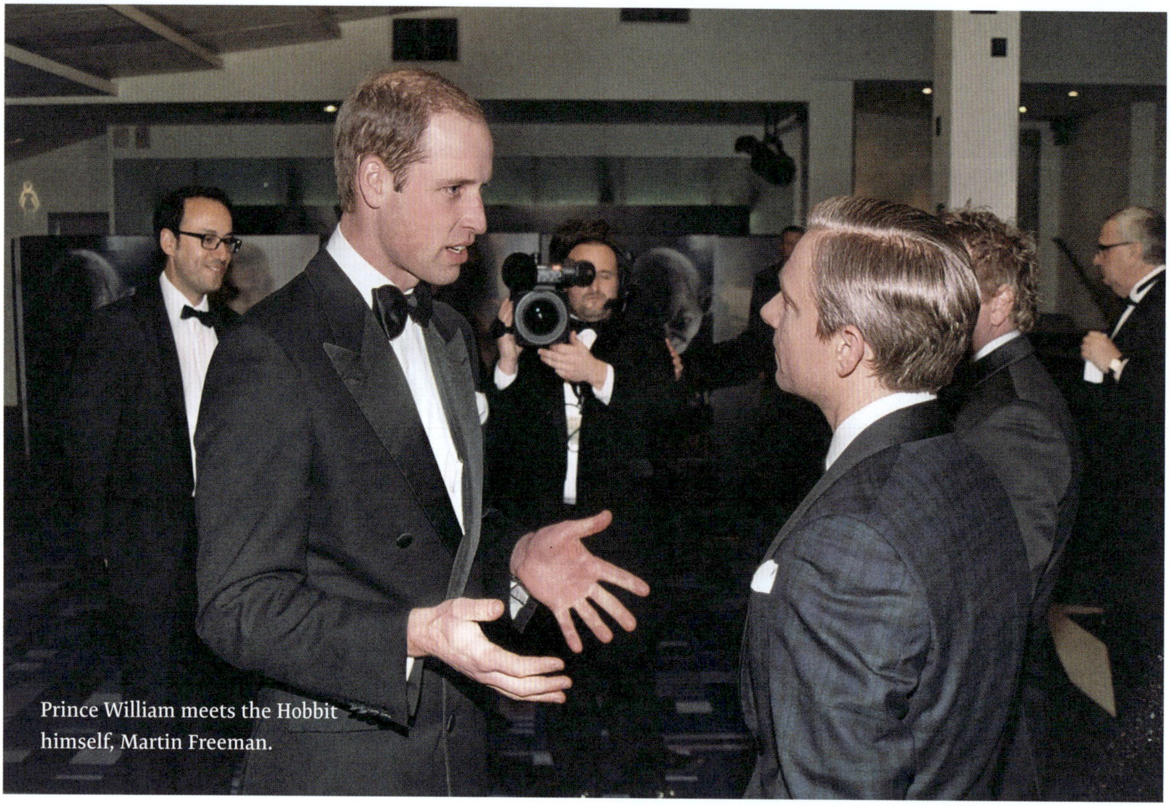

Prince William meets the Hobbit himself, Martin Freeman.

The evening was another resounding success, except for the moment when a rather overenthusiastic fan ran down the stairs of the Circle towards Peter Jackson, who was standing with the royal party, to get his autograph. He might have thought twice about his actions had he realised the royals always travel with a plain-clothes police officer carrying a gun.

Not surprisingly, the Royal Film Performance has the tightest security. On the day itself, a full security sweep takes place inside the cinema with police sniffer dogs, and while the royal premiere is taking place the cinema is in total lockdown.

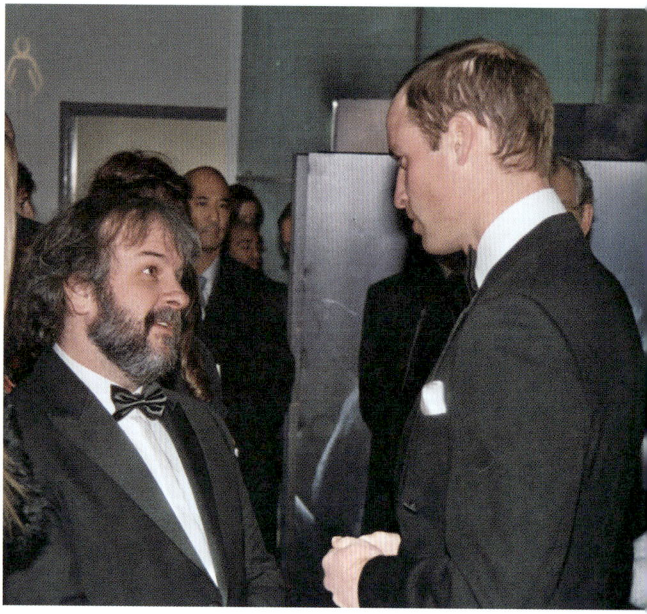

Director Peter Jackson chats with His Royal Highness.

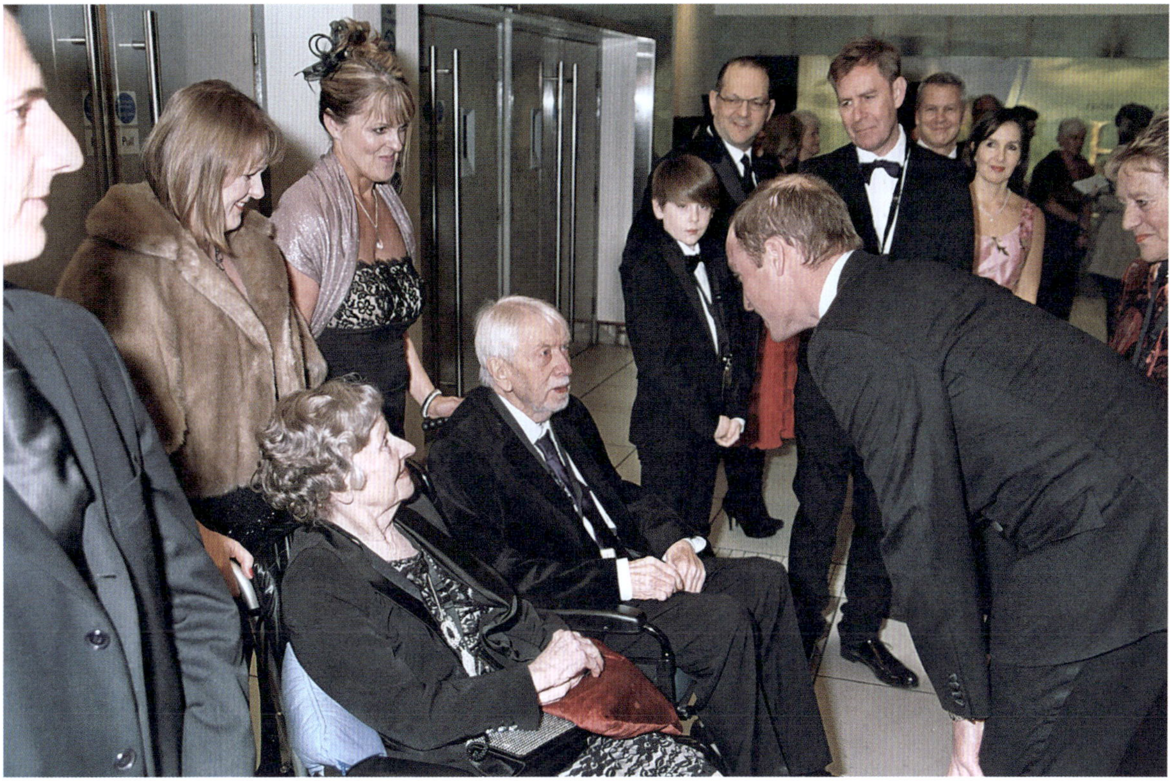

Prince William meets some Glebelands residents who are attending the Royal Film Performance.

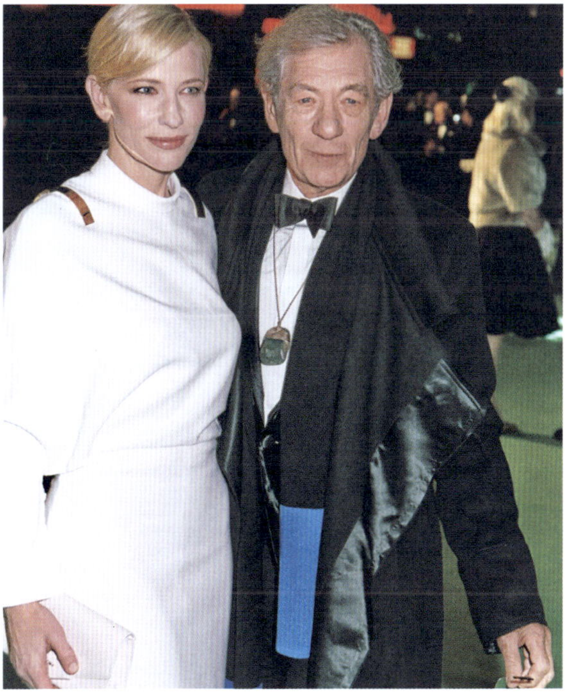

Stars Cate Blanchett and Sir Ian McKellen arrive at the Odeon.

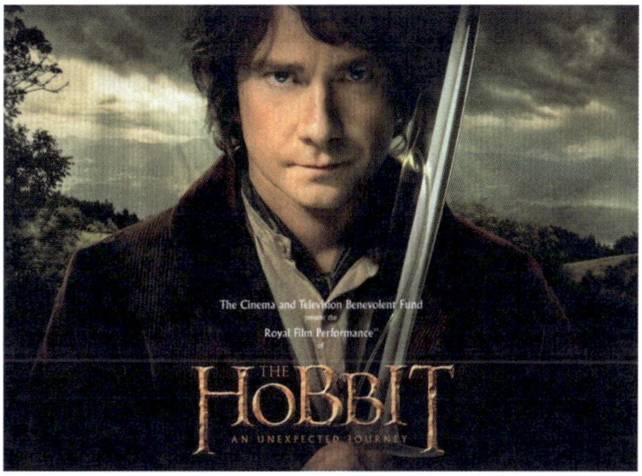

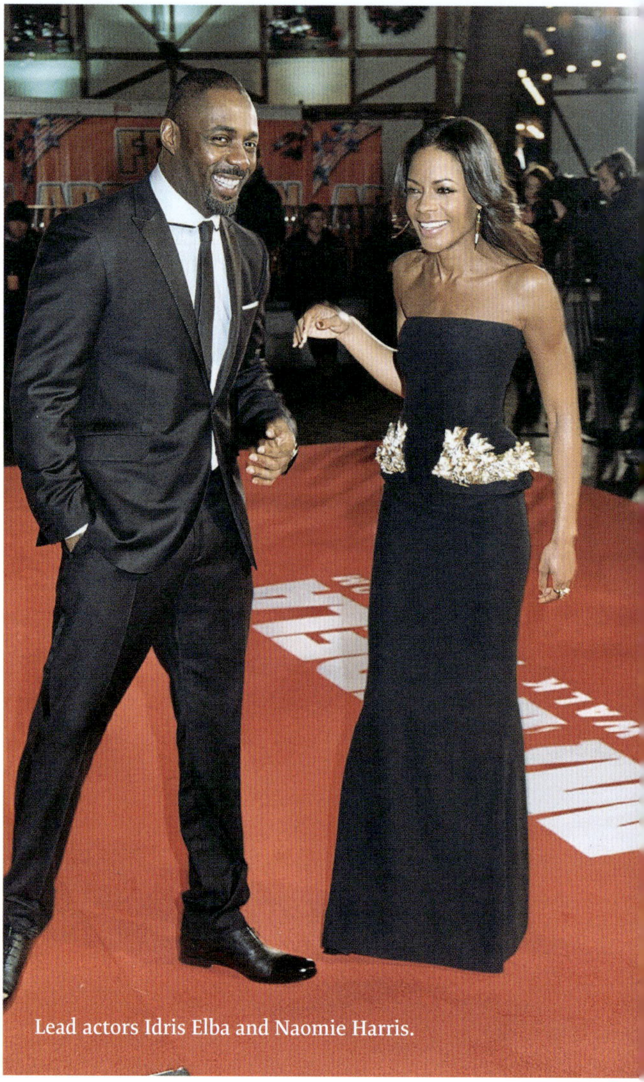

Lead actors Idris Elba and Naomie Harris.

2013 *Mandela: Long Walk to Freedom*

This film was based on Nelson Mandela's autobiography, which chronicled his early life and twenty-seven years in prison before becoming President of South Africa and working to rebuild a country that had been ravaged by the stain of apartheid. It was a fitting gesture that it had been chosen for the Royal Film Performance, yet nobody could have envisaged the very sad circumstance that was to befall that night.

Then 95 years of age, Nelson Mandela was too frail to make the long trip to London. Instead, his two youngest daughters, Zindzi and Zenani, represented the family and were introduced to Prince William and Catherine, Duchess of Cambridge. Also present were the stars of the film, Idris Elba, who played Mandela, and Naomie Harris.

Cameron Saunders was in the audience that night. He was there on behalf of 20th Century Fox who, through their subsidiary division Pathé, were distributors of the *Mandela* picture:

> The film had started, and I distinctly remember being sat in the Royal Circle and my phone vibrating. In that situation you're not quite sure if something's happened so you check your emails because there might be something I'm needed for. And I looked down and it was a Sky newsflash, Mandela has just died. It was shocking news.

In the Circle, Cameron could see downstairs into the Stalls. 'And I could see little screens lighting up. And that was quite rare for a Royal Film because normally your phones are away out of respect.' The news was beginning to spread throughout the auditorium. Quietly, Mandela's daughters received the news of their father's passing. As they were led out,

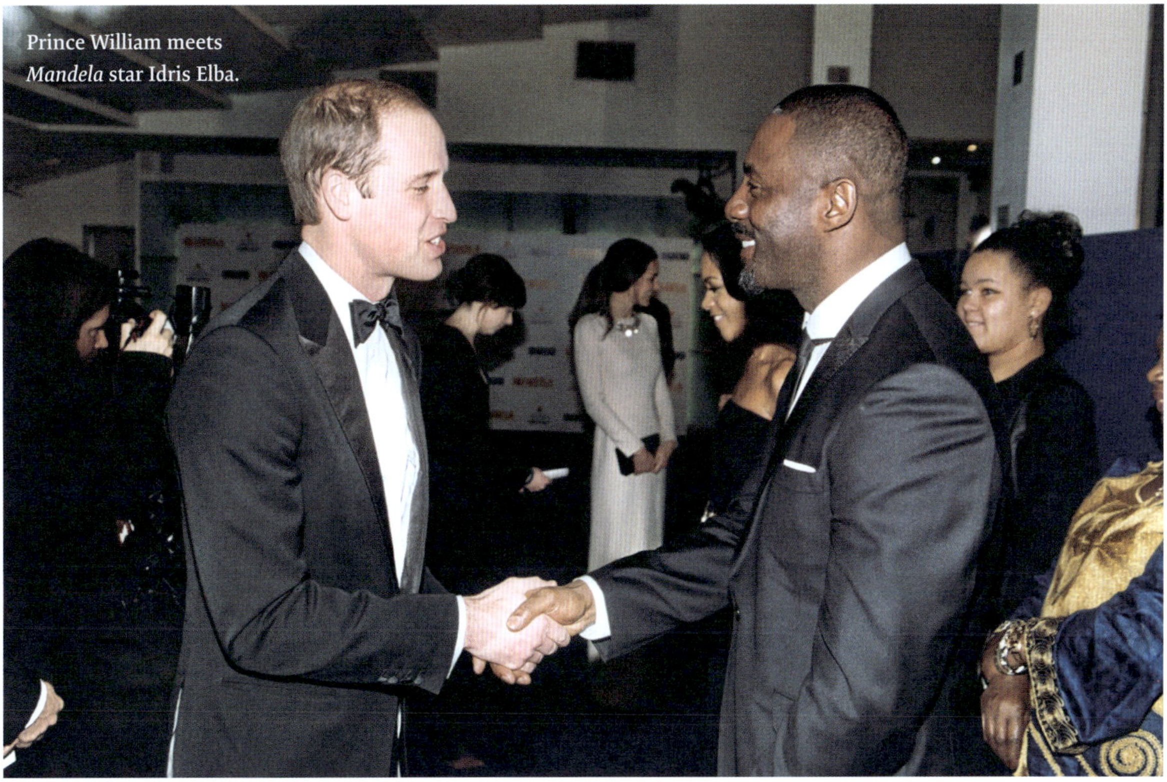

Prince William meets *Mandela* star Idris Elba.

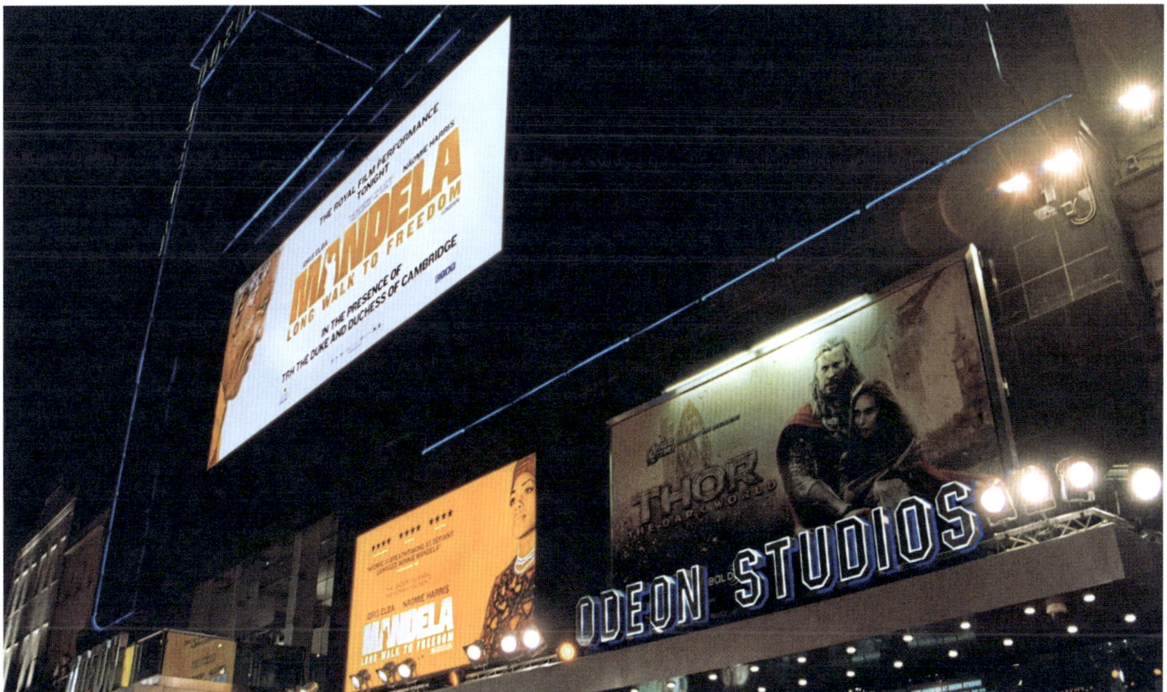

both requested that the film continue. 'But by that point whole rows of people were leaving,' reveals Cameron:

> ... because if you're representatives of Pathé or the royal advisers it was, how do we handle this? Obviously, they would have prepped and have stuff in place, but you probably wouldn't have anything in the case of Mandela dying in the middle of his own film. It was a unique situation.

When the picture came to an end, the film's producer Anant Singh announced the death to the audience and there was a minute's silence. Prince William and Catherine were the first to leave, as protocol dictates, and faced a barrage of cameras and reporters outside the cinema. 'Normally at a premiere when you walk in, it's cameras and media everywhere,' says Cameron. 'When you walk out it's all dismantled and you just go home. But that night it was like the whole of the world's media was there interviewing people coming out. It was a whole media frenzy.' Standing in front of the world's press, Prince William gave a sombre tribute, closing what must go down as the most momentous Royal Film Performance of them all.

2015 *The Second Best Exotic Marigold Hotel*

After the surprise and delightful success of *The Best Exotic Marigold Hotel* in 2011, about a group of British pensioners moving to a retirement hotel in India – which was made for $10 million and grossed $136 million – screenwriter Ol Parker was signed to deliver a treatment for a sequel to Fox Searchlight Pictures in October 2012, with most of the cast agreeing to return along with a few new faces, including Richard Gere. 'This cast of actors is kind of a dream,' Gere told reporters. 'I loved the first one, and this was also a terrific script. It's not like it was a particularly difficult film, but I thought it would be fun to make, and it was.'

Returning director John Madden was determined to create another crowd-pleaser. 'I felt pressure to deliver something that wouldn't disappoint an audience,' said the Oscar-nominated director. 'The crucial thing was that I felt we had a story left to tell and actually to resolve. The second film really is a resolution of the first.'

On 17 February, Leicester Square was transformed with beautiful orange and pink drapes, hanging marigold floral decorations lined either side of a lavish orange carpet, like an aisle at an Indian wedding. A troupe of dancers, Karan's Bollywood Masterclass (KBM), put on a high-octane energy show that filled the mild London air with heavy bhangra and Bollywood beats.

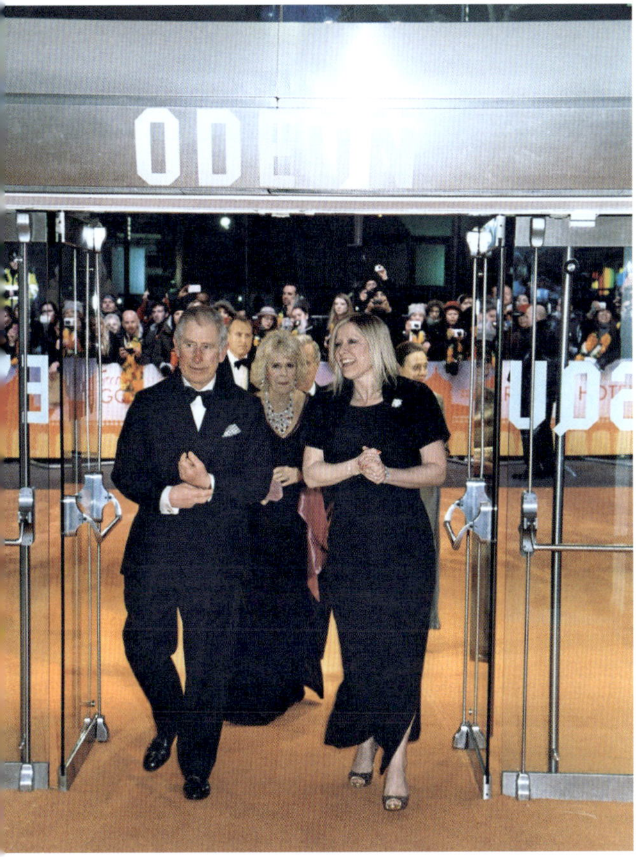

The royal party are welcomed by new Odeon manager Tessa Street.

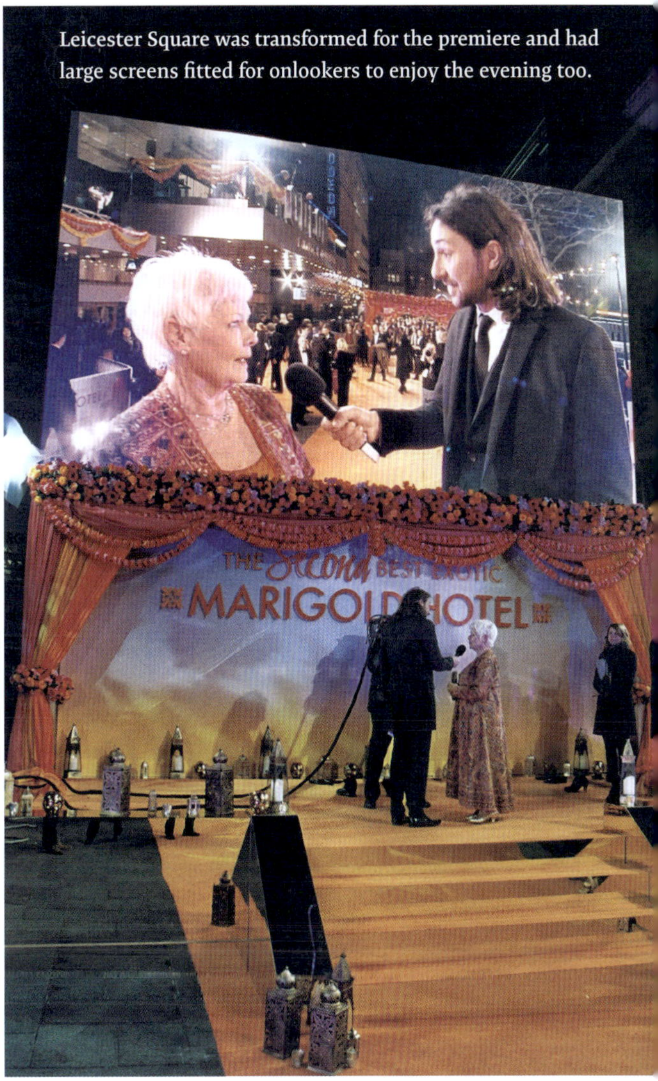

Leicester Square was transformed for the premiere and had large screens fitted for onlookers to enjoy the evening too.

Limousines and tuk-tuks delivered cast and crew members Judi Dench, Maggie Smith, Ronald Pickup, Celia Imrie, Diana Hardcastle, Tina Desai and director John Madden for the premiere in the presence of the Prince of Wales and Duchess of Cornwall. 'I couldn't wait to get back to India,' an enthusiastic Judi Dench told waiting reporters on the orange carpet, 'for another glorious eight weeks.' Pondering the runaway success of the first film, she added, 'I think it came at the right time … and we are all great friends – I've known Maggie Smith since 1958! – so it was like a theatre company coming together again.'

Cameron Saunders, managing director of UK theatrical at 20th Century Fox, welcomed the royal party and introduced the line-up:

> With Prince Charles I occasionally tried to put a name in his ear [who he was meeting], but he would gently move around informally – in the way that Prince Philip liked to – and be very jokey and jovial. [The Duke of Edinburgh] took a lot longer along the line than the Queen because he

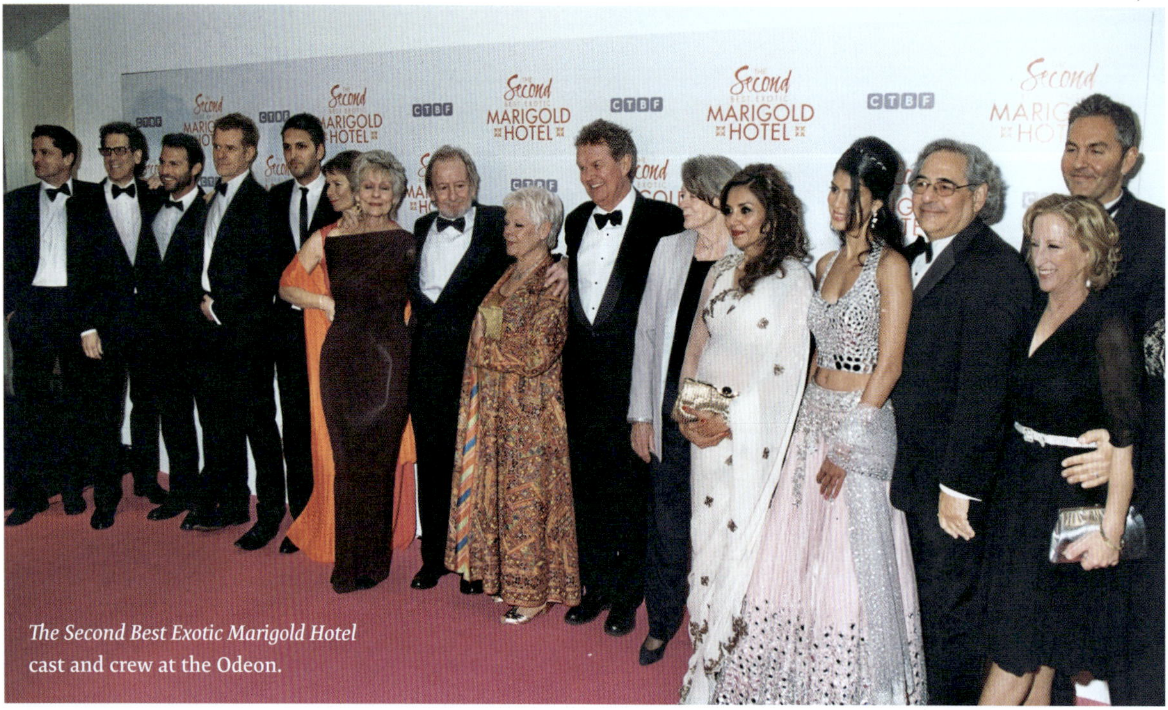

The Second Best Exotic Marigold Hotel cast and crew at the Odeon.

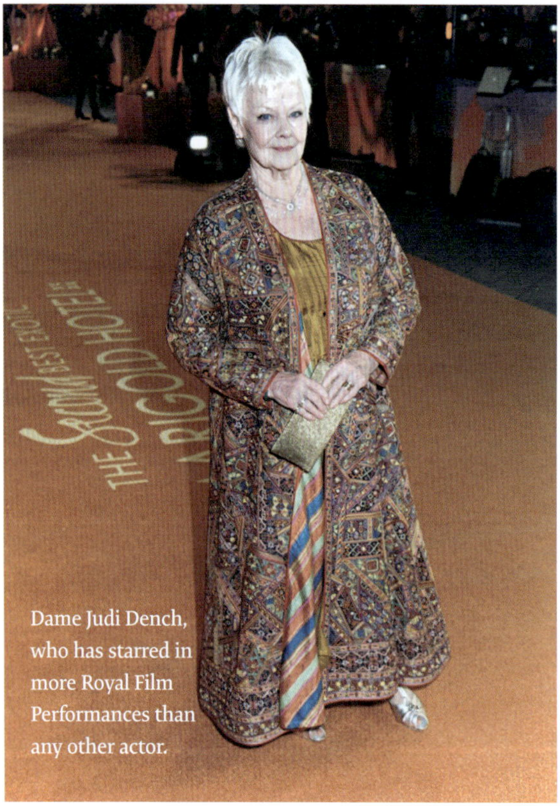

Dame Judi Dench, who has starred in more Royal Film Performances than any other actor.

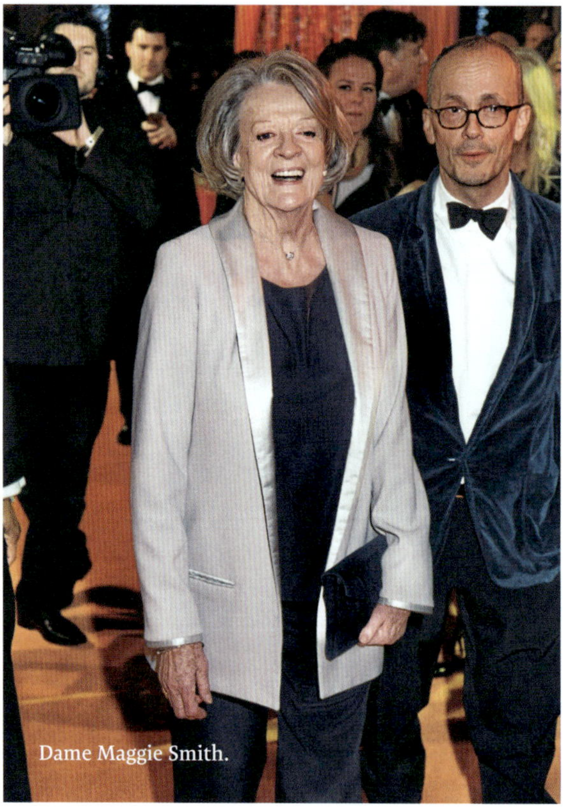

Dame Maggie Smith.

would make a point of pretty much talking to everyone and having a little bit of time with each person.

The line-ups would sometimes take up to thirty minutes, but everyone would come away feeling very special.

CTBF president Barry Jenkins said, 'At the end of our ninetieth-anniversary year, it is fitting that we can celebrate alongside such acclaimed British filmmaking talent. We are extremely grateful to the royal family for their continued support and to Fox Searchlight Pictures for sharing this opportunity with us.'

Sadly Dev Patel, Bill Nighy and Richard Gere were unable to attend due to filming commitments, and when the director was asked if another reunion might be on the cards, he replied, 'I would douse any expectations of that right now', stating that he hadn't even expected to direct a sequel:

> It is after all about people getting uncomfortably close to mortality, therefore it's going to start to deal with that fact. The truth is the audience doesn't want to see that – they want the same film again even if they won't appreciate it if it is the same. But instinctively they do. So quit while you're ahead, I say.

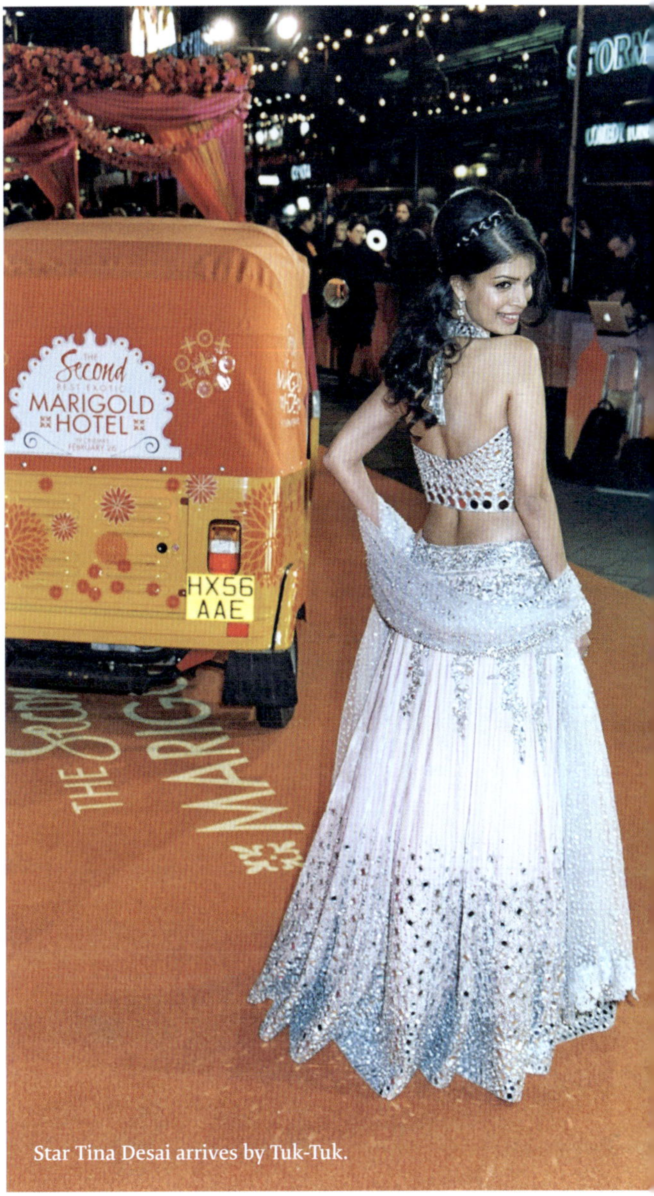

Star Tina Desai arrives by Tuk-Tuk.

2015 *Spectre*

Once again, the Royal Albert Hall provided a fitting setting for the world premiere of the latest James Bond adventure, the third 007 picture chosen for a Royal Film Performance, and the second Performance of the year. The hall's south steps were made over in an eerie but festive style featuring a huge masked and feathered skull which mirrored the film's opening sequence set during Mexico's Day of the Dead festival. The red carpet snaked practically all around the building and as guests arrived, huge speakers pumped out Bond themes from the past and scenes from *Spectre* played out on giant screens.

Attending were Prince William and Kate, along with Prince Harry. Daniel Craig, dressed in a Tom Ford tuxedo, was the first member of the cast to arrive and happily signed autographs and posed for selfies with fans. All the film's main cast were in attendance, including Bond girls Léa Seydoux and Monica Bellucci and baddie Christoph Waltz. The film's plot was a throwback to the 1960s Bond movies, where 007 faces the terror crime syndicate Spectre and arch foe Blofeld.

As is a tradition at Bond premieres, there were familiar faces from past films: Dame Shirley Bassey, Maud Adams (*Octopussy*), Maryam d'Abo (*The Living Daylights*) and Luciana Paluzzi (*Thunderball*).

Comedian David Walliams and TV presenter Susanna Reid hosted a live telecast that was broadcast around the world. Walliams (a well-known Bond fan) conducted interviews with the cast and crew on the red carpet. Inside the auditorium, director Sam Mendes introduced the cast on the stage prior to the screening.

For the first time ever at a Bond premiere, the film opened on the same night at cinemas across the UK and Ireland. As Sam Mendes told the press, 'I love the idea that cinemas around the country will be full tonight at the same time as we are during the royal premiere.' Unfortunately, the public missed out on the 'invitation only' post-premiere party held at the British Museum, where the Day of the Dead theme continued with costumed dancers and hanging skeletons adorning the vast rooms.

Slightly overshadowing proceedings were Daniel Craig's recent controversial comments that he would 'rather slash my wrists' than make a fifth Bond picture. Asked about them on the red carpet, producer Barbara Broccoli said she was determined to hang on to her star. Craig would indeed return one more time as 007.

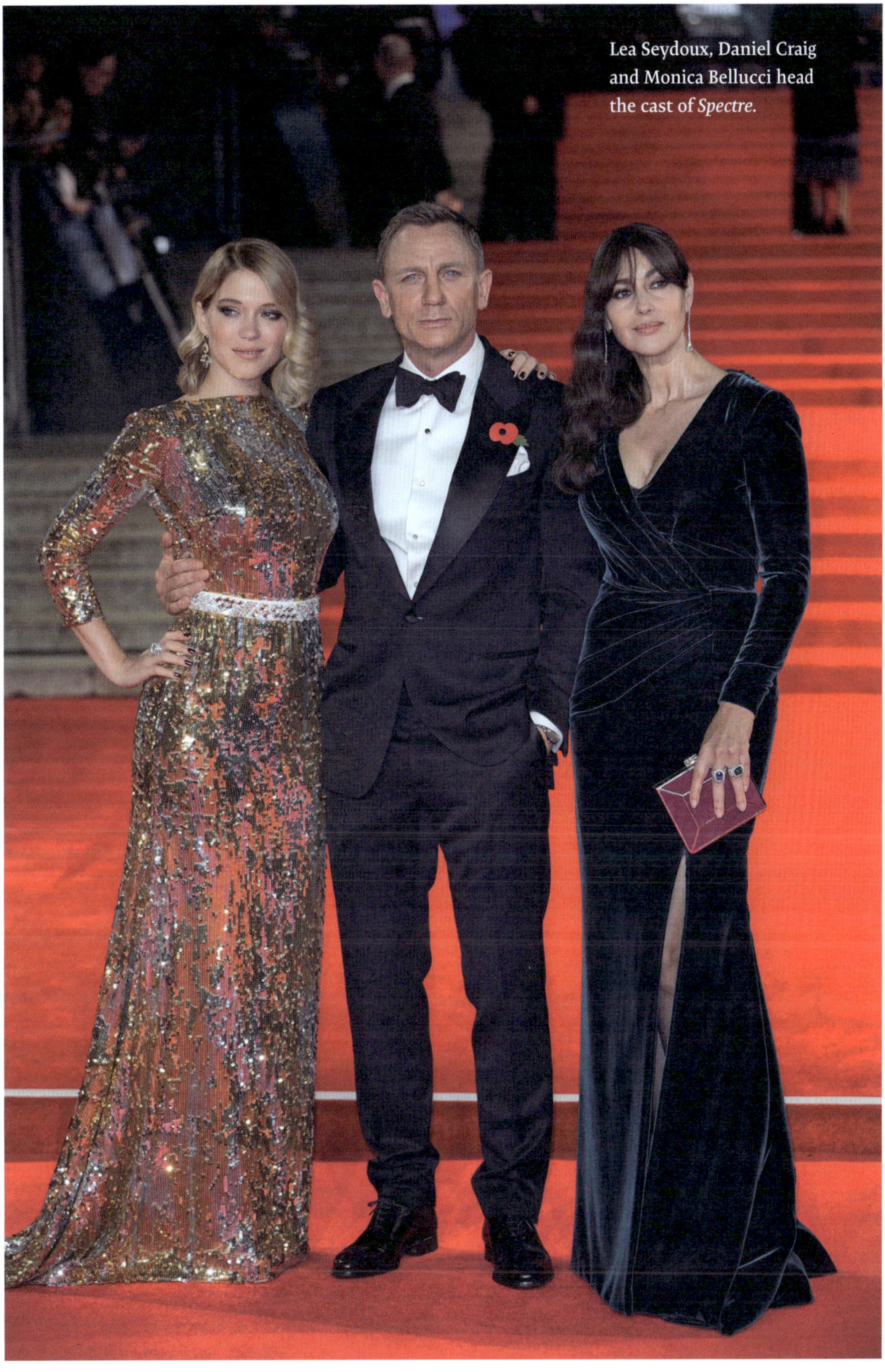

Lea Seydoux, Daniel Craig and Monica Bellucci head the cast of *Spectre*.

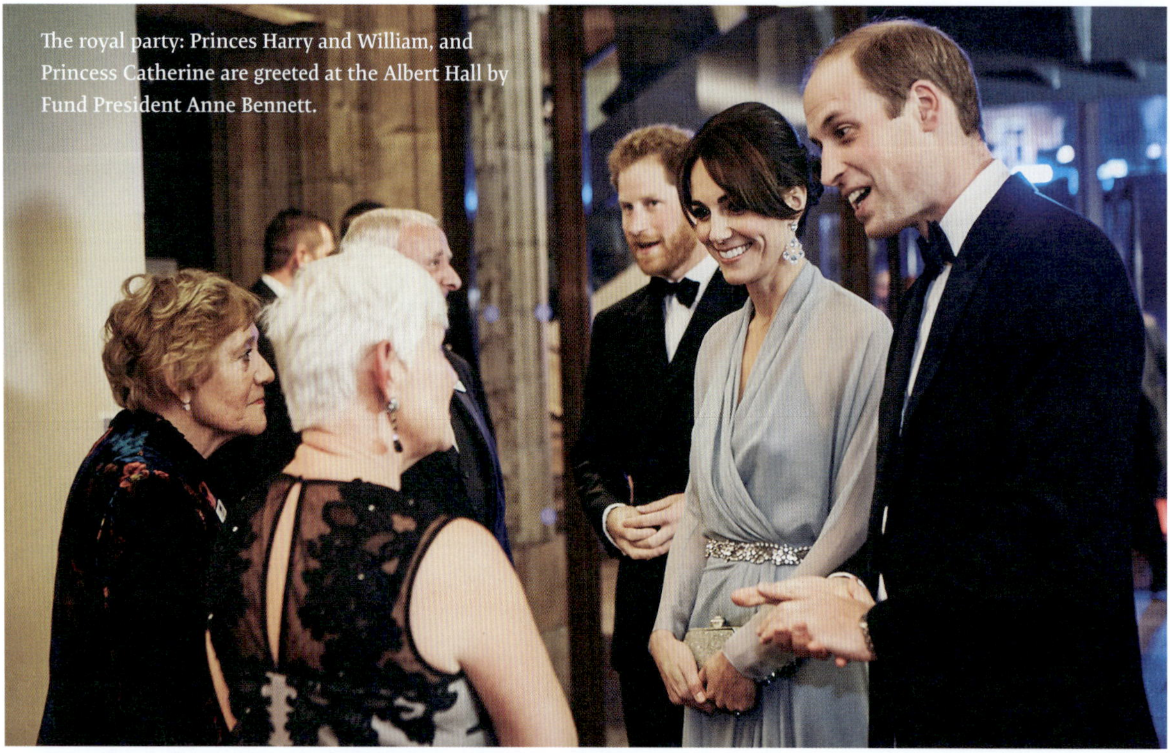

The royal party: Princes Harry and William, and Princess Catherine are greeted at the Albert Hall by Fund President Anne Bennett.

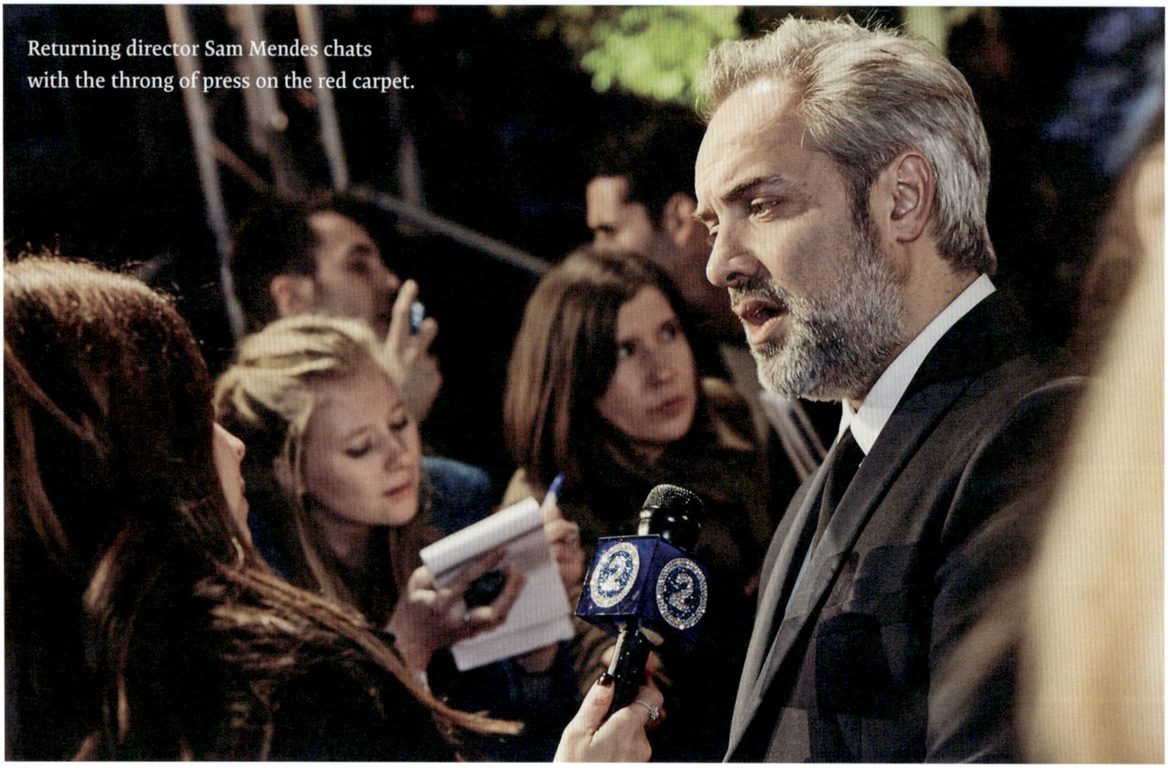

Returning director Sam Mendes chats with the throng of press on the red carpet.

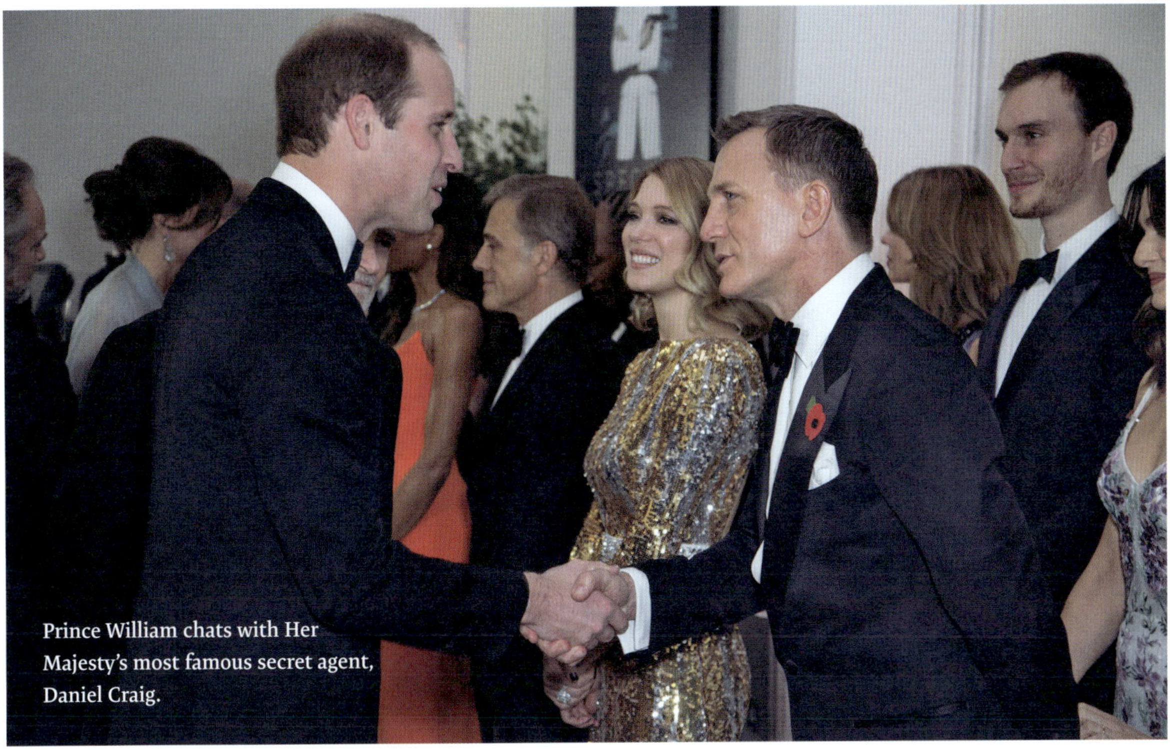

Prince William chats with Her Majesty's most famous secret agent, Daniel Craig.

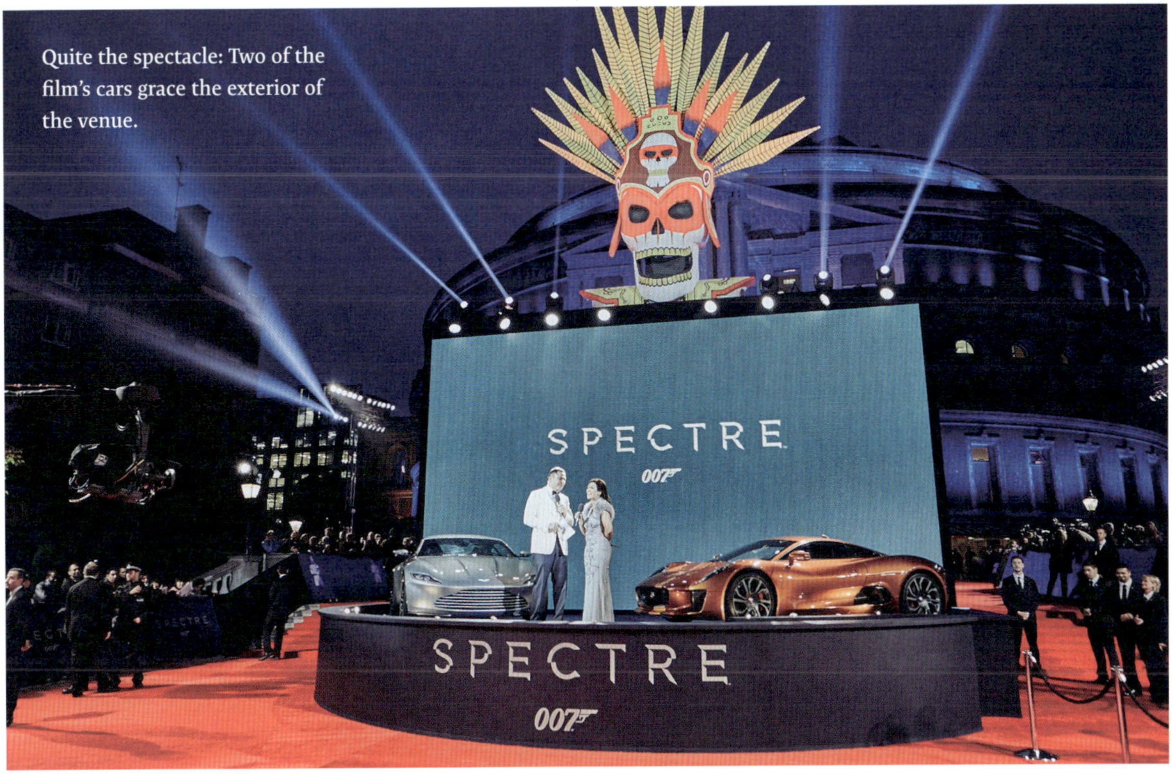

Quite the spectacle: Two of the film's cars grace the exterior of the venue.

2019 *1917*

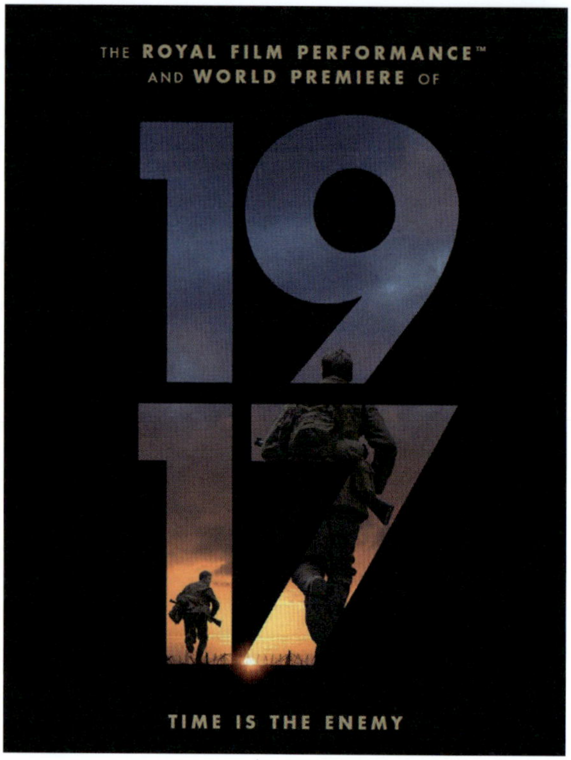

Due to changes at the charity, there had been no Royal Film Performance for three years. When it returned, the chosen film was once again directed by Sam Mendes and inspired by the war stories of his grandfather, Alfred Mendes, who enlisted as a 17-year-old and fought in the First World War on the Western Front. Alfred Mendes became a novelist but never spoke to his family about his war experiences until his mid-seventies. Out of all the stories Alfred told about what happened to him, it was the tale where he was tasked to carry a single message through no man's land in the winter of 1916 that stayed with the young Sam Mendes. It was this story, a very personal one set against a vast historical landscape, that became the basis for *1917*.

In the film, two young British soldiers, Blake and Schofield, are given a seemingly impossible mission. In a race against time, they must cross a hellscape of gouged-out trenches and burnt ruins to deliver a vital message that could save many lives, including Blake's brother. From the very beginning, Mendes saw the film as operating very much like a ticking-clock thriller and wanted the audience to experience every second along with the men. For this to work, Mendes came up with the idea that the film's running time of two hours would pass in real time and be made to appear like one continuous take. It was a bold gamble that won the film critical plaudits.

This, the seventieth Royal Film Performance, was the world premiere of *1917* and was attended by the Prince of Wales and the Duchess of Cornwall. Many of the film's cast and crew were in attendance, including Sam Mendes, Richard Madden, Andrew Scott, Mark Strong and the two young actors playing Blake and Schofield – Dean-Charles Chapman and George MacKay. The entire event was streamed live on both YouTube and Facebook.

The film went on to become a box-office winner, emerging as the biggest earner of 2020 in UK cinemas. Unfortunately, its run was cut short, thanks to the mass closures of cinemas that began with the first national lockdown that March during the coronavirus pandemic. Inevitably, this played havoc with release schedules and led to the cancellation of the next two Royal Film Performances. But the charity was determined to come back with a bang.

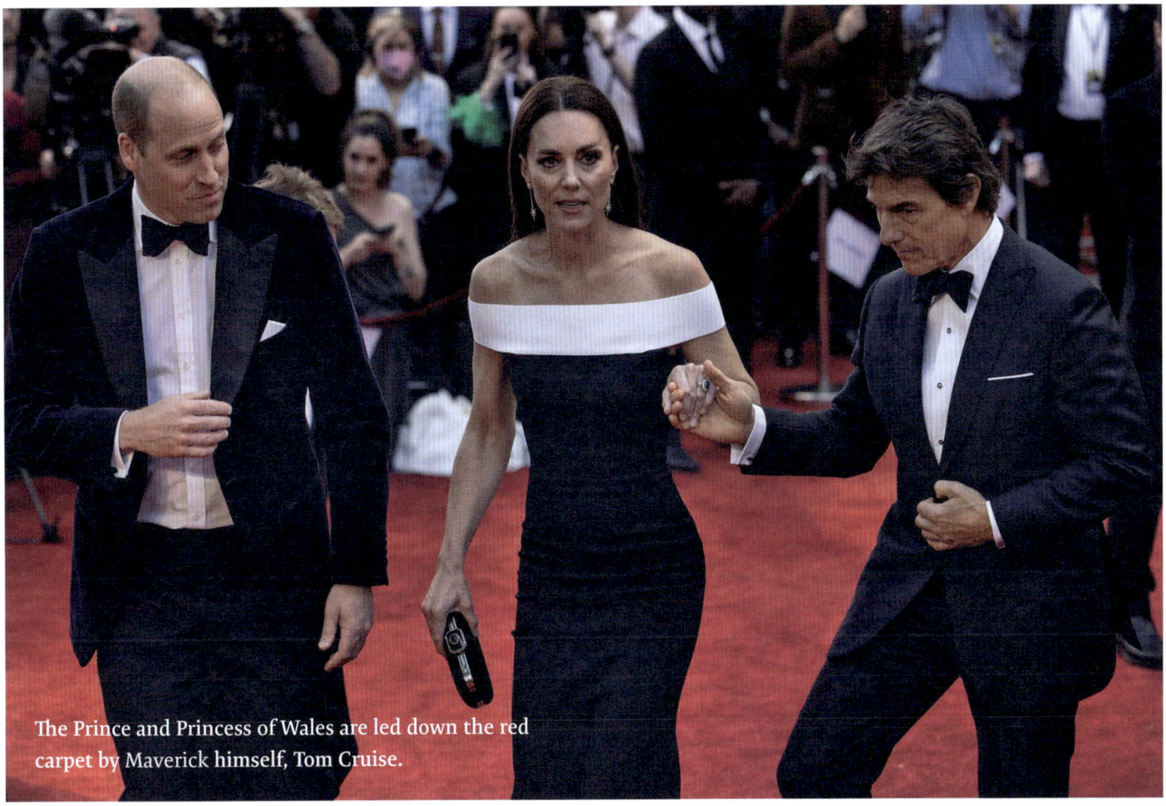

The Prince and Princess of Wales are led down the red carpet by Maverick himself, Tom Cruise.

2022 *Top Gun: Maverick*

The coronavirus pandemic scuppered many film release schedules. One of the most hotly anticipated films affected was the big-budget remake of 1986's *Top Gun*, starring Tom Cruise. Originally planned to open in the summer of 2020, a huge media blitz was planned. This included the possibility of Lady Gaga performing at Glastonbury, where the final song of her set was to be a track from the film. Cruise was to join her on the stage, followed by a flyover by the Red Arrows. Such high-profile premieres and PR stunts were to be repeated across Europe.

Alas, Glastonbury was scrapped, and *Top Gun: Maverick* was shelved until the world returned to some sort of normalcy. When

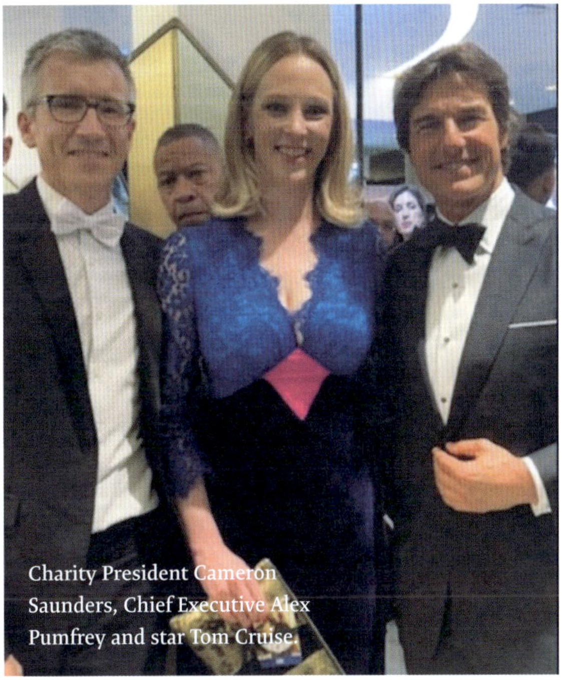

Charity President Cameron Saunders, Chief Executive Alex Pumfrey and star Tom Cruise.

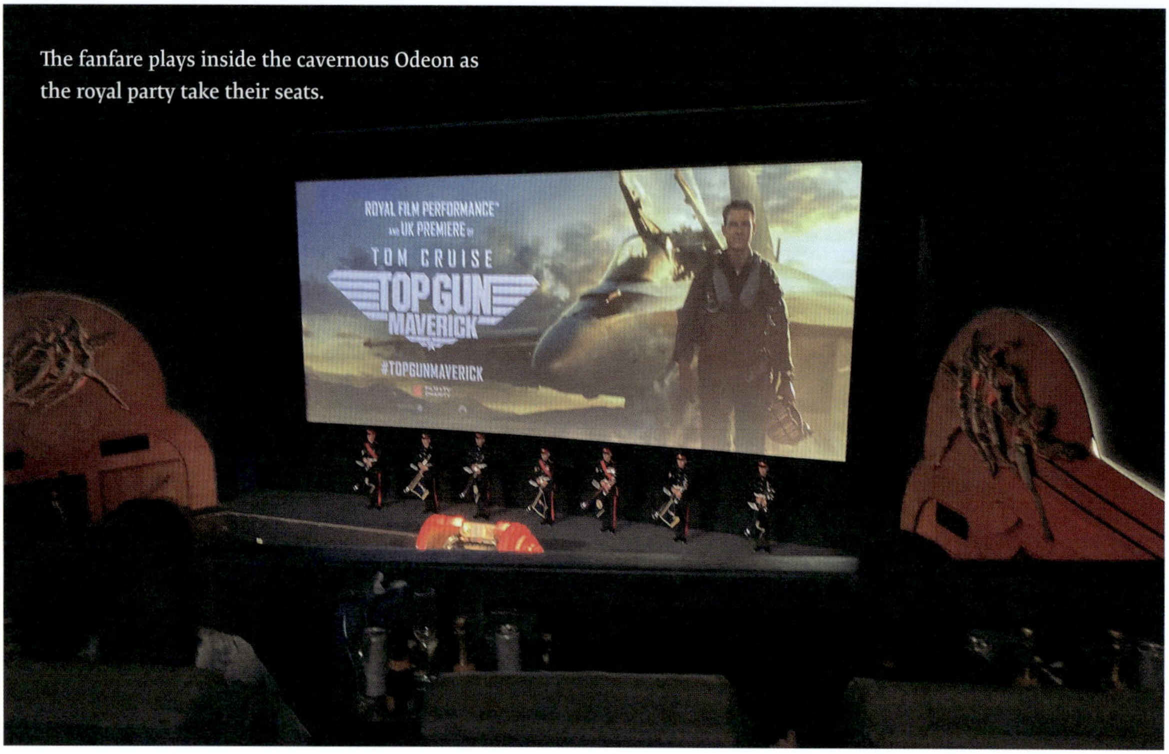

The fanfare plays inside the cavernous Odeon as the royal party take their seats.

dates began to be reconsidered for the film's opening, the possibility of it being a Royal Film Performance was discussed. Cruise was super keen, being a big anglophile and a fan of the royal family. He had huge respect for Charles and Camilla, but for him, his preference was always for William and Kate, not least because William was a die-hard fan of the original and the young royal couple represented what the film was about. Cruise's character is now a teacher training the next generation of pilots.

While it is never the case that filmmakers can influence which royals attend the premiere, it came back quickly from the Palace that William was extremely enthusiastic about attending, and indeed that turned out to be the case. On the red carpet, William sported special shoes featuring the *Top Gun* logo. When it came to the Royal Box, according to Cameron Saunders, then executive vice president of marketing and distribution at Paramount across Europe, Cruise wanted to sit next to Kate, 'but William wanted to sit next to Tom, so he could talk planes and stuff'. Prince William, of course, had served in the Royal Air Force.

Saunders had worked with Cruise before on a couple of films and found him both sincere and hands-on, 'He was really interested in the charity and what the charity did, about how it supported people in lockdown and the cost of living, and the various equality and diversity programmes. He was genuinely interested.'

As Royal Film Performances go, this was a big one. A spectacular full-size replica jet was on display outside the cinema. 'There was a moment on the red carpet when Kate slipped and Tom grabbed her hand,' recalls Saunders. 'He was in there straight away, saving the Princess, and it was a great shot for the press.'

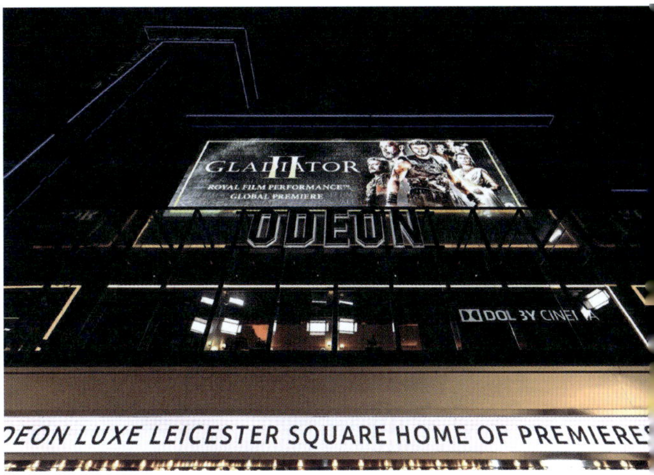

It was Saunders' duty to lead Kate and William down the line-up and he recalls them both being very informal and chatty. Kate was disappointed that the film had some swearing in it because they were hoping to show it to George. Saunders' daughter stepped in at the last moment when the girl originally to give a bouquet to Kate fell ill.

Top Gun: Maverick was a big hit with the audience on the night, which always helps. 'It was that point in time,' says Saunders:

> … when it was still early days post-Covid, of things coming back to normal, people in a cinema together, no face masks, no restrictions. And almost in a way it was a release, because the film had an exuberance and optimism, it was one of those films that was unashamedly blockbuster. It was such a cathartic release of energy, people were literally whooping and cheering, which was very unusual for a British audience. It felt like an American reaction to a movie.

In a throwback to the 1950s, this Royal Film Performance also had regional events, though rather than 'replica' premieres on different dates, it was live-streamed to various cinemas around the country, helping to raise additional income for the charity.

2024 *Gladiator II*

In September 2022, Queen Elizabeth II passed away at the age of 96.

The charity was asked to maintain her name as patron, albeit styled as 'The Late Queen Elizabeth II' until, following his coronation, King Charles confirmed he would be continuing the monarch's patronage of the charity.

During the early summer of 2023 industry rumours suggested Ridley Scott's epic biopic of *Napoleon* was being positioned to be the annual Royal Film Performance in the autumn; however, two major disruptions thwarted plans: the Writers Guild of America strike (2 May to 27 September) and the SAG-AFTRA actors' union strike (14 July to 9 November) all but paralysed Hollywood production. The actors' union strike was the longest in history and prevented members from not only taking part in filming but also in any promotion of projects they were involved with. Chat-show sofas remained strangely vacant of major stars, and West End cinemas were devoid of premieres.

With the actors' strike unresolved at the time, the Royal Film Performance planning and palace diary meetings took place, and

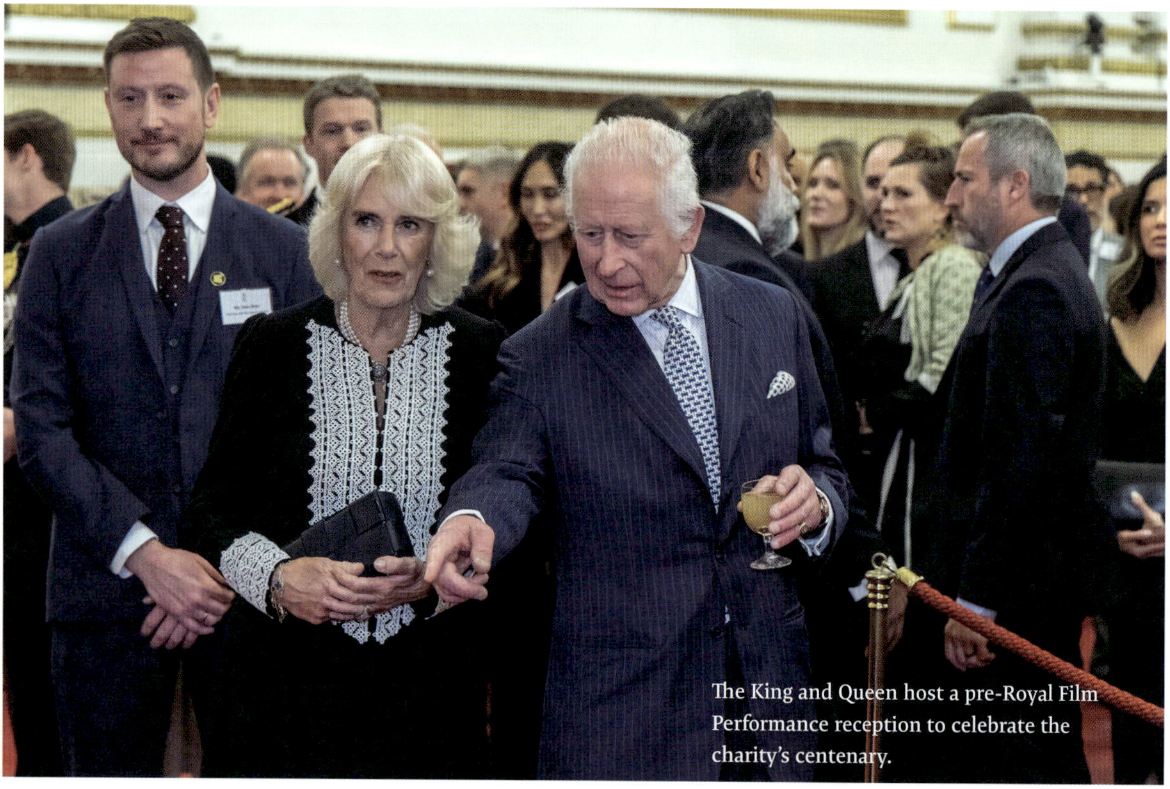

The King and Queen host a pre-Royal Film Performance reception to celebrate the charity's centenary.

it was decided to postpone the event until the following year. The *Gladiator* sequel was chosen to premiere on 13 November at a Leicester Square event at both the Odeon and Empire.

That same afternoon, His Majesty the King celebrated the UK's film and television industry at a Buckingham Palace reception ahead of the premiere with directors, actors, TV presenters, stunt performers and costume designers – plus the director of the *Gladiator* sequel, Sir Ridley Scott – in attendance. It marked the centenary of the Film and TV Charity.

Queen Camilla greeted Sir Ridley, coughed and, according to a Sky News report, said, 'I am so sorry I can't come [to the premiere] tonight. I'd be coughing all the way through!', referring to her reported recent chest infection.

Actress and filmmaker Emily Mortimer, speaking at the event, said the King demonstrating support towards the people who work in the British Film and TV industry was 'huge'. 'It means so much,' she said in a Sky News report of 13 November. 'You get older and older and you've been doing it longer and longer, and in most jobs that would mean some level of security – but in our job it doesn't. We're just freelance people – like circus people, in a way. So, the fact that there are people out there willing to support the industry, and people who are willing to take the risk to commit themselves and their lives to this profession, is so important.'

In the same report, Marcus Ryder MBE, the chief executive of the Film and TV Charity, said the event was intended to celebrate and show support 'to everybody in the TV and film industry'.

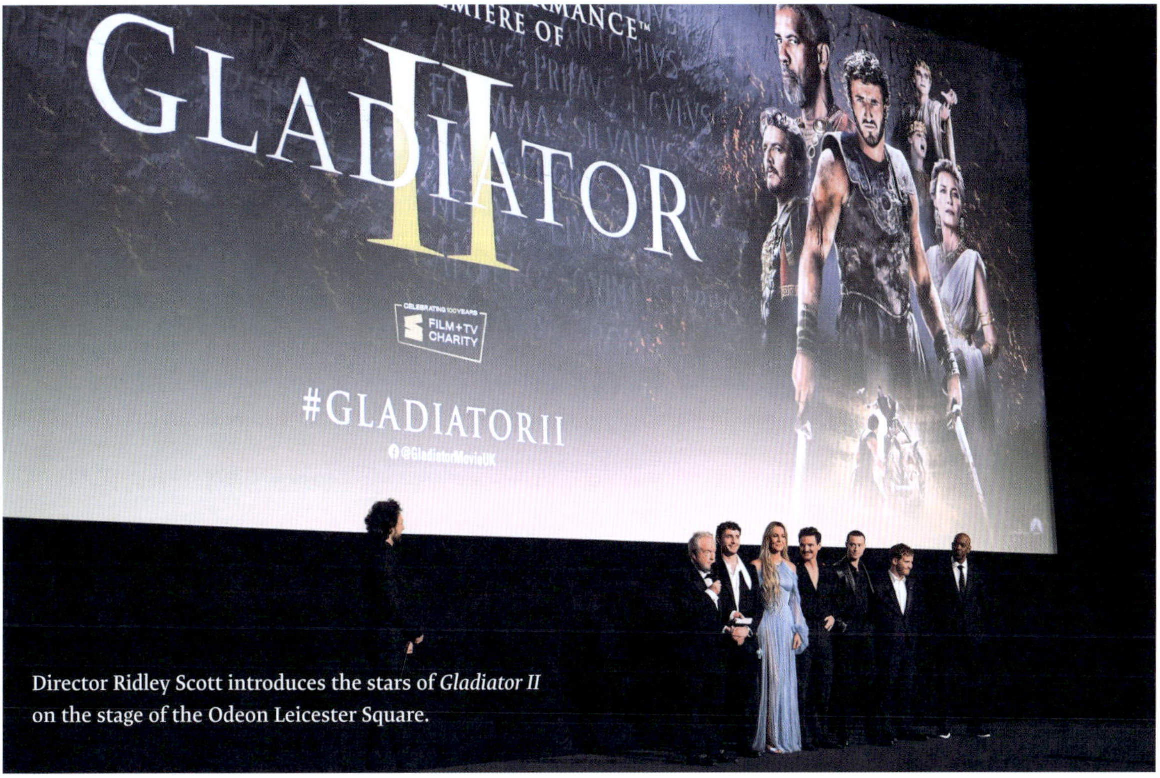

Director Ridley Scott introduces the stars of *Gladiator II* on the stage of the Odeon Leicester Square.

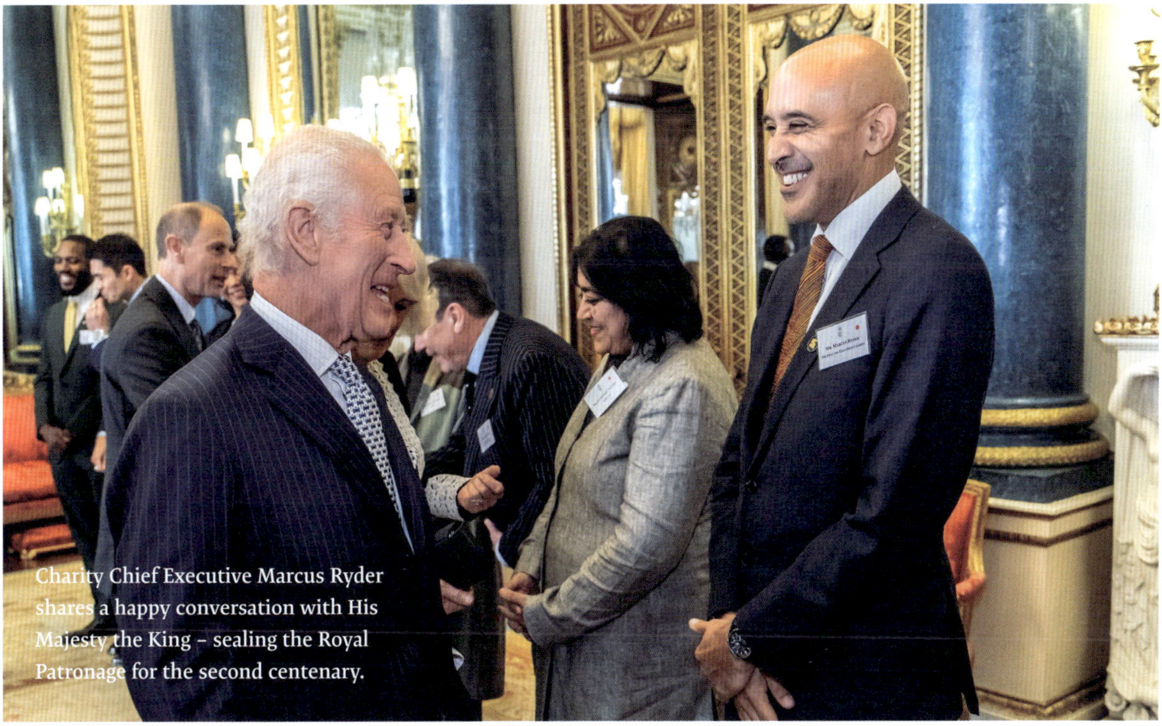

Charity Chief Executive Marcus Ryder shares a happy conversation with His Majesty the King – sealing the Royal Patronage for the second centenary.

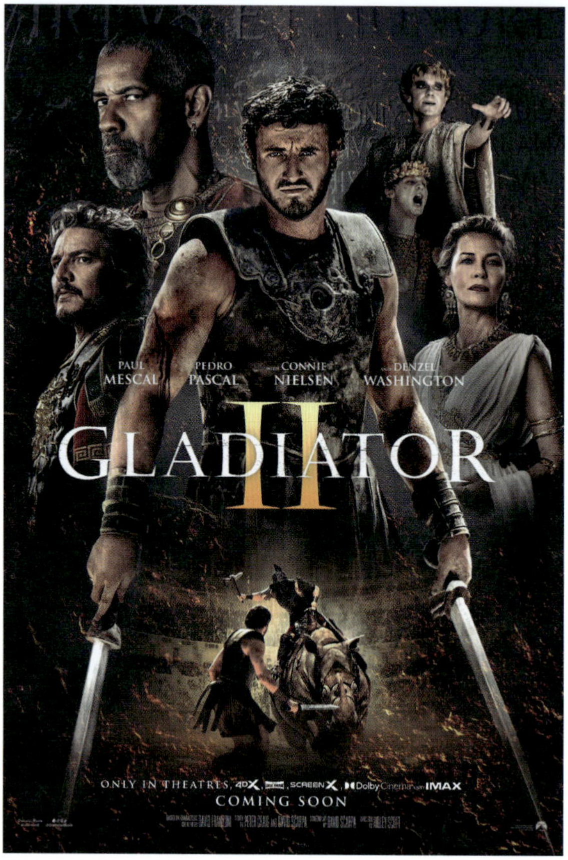

A number of costumes and props from films were on display at the palace, including costumes worn by Joseph Quinn in his role as Emperor Geta in *Gladiator II*; those worn by the late Bernard Hill in his role as Captain Edward Smith in James Cameron's *Titanic*; two of Russell Crowe's outfits from *Master and Commander: The Far Side of the World*; and the late Dame Maggie Smith's outfit from the 1982 film *Evil Under the Sun* – all of which were previous Royal Film Performances.

Meanwhile, over at Leicester Square, the red carpet was being laid and surrounded by pillars and columns of ancient Rome to await the arrival of stars Paul Mescal, Pedro Pascal, Denzel Washington, Connie Nielsen and director Sir Ridley Scott.

King Charles arrived to meet filmmakers and studio executives ahead of moving inside the Odeon auditorium for the Loyal Address and introduction, from where Scott and Mescal briefly crossed the Square to introduce the film to the audience at the adjacent Empire, as well as beaming introductions around selected UK cinemas.

Genuinely overwhelmed by the enormity of the occasion, Paul Mescal admitted on the red carpet, 'I'm genuinely struggling to string sentences together … how can you fathom any of this … I'm just not used to it.'

Producer of the original *Gladiator* as well as the sequel, Lucy Fisher added, 'We're the luckiest producers in the world to have this cast. We had to wait for Paul Mescal to be born before we could make this movie!'

The film carries a $250 million-plus budget and its impressive sets, including a full-size Colosseum, and battles – with gladiators, vicious apes, a rhino and sharks! – certainly proved a memorable event for the King's first premiere as monarch.

Appendix

The Film & TV Charity Governance

Presidents / Chairs of Trustees

1924 to 1925	None
1926 to 1944	Sir William F. Jury
1944 to 1956	Reginald C. Bromhead
1956 to 1960	Lord Rank
1960 to 1969	Sir Philip Warter
1969 to 1980	Cecil G. Bernstein
1981 to 1983	Sir John Davis
1983 to 1986	Sydney W. Samuelson CBE
1986 to 1989	Percy Livingstone CBE
1989 to 1992	James R.C. Higgins MBE
1992 to 1995	Sir Paul Fox CBE
1995 to 1998	Fred P. Turner
1998 to 2001	David S. McCall CBE DL
2001 to 2004	Ian Lewis
2004 to 2007	Stanley Fishman CBE
2007 to 2010	David Murrell
2010 to 2013	Anne Bennett
2013 to 2017	Barry Jenkins
2017 to 2021	John Pike
2022	Cameron Saunders (interim)
2022 to 2023	Andrew Wilson-Mouasher (interim)
2023 to present	Claire Tavernier

The Executive Directors

Prior to 1972, the role was 'Chairman' and post-holders were:

1924 to 1926	Position not filled
1926 to 1956	Reginald C. Bromhead
1956 to 1972	Ralph S. Bromhead

Then:

1972 to 1981	Major General Casimir Michael Grigg
1982 to 1996	Colonel Peter J.C. Ratcliffe OBE
1997 to 2000	Captain Don Hunsley MBE JP
2000 to 2009	Captain Peter Hore
2009 to 2012	Brian Robertson
2012 to 2016	Richard Wilson
2016 to 2017	D'Arcy Myers (interim)
2017 to 2023	Alex Pumfrey
2023 to present	Marcus Ryder

Acknowledgements

We would like to thank the following people and companies for their assistance in the compilation of this book:

Davina Belling
George Biggs
George Chakiris
Tom Courtenay
Charles Dance
Yvonne Dickens
Gayle Gover
Taylor Hackford
Robin Harbour
Nigel Havers
Robert Henrey
Chris Hilton
Peter Hore
Dame Virginia McKenna
Scott Myers
Dave Norris
David Parfitt
Lord Puttnam
Brian Robertson
Ilya Salkind
Cameron Saunders
Stephanie Wenborn (Eon Productions)